D1608223

This volume describes the six modern Celtic languages. Four of these, Modern Irish, Scottish Gaelic, Welsh and Breton, are living community languages; the other two, Manx and Cornish, survived into the modern period, but are no longer extant as community languages, though they are the subject of enthusiastic revivals. *The Celtic languages* sets them briefly in their Indo-European context, and states their general relationships within the broader Celtic language family. Individual linguistic studies are first placed briefly in their sociolinguistic and sociohistorical context. A detailed synchronic account of each language then follows, including syntax, morphology, phonology, morphophonology, dialect variation and distribution. Each description is based on a common plan, thus facilitating comparison amongst the different languages.

This latest volume in the Cambridge Language Surveys will be welcomed by all scholars of the Celtic languages, but has also been designed to be accessible to any reader with only a basic knowledge of linguistics. It is the only modern account to deal with all surviving Celtic languages in this detail.

THE CELTIC LANGUAGES

Cambridge Language Surveys

General editors: B. Comrie, R. Huddleston, R. Lass, D. Lightfoot, J. Lyons, P. H. Matthews, R. Posner, S. Romaine, N. V. Smith, N. Vincent

This series offers general accounts of all the major language families of the world. Some volumes are organised on a purely genetic basis, others on a geographical basis, whichever yields the most convenient and intelligible grouping in each case. Sometimes, as with the Australian volume, the two in any case coincide.

Each volume compares and contrasts the typological features of the languages it deals with. It also treats the relevant genetic relationships, historical development and sociolinguistic issues arising from their role and use in the world today. The intended readership is the student of linguistics or general linguist, but no special knowledge of the languages under consideration is assumed. Some volumes also have a wider appeal, like that on Australia, where the future of the languages and their speakers raises important social and political issues.

Already published:
The languages of Australia *R. M. W. Dixon*
The languages of the Soviet Union *Bernard Comrie*
The Mesoamerican Indian languages *Jorge A. Suárez*
The Papuan languages of New Guinea *William A. Foley*
Chinese *Jerry Norman*
The languages of Japan *M. Shibatani*
Pidgins and Creoles (Volume I: Theory and structure; Volume II: Reference survey) *John H. Holm*
The Indo-Aryan languages *Colin Masica*

Forthcoming titles include:
Korean *Ho-Min Sohn*
The languages of South-East Asia *J. A. Matisoff*
The Austronesian languages *R. Blust*
The Slavonic languages *R. Sussex*
The Germanic languages *R. Lass*
The Romance languages *R. Posner*

THE CELTIC
LANGUAGES

Edited by

DONALD MACAULAY

Professor, Department of Celtic,
University of Glasgow

 **CAMBRIDGE**
UNIVERSITY PRESS

Published by the Press Syndicate of the University of Cambridge
The Pitt Building, Trumpington Street, Cambridge CB2 1RP
40 West 20th Street, New York, NY 10011–4211, USA
10 Stamford Road, Oakleigh, Victoria 3166, Australia

© Cambridge University Press 1992

First published 1992

Printed in Great Britain at the University Press, Cambridge

A catalogue record for this book is available from the British Library

Library of Congress cataloguing in publication data
The Celtic languages / edited by Donald MacAulay.
    p.   cm. – (Cambridge language surveys)
  Includes index.
  ISBN 0 521 23127 2 (hardback)
  1. Celtic languages. I. MacAulay, Donald. II. Series.
  PB1014.C45 1992
  491.6– dc20 91–34570 CIP

ISBN 0 521 23127 2 hardback

TS

Tha an leabhar sa 'na chuimhneachan air fìor sgoilear agus deagh charaid An t-Ollamh Dáithí Ó hUaithne nach maireann a bha gu bhith air fear den luchd sgrìobhaidh.

CONTENTS

MAPS

CONTRIBUTORS

DONALD MACAULAY
Department of Celtic, University of Glasgow

CATHAIR Ó DOCHARTAIGH
Language Consultant, Bangor, North Wales

ELMAR TERNES
Phonetisches Institut, Universität Hamburg

ALAN R. THOMAS
Department of Linguistics, University College of North Wales, Bangor

ROBERT L. THOMSON
formerly Reader in English and Celtic, University of Leeds

PREFACE

This volume aims to give a description of the six modern Celtic languages. Four of these, Irish and Scottish Gaelic, Welsh and Breton, are living community languages. As such, extended treatment (within the limits of the volume) is given to their phonology, morphology and syntax and a sketch of their sociological history and a sociolinguistic profile is provided. Two of the languages, Manx and Cornish, have recently, the former in the nineteenth and the latter in the eighteenth century, ceased to be spoken community languages – though both have been the subject of enthusiastic revivals. These two languages are given less intensive coverage, though a similar range of aspects is dealt with.

The descriptions are basically synchronic (though certainly informed by the writers' knowledge of their languages' histories). It was considered that an attempt to include a historical section on each language, that would be in any way adequate, would make the volume impossibly unwieldy. There would, indeed, be in such a historical examination sufficient material for a volume in itself. It was felt that the present volume, making a clear statement of the contemporary linguistic position of the living languages (in particular), would, in any event, be a desirable preliminary to that.

The volume was planned to present parallel descriptions. Contributors were all presented with identical sets of chapter, section and sub-section headings. As was anticipated, it proved impossible to follow this plan in its entirety, and it seemed best not to insist on it rigidly, as such an insistence might well have produced a distorted picture of some important areas of the different languages. Contributors were, however, encouraged to restructure their plan only within strict limits and when their intimate knowledge of the particular language indicated to them that that was necessary. By and large the relative coincidence of descriptive headings is very high indeed. This enables readers to make their own comparisons between the languages and to see the extent to which their structures and systems and the manner in which these are realised are comparable. A detailed explication of these comparisons makes a fascinating study. Such a study, however, would be an extensive one, and is beyond the scope of this volume.

The linguistic studies are placed in brief sociolinguistic and sociohistorical contexts because the writers are convinced that such information is vital to the understanding of how the languages present themselves. It provides the reader with a frame of reference which will help to explain the different directions that the development of the languages has followed, influenced by contact with other societies and other languages. Again, these contextual sections are necessarily curtailed by the limits of space.

The volume has taken some time in the making and some of the contributions were in fact written a number of years ago. To be fair to those contributors affected, this should be made clear. The editor is grateful to them for their forbearance and to the publishers for their patience while problems were overcome which threatened at one stage to end his participation in the project altogether.

NOTE

Readers may have initial difficulties with examples if they are not acquainted with the more unusual features of the Celtic languages, such as initial mutations: changes that affect consonants at the beginnings of words (see, for example, 1.6.2); or the variation in verb stems, for example Scottish Gaelic *chi* 'sees', (*chan*) *fhaic* '(does not) see', *chunnaic* 'saw', (*chan*) *fhaca* '(did not) see', or the order of verb and subject *chan fhaca e* [not + saw + he] 'he did not see'. It is, unfortunately, not possible to find viable examples that do not utilise these features, and it is not feasible to refer constantly to sections where these features are explained. We recognise the difficulties, however, and we have tried to minimise them.

ACKNOWLEDGEMENTS

Thanks are due to the Dublin Institute for Advanced Studies for permission to reproduce maps from Jackson 1967 (7.1 and 7.2); to the Association for Scottish Literary Studies for permission to use maps from MacKinnon 1986 (4.2 and 4.3) and from Withers 1979 (4.1). Thanks are also due to these authors; and to Dr Seumas Grannd for useful information about the distribution of some Scottish Gaelic dialect forms.

ABBREVIATIONS

ABST	abstract
ADJ	adjective
ADV	adverb
AFF	affirmative
ART	article
ASPIR	aspiration
COLL	collective
COMP	comparative
COND	conditional
CONJ	conjunction
COP	copula
DEF	definite
DEM	demonstrative
DEP	dependent
DIM	diminutive
DIR	directional
DU	dual
EMPH	emphatic
EQ	equative
FEM	feminine
FUT	future
GEN	genitive
HAB	habitual
IMPERF	imperfect
IMPERS	impersonal
IMP(v)	imperative
INDEF	indefinite
INDEP	independent
INDIC	indicator
INF	infinitive
INTER/Q	interrogative

LOC	locative
MASC	masculine
NEG	negation
NOM	nominative
NUM	numeral
O	object
P	predicate
PERF	perfective
PL	plural
POS	positive
POSS	possessive
PPART	past participle
PREF	prefix
PREP	preposition(al)
PRES	present
PRET	preterite
PREV	preverbal
PRO	pronominal
PROG	progressive
PRON	pronoun
PT	particle
RECIP	reciprocal
REFLEX	reflexive
REINF	reinforcing
REL	relative
S	subject
SG	singular
SGT	singulative
SIT	situational
SPEC	specific
ST	stem
SUBJ	subject
SUBJUNCT	subjunctive
SUBORD	subordinate
SUFF	suffix
SUP	superlative
V	verb
VN	verbal noun/verb–noun
VPT	verbal particle

1

The Celtic languages: an overview

DONALD MACAULAY

1.0   THE CELTS: ORIGINS, MIGRATIONS,
        DISTRIBUTION

The original homeland of the Celts (if that is indeed a valid historical concept) is unestablished: no hypothesis of the many proposed has found general acceptance. The earliest named Celts (in Greek and Latin sources) are associated with two major central European Iron Age cultures, the Hallstatt, dated to the seventh century BC, and La Tène, dated to the fifth century BC. The archaeological evidence suggests a cultural continuity backwards through the late Bronze Age Urnfield Culture with no material evidence that the Celts were newcomers to the region.

During the Hallstatt and La Tène eras the Celts enjoyed a period of great power and expansion. They spread from their central domain in different migrations over the whole of Europe: east and south through the Balkans to Asia Minor (crossing through the Hellespont in 278 BC), south into Italy (Rome was captured in 390 BC), west into the Iberian Peninsula, north to the Atlantic coast and across into Britain and Ireland, where they were a dominant force by the third century BC.

With the rise of Roman power and expansion, the Celts lost their dominance in western Europe and southern Britain before the end of the first century AD. With the withdrawal of the Roman power from Britain in the second decade of the fifth century, British leadership sought to re-assert control and defend themselves against incursions from the Germanic tribes who settled on the east coast and expanded inland. These had conquered the greatest part of the territory of the former Roman province of Britain by the seventh century, confining the British kingdoms to the west.

The Britons also had to contend with the Irish, who had remained outside the sphere of direct Roman power and were in an expansion posture during the late fourth and the fifth centuries. They established settlements along the coast of western Britain; and under the combination of pressures exerted by them and by the Saxons from the east, there was a large-scale emigration back to the continent from south-west Britain to north-west Gaul, giving rise to the territorial name, Brittany. The most permanent Irish settlement, however, was in north Britain. It is not clear when settlement began, but the colony of Dál Ríata was well established by 500 BC and descendants of these settlers eventually conquered the whole of 'Scotland' (a name derived from *Scotus*, the Latin name for 'Irishman').

1.1   CONTINENTAL CELTIC

The term Celt is, in the first place, a linguistic term: the first mentions of Celts are to be found in the writings of Greek and Roman ethnographers and historians, who identified them as a separate people speaking a distinctive kind of language. This language, referred to generally as Continental Celtic, is partially reconstructed from various sources such as place names, inscriptions, items borrowed into Germanic or Italic and references in Latin texts. It had a range of dialects, precisely how many we do not know. These dialects are reflected in the distinctive remains of Gaulish, Celtiberian and Lepontic (northern Italy) (see De Hoz 1988; Fleuriot 1988; Evans 1979; Schmidt 1986). No substantive remains of Galatian (Asia Minor) are extant, although it is reported as surviving into the fourth century AD. A distinctive tongue, Narbonensic, the language of the Narbonenses (southern France), has been postulated, along a number of other Gaulish dialects. Celtic speech, apart from possible enclaves, appears to have died out on the European continent by AD 500.

1.2   INSULAR CELTIC

In the British Isles, however, Celtic survived. Scotland north of the Forth–Clyde line, the territory of the Picts, avoided Romanisation and, along with Ireland, kept its Celtic tongue (or tongues) intact. Within the Roman province and its spheres of influence the British tongues were, in different degrees, affected by Latin but survived the occupation, and the later English settlement, developing northern and southern varieties which were the ancestors of Welsh and of Cornish and Breton, respectively. Cornish ceased to be a spoken community language in the eighteenth century.

'Pictish' was superseded by the Gaelic brought in by the Irish settlers, establishing a Gaelic continuum covering Ireland and Scotland. This 'common

Gaelic' developed into Irish, Manx and Scottish varieties. Manx ceased to be a spoken community language in the nineteenth century.

1.3   THE SURVIVING CELTIC LANGUAGES

The surviving Celtic-language communities are located on the peripheries of states with other majority languages. (Irish is, of course, the designated national language of the Irish Republic.) In Brittany, Wales and Ireland there are in the region of half a million valid speakers and in Scotland there are around 80,000 speakers.

Many *émigré* Celts are dispersed in loose networks or as family groups or individuals throughout other majority populations around the world. Ethnic communities were established in America, notably by Scottish Gaels in Nova Scotia from the late eighteenth century and by the Welsh in Patagonia in 1805. A number of native speakers of Patagonian Welsh and Cape Breton Gaelic still remain.

1.4   LINGUISTIC AFFINITIES

Celtic has been long recognised as a branch of the Indo-European family of languages. Its most distinctive phonological innovation is the loss of Indo-European *$*p$*, which occurred both initially and medially: for example Gaelic *éan*, Welsh *edn* 'bird', compared with Latin *penna*, Greek *pterón*, English *feather* ($p > f$) 'feather'; Gaelic *caora* 'sheep' compared with Latin *caper* 'he-goat', Greek *kápros* 'boar' (Lewis and Pedersen 1937: 26–7 and ch. 1 *passim* for the full range of correspondences).

1.4.1   Whereas it is easy to demonstrate the status of Celtic as an Indo-European language, it has proved more difficult to find a consensus about its place in the language family, and various theories have been advanced about its genetic relationships.

Celtic is regarded as having archaic features. Typical of these are the lack of a fully developed infinitive, the lack of a verb 'have' (still true of the modern languages), the differentiation of gender in the numerals 3 and 4 (still surviving in Welsh) and the ancient SOV word order in Celtiberian and Lepontic (and still the order to be found in embedded non-finite clauses in Scottish Gaelic, and in Irish in a restricted range; see Schmidt 1986: sect. II). This has sometimes been related to its being a 'peripheral' language, that is, removed from an innovating centre.

1.4.2   'Proto-Celtic', reconstructed from the evidence of the earliest surviving fragments together with extrapolation from later materials, has been seen in the context of 'Old European' and of 'Western European'; as having a special relationship with Italic, to the extent of deriving from an Italo-Celtic common ancestor; and as having a special relationship with Germanic. The proponents of these theories have all had substantive and important data to present. However, as we get more information about early Celtic remains, about ancient languages in the Celtic contact areas and about languages of Indo-European origin elsewhere, the strong versions of these hypotheses have tended to dissolve as it becomes clear that what were considered defining criteria can no longer be regarded as restricted to the 'languages' concerned (e.g. 'Old European' and 'Italo-Celtic'; Bednarczuk 1988). Again new sources of information open out the possibilities of moving to new or revised positions along a positive rather than a negative path (e.g. the 'Western European' thesis). The evidence may, for instance, point more strongly to an early period of interlanguage contact rather than the presence of a genetic relationship. Indeed, it seems clear that this is the case with Celtic–Germanic relationships, and it is becoming increasingly acceptable to see the other cases we have cited primarily in those terms. It is certainly the case that similarities between the modern Celtic languages and genetically related tongues (such as English and French) owe much to contact. We are in the happy position, of course, in most of these cases, of having the data to enable us to distinguish innovation from survival (see Schmidt 1988; Evans 1979).

1.5   INTRA-CELTIC VARIATION

It has been common practice to divide the Celtic languages into Continental Celtic and Insular Celtic (as we have done above). This dichotomy as a historical and working definition serves its purposes: for example, when we speak of Continental Celtic we are talking of a very early period in the development of the Celtic languages, and when we speak of Insular Celtic we are talking about the direct ancestors of the modern tongues. Linguistically, however, the picture is different.

1.5.1   Two basic criteria (along with a supporting set of less distinctive ones) have been used to establish the primary linguistic division within Celtic. The first of these is the development of Indo-European $^*k^w$ (and $^*k + {}^*u$, which came together with $^*k^w$) which has different reflexes in different Celtic languages:

(a) It appears as /kụ/ in Celtiberian, in some dialects of Gaulish (where this is regarded as a mark of their archaism) and in Ogam inscriptions (where the symbol has been transliterated as Latin *q* – hence the term Q-Celtic). This yields /k/ in the historical Goedelic languages (Irish, Manx and Scottish Gaelic).

(b) It appears as /p/ in Gaulish, Brittonic and Lepontic.

This gives us early Gaelic, for example, *cenn*, Welsh, *pen(n)* 'head' and Gaelic *mac(c)*, Welsh *map*, 'son'. The latter is also attested in Ogam *maq(q)i* and Gaulish *Maponos* (the name of a divine being).

The second criterion is the development of syllabic nasals $^*m$ and $^*n$ which, unsupported and before stops, gives $^*em$, *en* in Goedelic but $^*am$, *an* in Brittonic, Gaulish and Celtiberian (the usage in Lepontic is doubtful: Schmidt 1988: 234). Examples are: Gaelic privative prefix *in-* as against Welsh *an-*; Early Gaelic *dét* (with loss of *n* and compensatory length) 'tooth', Welsh *dant*, etc. This second criterion separates Goedelic from the other early Celtic languages:

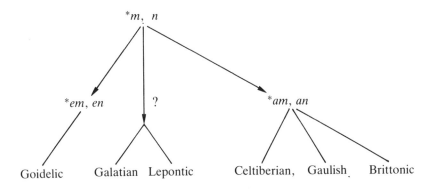

The first criterion shows relationships between Goedelic and Celtiberian and archaic Gaulish dialects:

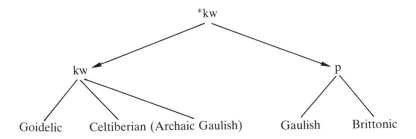

1.5.2   Modern Celtic languages

The relationships between the modern Celtic languages are as follows:

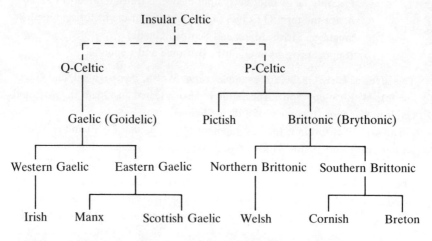

1.6   TYPOLOGICAL FEATURES OF MODERN CELTIC LANGUAGES

Some of the special typological features of the Celtic languages are archaic or conservative and some are innovative. Amongst the archaic features are the lack of a verb 'have' and the expression of the notion of possession by noun (possessed) + noun (gen.) (possessor) juxtaposition or by a noun (possessed) + locative preposition + noun (possessor) structure: *cù Chaluim/an cù aig Calum*, 'Calum's dog'; and, for example, the marking of gender in numerals 'three' and 'four' in Welsh: *tri, pedwar* (masc.) and *tair, pedair* (fem.), and perhaps the object–verb order in embedded non-finite clauses.

Locative structures, as well as being used to express 'location' and 'possession', are used to express aspectual modes. This covers the range of aspects, progressive, prospective and perfective in Scottish Gaelic and Welsh and optionally in Irish. Breton and Irish have innovated on the basis of their 'majority' contact languages, French and English respectively, to develop new perfective constructions. Contact with these languages is, as is demonstrated in the sections on the different languages below, a prime and accelerating source of innovation in all Celtic tongues.

1.6.1   Typologically, Celtic languages are VSO languages: that is, the order of elements in the structure of free, transitive, matrix sentences is verb–subject–object. This is accompanied by a structural highlighting device in which the copular verb is utilised in an equative sentence with the highlighted element as its subject (or at least as the first element following the verb). Compare the simple Scottish Gaelic sentence, 'I am at the door' *Tha mi aig an dorus* (is I at the door) with its 'equivalent' with *mi* highlighted. *Is mi a tha aig an dorus* (is (copular V) I REL is (existential V) at the door). Such sentences are common in discourse, in all the languages, with the initial verb elided. Breton has developed this structure as its unmarked form.

As is usual in VSO languages, the adjective follows the noun in the noun phrase.

1.6.2   Distinctive also, and an innovative feature, is the exploitation of sets of systemically related consonants, historically derived from their positional conditioning, to denote morphological distinctions. This happens most notably in the initial consonants of nouns, and we can illustrate it briefly by looking at the noun *cù* 'dog' and the phrases 'his dog' and 'her dog' in Irish and Scottish Gaelic, in Welsh and in Breton.

	'dog'	'his dog'	'her dog'
Irish	cú /kuː/	a chú /ə xuː/	a cú /ə kuː/
Scottish Gaelic	cù /kuː/	a chù /ə xuː/	a cù /ə kuː/
Welsh	ci /kiː/	ei gi /i giː/	ei chi /i xiː/
Breton	ki /kiː/	e gi /e giː/	e c'hi /e xiː/

We note that the possessive pronouns are realised identically (phonologically) in all languages for both genders: that is, the distinction is carried by the form of the mutation of /k/. We note also that this distinction is realised in the same manner in both Gaelic languages and in both neo-Brittonic languages, and that the two groups differ from each other in this realisation (maintaining an ancient distinction in the treatment of intervocalic stops). We are unable, for reasons of space, to give more examples here. However, further examples of these systems and of the other points raised in this section, and indeed of many other typologically relevant topics relating to Celtic, are to be found in the relevant chapters of the description of the individual languages below.

REFERENCES

Bednarczuk, L. 1988. The Italo-Celtic hypothesis from an Indo-European point of view. In G. W. MacLennan (ed.), *Proceedings of the first North American Congress of Celtic Studies*, Ottawa : Ottawa University Chair of Celtic, 175–90.

8   *Donald MacAulay*

De Hoz, J. 1988. Hispano-Celtic and Celtiberian. In *Proceedings of the First North American Congress of Celtic Studies*, Ottawa: Ottawa University Chair of Celtic, 191–208.

Evans D. E. 1979. *The Labyrinth of Continental Celtic* (John Rhŷs Memorial Lecture, British Academy, 1977), London: Oxford University Press.

    1988. Celtic origins. In *Proceedings of the First North American Congress of Celtic Studies*, Ottawa: Ottawa University Chair of Celtic, 209–22.

Fleuriot, L. 1988. New documents on Ancient Celtic and the relationship between Brittonic and continental Celtic. In *Proceedings of the First North American Congress of Celtic Studies*, Ottawa: Ottawa University Chair of Celtic, 223–30.

Lewis, H. and H. Pedersen 1937. *A Concise Comparative Celtic Grammar*, Göttingen: Vandenhoek and Ruprecht.

Schmidt, K. H. 1986. The Celtic languages in their European context. In D. E. Evans, J. G. Griffith, and E. M. Jope (eds.) *Proceedings of the seventh International Congress of Celtic Studies*, Oxford: 199–221

    1988. On the reconstruction of Proto-Celtic. In *Proceedings of the First North American Congress of Celtic Studies*, Ottawa: Ottawa University Chair of Celtic, 231–48.

PART I

The Gaelic languages

2

The Irish language

CATHAIR Ó DOCHARTAIGH

HISTORICAL AND SOCIAL PERSPECTIVE

2.0   EXTERNAL HISTORY OF THE LANGUAGE

The Irish language (*Gaeilge*) is, together with Scottish Gaelic and Manx, a member of the Q-Celtic grouping of Insular Celtic. Although it has existed in Ireland from at least the early centuries of the Christian era, the date of its introduction into the country is unknown and a number of theories have been proposed. One attempts to derive the language from a suggested invasion of an Indo-European warrior aristocracy in the first millennium BC as part of the large-scale expansions of the early Bronze Age from a central European heartland. An alternative suggestion is that the early Celtic inhabitants of Ireland were P-Celtic speakers rather than Q-Celtic (or, to be more accurate, spoke a language which later gave a form of Insular P-Celtic) and that the introduction of the Q-Celtic dialects into the country came about as the result of the dislocations and tribal movements in Gaul following the expansion of Roman power into that region and its subsequent incorporation into the Roman Empire. This latter suggestion would obviously place the origins of the Q-Celtic-speaking Gaels very much later than the alternative theory and unfortunately there is no definitive external evidence to allow us to decide between the two competing theories. From a linguistic point of view, the only suggestions to support the latter proposal are a number of words in Irish (such as *peata* 'pet' or *portán* 'crab') which appear to be old but which cannot be genuine Q-Celtic forms. It has been suggested that these represent the relics of the P-Celtic substratum in Ireland, as words which were part of the speech of the ordinary people which was displaced by that of the mainly warrior class involved in the late incursion from Gaul. For a summary of the position from the viewpoint of the first theory see Dillon and Chadwick (1973) and for the alternative suggestion see the discussion in O'Rahilly (1946); an up-to-date summary of the whole question can be found in Greene (1983) and Piggott (1983).

The earliest evidence we have for the presence of Q-Celtic in Ireland dates from the period of the Ogam inscriptions between the first and the sixth centuries AD. These lithograph inscriptions are found extensively in the southern half of the country and make use of a native cryptographic system possibly derived from a modification of the Latin alphabet (see Carney 1975). Unfortunately, the formulaic nature of these inscriptions is such as to give us very little evidence on matters of verbal morphology or syntax, but a good deal can be gleaned from them regarding the phonology and, to some extent, the noun morphology of the language underlying them. An examination of these features shows clearly a Q-Celtic language and to an extent allows us to trace some of its historical development in this essentially preliterate period. A collection of all known Ogam inscriptions is provided in Macalister (1945) and the linguistic evidence to be gleaned from them is outlined in Pedersen (1913), Thurneysen (1946), Lewis and Pedersen (1962) and Pokorny (1969).

Christianity was introduced into the country in the course of the fifth century and brought in its wake a new literacy in so far as the traditional Latin alphabet was adapted for the native language. Although we have no direct contemporary evidence for the use of this new alphabet in Irish, there is clear evidence to suggest that it was employed from an early stage and has served, with relatively minor modifications to the conventions, down to the present day. This contact with Christianity was mediated through the Church in Britain, which at this stage was Welsh-speaking (or at least spoke a form of P-Celtic which later developed into Old Welsh) and through this medium the Irish language came into contact with the classical languages, in particular Latin, mainly in ecclesiastical and high-literate contexts. This contact brought with it a series of loans from Latin (or from Greek through Latin) and appears to have extended over a period of about a century, lasting down to the middle of the sixth century. Two major periods of borrowing can be distinguished on linguistic grounds, and between them they enable us to create a relative chronology for a massive series of phonological changes undergone by the language between the fifth and seventh centuries. This set of changes marks the boundary between, on the one hand, the language of the Ogam inscriptions with its close phonological relationship with the Continental Celtic of late Gaul and its contemporary P-Celtic language in Britain and, on the other, the distinctively Irish form which emerged after this upheaval (see Jackson 1953 and MacManus 1984 for a discussion of these Latin borrowings into Irish).

The Old Irish period from about the early seventh century (Archaic Old Irish) to the ninth (Late Old Irish) is fairly well represented linguistically in a number of texts, though the only items which are still available to us in a contemporary form are the glosses and marginalia on the Scriptures and various Latin texts which have been preserved mainly in continental monastic libraries, taken there as part of the Gaelic religious diaspora of the eighth and ninth centuries. For the rest, the texts are preserved only in later manuscripts (some as late as the seventeenth century giving poems of the eighth with a clear history of textual transmission) and have not unexpectedly suffered to a greater or lesser degree in this transmission. The period of Old Irish also represents probably the widest geographical spread of Irish speech in Ireland, as by this time it is reasonable to assume that the remaining traces of any autochthonous P-Celtic speech (following O'Rahilly's (1946) views) had disappeared and the Vikings were yet to make their appearance on the Irish scene, an appearance which was to lead to the establishment of a number of large-scale colonies in various parts of the country.

These Viking incursions began in the late eighth century, and by the middle of the following century we find substantial settlements of Norse speech and with them the beginnings of urbanisation in areas such as Dublin, Wexford and Limerick, with minor sites elsewhere around the coastal regions. The linguistic effect of these Norse colonies on the Irish language was fairly limited as compared with Scottish Gaelic, of which some dialects underwent a substantial degree of close social and linguistic contact with the major Norse settlements. In the main, the effects on Irish were limited to lexical borrowings, mainly connected with seafaring, and it is clear that the social and political effects of the settlements became of decreasing importance after the battle of Clontarf in 1014, though it is likely that the language survived somewhat longer in major settlements such as Dublin until its final disappearance under the social and linguistic pressures of the Anglo-Norman invasions of the twelfth and thirteenth centuries.

This period also ushers in a wide-ranging series of modifications to the morphology of the language, changes which spread over the era of Middle Irish (ninth to twelfth centuries). Where the previous set of phonological changes in the fifth and sixth centuries had served to further the development of the language away from its close relationship to its Indo-European origins, they had left the morphological system relatively unaffected. Thus, in the *o*-stem nouns, the five-case system of the Ogam period remains into Old Irish, though naturally with different morphophonological correlates following on the massive series of sound changes. This means that the language of the Old Irish period shows a phonological structure which is substantially the same as that of some at least of the more conservative modern northern dialects, whereas its morphological system, particularly in the verb, is more similar to that of other earlier Indo-European dialects. All this was to be drastically modified in the sweeping series of morphological changes which affected the language over the period of Middle Irish and which by the thirteenth century left the language more or less in its modern form.

This modern period of Irish is usually divided into two – Early Modern (or Classical) Irish from *c.* 1250–1650 and Modern Irish from 1650 – although the reasons for this division are more sociohistorical than purely linguistic. After the changes of the Middle Irish period, the language emerged into a world where one major social caste, the literati and in particular the poets, had taken over the codification of the language and its use in formal literary domains. This hold, which they succeeded in maintaining over the course of the next four centuries, was strengthened by the internal structure of the bardic order, which was essentially a closed craft guild maintaining itself from within its own family ranks, and, more importantly, by inducting its aspirants through a rigid schooling system. The operation of this coherent structure, based on schools rather than a single 'school', in a Gaelic world where the tribal system with all its political fragmentation was otherwise the norm, led to the accumulation of linguistic power in the hands of the bardic order and other groups, such as the legal orders, closely associated with them in their high-status position. The result of this hold over the 'official' literary output of Classical Gaelic was a standardisation of the language, essentially in the form in which it had emerged from the changes of the Middle Irish period. This new literary tradition had two major sociolinguistic consequences. On the one hand, it served to ensure that some form of a high-register standard prevailed throughout the medieval Gaelic world of Ireland and Gaelic Scotland, at least in so far as formal poetic compositions were concerned. However, it also ensured that no detailed traces of the diachronic development of the language over this period emerged in the official literary manuscript output, thus effectively masking from view the emergence of the modern dialects (including the major differentiation of the language into Irish and Scottish Gaelic forms) over the course of these four centuries.

This literary and linguistic conservatism of the bardic order also served to conceal the linguistic effects of a series of historical events which had the most far-reaching consequences for the Irish language. The Anglo-Norman invasion of the country which began as a follow-through of the momentum of the Norman invasions of England and Wales in the eleventh century led in Ireland

to a nine-century-long series of adstratum contacts between Irish and English
which had the most profound effects on the language, from the phonological
system right through to a sociolinguistic situation where the continuing existence
of Irish is now seriously threatened. These contacts with English, from its
earliest Anglo-Norman form through to the language of the present day, have
given rise to a massive series of lexical borrowings and calques and there is
strong evidence for a range of syntactic, morphological and phonological
modifications to the language (see Bliss 1984 for a summary of Anglo-Norman).

Other linguistic contacts over the Classical Irish period were relatively minor
by comparison. With an increasing awareness of the world of medieval
European learning in the later Middle Ages, classical influences appear in the
language, mainly in the form of Latin loans which were clearly borrowed under
conditions of a high literate tradition. The conservatism and relative linguistic
isolation of the native tradition is further illustrated by one other source of Latin
influence in this medieval phase. This appears through the growing connections
with the European medical writers with their handbooks of symptoms, diseases
and remedies, a number of which appear to have been translated into the
vernacular for use by the Irish medical classes. Loans from French, particularly
in the Anglo-Norman period, are discussed in Risk (1968–74). Apart from
these, the only other linguistic borrowings which can be attributed to this period
appear to date in the main from the fifteenth and sixteenth centuries, when
closer links between the ordinary Irish (as opposed to the learned orders) and
the Continent were established, leading to a number of borrowings of a popular
nature such as some card-playing terminology.

The seventeenth century marks an abrupt watershed in the fortunes of the
language. After the defeat of the remnants of the native tribal order at the battle
of Kinsale in 1601, the old high-literary tradition, which was predicated on a
close-knit hierarchical and familiar society, collapsed, and with it was washed
away the standardised common written language practised previously. In its
place we find the emergence into the manuscript tradition of the distinctive
forms of the three main dialect areas of Modern Irish: Munster, Connacht and
Ulster. Essentially, the picture presented by the late seventeenth-, eighteenth-
and nineteenth-century texts shows language forms to all intents and purposes
(at least as far as information can be gained from the orthographic conventions
used) identical to those found in the twentieth-century dialects. It should be
noted that, although there was a clear break in the social and literary tradition in
the course of the seventeenth century, there is no such clear change-over to new
sets of orthographic conventions and these later texts preserve in the main the
spellings of the earlier period. This means that very little evidence shows

through these spellings to enable phonological statements to be made; rather, we are confined in the main to morphological, syntactic and lexical observations. It may be noted here that printing in Irish did not become widespread until the late nineteenth century and was then associated mainly with the new language revival movement, rather than the native tradition: in fact the manuscript tradition continued relatively untouched by the outside world until the mid nineteenth century.

This modern period also presents us with the first descriptive grammars of the language and with the beginnings of major lexicographical work. The grammatical treatises of the earlier Classical Irish period were intended primarily as texts for aspiring poets and are essentially prescriptive commentaries. In addition, there exist a number of short glossaries which concentrate on unfamiliar and obviously very literate, or even exotic, words and forms. The earliest of these is Cormac's Glossary, which dates from the late tenth century, and this tradition continued unabated in the manuscripts down to the nineteenth century. The native grammatical tradition was fertilised by a number of late medieval attempts at composing descriptive grammars for the language, based on the classical models of Latin grammar. It is these newer models which are followed in the grammars of the eighteenth and nineteenth centuries and the codification of the language contained in these still has considerable influence on the conventional wisdom of grammar writers down to the present day. The earliest large-scale dictionary of Irish was put together in the mid seventeenth century, but exists only in manuscript form. The first combined grammar and dictionary is in Lhuyd's *Archaeologia Britannica*, published in 1707 and containing partial grammars of all the Celtic languages, together with extensive vocabulary listings. The standard modern dictionaries are de Bhaldraithe (1959; English–Irish) and Ó Dónaill (1977; Irish–English).

2.0.1   Historical position

2.0.1.1   Areal distribution
As already noted, the late Old Irish period must represent the high watermark of the geographical spread of the language in Ireland and the picture since then is one of a language under increasing social and linguistic pressures. Maps 2.1, 2.2 and 2.3 present very approximate pictures of the linguistic situation in Ireland in 1300, 1500 and 1700. Map 2.1 illustrates the extent of the Anglo-Norman conquests of the previous century, conquests which were not entirely successful in a linguistic sense in so far as large areas of the south of the country

Map 2.1   Height of the English lordship *c.* 1300

Map 2.2   High point of Gaelic resurgency *c.* 1500

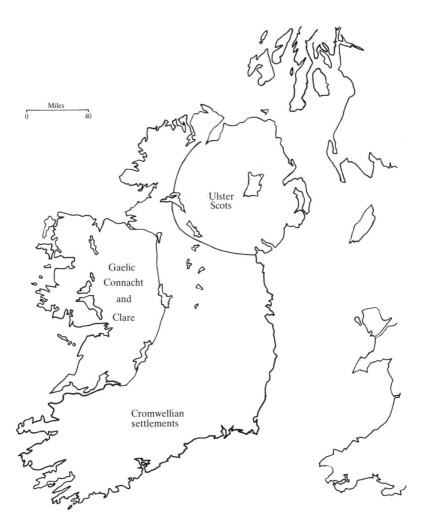

Map 2.3   The aftermath of the Cromwellian settlements *c*. 1700

which had been settled from Britain were re-Gaelicised as a result of a decreasing interest in the country by the English crown. Map 2.2 attempts to show some of the effects of this re-Gaelicisation and map 2.3 illustrates the outcome of the wars of the sixteenth and seventeenth centuries and the increasing plantations from Britain.

2.0.1.2   Demographic distribution

We have no accurate figures for the Irish-speaking population until the nineteenth century, but based on a figure of *c.* 5 million for the total population in 1800 (Connell 1950: 25), one might estimate that Irish speakers would have numbered around 3.5 million.

2.0.1.3   Status, institutionalisation, functional range, literacy

The learned orders of the Classical Irish period made use of a standardised form of Irish, and the language appears to have contained a full range of high and low registers with appropriate domains of usage. It seems likely that the low-register forms diverged more and more from the high-register standardised form and it is clearly these forms – presumably with a strong geographical bias – which form the basis of the dialectal varieties which make their literary appearance in the seventeenth century. There is no evidence at all for utilisation of the low-register popular forms in the writings of the Classical Irish period – not even in literary texts where one might have expected to find them used for stylistic purposes; in fact any such forms noted in the prescriptive grammatical tracts are disparaged as 'colloquial'.

From the point of view of the various groups of English-speaking settlers who appeared in the country over the centuries, the Irish language was felt to be an undesirable trait of the native population. Moreover, in order to defend their social polity against the surrounding Irish speakers, numerous decrees were passed forbidding the English to have any truck with Irish and encouraging them to ensure that their children were educated in English, though this official attitude appears to have been countered by a creeping assimilation of numbers of the settlers to the Irish way of life, and most of these decrees, at least down to the time of the Tudor expansions in Ireland, appear to have been more honoured in the breach than in the observance (see Ó Cuív 1951: ch. 1 for a detailed account of the external history of the language over this period).

The functional range of the language in the classical period appears to have encompassed the whole range of sociocultural life, with the exception of the dealings between the native chieftainry and the foreign-dominated governmental system. It was used for all aspects of native literary compositions, poetry, heroic tales, history and genealogy. The learned orders used it exclusively in matters of medicine (to judge from their manuscript handbooks, though they were clearly also familiar with Latin) and most particularly in the legal sphere where an extremely complex native legal code had existed from an early period.

On the question of literacy, it would appear that this was in the main confined to the native learned orders – the poets, law-givers and physicians – and presumably also was shared by the better-educated clerics of the period. Apart from these, there is little, if any, evidence for literacy among the populace at large and it would seem that even chieftains were not necessarily expected to be able to deal with written materials. Essentially, the culture was an oral one, with the poets in particular placing a strong emphasis on the memorising of large numbers of stories and poems. From the evidence which we have from much later in the Irish tradition, it seems that this oral tradition was extensively shared by the ordinary people and this particular group never seems to have been able to join the ranks of the literate, even in the period of the modern language in the eighteenth and nineteenth centuries. A comparison with the situation in Gaelic Scotland or Welsh Wales suggests that one of the reasons for this non-attainment of a more general literacy was the failure of the Reformation in Ireland and the consequent lack of a religious tradition of Scripture reading both in church services and in private (see Durkacz 1983). In addition, the failure of the language to appear in print to any great degree and the generalised lack of any effective native schooling tradition from the seventeenth century on would also have served as a potential damper on attempts to spread literacy more widely.

2.0.2   Contemporary position

The position and fortunes of the Irish language from the mid nineteenth century to the present day present a picture very different from that of any of the other contemporary Celtic languages. It is clear that, by the time of the first census of Ireland to include a language question, held in 1851, the language, although having over 1.5 million speakers, was on the point of extinction. This figure represents about one-quarter of the population of Ireland but the only areas which show an Irish-speaking population of over 50 per cent are most of west Connacht, parts of Munster and a small area of County Donegal (Ulster Irish). Although we have no definitive data on the socio-economic structure of this Irish-speaking population, it is certain that they represented the poorest and least privileged section of the country. No town, large or small, is returned as having an Irish-speaking majority and we know from the political history of the country in the eighteenth and nineteenth centuries that, whatever aspects of local devolution were permitted to the populace, the major bases of political and economic power rested in the English-speaking world of Ireland. An illustration of this is provided by the career of Daniel O'Connell, who, although he was a native Irish speaker whose campaigns involved extensive public addresses to a mainly peasant audience, never used Irish in his speeches. Given this exclusion of the language from the centres of political and economic life, it seems certain that the pattern of decline of Irish over the following century was set to parallel that of Scottish Gaelic, Welsh and Breton. In fact, as far as the native Irish-speaking population of the country was concerned, this is precisely what has happened. The most recent Irish census shows an estimated population for the *Gaeltacht* (or Irish-speaking districts) of 70,000, but a more realistic study of the situation suggests that there may be as few as 30,000 living in active Irish-speaking communities (Fennell 1981: 36).

2.0.2.1   Areal distribution

The geographical distribution of these native speakers is illustrated in map 2.4, showing the language confined to small areas of the western seaboard, with these native speakers representing between 1 and 2 per cent of the total population of the country. These figures form an interesting parallel with the situation of Scottish Gaelic, which has declined since 1891 from approximately 250,000 or 6.3 per cent to 70,000 or 1.4 per cent of the population of Scotland.

The reasons for this decline and loss of the native language are too complex and various to be dealt with here. Fundamentally, there are two aspects to the problem: an inner, which represents the internal sociodynamics of the native language speakers and their self-perceptions as members of a larger and rapidly changing social and economic polity; and an outer aspect, which covers the externally perceived reality of the Irish-speaking community as seen from the high ground of nineteenth- and twentieth-century Irish society. This external perception of the Irish-speaking population has been analysed as one of internal colonialism, in parallel with the underlying attitudes and perceptions which fuelled the expansion of the British Empire in the late eighteenth and nineteenth centuries (see Hechter 1975 for a detailed analysis in these terms). Thus, the attitudes of the native population were regarded as obstacles to economic and social progress and the position of the governing bodies was one of a thorough-going paternalism which sought to integrate the social and economic backward-ness of the peasantry with their use of a barbarous language and to ameliorate their lot in the first instance by encouraging them to abandon the latter in favour

Map 2.4   The Gaeltacht in the 1980s

of English as a major language of trade, commerce, politics and religion – in short, a language of 'general civilisation'.

The other side of the coin is to be seen in the attitudes of the Irish-speaking population itself to its own language and traditions. Following the military suppression of the native chieftain class in the seventeenth century, the Irish-speaking peasantry were excluded from the wider political and social life of Ireland for almost two centuries. This exclusion led to a feeling of powerlessness which, coupled with the native perception of the conventional wisdom of the ruling classes regarding the use of Irish, created an unconscious acceptance by the oppressed of the external analysis of their condition. The final blow in this game of psychological warfare was probably the Irish Famine of 1847–8 which led to a halving of the overall population, from around 8 million to about 4 million. The major effects of this natural disaster were felt most keenly amongst the peasantry and, in parallel to the effects of the Highland Clearances on the Gaelic-speaking Highlands of Scotland in the early nineteenth century, served to demoralise the population completely. The native responses to this disaster were flight – flight from the land to the urban centres, emigration to the New World in particular and, finally, flight from the Irish language into the new world of English. This shift to English was made easier by the fact that by the middle years of the nineteenth century a large proportion of the Irish-speaking population was already bilingual in English: of the 1.5 million Irish speakers in 1851, roughly 80 per cent were bilingual to a degree. Though it is doubtful if, for most people, this was anything more than a functional bilingualism, it means that there already existed an acceptance of English among Irish speakers, particularly in those domains of the highest public prestige – trade, politics, education and, to a great extent, religion.

All of the above presents a picture familiar to those dealing with the decline of a minority language almost anywhere in Europe over the past few hundred years – its gradual exclusion from wider and wider domains of usage and its external branding and ultimately internal perception as a second-class medium until the gradual demographic decay turns to an outrunning tide. However, the Irish experience was, in important aspects, unlike that of other Celtic areas. The re-awakening of a national consciousness on the part of the rapidly expanding Catholic urban middle classes in the mid and later nineteenth century led to an increasing awareness of the existence of the Irish language and of the possibilities of its use as a badge of separate identity. This was necessary in order to emphasise the differences between the new English-speaking middle classes in Ireland and the English-speaking world of Britain and the British Empire.

The effects on the native Irish-speaking population of this new spotlight which was thrown on them have already been outlined above. The sort of attention which was paid to the very difficult social and economic problems of the Gaeltacht fringes of the country was insufficient to halt the demographic decay of this population and to a great extent the attraction of Irish for the new nationalists was of symbolic rather than practical value. However, and this is where Ireland differs radically in its recent linguistic history from the other Celtic countries, one result of this new attitude towards Irish was to encourage many of the monoglot English speakers of the country to attempt to learn and use it in as many as possible of their everyday activities. The main organisational driving force behind this movement in the late nineteenth century was the Gaelic League (founded 1893) and many of the learning structures established by it in that period have survived to the present day, in the form of local branches of the movement which gave members the social opportunities to meet and further their knowledge of the language. With the establishment of a national government in 1922, the new state took over most of the ideals of these language revivalists and attempted to press the process forward through the formal educational system. Basically the same approach has survived to the present, though there have been modifications to the details to take account of a number of criticisms of the revivalist ideas and of their realistic chances of success (see Edwards 1984 for a bibliography).

From the sociolinguistic point of view, this educational policy has created an interesting and probably unique situation in that there exist large numbers of people whose competence in the language ranges from an almost fully native-speaker command to a very low level indeed. These speakers are mainly urbanised and do not normally make use of Irish in most aspects of everyday working life, with the language tending to be confined to mainly informal networks of friends and acquaintances and in particular to use within the family. In the public domain, the use of Irish appears to have a symbolic function when employed by politicians and other public figures and it would be rare to find it used to any great extent in contacts between the general public (even those who are fluent Irish speakers themselves) and any public or private organisation.

2.0.2.2   Demographic distribution

As already noted, the current official census figures for Irish speakers are untrustworthy as an indication of the extent of actual use of the language in the country. It is interesting to observe that such a comment could also have been applied to the nineteenth-century census returns, but there the error margin appears to have operated in quite the opposite direction to that found in the contemporary reports. In the earlier period, it would seem that respondents were unwilling to announce themselves as Irish speakers, given the perceived official attitudes towards the language. The same factors now appear to apply in the reverse direction in the light of the current favourable public opinion. Because the census questions used are so general and because of the problems inherent in self-reporting, it is impossible to measure accurately from the official statistics the actual linguistic competence of the declared Irish speakers or to estimate the active use, as opposed to a passive understanding, of the language. This problem was addressed in the 1970s in a major sociolinguistic survey which attempted to assess various aspects of Irish-language use and public attitudes towards it. Of the adult population in the non-Gaeltacht parts of the country whose self reported linguistic abilities in Irish were high, it would appear that only about 4 per cent made any extensive use of Irish in everyday conversations – a possible total of around 100,000 in all, distributed over the whole of the country (CLAR 1975: ch. 4).

From the point of view of the native speakers living in the west, there are distinct economic advantages in the way of various public-works grants available for projects within the official Gaeltacht areas. The precise geographical definition of these areas is a matter of ministerial fiat and no clear-cut linguistic criteria are used in establishing their boundaries *vis-à-vis* the *Breac Ghaeltacht* (semi-Irish-speaking district) or areas of English speech. Not unnaturally, this has led to a certain tension between the rural population of the non-Gaeltacht west and their Gaeltacht neighbours in a situation where most of the social and economic problems are identical for both communities.

2.0.2.3   Status, institutionalisation, functional range, literacy

The language occupies an extremely ambiguous position both in regard to public attitudes towards it and in the practical implementation of these attitudes in the public domain. For most citizens of the Republic of Ireland it has a strong symbolic value as one of the indicators of national identity. In part, this attitude represents the modern reflex of the views of the politically motivated revivalists of the late nineteenth century, and its practical effects are to ensure that some ritualistic or formulaic use of the language appears on most important public occasions. In the Constitution, Irish is recognised as the first official language but there are no clearly defined statutory rights granted to it by specific Acts. It is also the case that in theory all branches of local and national government should be capable of dealing with the public in Irish, though this is not always true in practice, apart from large sections of the Department of Education and the Department for the Gaeltacht. Most people who have passed through secondary-level education have, in theory, a knowledge of the language, though few would be capable of holding a sustained conversation in it. All businesses, with the exception of a few based within the Gaeltacht areas and clearly connected with semi-state sponsorship, operate through English, and no real attempt is made to cater in any way for those wishing to transact affairs through Irish. Given a situation where almost everyone in the country is a native speaker of English, only those who regard themselves as revivalists and as committed to the preservation of the language will actually make any sustained use of it.

Irish is a compulsory subject throughout the primary- and secondary-school system and is a required matriculation subject for entry to the National University colleges but there are very few posts, and these almost exclusively in the public service (including teaching posts) or in semi-state bodies, for which a knowledge of the language is a requirement or in which much active use could be made of one's knowledge of it. There are inherent sociolinguistic divisions between a rural Gaeltacht population of native speakers of the language who have not made an active choice to use the language and the wider population of mainly urbanised native speakers of English who have opted to speak Irish in as wide a range as possible of everyday contexts. These divisions are reflected most clearly in two aspects of actual linguistic performance. In the realm of pronunciation, the language of these non-native speakers is quite naturally heavily influenced by English and there are few learners whom native speakers would consider as having anything other than some form of 'learners' Irish'. On the other hand, because of the prescriptive situation in which the language is usually learned in the educational system, learners will make far more of an attempt to use a range of composed modern lexical items when speaking of the new technological world around them. In a situation where all aspects of the modern world are mediated through the medium of English, it is more usual to find native Irish speakers, who are normally competent bilinguals, simply using the English terms when speaking of such matters. It also seems to be the case that code switching is more common among native speakers than among the linguistically more sensitised learners.

All speakers of Irish are in theory literate, but it seems to be mainly the learner group who make up the bulk of the Irish-reading public. There is one weekly newspaper and a number of monthly magazines in Irish and the daily English-language newspapers usually have one or two Irish columns per week, though actual reporting of news events in Irish is rare and then only if the story has some Irish-language interest. Book publishing covers a wide range of interests, from novels and short stories, through poetry and more literary materials to non-fiction reading matter, including a wide range of educational works, with a total of approximately eighty titles appearing annually.

In the broadcasting services, there is one radio channel entirely in Irish aimed mainly at a Gaeltacht audience and broadcasting about thirty-five hours per week. Otherwise, Irish shares air space with the main English-language channels – two national television and two radio channels, in addition to a number of other commercial stations beamed mainly at the major conurbation of Dublin. On the national radio system Irish takes about 4 per cent of the time, mainly in the general services broadcasting channel, as opposed to the more youth-culture-oriented second channel. Irish on television accounts for less than 4 per cent of air time, though as a proportion of home-produced programmes it amounts to about 11 per cent – approximately 60 per cent of programmes are bought in from overseas. Television and radio have also served as media of formal instruction in Irish and have recently combined in a multi-media course, though there is no national educational broadcasting service aimed at the schools or other learners.

It may be useful at this point to outline the recent history of the orthography of the language. As already mentioned, a more-or-less standardised system of spelling existed in the official manuscript literature of the medieval period and this system was by and large retained on the break-up of the old order in the seventeenth century. In the absence of printing, the manuscript tradition survived among the native Irish-speaking population down to the middle of the nineteenth century, and the orthographic system used, as well as the actual letter forms, remained fairly constant. Given an acquaintance with this system, it is possible to read as easily the written forms of the fourteenth century as those of the nineteenth.

With the adoption of Irish by the English speakers of the country, and particularly with its large-scale introduction into the educational system after independence, it was felt that this older system was no longer appropriate to modern usage. As far as the letter forms were concerned, the original non-cursive writing, itself based on an insular form of the Roman half uncial script, was replaced by a cursive form of the letters identical with that used in English. With regard to the actual spellings, the main problems lay in the area of diachronic changes in the spoken language which had broken some of the one-to-one relationships between sound and letter existing at the original standardisation of the orthography in the thirteenth century. These changes mainly consisted in various vocalisations of original non-initial voiced fricatives, with concomitant lengthening or diphthongisation of preceding vowels, though not all dialects had applied these diachronic changes in the same way. The new standardisation of the orthography was intended to answer a number of these problems of sound–letter correspondence while at the same time not giving undue orthographic recognition to one dialect over another. Like all such devices, the resulting *Caighdeán na Gaeilge* (Standard of Irish) satisfied no group entirely, either within the Gaeltacht areas or among the non-native speakers of the language who were to be its main consumers. However, the implementation of the new system was carried out through the schooling and publishing world over the course of the 1950s and 1960s and has by now gained a wide acceptance, at least on the part of the language learners. As an extension of this policy of gradual linguistic standardisation, an attempt is currently being made to introduce a standard pronunciation based on a compromise between the phonetic forms used in the three main dialect areas. It will be interesting to watch the public response to this initiative, considering the extent to which the introduction of the standard spelling was accompanied by argument and discussion.

2.1   SYNCHRONIC LINGUISTIC VARIATION

Although the non-native Irish-speaking population forms a majority of Irish speakers in the country, the remainder of this chapter will concentrate on a description of the language as it appears among native speakers in the traditional Gaeltacht areas. These core areas of Irish speech have been progressively shrinking over the past 400 years, with the major downturn coming in the course of the last 150, and what we are faced with at present are a number of isolated areas surrounded by a sea of English. This fragmentation of the Gaeltacht has had the major effect of disrupting inter-Gaeltacht communication, with the result that each dialect area still maintains its own fairly well defined speech forms and no accepted koine has emerged to replace the standardised variety which held sway in the medieval period. On the question of actual everyday use of Irish in the public domain within the Gaeltacht areas, it is probably only in south-west Connacht that a reasonably full range of daily activities can still take place through the medium of Irish without the intervention of English.

Within a particular dialect grouping one can find some register differences, though, because of the large-scale exclusion of Irish from the public domain in the past centuries, the only real example of a high register occurs within the world of the traditional story teller, who makes use of a range of lexical material and proverbial and formulaic expressions not found in the language at large. Most dialects of Irish appear to be undergoing widespread linguistic change as their use declines in their communities, and this is reflected in marked differences between the generations, usually consisting of lexical impoverishment, a simplification of the traditional morphological system of the noun and various influences from the syntax of English.

Scientific linguistic descriptions, chiefly phonetic and phonological monograph studies of the dialects, have been carried out since the late nineteenth century in all major dialect areas, ranging from Rathlin Island in the extreme north-east to dialects of Waterford, Cork and Kerry in the south. Unfortunately, very few of these useful and detailed works were conceived of as parts of an integrated overall series of studies of Irish dialects and we are presented with a disparate set of studies which vary greatly both in terms of their actual coverage of the dialects concerned (some, for example, including a detailed commentary on various diachronic developments) and with regard to the extent of their commonly shared phonetic and phonological theories (see, for example, Quiggin 1906; Sommerfelt 1922; Ó Cuív 1944; de Bhaldraithe 1945; Breatnach 1947; de Búrca 1958; Wagner 1958; Holmer 1962). The major work of linguistic geography, which avoids these problems of cross-interpretation of differing scholarly traditions and viewpoints, is the four-volume *Linguistic atlas and survey of Irish dialects* (Wagner 1958–69) based on fieldwork undertaken in the early 1950s mainly with informants of the older generation and representing the usages of the language in the last quarter of the nineteenth century.

2.1.1   Dialect differentiation

As suggested earlier (and as illustrated in map 2.4), there are three quite distinctive dialect areas still existing – those of Munster, Connacht and Ulster Irish (Ulster Irish is the generally used linguistic term to cover Donegal Irish) – and each of these presents varying degrees of internal geographical differentiation. Overall, a fundamental distinction can be made between northern and southern Irish, with Connacht and Ulster falling into the first grouping and Munster Irish into the latter. Dialects differ at all linguistic levels, though, as might be expected, the range of syntactic differences is very small, whereas the variation in the realms of the phonetics and phonology is quite large. With regard to their diachronic development, the dialects of Munster Irish could be categorised as the most conservative in terms of their morphology where their phonological system is most different from that of Classical Irish. Northern dialects, and in particular those of Donegal, show the most conservative phonological systems and the most innovatory morphology, particularly that of the verbal system.

2.1.2   Vocabulary

To the non-linguist the area of lexical differentiation is perhaps the most obviously noticed and is certainly that which is most commented upon by native speakers who are acquainted with other dialects. Although the core vocabulary is by and large common to all dialects of Irish, there is a wide range available in the non-core or peripheral vocabulary and, in general, words which are specific to one dialect area and which are part of the active vocabulary there would not necessarily form part of even the passive vocabulary of speakers of other dialects. The reasons for this non-congruity in the passive vocabulary probably has to do with the decline in the oral literacy of the culture over the past hundred years, with fewer and fewer speakers being exposed to language materials which might expand their passive range of lexical materials. This is particularly clear in the case of the post-1945 generation, who appear to have lost (or at least be losing) a whole range of terminology. This includes not only those terms which one might expect to disappear in any case with technological innovations and the decline of the traditional ways of life (for instance, the use of terminology connected with sailing boats), but even words which one might have thought to be essential for normal everyday living are being lost. In a number of cases this has led to an extension of the use of indefinite nouns (*rud* 'a thing' being a good example) but increasingly common is the simple substitution of an English term. For example, I have noted the phrase *ag coimhlint* 'competing, striving' not being understood by a younger person in a discussion about a football match and the phrase *bhí sí ag slipeáil air sin* 'it was slipping on that' used where there exists a perfectly good Irish equivalent.

2.1.3   Syntax and morphology

There are no instances of major syntactic differentiation, and the morphology mainly shows variation in the nominal and verbal paradigms. With the nouns, the use of particular plural markers of the strong type (that is, those which add a plural ending) tends to be dialect-specific, with Connacht dialects favouring the *-acha(í)* form with certain classes of noun where Donegal dialects tend to use *-annaí*. There also appears to be an increasing generational differentiation based on various simplifications of the case system and this change is not confined to any one dialect: for example, the progressive loss of the genitive case in a number of constructions is a marked feature of most of the younger generation of Irish speakers.

Within the verbal system, the chief dialect differentiator is the use of synthetic forms in a large number of Munster dialects, where other dialects prefer in the main to use analytic constructions with the subject pronoun appearing as a separate morpheme.

(1)   *chuiris*   *chuir tú*   *tógfad*   *tógfaidh mé*
         put-PAST-2SG   put-PAST you   lift-FUT-1SG   lift-FUT   I
         'you put'   'I will lift'

One apparently fairly recent development is the use of an auxiliary verb *déan* 'to do', which serves two functions. It may be used as a straightforward auxiliary, particularly in the future tense:

(2)   *dhéanfaidh mé sin a   cheannacht duit*   = *ceannóidh mé sin   duit*
         do-FUT   I   that VPT buy   to+you   buy-FUT   I   that to+you
         'I will buy that for you'

It may also appear in responses where one would normally expect the repetition of the verb of the question to indicate a positive or negative response:

(3)   *ar*   *chuir*   *tú amach an   bhó?* *rinne* = *chuir*
         WH-PAST put-PAST you out   ART cow   do-PAST put-PAST
         'Did you put the cow out?   Yes'

2.1.4   Sound system

The major set of phonological differences between Irish dialects lies in the realm of the operation of both synchronic and diachronic word-stress rules and their effects mainly on the quantity of vowels within unstressed syllables. Historically, it appears to have been the case that Irish developed a strong stress accent on the initial syllable of words during the pre-Old Irish period of the Ogam inscriptions, leading to a reduction of original long vowels in unstressed syllables. The re-introduction of long vowels into such syllables came about as a result of the vocalisation with compensatory lengthening of the by now lenited /g/ in the Ogam ending *-agnos*, to give the common diminutive ending *-án*. In addition, the borrowing of a Welsh diminutive to give Irish *-óg* and the introduction of long vowels in a number of Classical loans helped with an acceptance of this type of word structure. The process was later encouraged within the verbal system by the Late Middle or Early Classical Irish vocalisation of voiced fricatives in unstressed syllables with compensatory lengthening and, again with nouns, by the Irish adaptation of various Anglo-Norman words which, on account of their stress pattern, were interpreted as having long vowels in unstressed position: e.g. *garsún*, taken ultimately from French *garçon*, *buidéal* from English *bottle*.

Of the modern dialects, the only area which preserves this earlier system more or less intact is that of west Connacht Irish, which shows both initial word stress and the presence of long vowels in unstressed syllables. Within the dialects of Munster, and to a lesser extent in east Connacht, this original system has been changed almost completely to one where vocalic length and the presence of stress are taken as coextensive, with words of the structure *bradán* showing stress on the *-án* and a qualitative reduction of the vowel in the first syllable (/br'da:n/ as opposed to Connacht /'bruda:n/). In Ulster dialects the opposite has happened, in that word stress has remained on the initial syllable throughout and original unstressed long vowels have been shortened and in some east Ulster dialects been qualitatively reduced as well.

Perhaps connected with this pattern of Munster stressing is a diachronic development whereby in a number of word final situations the southern dialects show a strengthening of a Classical Irish voiced fricative to its homorganic stop where in the northern grouping the same fricative would be simply vocalised. For example the word *marcaigh* 'horsemen' can give Munster /'markig'/, Connacht /'marki:/ or Ulster /'marki/, the last showing the northern shortening of the unstressed long vowel.

Within each of the three major dialect areas there are clear internal distinctions, based mainly on phonetic differences. For instance, there appears to be a gradual vocalisation of the voiceless velar fricative in a number of environments within the Irish of Ulster, with progressive phonetic weakening of this segment through some sort of [h] sound to zero as one moves from south-west to north-east Ulster. Similarly in Munster dialects, where the eastern part of the area in County Waterford shows features different from the more central southern dialects.

2.1.5   Other features of linguistic differentiation

Intonation patterns are distinctive dialect markers, though, in the absence of any detailed and comparable descriptions of the systems involved, it is impossible to give any sensible account of the distinctions here.

Apart from features of lexical differentiation between the generations mentioned above, where the younger age groups use many more English borrowings, it is also possible to note some dialectal differentiation based on loans from two external sources. Although most Irish dialects have come into close contact with English through the medium of Hiberno-English and have attracted loans from that language, dialects of Ulster have had a closer connection with Ulster Scots (introduced into the northern counties of the country as part of the plantation policies of the early seventeenth century) and this has formed the main source of their loans, at least up to the beginning of the present century and the increasing contacts with mainstream English.

For an extensive study of Irish dialect differentiation based in the main on a diachronic approach see O'Rahilly (1972), though it should be noted that the range of information available to him at this period was such as to render a number of his conclusions open to correction in matters of detail.

SYNTAX

2.2   SENTENCE STRUCTURE

The syntax and morphology of Irish are well described and illustrated, though in a somewhat traditional format, in *Graiméar* (1960). The best overall structural survey is Mac Éinrí (1970). Stenson (1981) provides an excellent account of a number of features of Irish syntax. Ó Muirí (1982) gives a detailed taxonomic description of a large corpus of sentences from a dialect of Donegal Irish. A recent study of grammatical structure which covers examples from different dialect areas is Ó Siadhail (1989).

2.2.1   Simple and complex sentences

Simple sentences, apart from imperatives, consist of at least two elements – verb and subject – with the addition of a complement to contain certain obligatory elements such as direct and indirect object.

Compound sentences contain two or more simple sentence structures linked by either co-ordinating or subordinating conjunctions. The former group is illustrated by words such as *agus* 'and', *ach* 'but', *nó* 'or', *ó* 'since', which are followed by full independent clauses:

(4)   *thóg   mé an guthán ach níor   labhair   mé leis*
        lift-PAST I ART phone but NEG-PAST speak-PAST I with-him
        'I lifted the phone but I didn't speak to him'

Simple subordinating conjunctions such as *dá* 'if', *mura* 'unless' are not common in Irish and most conjunctions are complex forms consisting of an element followed by one or other of the preverbal particles *go* and *a*: for example, *go dtí go* 'until', *ar eagla go* 'lest', *fhad is a* 'while'.

2.2.2   Parataxis and hypotaxis

Instances of parataxis are not common in the spoken language. They are usually marked by intonation (a rise to indicate an incomplete statement) and have a listing function:

(5)   *d'éirigh sé, d'fhoscail sé an   doras agus d'imigh amach*
        rise-PAST he open-PAST he ART door and go-PAST out-DIRECTION
        'He got up, opened the door and went out'

Instances of hypotaxis are found with subordinate clauses, usually introduced by the preverbal element *go* (negative, *nach*), which is followed by the so-called dependent form of the verb (see 2.7):

(6)   *dúirt   sé go raibh   sé tinn*
        say-PAST he VPT be-PAST-DEP he ill
        'He said that he was ill'

Compare (7):

(7)   *bhí   sé tinn*
        be-PAST-INDEP he ill
        'He was ill'

In conditional sentences we have a conditional verbal form, with, as required, the conjunctions *dá* 'if' or *mura* 'if not', and the dependent clause must also have a conditional verb here:

(8)   *cheannóinn   sin duit   dá mbeadh airgead go   leor   agam*
        buy-COND-1SG that to-you if be-COND money ADV.PT sufficient at-me
        'I would buy that for you if I had enough money'

Note the difference between this modal sentence and similar structures containing *má* 'if':

(9)   *ceannóidh mé sin duit   má bhíonn airgead go   leor   agam*
        buy-FUT   I   that to-you if be-PRES money ADV.PT enough at-me
        'I will buy that for you if I have enough money'

2.2.3   Elements of structure and elliptical sentences

Sentences may consist of up to four possible places of structure. The minimum sentence consists of only a verbal element, as in imperatives:

(10)   *imigh*
        'Go away'

Two-place sentences consisting of verb + subject are found with intransitives:

(11)   *thuit   sé*
        fall-PAST he
        'He fell'

Transitive sentences consist of three places, verb + subject + direct object:

(12)   *chonnaic sí   Seán*
            see-PAST she John
            'She saw John'

Transitive sentences which are transactional consist of four places, with the normal order of verb + subject + direct object + indirect object:

(13)   *thug   mé an leabhar do Mháire*
            give-PAST I   ART book   to Mary
            'I gave the book to Mary'

All *yes/no* responses normally involve some ellipsis, and the normal unmarked pattern consists of a repetition, in a positive or negative form as appropriate, of the verb of the preceding question, without any subject pronoun or verbal complement:

(14)   *an bhfaca   tú   é? chonnaic*
            WH see-PAST-DEP you him see-PAST-INDEP
            'Did you see him? Yes'

(15)   *nach   raibh   imní   ort?   ní   raibh*
            WH-NEG be-PAST-DEP anxiety on-you NEG be-PAST-DEP
            'Weren't you anxious? No'

In responses to copular sentences, the copula is normally echoed, together with another element (see 2.2.7.1 for the responses to existential questions). With idiomatic constructions consisting of the copula followed by an adjectival element followed by a conjugated preposition, the response includes the adjectival element:

(16)   *an   maith leat   Pádraig? ní   maith*
            WH-COP good with-you Patrick   NEG-COP good
            'Do you like Patrick?   No'

The appearance of the subject pronoun in responses is usually marked by the presence of a strong stress on it, together with a falling intonation and sometimes a preceding silent stress and such appearance of a subject implies that the response is emphatic:

(17)   *ar labhair   tú leis?   níor labhair   mé*
            WH speak-PAST you with-him NEG speak-PAST I
            'Did you speak to him?   I did not indeed'

The present-tense form of the substantive verb *bí* may appear without a subject as a semantically empty introductory pro-verbal element in responses to *wh*-questions, usually marked off by a falling intonation pattern and a following silent stress:

(18) *cá háit a bhfaca   tú Seán? tá,   ag an droichead*
      WH place PT see-PAST-DEP you John be-PRES at the bridge
      'Where did you see John? At the bridge'

2.2.4   Order of elements

The verbal element in the sentence is followed immediately by the subject, whether noun or pronoun (some verbal forms show morphologically more complex synthetic forms, with an incorporated postverbal subject morph – see 2.7.1). This in turn is followed by the complement, whether direct or indirect object, etc. Optional adjuncts such as adverbs follow the complement. Complements containing both direct and indirect objects have the order direct + indirect, except where the direct object is a pronoun, where the unmarked position is at the end of the clause:

(19) *thug   mé an leabhar do Sheán inné*
      give-PAST-INDEP I ART book   to John yesterday
      'I gave the book to John yesterday'

(20) *chuala   mé Seán ins an tseomra*
      hear-PAST-INDEP I John in ART room
      'I heard John in the room'

but:

(21) *thug   mé do Sheán inné   é*
      give-PAST I to John yesterday it
      'I gave it to John yesterday'

(22) *chuala   mé ins an tseomra é*
      hear-PAST I in ART room   him
      'I heard him in the room'

2.2.5   Affirmatives, interrogatives, negatives

In the simple declarative sentence the structure is as outlined in the preceding sections, with the normal unmarked order being verb + subject + complement. With interrogative and negative sentences, the order of elements remains the same, with only the presence of a preverbal particle to mark the syntactic class of the sentence and both *yes/no* and NEG-sentences are structurally identical:

(23) *chonnaic   mé an t-eitleán*
      see-PAST-INDEP I ART plane
      'I saw the plane'

(24)   *an bhfaca   tú   é?*
          WH see-PAST-DEP you it
          'Did you see it?'

(25)   *ní   fhaca   mé é*
          NEG see-PAST-DEP I   it
          'I didn't see it'

wh-questions consist of an initial interrogative element followed by the verb, which is in the morphologically independent form apart from when it follows the element *cá háit* 'where':

(26)   *caidé chonnaic   tú?*
          WH   see-PAST-INDEP you
          'What did you see?'

(27)   *cá háit a bhfaca   tú é?*
          WH place PT see-PAST-DEP you it
          'Where did you see it?'

Questions may also appear as a statement followed by a tag question, where the polarity of the tag is the reverse of that in the main clause and such tags show ellipsis of the subject pronoun:

(28)   *thug   sé leis   é, nár   thug?*
          bring-PAST-INDEP he with-him it, WH-NEG-PAST bring-PAST-DEP
          'He brought it with him, didn't he?'

(29)   *níor   thóg   tú sin, ar   thóg?*
          NEG-PAST lift-PAST-DEP you that, WH-PAST lift-PAST-DEP
          'You didn't lift that, did you?'

In phrasal complements, negation may extend over the whole phrase, using *gan* 'without':

(30)   *d'iarr   mé ort   gan   an t-airgead a thabhairt dó*
          ask-PAST-INDEP I on-you without ART money   PT giving   to-him
          'I asked you not to give the money to him'

2.2.6   Impersonal and passive sentences

Morphologically distinctive verbal forms which function as impersonals are found:

(31)   *labhairtear   Gaeilge anseo*
          speak-PRES-IMPERS Irish   here
          'Irish is spoken here'

(32)   *níor   moladh   é*
          NEG-PAST recommended-PAST-IMPERS him
          'He wasn't recommended'

Passive sentences as such consist of an appropriate tense form of the substantive verb *bí* together with a non-finite verbal form (the verbal adjective) and the logical subject expressed after the preposition *ag* 'at':

(33)   *tógann Máire an cat*   ~   *tá   an cat tógtha ag Máire*
         lift-PRES Mary ART *cat*   be-PRES ART cat lifted at Mary
         'Mary lifts the cat'   'The cat is lifted by Mary'

In passive sentences derived from aspectually marked sentences containing the substantive verb as auxiliary (see 2.2.9) passivisation involves a non-finite verbal form (the verbal noun) governed by the preposition *do* 'to' in combination with a possessive pronoun anaphoric to the grammatical subject:

(34)   *tá   Úna ag tógáil an chait*   ~   *tá   an cat dá   thógáil ag Úna*
         be-PRES Úna at lifting ART cat-GEN   be-PRES ART cat to-its lifting at Úna
         'Úna is lifting the cat'   'The cat is being lifted by Úna'

Sentences such as (34) may also appear without an expressed agent:

(35)   *tá   an cat dá   thógáil*
         be-PRES ART cat to-its lifting
         'The cat is being lifted'

2.2.7   'Being' sentences

The substantive verb *bí* is used principally to indicate existence, position or state and also as an auxiliary verb in aspectually marked sentences (see 2.2.9). The order of elements in these sentences is verb + subject + complement and the elements which can appear in the complement position are adjectives, adverbs or prepositional phrases (including verbal elements when aspectual forms are expressed). The appearance of nouns in this complement position is restricted and they are only found in expressing certain relationships, age and weights where the subject is [+Human] and, in addition, with expressions of time.

(36)   *tá   an carr sa   gharáiste*
         be-PRES ART car in-ART garage
         'The car is in the garage'

(37)   *bhí   an leabhar go   maith*
         be-PAST ART book   ADV.PT good
         'The book was good'

(38)   *bím   ag obair   ann go   minic*
         be-PRES-HABIT-1SG at working there ADV.PT often
         'I often work there'

(39)   *tá   sé a trí   a chlog*
         be-PRES it PT three o'clock
         'It is three o'clock'

(40)   *tá   muid an dá ó*
         be-PRES we   ART two grandchild
         'We are first cousins'

(41)   *tá   sí trí clocha déag*
         be-PRES she three stones -teen
         'She weighs thirteen stone'

2.2.7.1   Existential sentences

In existential sentences *bí* is used in conjunction with the element *ann* (literally
the third-person singular masculine of the conjugated preposition *i* 'in'):

(42)   *bhí   rí   ann fadó*
         be-PAST king in-it long ago
         'There was a king long ago'

(43)   *tá   droch lá ann inniu*
         be-PRES bad   day in-it today
         'It is a bad day today'

In the case of complex sentences, the *ann* may be omitted:

(44)   *bhí   rí   fadó   agus caisleán ar an oileán aige*
         be-PAST king long-ago and castle   on ART island at-him
         'There was a king long ago with a castle on the island'

2.2.7.2   Classificatory sentences

In these sentences the copula is used and the order of elements is copula +
complement + subject, though the copula may be optionally deleted if it is in the
present tense and positive and the complement consists of more than a simple
noun. The complement may be an indefinite noun or noun phrase – neither a
definite noun nor a personal pronoun may appear as principal complement in
classificatory sentences. In those cases where the logical subject is a personal
pronoun, it appears in the oblique case, where such a distinction is made (2.6.8).

(45)   *is   tiománaí maith í*
         COP driver   good her
         'She is a good driver'

(46)   *ní   baile deas Béal Feirste*
         NEG-COP town nice Belfast
         'Belfast is not a nice town'

(47)   *ba   rí   é*
         COP-PAST king him
         'He was a king'

(48)   *nach   ainmhí deas an cat?*
         WH-NEG-COP animal nice ART cat
         'Isn't the cat a nice animal?'

In the case of present-tense declarative constructions with a noun complement we may have optional deletion of the copula *is*. Thus, from (45) we may derive:

(49)   *tiománaí maith í*
         'She is a good driver'

With constructions such as (46) or (48) with a definite subject, we may optionally have a pronoun in apposition to the subject:

(50)   *is   baile breá é Doire*
         COP town fine it Derry
         'Derry is a fine town'

In addition to the above classificatory sentences with the copula, we also find a construction with the substantive verb in combination with the preposition *i* 'in' and a possessive pronoun anaphoric to the subject:

(51)   *tá   sí   ina   tiománaí maith*
         be-PRES she in-her driver   good
         'She is a good driver'

(52)   *tá   Doire ina   bhaile breá*
         be-PRES Derry in-its town   fine
         'Derry is a fine town'

Traditionally, it has been suggested that the difference between the copular and the substantive constructions here lies in the fact that the former indicates a permanent state, where the latter has a more temporary attribute. Thus we can distinguish between (53) and (54):

(53)   *is   fear é*
         COP man him
         'He is a man'

(54)   *tá   sé ina   dhochtúir*
         be-PRES he in-his doctor
         'He is a doctor'

However, it is very doubtful if this distinction would be maintained in the current language, particularly in spoken forms, and it would appear that both may be used interchangeably.

Although the above examples represent the normal unmarked construction in classificatory sentences, it is more common to find a construction where the complement is emphasised by raising. Here there are two possibilities, using either the copula (which may optionally be dropped if simple present, particularly in the spoken language) or a relativised form of a construction with *i* 'in' transformationally derived from the substantive construction as in (51) and (52) above. The copular construction appears with positive clauses only, whereas the substantive construction can occur with any sentence type. Thus, in parallel to the sentences in (51), (52) and (46) above, we have:

(55)   *tiománaí maith atá*   *innte*   *tiománaí maith is   ea*   *í*
        driver   good REL.PT-be-PRES in-her   driver   good COP IMPERS.PRON she
                        'She is a good driver'

(56)   *baile breá atá*   *i nDoire*   *baile breá is   ea*   *Doire*
        town fine REL.PT-be-PRES in Derry   town fine COP IMPERS.PRON Derry
                        'Derry is a fine town'

(57)   *ní*   *baile deas atá*   *i mBéal Feirste*
        NEG-COP town nice REL.PT-be-PRES in Belfast
        'Belfast isn't a nice town'

The substantive construction really falls into the category of simple topicalisation with a raised head which may or may not be supported by the declarative
copula (see 2.2.12 for a discussion). There appears to be a difference in dialectal
usage between the two types of construction illustrated in (55)–(57) in so far as
the forms with the anaphoric impersonal pronoun *ea* are not common in
northern dialects, and are completely lacking within Donegal (Ulster) Irish.

The response to a classificatory question consists of the copula, positive or
negative, present or past (*is* and *ní*, *ba* and *níorbh*), followed by the impersonal
pronoun *ea*:

(58)   *an*   *duine maith é?*   *is   ea /*   *ní   hea*
        WH-COP man good him   COP IMPERS.PRON / NEG-COP IMPERS. PRON
        'Is he a good man?   Yes / No'

(59)   *an*   *leabhar maith atá*   *ann?   is ea / ní hea*
        WH-COP book   good REL.PT-be-PRES in-it
        'Is it a good book?   Yes / No'

(60)   *ar*   *leabhar maith é? ba*   *ea /*   *níorbh*
        WH-COP-PAST book   good it COP-PAST IMPERS.PRON / NEG-COP-PAST
        ea
        IMPERS.PRON
        'Was it a good book?   Yes / No'

There is a subset of these classificatory sentences where the logical subject
consists of a demonstrative pronoun (see 2.6.8). In these cases an anaphoric
accusative pronoun, inflected for gender and number, appears between the
main complement and the subject, in a construction similar to that illustrated in
(50). With the simple present-tense declarative forms of this set it is probably
more common to find a construction with the demonstrative pronoun in first
position and the copula deleted.

(61)   *is   leabhar é*   *seo*   ~   *seo leabhar*
        COP book   it (MASC) this   this book
                        'This is a book'

(62) *is   cailín deas í   sin*   ~   *sin cailín deas*
      COP girl   nice her that   that girl   nice
                  'That is a nice girl'

(63) *is   daoine saibhre iad   siúd*   ~   *siúd daoine saibhre*
      COP people rich-PL them that   that people rich
                 'Those are rich people'

but:

(64) *ní   daoine deasa   iad   sin*
      NEG-COP people nice-PL them that
      'Those are not nice people'

with no alternative form with initial demonstrative. With this we may compare the optional deletion of *is* in (49), where it is similarly impossible to delete any of the other forms of the copula (negative, interrogative, past).

Complements with nominal plus conjugated preposition

There exists an important group of idiomatic copular constructions with complements consisting of a noun or adjective followed by a conjugated preposition to express the underlying subject, followed by the logical object. Responses to the question forms of this construction usually repeat the copula and following nominal or adjectival element, without the preposition, though for emphatic responses the preposition will appear, together with an object pronoun.

(65) *is   fuath liom   madaidh*
      COP hate with-me dog-PL
      'I hate dogs'

(66) *an   maith leí   cait?   is maith*
      WH-COP good with-her cat-PL COP good
      'Does she like cats? Yes'

The copula is also used in comparative constructions, though chiefly in southern dialects, whereas in northern Irish we find *bí*:

(67) *is   fearr Úna ná   Máire*
      COP better Úna than Mary
      'Úna is better than Mary'

(68) *tá   Úna níos   fearr ná   Máire*
      be-PRES Úna COMP.PT better than Mary
      'Úna is better than Mary'

2.2.7.3   Equative sentences

The copula is again used in these sentences where the grammatical subject is always a definite noun (e.g. proper name, article plus noun, noun followed by definite dependent genitive) and the complement usually also definite. There are two types of construction, depending on whether the complement or the subject follows the copula. The copula may also only be followed immediately by a pronoun and if the complement or subject following it is a noun, then an auxiliary third-person pronoun agreeing in gender and number with the noun appears in this position as a subcomplement. As previously noted, the simple present-tense declarative form of the copula may optionally be deleted.

(69)(a) *(is)*   *mise   an deoraí*
                                 I-INDIC ART exile
         'I am the exile'
    (b) *an*   *tusa   Seán?*
         WH-COP   you-INDIC John
         'Are you John?'
    (c) *ba   é*   *Éamann an duine*
         COP-PAST him   Éamann ART man
         'Éamann was the man'
    (d) *nach   í*   *Úna í?*
         WH-COP   her   Úna her
         'Isn't it Úna?'
    (e) *arbh   iad*   *na buachaillí iad?*
         WH-COP-PAST them   ART boy-PL   them
         'Were they the boys?'

The second type of construction with the complement in final position is usually found in situations with complex noun phrase subject or complement.

(70)   *is é cuspóir na ndaoine   an leabhar a dhíol*
         COP it purpose ART people-GEN-PL ART book   VPT sell
         'The purpose of the people is to sell the book'

(71)   *ba   é an rud a   bhí   ann cat mór*
         COP-PAST it ART thing REL.PT be-PAST in-it cat big
         'What it was was a big cat'

(72)   *is é mo   bharúil go raibh   sé ag obair ann*
         COP it POSS-1SG opinion VPT be-PAST he at working in+it
         'It is my opinion that he was working there'

In some dialects it is common in sentences of the type in (70) or (71) for a semantically empty introductory *ná* to appear before the complement:

(73)   *is é an rud a   rinne   sé ná an coisí   a bhuaileadh*
         COP it ART thing REL.PT do-PAST he than ART pedestrian VPT hit
         'What he did was to hit the pedestrian'

Wh-questions in equative sentences appear as:

(74)   *cé hé Colm?*
         WH him Colm
         'Who is Colm?'

(75)   *cé an carr é sin?*
         WH ART car it DEM
         'Which car is that?'

(76)   *cé sibhse?*
         WH you-PL-INDEP
         'Who are you?'

This construction is also used with the superlative adjective as complement:

(77)   *ní   hé Pádraig is   fearr*
         NEG-COP him Patrick SUP.PT best
         'Patrick is not the best'

(78)   *(is) iadsan   is   measa*
         COP them-INDEP SUP.PT worst
         'They are the worst'

2.2.8   Locative and possessive sentences

Locative sentences use the substantive verb *bí* with the complement expressing the location:

(79)   *bhí   an ríomhaire ar an tábla*
         be-PAST ART computer on ART table
         'The computer was on the table'

Possession is indicated by means of the substantive verb in combination with the preposition *ag* 'at':

(80)   *bhí   cupla carr agSeán an uair úd*
         be-PAST couple car at John ART time DEM
         'John had a couple of cars at that time'

(81)   *níl   an leabhar agam anois*
         be-PRES-NEG ART book   at-me now
         'I haven't the book now'

Ownership is usually expressed by means of a copular construction with the preposition *le* 'with' appearing in the complement governing the logical subject. Responses repeat the copula and preposition in an appropriate conjugated form:

(82)   *ba   le Dónall an madadh*
         COP-PAST with Donald ART dog
         'Donald owned the dog'

(83)   *an   le Séamas an leabhar? ní   leis*
         WH-COP with James ART book   NEG-COP with+him
         'Does James own the book?   No'

2.2.9   Aspectually marked sentences

Aspect is signalled in the complement of sentences with the substantive verb *bí* as an auxiliary verb carrying tense and person. The aspectual marker is usually a preposition, and this is used in combination with a non-finite form of the verb (verbal noun) which carries the semantic information in the sentence (see Greene 1979). We can distinguish three major aspectual categories in Irish, progressive, completive and prospective, with some possibilities of indicating the relative distance of the action from the point of speaking, proximate or non-proximate. Progressive aspect can be illustrated by (84):

(84)   *tá   Máire ag scríobhadh na   litre*
          be-PRES Mary at writing   ART letter-GEN
          'Mary is writing the letter'

In this construction the logical object is placed after the verbal noun and is in the genitive case as it depends directly on the preceding noun (see 2.3.3).

The perfective aspect has two possible constructions, one with the verbal noun and one with the verbal adjective:

(85)   *tá   Máire tar éis an litir a   scríobhadh*
          be-PRES Mary after   ART letter VPT write
          'Mary has written the letter'

(86)   *tá   an litir   scríofa ag Máire*
          be-PRES ART letter written at Mary
          'Mary has written the letter'

As an alternative to *tar éis*, we may also find the preposition *i ndiaidh* – the distribution of these two seems to have a geographical basis, with northern dialects favouring the latter. Proximate forms here may be indicated by means of the adverb *díreach* 'directly' placed in front of the preposition:

(87)   *tá   sí díreach i ndiaidh an siopa a   dhruid*
          be-PRES she directly after   ART shop VPT close
          'She has just closed the shop'

or alternatively with the verbal adjective:

(88)   *tá   an siopa díreach druidte aice*
          be-PRES the shop directly closed at-her
          'The shop has just been closed by her'

Note that in the verbal-noun construction the logical object now precedes the verbal element and is in the nominative case, unlike the situation with the progressive aspect.

It is also possible to combine a perfective with a progressive aspect:

(89)   *tá   mé díreach i ndiaidh bheith ag caint   leis*
          be-PRES I   directly after   be   at speaking with-him
          'I have only just been speaking to him'

Prospective aspect may also be indicated by two different constructions, the first using the prepositions *ar tí* (proximate), *chun* or *le* (to express intention), the second using the verbal noun *ag dul* 'going' (expressing intention), possibly as a calque on English.

(90)   *tá   sí ar tí bróga a   cheannacht*
          be-PRES she about shoe-PL VPT buy
          'She is about to buy shoes'

(91)   *tá   muid ag dul a   dhíol an tí*
          be-PRES we   at going VPT sell ART house-GEN
          'We are going to sell the house'

This construction may also be combined with progressive aspect as in (89):

(92)   *tá   mé le bheith ag obair   anseo i rith   na hoíche*
          be-PRES I   with be   at working here in course ART night-GEN
          'I am to be working here all night'

2.2.10   Complementation

Complements of the verb *bí* and of the copula have already been discussed in 2.2.7 and its subsections. In transitive sentences we chiefly find adjectival complements, with some instances of prepositional phrases:

(93)   *tá do chuid lámh   salach*
          is your share hand-GEN-PL dirty
          'Your hands are dirty'

(94)   *d'iarr   mé ort   do chuid lámh   a   bheith glan*
          request-PAST I on-you your share hand-GEN-PL VPT be   clean
          'I asked (you) that your hands be clean'

(95)   *an bhfuil   sibh   éirithe fallsa?*
          WH be-PRES-DEP you-PL risen   lazy
          'Have you become lazy?'

(96)   *d'imigh sé leis   ina   amadán críochnaithe*
          left-PAST he with-him in-his fool   finished
          'He left as a complete fool'

Indirect speech is introduced by the particles *go* 'that', *nach* 'that not', *gur* 'that-PAST' or *nár* 'that not-PAST' which are followed by the appropriate dependent form of the verb in the subordinate clause:

(97)   *chuala   mé gur imigh   tú   ann   Dé Luain*
            hear-PAST I   that go-PAST-DEP you there Monday
            'I heard that you went there on Monday'

2.2.11   Modal sentences

Modals are usually expressed by means of *bí* or the copula in conjunction with a
personal form of a preposition (see 2.10) to indicate the subject and followed by
a nominal phrase with a non-finite verb. One may also use the future (and
occasionally the past) of the verb *caith* together with a subject pronoun and a
nominal complement. Some examples of these constructions are given, based on
the translation equivalents of 'I must sell the car':

(98) (a)   *tá orm*
            is on-me
     (b)   *tá (sé)d'iallach   orm*
            is (it) of-requirement on-me
     (c)   *ní   mór dom*   *an   carr a dhíol*
            NEG-COP big to-me   ART car to sell
     (d)   *ní   foláir dom*
            NEG-COP 'excess' to-me
     (e)   *caithfidh   mé*
            'must'-FUT I

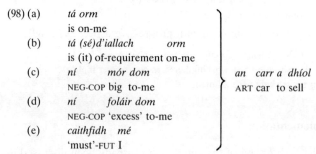

The negation of the complement in all the above forms is indicated by prefixing
it with *gan* 'without':

(99)   *tá orm   gan   an carr a dhíol*
            is on-me without ART car to sell
            'I have to not sell the car'

Compare:

(100)   *níl   orm   an carr a dhíol*
            is-NEG on-me ART car to sell
            'I don't have to sell the car'

Similarly, notions of 'ought' and of intention may be expressed by use of the
auxiliaries:

(101)   *ba   cheart dom an carr a dhíol*
            COP-COND right to-me ART car to sell
            'I ought to sell the car'

(102)   *tá agam leis an charr a dhíol*
            is at-me with ART car   to sell
            'I have to sell the car'

2.2.12   Topicalisation

Irish does not make very much use of pitch, stress or loudness to emphasise elements of sentences. Instead, as suggested earlier, any element which it is desired to emphasise is raised to the sentence-initial position. All such topicalisations use the copula to support the raised element, following the rules for copular sentences adduced in 2.2.7.2 and 2.2.7.3 above, though it may optionally be deleted if simple present. The topicalised word or phrase is followed by the original sentence as a relativised dependent clause. Taking the sentence of (103), we may illustrate the topicalisation of each item in turn, where the topicalised element is introduced by the simple present of the copula in each case (optional in (104)). It would, of course, be possible to find other tense forms, as well as negatives and interrogatives, as forms of the introductory copula.

(103)   *bhuail   carr an   coisí   ólta   ar an   droichead aréir*
          hit-PAST car   ART pedestrian drunk on ART bridge   last+night
          'A car hit the drunk pedestrian on the bridge last night'

For the subject:

(104)   *(is)   carr a   bhuail an coisí ólta ar an droichead aréir*
          COP-PAST car   REL.PT
          'It was a car which hit the drunk pedestrian on the bridge last night'

The object:

(105)   *is é an coisí ólta a bhuail carr ar an droichead aréir*
          'It was the drunk pedestrian whom a car hit . . . '

The prepositional phrase:

(106)   *is ar an droichead a bhuail carr an coisí ólta aréir*
          'It was on the bridge that a car hit . . . '

The adverb:

(107)   *is aréir a bhuail carr an coisí ólta ar an droichead*
          'It was last night that a car hit . . . '

Finally, the whole sentence may be emphasised by using the noun *rud* 'a thing':

(108)   *is   é rud   a   bhuail   carr an coisí ólta ar an droichead aréir*
          COP-PAST it thing REL.PT hit-PAST
          'What happened was that a car hit . . . '

Or by means of the adverb *amhlaidh* 'thus, so':

(109)   *is amhlaidh a bhuail carr an coisí ólta ar an droichead aréir*
          'It was the case that a car hit . . . '

2.2.13   Other sentential features

There is a sentence type which contains a phrase introduced by *agus* 'and', usually containing a non-finite verbal form (the verbal noun) in conjunction with one of the aspectual particles (2.2.9) to indicate an action or state contemporary with that of the main verb:

(110)   *tig   sé amach agus é   ag gáire*
come-PRES he out   and him at laughing
'He comes out laughing'

(111)   *d'imigh sé agus é   i ndiaidh an   deoch a ól*
go-PAST he and him after   ART drink to drink
'He went off having had the drink'

(112)   *tháinig   siad isteach agus iad   fliuch go craiceann*
come-PAST them in   and them wet   to skin
'They came in soaked to the skin'

Optative sentences are usually expressed after the particles *go* or *nár*:

(113)   *go mairí   an bhainríon!*
POS live-SUBJUNCT the queen
'Long live the queen!'

(114)   *nár aifrí   Dia orm   é!*
NEG rebuke-SUBJUNCT God on+me it
'May God forgive me!'

STRUCTURE OF THE PHRASE

2.3   THE NOMINAL PHRASE

Noun phrases consist of at least a noun or other nominal element as head with various optional elements occurring as modifiers. We may analyse such phrases in terms of those elements which may occur before, and those which may occur after, the phrasal head. The former category is fairly restricted and contains only the article and various adjectivals such as possessives, numerals and a limited set of prefixed adjectives, usually with an intensive force. The latter consists of descriptive adjectivals, various determinative forms, adverbs, nouns (in genitive case), noun phrases and relative clauses.

2.3.1   Order of elements: pre-head position

(115)   DEF ART   *uile*   ORDINAL   CARDINAL   ADJ
            gach   *aon*
            POSS ADJ
            cibé

Of the forms in the first column, the first three are definite (*gach* = 'each' or
'every'), the last (WH + 'ever') an indefinite modifier. In the second column, *aon*
(literally 'one') may be used alone as an indefinite modifier, 'any', or in
combination with the definite article to mean 'only'. Only a few adjectives such
as *sean* 'old', *príomh* 'chief' and some colour terms used as intensifiers can
appear in pre-noun position. Some examples of these premodifier combinations
are given in (116)–(118).

(116)   *na chéad trí chat* 'the first three cats'
            gach uile dara duine 'every single second person'
            mo chéad leabhar 'my first book'

(117)   *cibé duine* 'whichever person' = 'whoever'
            cibé uair 'whatever time' = 'whenever'
            cibé dóigh 'whatever way' = 'however'

(118)   *an t-aon droch chapall* 'the only bad horse'
            dearg ádh 'very good luck' (lit. 'red luck')

2.3.1.1   Postmodifier elements
Following the nominal head we have the following possibilities:

(119)   DESCRIPTIVE ADJ   DETERMINER   ADV   PREP PHRASE   REL CLAUSE
                                                       NOUN PHRASE

Within the grouping of descriptive adjectives, the order of elements is usually
size + age + colour + quality + provenance:

(120)   *an   leabhar beag úr   dearg míofar Síneach*
            ART book   small new red ugly   Chinese
            'the little new red ugly Chinese book'

though the ordering will depend on a number of factors, including the precise
semantic relationships with the head and between the adjectival elements.

Prepositional phrases and relative clauses as modifiers are dealt with in the
following section and the appearance of a noun phrase as postmodifier is
covered in 2.3.3. Demonstrative adjectives are dealt with in 2.3.4. Some
examples of the first three groups of modifiers are:

(121)   (a) *an cat deas istigh* 'the nice cat inside'
            (b) *cat mór éigin* 'some big cat'

(c) *cat beag bán eile* 'another little white cat'

(d) *an cat mór Manannach céanna* 'the same big Manx cat'

2.3.2   Embedding: phrasal and clausal modifiers

Modifiers may take the form of prepositional phrases:

(122)   *an cat beag ar an chathaoir*
          'the little cat on the chair'

The more important category, however, is that of relative subordinate clauses. Irish has two types of such clause, the so-called direct and indirect, depending on whether the antecedent or nominal head is regarded as the subject or object of the subclause or whether it exists in some other grammatical relationship (i.e. in the genitive case or within a prepositional phrase) within that clause. The two types differ in the form of relative pronoun used and also in the form of the verb in the subclause following the pronoun, although this distinction is only maintained with positive relative clauses. Examples are given below of the various types of relative construction, using an irregular suppletive verb to illustrate clearly the differences between the two types. For an extremely detailed analysis of the Irish relative see MacCloskey (1979).

Antecedent as subject or object of relative clause:

(123)   *an fear a   chonnaic Máire sa   charr*
          ART man REL.PT see-PAST Mary in-ART car
          'the man who saw Mary in the car' *or* 'the man whom Mary saw in the car'

Note the inherent ambiguity in such direct relative clauses regarding the distinction between subject and object when the verb is such as to allow the possibility of a [+Animate] subject. Compare (123) with (124):

(124)   *an fear a   chonnaic an carr*
          ART man REL.PT see-PAST ART car
          'the man who saw the car'

Where necessary, when the antecedent is the object this ambiguity may be avoided by means of an indirect relative construction:

(125)   *an fear a   bhfaca   Máire sa   charr é*
          ART man REL.PT see-PAST-DEP Mary in-the car   him
          'the man whom Mary saw in the car'

Antecedent within prepositional phrase: starting from the sentence:

(126)   *chonnaic mé leis an fhear thú*
          see-PAST I with ART man you
          'I saw you with the man'

we may derive:

(127)   *an fear lena   bhfaca   mé thú*
ART manwith-REL.PT see-PAST-DEP I   you
'the man I saw you with'

or alternatively:

(128)   *an fear a   bhfaca   mé leis   thú*
ART man REL.PT see+PAST-DEP I   with+him you
'the man I saw you with'

where in this case the preposition within the clause must show the appropriate personal and gender form. In the negative relative subclause we can only have:

(129)   *an fear nach   bhfaca   mé leis thú*
ART manREL.PT+NEG see+PAST-DEP
'the man I didn't see you with'

Constructions such as (130) are not found in the modern language:

(130)   *an fear le nach bhfaca mé thú*

With the antecedent in a genitival relationship within the clause we have:

(131)   *an fear a   bhfaca   mé a   mhadadh*
ART manREL.PT see+PAST-DEP I   POSS.ADJ-3SG-MASC dog
'the man whose dog I saw'

where the subordinate clause will contain an anaphoric possessive adjectival pronoun governing the possessed object. The clause in (131) may be taken as derived (somewhat simplistically – see McCloskey 1979 for a fuller discussion) by means of relativisation from the sentence:

(132)   *chonnaic mé madadh an   fhir*
see-PAST I   dog   ART man-GEN
'I saw the man's dog'

2.3.3   Definiteness and indefiniteness

There is no indefinite article in Irish and marking of definiteness is carried by the definite article or possessive adjective in position before the noun, or within a noun phrase adjunct to the noun. The article and possessive adjective are, not unexpectedly, mutually exclusive, but there also exists an exclusive relationship between a pre-head article and a following noun phrase, with definiteness only being marked once within the nominal phrase. This may be illustrated by means of the examples:

Indefinite noun:

(133)   *lámh*   *lámh fhir*
              hand 'a hand'   hand man-GEN 'a man's hand'

Definite noun:

(134)   *an   lámh   mo*   *lámh*   *lámh Sheáin*   *lámh an   fhir*
              ART hand POSS.ADJ-1SG hand   hand John-GEN   hand ART man-GEN
              'the hand'   'my hand'   'John's hand'   'the man's hand'

The above implies that one cannot have **an lámh an fhir* or **an lámh Sheáin* to
translate English 'the hand of the man' or 'the hand of John's'.

2.3.4   Demonstratives

There are three demonstratives in Irish: proximate, corresponding to the first
person in a deictic frame; non-proximate, corresponding to the second person;
and remote, corresponding to third person, with this last term being non-
proximate both in time and space. They occur postnominally in the determiner
position with the definiteness of the head noun being marked either by the
presence of a preceding definite article or, in the case of the genitival
construction described in the preceding section, by the definite marker of the
second noun.

(135)   *an lamh seo*   *an fear sin*   *an leabhar úd*
              'this hand'   'that man'   'that book'

(136)   *lámh seo an fhir* 'this hand of the man'
              leabhar sin Shéain 'that book of John's'

The demonstratives are invariable and are not declined for case or number
concord with their head, nor are they initially mutated in the way in which a
normal adjective would be in this postnominal position (see 2.16). For a
discussion of some aspects of deictic categories in Irish see Ó Baoill (1975).

2.3.5   Reflexives

The element *féin* 'self' is used to express reflexiveness, being attached to the
nominal head following any determiner that is present. It may also be attached
directly to independent pronouns or to conjugated pronominal forms (synthetic
verbal forms or conjugated prepositions):

(137)   *an fear féin* 'the man himself'
              mholfainn féin é 'I myself would praise him'
              sinn féin 'we ourselves'

2.3.6   Enumeration

For the numeral 'one' we have the choice of several constructions with the noun:

(138)   *aon mhadadh (amháin)   madadh amháin   madadh*
          one dog   only

all glossed as 'one dog'. With numerals above 'one' there are two possible constructions, the first consisting simply of the numeral followed by a singular or plural noun, the second consisting of the numeral in conjunction with an indefinite pronoun (actually the word *ceann* 'head', singular or plural) followed by the preposition *de* 'of' and a plural head noun. This second construction is particularly common where the noun is qualified by any following adjectival element, but it does also appear with the simple nominal heads.

(139)(a)   *aon cheann déag de chaoirigh mhóra* 'eleven sheep'
     (b)   *dhá chéad is trí cinn d'ubhlaí* '203 apples'

Numerals formed by a combination of a simple ordinal ('one' to 'nine') with the element *déag* '-teen' show the *déag* in postnominal position following any attributive adjective. Combinations with multiples of ten show the structure of a simple numeral, followed by the noun, followed by *is* (= *agus* 'and'), followed by the appropriate multiple (*fiche* 'twenty', *daichead* 'forty', etc.).

(140)   *trí chapall déag   ceithre charr is fiche*
          'thirteen horses'   'twenty-four cars'

There is a limited group of special numeral forms ('two' to 'ten' and 'twelve' only) used for counting persons, which may also appear alone as indefinite numerals referring to people (and in some northern dialects with a wider reference as general indefinites).

(141)   *beirt fhear* 'two men'   *ceathrar garda* 'four policeman'

2.3.7   Possession

Possession is usually indicated by means of the possessive adjective or a postposition nominal in the genitive case, or alternatively, by means of a prepositional phrase with *ag* 'at'. The precise repartition between these two constructions is not entirely clear: the use of the first type appears normal in cases of inalienable possession – parts of the body, relations, clothes, etc.; the second seems more common in the case of third-person forms where alienable possession or proper names are involved or in partitive meaning:

(142)(a)   *mo dheirfiúr* 'my sister'
     (b)   *deirfiúr Mháire* 'Mary's sister'
     (c)   *Máire 's agaibh-se* 'your (EMPH) Mary'

(d)   *an teach 's aige* 'his house'
(e)   *an croí seo agam-sa* 'this heart of mine'

2.3.8   Concord

Concord within the noun phrase exists between the head noun and following adjectives, which may be inflected for number, gender and case, though not all the possibilities here actually show inflectional concord. This particular feature is one which is highly sensitive to generational differentiation, at least in respect of the appearance of concord in singular oblique cases. The 'classical' modern paradigm of noun and adjective declension for a masculine and a feminine noun with following adjectives is given in (143):

(143)   *Singular*
         NOM. *an fear mór* 'the big man'   *an fhaoileog bhán* 'the white gull'
         GEN. *an fhir mhóir*   *na faoileoige báine*
         PREP. *an fhear mhór*   *an fhaoileoig bháin*

         Plural
         NOM. *na fir mhóra*   *na faoileogaí bána*
         GEN. *na bhfear mór*   *na bhfaoileogaí bána*
         PREP. *na fir mhóra*   *na faoileogaí bána*

2.3.9   Adjective phrase

An adjective may appear as the head of a phrase with various modifiers:

(144)   *ró-mhór = iontach mór = fíor-mhór* 'very big'
(145)   *tá sé leath chomh mór leatsa*
         is he half as   big with-you-EMPH
         'He is half as big as you'

2.4   THE VERBAL PHRASE

The verb phrase consists of an independent finite verbal head showing formal contrasts in tense and mood, followed (except in the case of imperatives) by a subject. It may also show certain preverbal elements connected with negation and question forms, with the form of the verb under these circumstances being normally morphologically marked with respect to the independent form (see 2.7.1). As described in 2.2.9, there is also the possibility of marking aspect in the phrase and this is usually done by means of a construction with the auxiliary verb *bí* 'to be' to carry tense and mood information, used in conjunction with various prepositional elements and a non-finite form of the verb. It may also be noted that with a pronominal subject there are two possibilities: either the subject is shown as an enclitic pronoun separable from the tense-marked verbal ending or as a single unanalysable ending containing both tense and personal information – see 2.7.1. We may illustrate the structure of the verb phrase as:

(146)   (PREMODIFIER) + VERB + (SUBJECT) + (ASPECTUAL MARKER) +
          (NON-FINITE VERB)

2.4.1   Preverbal modifiers

These consist of the interrogative and negative particles which show a variety of morphological shapes depending on the tense of the following verb. It may be noted here that the *wh*-interrogative particles require a structure identical to that found in relative subclauses and have been so analysed in McCloskey (1979).

(147)(a)   *ní   thógfaidh mé an   leabhar*
             NEG lift-FUT   I   ART book
             'I will not lift the book'

   (b)   *níor   bhuail   mé an   cat*
             NEG-PAST hit-PAST I   ART cat
             'I didn't hit the cat'

(148)(a)   *cé   dhéanfadh sin   dom?*
             WH do-COND   that to-me
             'Who would do that for me?'

   (b)   *caidé chuir   sé ansin?*
             WH   put-PAST he there
             'What did he put there?'

2.4.2   Auxiliary verb

Occasional use is made of the auxiliary *déan* 'to do' in combination with a non-finite form of the verb preceded by a particle. This appears to be a stylistic use intended to avoid adding a further enclitic syllable to polysyllabic verbs in certain morphological forms such as the impersonal or future.

(149)   *dhéanfaidh mé an   carr a   thiomáint duit*
          do-FUT   I   ART car VPT drive   to-you
          'I'll drive the car for you'

By far the most common use of an auxiliary construction is in the aspectually marked sentences previously described. The only additional point which may be

made here concerns the object marking in such constructions which differs
between the various aspectual forms and also between noun and pronomial
object. In the case of the latter, the object appears as a possessive adjective
preceding and governing the non-finite verbal element. A noun object appears
before the infinitive in the case of the prospective and completive aspects and
after the infinitive in the case of the progressive.

(150)   *tá   sé ag tógáil an   leabhair   tá sé dhá thógáil*
         be-PRES he at lifting ART book-GEN   at-its lifting
         'He is lifting the book'   'He is lifting it'

(151)   *tá   sé i ndiaidh an leabhar a   thógáil   tá sé i ndiaidh é a   thógáil*
         be-PRES he after   ART book   VPT lifting   after   it VPT lifting
         'He has lifted the book'   'He has lifted it'

2.5   THE PREPOSITIONAL PHRASE

These phrases consist typically of a preposition followed by a complement
consisting of a nominal element – a noun phrase or verbal noun phrase. There
are two prepositional types in Irish, simple and compound, with the latter being
structured as a combination of a simple preposition and a following nominal. In
many cases this noun also occurs independently, for example *ar aghaidh* 'in front
of' has *aghaidh* 'face', but in others we have petrified earlier nouns which no
longer have an independent existence, for instance *faoi dhéin* 'for'. Simple
prepositions are followed by either nominative or dative case of the noun;
compound forms take the genitive, in accordance with the rule noted in 2.3.3.

2.5.1   Prepositions with noun phrase

In the noun phrase the preposition comes first, preceding the article or
possessive adjective of 2.3.1.1. There are a number of simple prepositions which
show morphological variants in position before the article, and some which end
in a vowel drop it before nouns beginning with a vowel. Examples of simple
prepositions are given in (152) and (153):

(152)   (a) *do Sheán* (b) *le casúr*   (c) *ar tábla*   (d) *in uisce*
         'to John'   'with a hammer'   'on a table'   'in water'
         (e) *faoi chathaoir*
         'under a chair'

(153)   (a) *don fhear* (b) *leis an chasúr* (c) *ar an tábla* (d) *san uisce*
         'to the man'   'with the hammer'   'on the table'   'in the water'

Compound prepositions are illustrated in (154):

(154) (a) *le   cois   trá*
              with 'foot' beach-GEN
              'beside a beach'
       (b) *faoi   bhráid   Dhónaill*
              under 'throat' Donald
              'in front of Donald'

With regard to case marking following prepositions, forms such as *gan* 'without', *idir* 'between' or *seachas* 'apart from' take the nominative. The simple prepositions take the dative, with the exception of a few, such as *trasna* 'across' and *chun* 'towards', which are followed by the genitive (these represent petrified forms of earlier nouns and hence follow the rules of 2.3.3). Compound prepositions are followed by the genitive. Due to the fairly generalised simplification of the traditional noun morphology (see 2.6), it is only in certain instances that one finds clear case marking in following noun phrases.

2.5.2   Prepositions with pronominals

Simple prepositions which normally take the dative of a noun, when followed by a pronominal element show complex forms with enclitic pronouns – see 2.10. Simple prepositions (apart from *idir* 'between') which take the nominative are followed by oblique-case pronouns (see 2.6.8).

(155)(a)   *gan é*
              'without him'
     (b)   *go dtí sibh*
              'towards you'

Compound prepositions in combination with pronomials show the disjunct structure already illustrated in the non-finite aspectual verbal phrases of 2.4.2, with a possessive adjective intercalated between the simple prepositional first element and the nominal second element.

(156)(a)   *le   mo chois*
              with 1SG side
              'by my side'
     (b)   *ar do shon*
              on 2SG sake
              'for your sake'
     (c)   *i m' fhianaise*
              in 1SG witness
              'in my presence'

2.5.3   Prepositions with verb phrases

These are used with the non-finite form of the verb, and in aspectual usage with the verb *bí* 'to be' only a few prepositions can appear in the complement. The preposition *gan* 'without' is used with nominal complements containing a non-finite verb to express a negative:

(157)(a)   *d'iarr   mé air   sin a   dhéanamh*
          ask-PAST I   on-him that VPT do
          'I asked him to do that'
    (b)   *d'iarr mé air gan   sin a dhéanamh*
                    without
          'I asked him not to do that'

The element *a* 'to' only appears before verbal nouns to fill a variety of functions and I have normally described it in examples above as a verbal particle (it seems to be a reduced form of earlier *do* 'to').

One important type of prepositional phrase with a verbal element appearing as a complement in sentences with *bí* 'to be' is the so-called 'stative' construction, consisting of the preposition *i* 'in', followed by a possessive adjective anaphoric to the subject and agreeing with it in number and gender, followed by a governed verbal-noun element. Thus:

(158)(a)   *tá   mé i mo   shuí*
          be-PRES I   in POSS.ADJ-1SG sitting
          'I am sitting'
    (b)   *tá   Seán ina   chodladh*
          be-PRES John in-POSS.ADJ-3SG-MASC sleeping
          'John is asleep'
    (c)   *tá   muid inár   luí*
          be-PRES we   in-POSS.ADJ-1PL lying
          'We are lying'

MORPHOLOGY

Unlike matters of syntax, studies in Irish morphology are widely available, though normally couched in a somewhat traditional format and usually articulated in the form of prescriptive grammars intended for language learners. To this extent, they present a somewhat idealised and standardised view of the language and do not generally deal in any detail with the micro-realities of the spoken dialects. Good general studies are provided in *Graiméar* (1960), *Gramadach na Gaeilge* (1968) (both in Irish) and *New Irish grammar* 1980 (a shortened English version of *Graiméar* 1960). A detailed morphological study of a Connacht dialect is de Bhaldraithe (1953; in Irish), and Lucas (1979) covers the same ground for a north Donegal dialect.

2.6 NOUNS

The noun is marked for gender, number and case and, to a limited extent, person (in vocative case nouns) by means of various combinations of initial-consonant mutations (see 2.16.1), base-vowel mutations or ablaut, final-consonantal mutations (see 2.16.2), the addition of endings or suppletion. Of these, base mutations and final-consonant mutations are mostly used for case differentiation within the singular and suffixation is mainly used to form the so-called 'strong' plurals. Root suppletion is only found with a limited number of irregular nouns. Initial mutations, found after the article, are most common in the singular but also appear in the genitive plural.

2.6.1 Structure: stems and endings

The simple stem, as in *iasc* 'fish', represents the minimal free form of the noun, and from this we may derive by suffixation forms such as *iascaire* 'fisherman'. There are instances of compound forms such as *iaschmheall* 'fish-ball' and diminutives with suffixation are fairly common, for example *iascán* 'small fish'. Compounds formed by a combination of a prefixed adjective and a noun are common, for example, *dubhaois* 'great age' (lit. 'black age'). Occasional collectives of the form *iascra* 'fish' are also found. Apart from these derivational suffixes, most instances of suffixation are to be found in the wide range of plural formatives and, to a lesser degree, in case marking.

2.6.2 Inherent classes

The only morphologically marked inherent classes are gender-based, with masculine and feminine nouns showing some differentiation in singular case marking and in mutational effects on a following adjective.

2.6.3 Animate/inanimate

There are no morphological correlates of animate versus inanimate. The only marginal instance of such a distinction is to be found in the interpretation of the locative/possessive construction of 2.2.8 where the preferred reading as possessive after the preposition *ag* 'at' depends on the governed noun being animate. Otherwise, the preferred interpretation is a locative one.

2.6.4   Gender

Irish has two gender categories in the noun, masculine and feminine, usually corresponding to natural gender, and normally collocating with the appropriate third-person singular pronoun. The distinction between the two genders is carried in the initial mutations found in the noun after the article in various case forms and in initial-mutation effects on following adjectives.

2.6.5   Number

Irish nouns show two numbers, singular and plural, with the nominative singular being the unmarked base form. In enumeration (see 2.8.6.1) plurals begin with 'three'. There are two types of plural formation. In the weak form, the plural marker consists of a mutation of the final consonant or consonant cluster of the singular, sometimes coupled with stem-vowel mutation, or else the simple addition of *-a* (phonetically a schwa) to the singular. The consonantal mutation here almost always involves a change from a neutral to a palatalised segment (or occasionally the opposite) – see 2.16.5. For the strong plurals, a suffix is added to the singular, sometimes with stem ablaut or syncope of an unstressed syllable or with mutation of the final consonant of the singular. Common plural markers are *-ta, -tha, -anna, -acha, -na* and *-í*, and it would appear that some dialects favour some endings in particular. The examples which follow are intended to illustrate only some of these plural formatives.

(159)   *Weak plural with palatalisation*

	Singular		Plural
	cat /kat/	'cat'	*cait* /kat'/
	bád /ba:d/	'boat'	*báid* /ba:d'/
	bradán /brada:n/	'salmon'	*bradáin* /brada:n'/
	marcach /markax/	'rider'	*marcaigh* /marki:/
	tarbh /tarv/	'bull'	*tairbh* /tir'v'/

(160)   *Weak plural by vowel suffix*

	Singular		Plural
	cos	'foot'	*cosa*
	cleas	'trick'	*cleasa*
	clann	'family'	*clanna*

bróg	'shoe'	*bróga*
neantóg	'nettle'	*neantóga*

(161) *Strong plural with vowel suffix and stem mutation*

Singular		Plural
uasal	'noble'	*uaisle*
scian	'knife'	*sceana*

(162) *Strong plural with suffix*

Singular		Plural
pian	'pain'	*pianta*
tír	'land'	*tíortha*
cith	'shower'	*ciothanna*
ubh	'egg'	*uibheacha*
monarcha	'factory'	*monarchana*
tincéir	'tinker'	*tincéirí*

(163) *Irregular plural formations*

Singular		Plural
bean	'woman'	*mná*
mí	'month'	*míosa/míonna*
lá	'day'	*lae/laethanta/laethe*
leaba	'bed'	*leapacha*

2.6.6   Case

There are four cases in Irish, though morphological case marking is not common within the noun itself, being more obvious in the mutational effects on the initial of the noun after the article or in the initial of a following adjective. The cases are nominative or base form, genitive, dative or prepositional case and vocative case, used after the vocative particle *a*. The most obviously marked forms are in the singular, with the genitive and vocative in particular usually showing clear marking. Only the weak plurals show any case differentiation and that only in the genitive. All genitive plurals are subject to initial mutation after the article. Case marking is usually accomplished within the noun by means of mutation of the final consonant or consonant cluster, with variation between neutral and palatalised consonants (2.16.5).

(164) *Masculine noun*

an mac	*ah mhic*	*don mhac*	*a mhic*
'the son'	'of the son'	'to the son'	'son' (vocative)

na cait	*na gcat*	*do na cait*
'the cats'	'of the cats'	'to the cats'

(165)   *Feminine noun*

an phóg   na póige   leis on phóig/phóg
'the kiss' 'of the kiss' 'with the kiss'

na craobhacha   na gcraobhacha   ins na craobhacha
'the branches'   'of the branches' 'in the branches'

The vocative is only found in a limited number of common nouns, for example *mac* 'son', *leanbh* 'child', *buachaill* 'lad', but is required in all direct-address forms with personal names. With masculine nouns which form their genitive singular by palatalisation of the final consonant, the vocative is identical to the genitive. With other masculine nouns and all feminine ones, the vocative is identical to the nominative or base form. The vocative plural of strong plurals is identical to the nominative plural. If a weak plural ends in a vowel (-*a*), the vocative is identical to the nominative; if it ends in a consonant, the vocative is formed from the genitive plural by the addition of -*a*. The vocative forms are preceded by the particle *a*, which causes lenition of the initial consonant of the noun and which is lost in the spoken language before a word beginning with a vowel:

(166)   *a Dhónaill* (to *Dónall* 'Donald') *a mhic* (to *mac* 'son')
        a Bhríd (to *Bríd* 'Brigid')   *a bhuachaill* (to *buachaill* 'lad')

2.6.7   Declensional classes

Although the plurals are various and generally speaking non-predictable from the form of the nominative singular, there none the less appears to be a fairly clear-cut set of declensional classes based on the behaviour of the noun in the singular form, where the main variation is in the quality of the final consonant. Traditional grammars have recognised five declensions and these may be outlined in table 2.1, which, however, represents the 'classical' or old-fashioned paradigm. It should be noted that the nominative and dative have fallen together in the second declension (except in some Donegal dialects) and even the genitive is starting to disappear among the younger generation in most dialect areas. Table 2.1 also gives an indication of the main gender affiliations of the members of each declension.

2.6.7.1   Article

In the paradigm below the superscript letters indicate mutations ([L] = lenition, [H] = provection, [N] = nasalisation) – see 2.16.

Table 2.1. *Noun declensions*

Declension	Nominative singular	Genitive singular	Gender class
First	Neutral C	Palatalised C	Masculine
example	*fear* /f′ar/	*fir* /f′ir′/'man'	
Second	Usually neutral C	Palatalise C and add -*e* (schwa)	Chiefly feminine
example	*bróg* /bro:g/	*bróige* /bro:g′ə/ 'shoe'	
Third	Neutral or palatalised C	Neutral C and add -*a* (schwa)	Masculine
example	*stiúrthóir*	*stiúrthóra* 'director'	
Fourth	Vowel or -*ín*	No change	Masculine and
example	*cóta, cailín*	*cóta* 'coat', *cailín* 'girl'	feminine
Fifth	Vowel or palatalised C	Neutral consonant	Mostly feminine
example	*caora, cathair*	*caorach* 'sheep', *cathrach* 'city'	

(167)

		Singular		Plural
		Masculine	Feminine	Both genders
	NOM	*an*	*an*^{L}	*na*^{H}
	GEN	*an*^{L}	*na*^{H}	*na*^{N}
	DAT	*an*$^{L/N}$	*an*^{L}	*na*^{H}

2.6.8   Pronouns

Pronouns vary along the dimensions of person and number with some variation for case and gender. Example (168) lists the main types (the distinction between *muid* and *sinn* is one of dialect, with *muid* being more common in northern areas).

(168)

		Singular		Plural	
		Subject	Object	Subject	Object
1		*mé*	*mé*	*sinn/muid*	*sinn/muid*
2		*tú*	*thú*	*sibh*	*sibh*
3	MASC	*sé*	*é*	*siad*	*iad*
	FEM	*sí*	*í*		

These pronouns are all enclitic, with the subject forms only occurring as verbal suffixes and the object pronouns only as a verbal complement. Independent pronouns are identical with the emphatic varieties shown in 2.6.10 below. The distinction between second-person singular and plural is one of number only, with no honorific use of the plural pronoun.

2.6.9   Possessive adjective

The personal forms of the possessive adjective, including forms used before vowels, are shown in (169):

(169)		Singular	Plural
1		$m(o)^L$	$ár^N$
2		$d(o)^L$	$bhur^N$
3	MASC	a^L	a^N
	FEM	a^H	

2.6.10   Emphatic forms

The emphatic or independent forms corresponding to the pronouns in (168) are shown in (170):

(170)		Singular		Plural	
		Subject	Object	Subject	Object
1		*mise*	*mise*	*sinne/muidinne*	*sinne/muidinne*
2		*tusa*	*thusa*	*sibhse*	*sibhse*
3	MASC	*seisean*	*eisean*	*siadsan*	*iadsan*
	FEM	*sise*	*ise*		

It is also possible to add emphasising particles to any personal verbal ending or personal form of the prepositions (see 2.10), for example *chuirfinn-se* 'I (EMPH) would put'. Where it is desired to emphasise one of the possessive adjectives, this is achieved by adding the emphasising particle to the noun in the possessive construction or, if the noun is qualified by an adjective, to the adjective:

(171) (a) *mo chatsa* 'my (EMPH) cat'
       (b) *do mhadadh bochtsa* 'your (EMPH) poor dog'
       (c) *a chótasan* 'his (EMPH) coat'
       (d) *a bróg bheagsa* 'her (EMPH) small shoe'
       (e) *ár gcuidne aráin* 'our (EMPH) share of bread'
       (f) *bhur mbádsa* 'your (EMPH) boat'
       (g) *a n-athair mórsan* 'their (EMPH) grandfather'

2.7   VERBS

Morphological variation in the Irish verb is used to mark tense (present, past and future), aspect (perfect versus imperfect), mood (indicative, conditional and imperative, with some instances of subjunctive), person and number, as well as non-finite forms, though not all of these categories are necessarily formally marked in every instance. The verbal system derives historically from an earlier stage similar to Latin or Greek conjugations, where pronomial subjects appeared as integral suffixes to the verb, together with some tense-marker morphs. This system has mostly been replaced over the centuries by one where the subject pronouns appear as clitic suffixes, and the synchronic situation is one which shows marked geographical differentiation based on these two processes. In general, the morphologically conservative dialects of Munster Irish show greater instances of the so-called synthetic forms, while northern dialects have more analytic forms (the subject pronoun is now always written separate from the verbal form), though no dialect of the language has a completely synthetic or a completely analytic verbal paradigm. See Wigger (1972) for a generative statement of South Connacht Irish verb morphology.

Those instances of initial mutations of verbs where the mutation is an exponent, or partial exponent, of tense or mood categories (i.e. in the past tense, in the imperfect and in the conditional mood) derive diachronically from Old Irish paradigms where the mutation was the result of the presence of a preverbal particle (*ro* or *no*, later both giving *do*). Before a consonant this particle has survived only in a number of Munster dialects.

In terms of the traditional grammar, two conjugations are recognised, with the second consisting mainly of polysyllabic verbs ending in -(*a*)*igh* and some in -*il*, -*in*, -*ir*, -*is*, with the irregular verbs as a separate grouping. The chief difference between the first and second conjugations lies in the form of the suffix of the future morpheme, -*f*- and -(*e*)*ó*-, respectively.

2.7.1   Stems and endings

The system may most conveniently be analysed as showing a verbal stem followed by one or two suffixes, with the combination of suffixation and possible initial mutation of the stem serving as exponents of the various categories mentioned in the preceding section. The basic stem form is the verbal root and is identical with the second person singular imperative. Occasional instances of more complex stems are found where a simple stem is compounded with a prefix such as the privative *dí*- or the iterative *ath*-.

Within the finite verbal paradigm, the normal order of elements is root + tense marker + person (and number) marker (e.g. *mol+f+aidh mé* 'I will praise'), though, as already noted, the tense marker may appear either as a suffix (sometimes zero), as an initial mutation of the stem (e.g. *mhol mé* 'I praised') or as a discontinuous morpheme realised with both initial mutation and a suffix (e.g. *mhol+f+ainn* 'I would praise').

2.7.2   Verb systems: finite/non-finite; dependent/independent

Non-finite verbal forms (the verbal noun and past participle) usually consist of a stem followed by a suffix (which may be zero in the case of verbal nouns). Some verbal nouns may show instances of mutation of the final consonant of the stem, with or without suffixation and a few verbs in the irregular conjugations use suppletion. Examples of these are given in (173).

The verbal adjective is the simpler of these two categories in terms of its formations. The suffix is *-ta/-te* or *-tha/-the* (the latter pair both pronounced /-hə/. The distinction between 'broad' and 'slender' endings (in *-a* and *-e*, respectively) here is discussed in 2.11 and the choice of the stop or the fricative is governed by the phonetic class of the final consonant of the stem, though unfortunately the twentieth-century spelling reforms have served to obscure some of the underlying patterns and conditioning factors involved. In the standard paradigm, stems ending in *-b*, *-c*, *-f*, *-g*, *-p*, *-r* take the suffix *-tha/-the*, stems in *-bh* and *-mh* drop the final consonant and show *-fa* (which arises by devoicing of the stem final by the originally following /h/ of the suffix), otherwise *-ta/-te* appears.

(172)   *glac*   →   *glactha*   *caith*   →   *caite*   *gabh*   →   *gafa*
             'take'   'taken'   'spend'   'spent'   'accept'   'accepted'

             leá   →   *leáite*
             'melt'   'melted'

Although the above rules represent the general pattern, there is a range of variation in the individual dialects with regard to the choice of /-t-/ or /-h-/ type suffixes when the root ends in a liquid consonant (/r l m nŋ/). I have discussed some of the phonological processes involved here in Ó Dochartaigh (1979). Ó Buachalla (1980) deals with the geographically limited use of the verbal adjective morph *-iste*.

The verbal noun shows a wide range of formations and there are no morphological rules for predicting the type which will appear. The most common suffix is *-(e)adh* (confined almost entirely to verbs of the first conjugation) and others are *-(e)áil* (apart from its appearance with native stems, this is the suffix used to Gaelicise the very large numbers of loans from English – *murdaráil*, *slipeáil*), *-(i)ú* (confined to the second conjugation and replacing the *-(a)igh* of the stem ending), *-t*, *-e*, *-(e)amh*, *-í*, zero and the substitution of a phonologically neutral stem-final consonant for the root-final palatalised con- gener, with or without the addition of a suffix. Suppletion is found mainly with the irregular verbs. The genitive of the verbal noun is often identical to the form of the verbal adjective noted above, though there are many exceptions where the verbal noun is declined as though belonging to one or other of the five declensions mentioned in 2.6.7.

(173)

Stem	Verbal noun	
mol	*moladh*	'praise'
fág	*fágáil*	'leave'
ceil	*ceilt*	'conceal'
cosain	*cosaint*	'defend'
scrúdaigh	*scrúdú*	'examine'
suigh	*suí*	'sit'
déan	*déanamh*	'do'
léim	*léim*	'leap'
dóigh	*dó*	'burn'
éist	*éisteacht*	'listen'
ól	*ól*	'drink'
teilg	*teilgean*	'cast'
lean	*leanúint*	'follow'
clúdaigh	*clúdach*	'cover'
dúisigh	*dúiseacht*	'waken'
cuir	*cur*	'put'
buail	*bualadh*	'hit'

Some suppletive and other formations:

(174)

Stem	Verbal noun	
abair	*rá*	'say'
bligh	*bleán*	'milk'
soláTharaigh	*soláthar*	'provide'
iarr	*iarraidh*	'ask'
seinn	*seinm*	'play music'
druid	*druidim*	'close'

Old Irish had a distinction of independent/dependent within the verbal paradigm, with the latter occurring in conjunction with preverbal particles. In the modern language the only traces of this are to be found in some irregular verb paradigms, where what appears to be suppletion is used to signal the difference. In fact, this is not suppletion but rather the reflexes of a combination of the original root with a preverbal particle, a particle on which the stress fell in the dependent forms, for example *chuaigh* (from earlier *do-coid*, with stress on the *-coid*) 'went', *ní dheachaigh* (earlier *ní-dechuid*, with stress on the *-de-*, where this represents a form of the preverb *do-*) 'did not go'. The distinction is between verbal forms preceded by a particle (negative, interrogative, subordinating, etc.) which show dependent forms and those with no preceding element which show independent forms. Some examples:

(175)(a)   *chonaic mé*   *an   bhfaca   mé*
            see-PAST I   INTER see-PAST-DEP I
            'I saw'   'Did I see?'
    (b)   *rinne   siad*   *nach   ndearna   siad*
            do-PAST they   INTER-NEG do-PAST-DEP they
            'they did'   'Didn't they do?'
    (c)   *gheobhaidh tú*   *go   bhfaighidh tú*
            get-FUT   you   SUBORD get-FUT-DEP you
            'you'll get'   'that you will get'

Verbs which follow the positive direct relative particle *a* normally appear in the independent form for most tenses. However, the suffix *-(e)as* may be used in the present and future tenses, and this is common in most dialects:

(176)   *an   fear a*   *bhuaileas   (bhuaileann) an   madadh*
            ART man REL.PT   hit-REL-PRES (hit-PRES)   ART dog
            'the man who hits the dog'

2.7.3   Verb classes

The only morphologically marked aspectual distinction is to be found in the stative verb *bí*, which distinguishes between simple present (*tá*) and habitual aspect (*bíonn*).

2.7.4   Tense, aspect and mood

The following paradigm of the regular verb *tóg* 'lift' will serve as an illustration of a number of matters to be raised in this section. It shows a maximal system with both synthetic and analytic personal forms, together with the various impersonals:

(177)

		Present	Future
SG	1	*tógaim*	*tógfad / tógfaidh mé*
	2	*tógair / tógann tú*	*tógfair / tógfaidh tú*
	3	*tógann sé/sí*	*tógfaidh sé/sí*
PL	1	*tógaimid / tógann muid*	*tógfaimid / tógfaidh muid*
	2	*tógann sibh*	*tógfaidh sibh*
	3	*tógaid / tógann siad*	*tógfaid / tógfaidh siad*
	IMPERS	*tógthar*	*tógfar*

		Imperfect	Conditional
SG	1	*thógainn*	*thógfainn*
	2	*thógthá*	*thógfá*
	3	*thógadh sé/sí*	*thógfadh sé/sí*

PL	1	thógaimis / thógadh muid	thógfaimis / thógfadh muid
	2	thógadh sibh	thógfadh sibh
	3	thógaidís / thógadh siad	thógfaidís / thógfadh siad
	IMPERS	thógthaí	thógfaí

		Past	Present subjunctive
SG	1	thógas / thóg mé	tógad / tóga mé
	2	thógais / thóg tú	tógair / tóga tú
	3	thóg sé/sí	tógaidh sé/sí / tóga sé/sí
PL	1	thógamar / thóg muid	tógaimid
	2	thógabhar / thóg sibh	tógaidh sibh / tóga sibh
	3	thógadar / thóg siad	tógaid / tóga siad
	IMPERS	tógadh	tógthar

		Imperative
SG	1	tógaim
	2	tóg
	3	tógadh sé/sí / tóga sé/sí
PL	1	tógaimis
	2	tógaid / tógaigí
	3	tógaidís / tóga siad
	IMPERS	tógtar

The Irish verb has four tenses, present, future, past and imperfect, with the last representing habitual or reiterative action in the past. The morphological exponents of the tense categories are:

(178) Present: zero
       Future: -f- (pronounced /-h-/ or zero with devoicing of a stem-final voiced consonant)
       -eó- (in 2nd conjugation)
       Past: lenition of stem (with or without preverbal particle do)
       Imperfect: lenition of stem (with or without preverbal particle do)

There are four moods, indicative, imperative, conditional and subjunctive, with the following exponents:

(179) Indicative: zero
       Imperative: zero
       Conditional: -f- or -eó-, depending on conjugation, together with lenition of stem (with or without preverbal particle do)
       Subjunctive: zero

In addition to the above, it must be noted that analytic verbal forms with enclitic pronouns show suffixes which tend to be tense specific:

(180) Present: -(e)ann
       Past: zero

Future: -(*a*)*idh*
Imperfect, conditional and imperative: -(*e*)*adh*

2.7.5   Personal/impersonal; active/passive

The Irish verb has three persons and two numbers, though in most cases it is the enclitic pronouns of 2.6.8 which are used to signal these categories. Some of the synthetic verbal personal suffixes are as follows (there is no third person singular marker):

(181)   1st singular   *-m/-d/-inn/-as*
           2nd singular   *-r/-thá/-is*
           1st plural   *-míd/-mís/-mar*
           2nd plural   *-í/-air*
           3rd plural   *-dís/-adar*

In addition to the above, there is a set of impersonal suffixes which, when they occur with an intransitive verb, indicate an impersonal usage where with a transitive verb the interpretation is a passive one:

(182)(a)   *téitear   ann go   minic*
            go+PRES+IMPERS there ADV.PT often
            cf. French 'On y va souvent'

    (b)   *feictear   ann go   minic é*
            see+PRES+IMPERS there ADV.PT often him
            'He is seen there often'

2.7.6   Concord

There is no concord between a verb and its following noun subject, and both singular and plural noun subjects require a form of the verb identical to that used with the third person singular pronoun.

2.7.7   ·   Other verbal conjugations

As already noted, the major difference between the first-conjugation verb illustrated in (177) and those of the second conjugation is the appearance of the morph -(*e*)*ó*- instead of -*f*- in the future and conditional, together with syncope of the unstressed vowel in verbal stems ending in -*il*, -*in*, etc. (e.g. *cosain* 'defend' → *chosnóinn* 'I would defend').

Verbs beginning in a vowel are conjugated as in (177) above, apart from the presence of a morph *d'*- before those forms which would show initial lenition of a consonant (e.g. *ól* 'drink' → *d'ólfadh sé* 'he would drink'). Verbs in initial *f*-show lenition of this consonant where appropriate, together with the *d'*- morph (e.g. *fan* 'wait' → *d'fhan mé* 'I waited').

There are eleven verbs which are in varying degrees irregular in their conjugation: *beir* 'bear', *cluin/clois* 'hear', *déan* 'do', *deir* 'say', *faigh* 'get', *feic* 'see', *ith* 'eat', *tar* 'come', *téigh* 'go', *tabhair* 'give' and *bí* 'be'. In general, they form their paradigms by root suppletion, with the approximate pattern:

(183)   Root 1 present, imperfect, subjunctive and imperative stem
             Root 2 future and conditional stem
             Root 3 past stem
             Root 4 non-finite stem

For example, with the verb *téigh* 'go', we have:

(184)(a)   *téann sé / théadh sé* 'he goes'/'he used to go'
   (b)   *rachaidh sé / rachadh sé* 'he will go'/'he would go'
   (c)   *chuaigh sé* 'he went'
   (d)   *dul* 'going'

2.7.8   Preverbal particles

Sentential particles such as the interrogative, the negative, the relative pronoun and the subordinating particles all show two major forms, one used before a verb in the past tense (apart from some of the irregular verbs) and the other used elsewhere. All the past forms end in *-r* and in origin they represent a combination of the general preverbal form with the earlier preverbal perfective marker *ro*.

(185)(a)   *an dtógfaidh tú é?*   (b) *ar thóg tú é?*
             'Will you lift it?'   'Did you lift it?'

2.8   ADJECTIVES

The predicative adjective is invariable and only the attributive adjective is morphologically marked. In general, it follows closely on the marking of its head noun, with the variation for case, number and gender being similar to that found in the noun class (2.6.5–7). It is also marked for comparison.

2.8.1   Structure: stems and endings

The simple stem, as in *mór* 'big', is the minimum unit of adjectival structure. Compound forms consisting of two simple stems occur: *úrnua* 'brand new' (from *úr* 'new' and *nua* 'new'). Other derived adjectives may be formed from a prefix plus a stem, for example the privative *ain-* plus *eolach* 'knowledgeable' gives *aineolach* 'ignorant', or the privative *dí-* plus *buíoch* 'thankful' gives *díomaíoch* 'ungrateful'. It is not uncommon for adjectives to be formed from nouns by the addition of various suffixes:

(186)   *eolas* 'knowledge'   → *eolach* 'knowledgeable'
          fios 'knowledge'   → *fiosrach* 'curious'
          leisce 'laziness'   → *leisciúil* 'lazy'
          grá 'love'   → *grámhar* 'loving'

Initial mutations of the adjective within the nominal paradigm are dealt with in 2.16.6. Final mutations in the singular generally follow one or other of the first two noun declensional classes outlined in 2.6.7, with adjectives following a masculine noun being declined to show palatalisation of the final consonant in the genitive singular and those following feminine nouns showing palatalisation of the final consonant with the addition of an *-e*, as illustrated in the declensional paradigm of (143).

Plural adjectives are usually formed by adding *-a/-e* (i.e. a schwa) to the singular base form, again with syncope of certain types as above. As already noted in the discussion of noun declension, this is an area of Irish morphology which is undergoing rapid change and simplification and the same general changes apply to the adjectival declensions.

2.8.2   Comparison

There is only one degree of morphologically expressed comparison in Irish. It is formed from the base adjective usually by palatalisation of the final consonant and the addition of *-e*, with some examples of suppletion or root ablaut in the ten or so irregular comparatives. The base adjective is used in conjunction with *comh . . .le* ('as' . . . 'with') to express the equative. To handle the comparative we have *níos . . . ná* (particle . . . 'than') and for the superlative *is . . .* (particle . . .), where in these instances the comparative form of the adjective appears after the particle.

(187)   *bán* 'white'   *deacair* 'difficult'
          comh bán le 'as white as'   *comh deacair le* 'as hard as'
          níos báine ná 'whiter than'   *níos deacra ná* 'more difficult than'
          is báine 'whitest'   *is deacra* 'most difficult'

Some irregular forms:

(188)   *beag* 'small' → *lú*   *fada* 'long' → *faide*   *te* 'hot' → *teo*
          maith 'good' → *fearr*   *olc* 'bad' → *measa*   *mór* 'big' → *mó*

2.8.3   Adjective classes

The possessive adjectives have been dealt with in 2.6.9, the demonstrative triad in 2.3.4 and the small subset of prefixed adjectives has been mentioned in 2.3.1.1. Indefinite postposition attributive adjectives such as *áirithe* 'certain', *céanna* 'same' or *eile* 'other' are not declined. Apart from these, adjectives do not form morphologically distinct classes in Irish.

2.8.4   Adverbs

Adverbs do not constitute a separate morphological class in Irish, being generally identical to their corresponding adjectives. The only formal adverbial marking is the occasional presence of the particle *go* before an adjective which has the mutational effect of *h*-provection on a following initial vowel (2.16.3).

(189)   *carr mall* 'a slow car'   →   *téann sé go mall* 'It goes slowly'

2.8.5   Adverb classes

There is a range of morphologically interrelated adverbs connected with spatial orientation and direction of movement which fall into four groups depending on whether location is at the speaker or at a distance and on whether the motion is directed towards or away from the speaker (see Ó Baoill 1975 for a discussion). The adverbs consist of a bound-form stem preceded by various enclitics and there are two major types, one concerned with location in terms of inside/ outside and the other with orientation in two- or three-dimensional space. They are much more widely used in Irish than might seem to be the case from their English.

   Inside/outside:

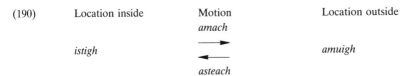

(190)	Location inside	Motion	Location outside
		amach	
	istigh	→	*amuigh*
		←	
		asteach	

The forms in the location column here always occur with a state verb, those in the motion column always with verbs of motion:

(191) (a)   *tá sé istigh/amuigh agam*   (b)   *d'fhág mé   istigh é*
              is it inside/outside at-me   leave-PAST I inside it
              'I have it inside/outside'   'I left it inside'

(192)   *fágfaidh   mé isteach duit   é*
             leave-FUT I   inside for-you it
             'I will leave it inside for you'

(193)   *tháinig   sé isteach/amach*
             came+PAST he in/out
             'He came in/out'

Horizontal adverbs:

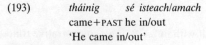

(194)   Location here   Motion   Location there
                                        anonn/sall
                                        ———————▶
                 abhus   *thall*
                                        ◀———————
                                         anall

Vertical adverbs:

(195)   *thuas*

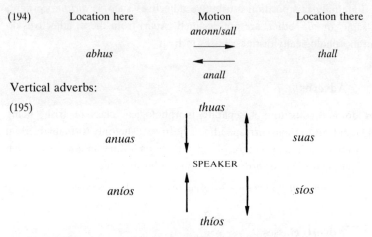

             anuas   *suas*

                                        SPEAKER

             aníos   *síos*

                                        thíos

Compass orientation:

(196)   *thuaidh*

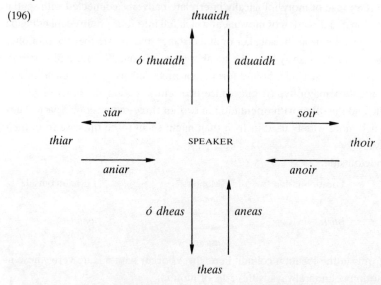

                       ó thuaidh   *aduaidh*

                  siar   *soir*
       thiar   SPEAKER   *thoir*
                 aniar   *anoir*

                       ó dheas   *aneas*

                                   theas

In addition to the above adverbs, there is a complex location class, consisting
of the prefix *la(i)st-* in combination with the basic stem, to indicate location with
respect to a particular position (in northern dialects a compound adverb
consisting of *taobh* 'side' and the simple location adverb is used). Its most
common usage is with the preposition *de* 'of' and a following location noun:

(197)   *tá sé laistigh /taobh istigh den   doras*
             is he inside   of-ART door
             'He is inside the door'

For a detailed discussion of these deictic adverbs in Ulster Irish see Ó Baoill (1975).

2.8.6   Numerals

The Irish numerals are mainly based on the decimal system, with quite a few instances of vigesimal counting.

2.8.6.1   Cardinal numbers

(198)   1   *(aon) N amháin*
             2   *dhá*
             3   *trí*
             4   *ceithre*
             5   *cúig*
             6   *sé*
             7   *seacht*
             8   *ocht*
             9   *naoi*
             10   *deich*
             11   *(aon) N déag*
             12   *dhá N déag*
             20   *fiche*
             21   *N is fiche / N ar fhichead*
             22   *dhá N is fiche / dhá N ar fhichead*
             30   *tríocha / deich N is fiche / deich N ar fhichead*
             32   *dhá N is tríocha / dhá N déag is fiche / dhá N déag ar fhichead*
             40   *daichead*
             42   *dhá N is daichead*
             50   *caoga / leathchéad*
             52   *dhá N is caoga/leath chéad / dhá N déag is daichead*
             60   *seasca / trí fichead*
             70   *seachtó / deich N is trì fichead*
             80   *ochtó / ceithre fichead*
             90   *nócha / deich N is ceithre fichead*
             100   *céad*
             102   *dhá N is céad*
             1,000 *míle*
             1,002 *dhá N is míle*

Unless otherwise specified by N, the head noun occurs after the cardinal and with both *aon* and *dhá* the singular is used. The alternatives in the vigesimal counting (with *fiche/fichead*), where one may have either *is* (an abbreviated form of *agus* 'and') or *ar* 'on', occur up to 'thirty' and above this value only *is* is used.

2.8.6.2   Ordinal numbers

Apart from the numbers 'one' and 'two', the ordinals are formed from the cardinals by the addition of the suffix -(*i*)*ú* (or -*dú*) and usually occur with definite nouns, with the ordinal appearing between the article and the noun. Numerals of the extended form with *is* or *ar* only show the ordinal form before the noun, with the following extension appearing in its cardinal form.

(199)		
	1st	*an chéad*
	2nd	*an dara*
	3rd	*an tríú*
	4th	*an ceathrú*
	5th	*an cúigiú*
	10th	*an deichiú*
	11th	*an t-aonú N déag*
	12th	*an dara N déag*
	20th	*an fichiú N*
	21st	*an t-aonú N is fiche*
	30th	*an tríochadú*
	40th	*an daicheadú*
	50th	*an caogadú*
	60th	*an seascadú*
	70th	*an seachtódú*
	80th	*an t-ochódú*
	90th	*an nóchadú*
	100th	*an céadú*
	101st	*an céad is aonú N*
	1,000th	*an míliú*

2.9   WORD FORMATION

There are three common methods of word formation in the language: compounding from two existing words (2.9.1), by means of an affix, of which there are large numbers, both prefixes (2.9.2) and suffixes (2.9.3). Such processes have existed throughout the history of the language and there are instances where the compound has become synchronically opaque due to the loss of one or other of its elements as a separate word – compare *banaltra* 'nurse' and *bantiarna* 'lady', where the word *tiarna* 'lord' is still extant but the *altra* element is not. The best account of word formation is in *Graiméar* (1960: ch. 34).

2.9.1   Compound words

The elements used are nouns, verbs, adjectives and prepositions, though the latter two do not really represent a productive category. The syntactic and morphological class of the compound is usually decided by the second element (but see (203) and (204)), and normally the initial consonant of this is lenited except when two homorganic consonants come together. Stress is normally on the initial element, though a number of adjectival compounds retain more or less equal stress on both elements. In the examples below, the composition elements are indicated separately, though normally these compounds are written as single words. Some more complex compounds indicated in (205) do appear as separate words and here the stress pattern is that of the basic phrase.

Noun/adjective/preposition plus noun:

(200)	*muic+fheoil*	'pig+meat'	→	'bacon'
	cúl+chaint	'back+talking'	→	'gossip'
	leath+dhuine	'half+person'	→	'fool'
	gearr+scéal	'short+story'	→	'short story'
	mór+roinn	'large+division'	→	'continent'
	idir+linn	'between+period'	→	'interval'
	fo+líne	'under+line'	→	'(telephone) extension'

Noun/preposition plus verb

(201)	*coinneal+bháigh*	'candle+drown'	→	'excommunicate'
	cion+dáil	'share+apportion'	→	'ration'
	idir+dhealaigh	'between+separate'	→	'distinguish'
	idir+shuigh	'between+sit'	→	'interpolate'

Noun/adjective plus adjective:

(202)	*ceann+dána*	'head+bold'	→	'headstrong'
	béal+bhinn	'mouth+sweet'	→	'melodious'
	bán+dearg	'white+red'	→	'pink'
	fionn+rua	'white+red'	→	'(of hair) sandy'

Verbal noun plus adverb combined to give a noun:

(203)	*cur síos*	'putting down'	→	'description'
	cur amach	'putting out'	→	'experience'
	éirí amach	'rising out'	→	'rebellion'

Noun plus adjective combined to give a noun:

(204)	*tóin+fhionn*	'backside+white'	→	'cotton-grass'
	broinn+dhearg	'breast+red'	→	'robin'

Complex compounds or lexicalised phrases (no plural forms):

(205)	*cos ar bholg*	'foot on belly'	→	'oppression'
	cur i gcéill	'putting in sense'	→	'pretence'

éirí in airde	'rising upwards'	→	'hauteur'
uisce faoi thalamh	'water under ground'	→	'intrigue'

2.9.2   Compounds with prefixes

There is a very large number of prefixes, most of which are genuine enclitic particles, but some of which are in fact independent adjectives used as intensifiers or are compounding forms of nouns.

(206)	*dubh+aois*	'black age'	→	'great age'
	ban+tiarna	'woman+lord'	→	'lady' (compare *bean* 'woman')

There is a range of privative prefixes, *an-*, *amh-*, *dí-*, *mí-*, *neamh-*, etc.:

(207)	*an+aicme*	'class'	→	'bad breed'
	aimh+leas	'advantage'	→	'disadvantage'
	dí+mheas	'respect'	→	'disrespect'
	mí+chlú	'repute'	→	'disrepute'
	neamh+shuim	'interest'	→	'indifference'

Some examples of common prefixes:

(208)	*ath+bhliain*	're+year'	→	'new year'
	foir+ceann	'over+head'	→	'end'
	iar+ó	'after+grandchild'	→	'descendant'
	oll+mhór	'great+big'	→	'massive'
	réamh+fhocal	'pre+word'	→	'preposition'
	sain+mhiniú	'special+explanation'	→	'definition'

Two prefixes, *so-* and *do-*, occur as a contrastive pair:

(209)	*so+dhéanta* 'easily done'	*do+dhéanta* 'impossible'
	so+bhriste 'breakable'	*do+bhriste* 'unbreakable'
	soiléir 'clear'	*doiléir* 'unclear'
	suairc 'pleasant'	*duairc* 'unpleasant'
	sochar 'good fortune'	*dochar* 'harm'
	sonas 'good luck'	*donas* 'bad luck'
	soineann 'fair weather'	*doineann* 'bad weather'

2.9.3   Compounds with suffixes

There is a wide range of suffixes used to form nouns, adjectives and, more rarely apart from loans from English, verbs. Again, as noted above, because of the long history of such compounding in the language, a large number of the resulting compounds have become morphologically opaque. The examples of nominal and adjectival suffixes below are a selection of the range available.

Verbal suffixes:

(210)   *-áil*:   *pleanáil* 'plan', *rútáil* 'root', *póirseáil* 'rummage'
           -aigh: *bánaigh* 'desert', *giorraigh* 'shorten', *dreasaigh* 'urge'

Adjectival suffixes:

(211)   *-ach*:   *bradach* 'thieving', *mórtasach* 'boasting', *diúltach* 'negative'
           -da: *gallda* 'foreign', *rúnda* 'secret', *seanda* 'old'
           -mhar: *ceolmhar* 'musical', *ciallmhar* 'sensible', *lúfar* 'active'
           -(i)úil: *madrúil* 'churlish', *cairdiúil* 'friendly', *ceanúil* 'loving'

Nominal suffixes:

(212)   Diminutive: *-án, -óg, -ín* : *bradán* 'salmon', *cnocán* 'hillock', *bratóg* 'rag',
                         cailín 'girl', *báidín* 'little boat'
           Agentive: *-aí, -ach, -aire, -óir: fostaí* 'employee', *bratach* 'flag', *iascaire*
                         'fisherman', *fostóir* 'employer'
           Abstract: *-acht, -as: uaisleacht* 'nobility', *binneas* 'sweetness'
           Collective: *-ra, -laith: macra* 'youths', *éanlaith* 'birds, fowl'

2.10   CONJUGATED PREPOSITIONS

The prepositional system of Irish includes a set of fifteen prepositions which
show personal endings, traditionally referred to in Irish grammars as prepositional pronouns, though it would seem preferable to consider them simply as
prepositional phrases in which the governed noun-phrase element is marked for
person, number and (in the third person singular) gender. They are generally
composed of a bound form of the preposition followed by a suffix, but the third
person singular masculine form does not lend itself easily to this analysis and is
probably best taken as an unanalysable single morph.

The personal endings are:

(213) | | Singular | Plural |
|---------|----------|------------|
| 1 | *-m* | *-(a)inn* |
| 2 | *-(i)t* | *-(a)ibh* |
| 3 MASC | zero | *-u/-bh/-o* |
| FEM | *-i* | |

The bound stem of the preposition shows various forms in combination with the
personal endings, allomorphs which are usually formed by ablaut from the base
form. The examples below include a relatively unchanged stem and instances of
consonant-final and vowel-final prepositions.

(214) | | *ag* 'at' | *chuig* 'towards' | *do* 'to' | *trí* 'through' |
|-------|-----------|-------------------|-----------|-----------------|
| SG 1 | *agam* | *chugam* | *dom* | *tríom* |
| 2 | *agat* | *chugat* | *duit* | *tríot* |

3	MASC	*aige*	*chuige*	*dó*	*tríd*
	FEM	*aice*	*chuici*	*dí*	*tríthi*
PL 1		*againn*	*chugainn*	*dúinn*	*trínn*
2		*agaibh*	*chugaibh*	*daoibh*	*tríbh*
3		*acu*	*chucu*	*dóibh*	*tríothu*

Other prepositions, such as *timpeall* 'around' or *trasna* 'across', may give personal forms by attaching one of the conjugated prepositions to them:

(215)   (a) *timpeall orm* 'around me'   (b) *trasna liom* 'across me'

SOUND SYSTEM

The sound systems are by far the best-studied aspects of the various Irish dialects, and monograph descriptions of individual dialects have provided a wealth of phonetic and phonological detail. However, in the absence of a standardised pronunciation, there is no accepted standard phonological statement. Ó Siadhail and Wigger (1975) represent an attempt at providing such an overall statement, based on a generative phonological analysis which tries to take account of some of the major dialectal differences. Another useful discussion of this problem is Ó Murchú (1969). The series of dialect monographs published by the Dublin Institute for Advanced Studies from the 1940s to the early 1960s provides a convenient overview of a number of Connacht and Munster dialects in Ó Cuív (1944), Breatnach (1947), de Bhaldraithe (1945), de Búrca (1958) and Mhac an Fhailigh (1968). They are all based on fieldwork undertaken in the 1940s and follow closely on the linguistic paradigm established by Daniel Jones in his phoneme theory. Wagner (1958) is a study of a Donegal Irish dialect which, although published under the auspices of the Institute, does not belong to the same series of studies and is not immediately comparable with them. Sommerfelt (1965) is a useful phonemic analysis of the Donegal dialect which he worked on for his (1922) phonetic monograph. Because of the lack of a standard phonology, the discussion in the following sections must be read as a somewhat abstract one, which attempts to subsume as much as possible of the interdialectal variation.

2.11   CONSONANT SYSTEM

The consonant system of Irish illustrated in table 2.2 is based on a fundamental dichotomy between velarised and palatalised segments, with a full range of pairs

Table 2.2. *Consonant system*

p	p′	t	t′	k	k′		
b	b′	d	d′	g	g′		
f	f			x	x′	h	h′
v	v′			γ	γ′		
m	m′	N	N′	ŋ	ŋ′		
ṽ	ṽ′	n	n′				
		L	L′				
		l	l′				
		R					
		r	r′				
		s	s′				

Note: Unlenited nasals, vibrants and laterals are conventionally symbolised by capital letters.

distinguished by the presence or absence of the feature [Palatalised]. This opposition has its origins in the development of distinctive consonantal quality in the course of the fifth and sixth centuries through the loss of vowels in unstressed syllables – for a detailed discussion of these historical developments see Greene (1973).

The overall system of single consonants as illustrated in table 2.2 must be regarded as a maximal one and not all of the contrasts shown necessarily appear in all dialects. For instance, the distinctive feature of consonantal length in the liquids (e.g. /L/ : /l/) has been lost in most dialects outside Donegal and even there is on the decline.

The system shown does not distinguish between those consonants found in medial or final position within the word and those found initially, where, for instance, the segments /v x γ ŋ/ and their palatalised congeners are not found except as the result of initial mutations (see 2.16). In addition to the consonants noted here, one might also include alveolar /ţ ḑ/, the affricates /tʃ dʒ/ and the voiced fricatives /z ʒ/ as part of a subsystem of unassimilated loans from English.

2.11.1   Single consonants, clusters and consonant length

Consonant clusters in syllable-initial position are shown in (216) and final clusters in (217). With a few exceptions (/-xt′-/ and /-rt′-/), clusters show internal congruence of neutral or palatal quality and the illustrations following are couched in terms of the neutral members only. Medial clusters can generally be regarded as combinations of initial and final single consonants or clusters:

(216)   Trisegmental initial clusters:

C_1		C_2		C_3
/s/	+	voiceless stop	+	/l/
				/r/

Bisegmental initial clusters:

C_1 C_2

/s/   + $\begin{cases} /l/ \\ /n/ \\ /r/ \\ /m/ \\ \text{voiceless stop} \end{cases}$

C   C

stop   + $\begin{cases} /l/ \\ /n/ \\ /r/ \end{cases}$ (except /pn-/ and /bn-/)

/f/   + $\begin{cases} /l/ \\ /r/ \end{cases}$

/m/   + $\begin{cases} /n/ \\ /r/ \end{cases}$

(217)   Bisegmental final clusters:

C_1 C_2

$\left.\begin{array}{l} /l/ \\ /n/ \\ /r/ \end{array}\right\}$ +   voiceless stop

/s/   + $\begin{cases} /t/ \\ /k/ \end{cases}$

/x/   +   /t/

$\left.\begin{array}{l} /r/ \\ /l/ \end{array}\right\}$ + $\begin{cases} /b/ \\ /g/ \\ /m/ \end{cases}$

The last grouping in the final clusters represents instances of consonantal combinations which have given rise to epenthetic vowels in most dialects of the language and it is a moot point whether one assigns the resulting intercalated schwa to the vowel phonology or derives it by rule from the bisegmental clusters (see 2.13).

2.11.2   Consonant classes

The grouping of consonants into classes is implicit in table 2.2 and the fundamental distinction between neutral and palatalised is signalled by various phonetic means, depending on the primary articulation of the segments. With the labials, distinctive phonetic palatalisation within the segment has been lost in Donegal Irish and in other dialects is realised by a tensing and spreading of the lips in contrast to the neutral labials. In Donegal the palatalisation feature has been shifted outside the bounds of the segment, to appear as a *j*-like off-glide. With dental consonants, the palatalised member is usually realised as an alveolar with a greater or lesser degree of secondary phonetic palatalisation and in the stops with accompanying affricated off-glide. The velars indicate palatalisation by a fronting of the point of primary articulation to a palato-velar or palatal position, to give, for example, [k ç]. The phonemes /s/ and /s'/ are distinguished as [s] and [ʃ]. The /h/ phoneme is realised as a voiceless vowel, with its precise quality depending on the phonetic environment. To this extent it could be argued that the segment does not partake of the palatalisation opposition; however, for reasons of pattern congruity and for the most economical analysis of the system, I would prefer to take it as participating fully in this opposition.

The unlenited nasals, laterals and vibrants (symbolised with capital letters in table 2.2, following the established practice of Irish dialectologists) must be taken together as a group of segments which share a number of common features, including length re-assignment from coda to nucleus (see 2.13). There is some evidence for internal differentiation within the liquid class as far as relative vocalicness or syllabicity is concerned. For example, initial clusters in /sm-/ are treated under lenition on a par with clusters followed by a stop, rather than as a combination of /s/ with a liquid, with lenition being blocked in the former case.

2.11.3   Range of consonant realisations

Table 2.3 is an attempt to provide a guide to the phonetic realisations of the various phonemic segments of table 2.2. However, such a chart does not do justice to the inter- and intradialectal range of variation which is well illustrated in the dialect monographs or, more particularly, in the Irish linguistic atlas (Wagner 1958–69).

The stops show glottal settings similar to English, with the voiceless stops being realised initially with a degree of postaspiration and their voiced counter-

Table 2.3. *Phonetic realisations of consonants*

p	p̜	t̪	t̪ʲ	k	k̟⁺		
b	b̜	d̪	d̪ʲ	g	g̟⁺		
f	f̜			x	ç	h	h̨
v	v̜			γ	j		
m	m̨	ṉ̪ ː	ɲ ː	ŋ	ŋ̟⁺		
ṽ	ṽ̨	n̪	n̪				
		ɫ̪ː	ʎː				
		l	l̲				
		rː					
		ɾ	ʂ				
		s	ʃ				

parts in this position appear as phonetically voiceless and unaspirated. In medial and final position the voiced segments have full, or nearly full, voicing, and the voiceless appear, in some dialects at least, to have a glottal setting somewhat akin to that found in Scottish Gaelic dialects which show pre-aspiration here, though there is no auditorily perceptible pre-aspiration in Irish. The /r/ phoneme shows a range of variation, from a trill through a tap to a voiced retroflex fricative (this latter in combination with/s/). The biggest variation is to be found in the realisations of the palatalised dental series, which range from true palatals through various degrees of prepalatals to palatalised alveolars and alveodentals.

An important influence on the phonetic realisations of the individual phonemic segments is that of sandhi effects. The most comprehensive statements of these (for Donegal Irish dialects) are to be found in Quiggin (1906) and Sommerfelt (1922) and information for other dialects appears in the dialect monographs mentioned earlier. The principal effects appear to be assimilations of consonantal quality (neutral to palatalised and vice versa) and glottal setting (voiced to voiceless and vice versa) with the directions of assimilation being both progressive and retrogressive.

2.12   VOWEL SYSTEM

The vowel system is illustrated in (218) and, as was the case with the consonant system, represents a pandialectal system, not all of whose contrasts are necessarily to be found in any particular dialect. It is also the case that in many dialects we find a much wider range of diphthongs (in /-i/ and /-u/) which derive diachronically from the vocalisation of earlier voiced fricatives and some dialects appear to show some additional contrasts (see de Bhaldraithe 1945). In addition, the system shown does not distinguish between different subsystems operating under various conditions of word stress or syllable structure – for example, open versus closed or stressed versus unstressed syllables. The range of variation can be quite wide here, from those Connacht dialects which show five (or perhaps six) long vowels together with a schwa in unstressed closed syllables, to east Ulster dialects, where the subsystem has only a schwa.

(218)   i: i   u   u:
        e: e   ɔ: ɔ   o   o:
                a: a   ia   ua

2.12.1   Monophthongs, diphthongs and vowel length

Short and long monophthongs are distinguished by length and, in the case of the high vowels /i u/, by quality, with the short varieties being lowered and centralised from the position of the corresponding high vowels. In phonological terms, the two diphthongs /ia ua/ appear to pattern more with short vowels than with long. As noted above, a number of dialects show diphthongs or long vowels arising from loss of earlier voiced fricatives with loss of compensatory lengthening. In addition to these, southern dialects have re-allocation of segmental length into the nucleus from an original long liquid in a syllable coda, thus creating new /-i/ and /-u/ diphthongs.

(219)   (a) *Tadhg* [taig] or [te:g]
         (b) *adharc* [airk] or [e:rk]
         (c) *am*   [aum], [a:m] or [am:]
         (d) *ball*   [baul], [ba:l] or [bal:]
         (e) *binn*   [b̥ʲaiɲ̟], [b̥ʲi:n̥] or [b̥ʲiɲ:]

Given the range of dialectal variation in the synchronic realisations of these earlier combinations of vowel plus consonant, it would seem preferable to take them at the synchronic phonological level as still containing the consonant, whether fricative or liquid, though the precise sets of rules involved in the generation of the modern realisations are not always entirely clear (Ó Siadhail and Wigger 1975: 89–92).

2.12.2   Vowel classes

As noted above, the distinction between long and short vowels is a matter of both quantity and, with certain vowels, quality. The phonological distribution of long and short vowels is interesting at the syllabic level in so far as in unstressed syllables instances of long vowels derive diachronically either from compensatory lengthening in conjunction with the loss of voiced fricatives, or from external borrowings (Latin, Norman French and English). Original short vowels in these unstressed syllables found chiefly in dialects of Ulster Irish are mainly confined to instances of relatively recent shortenings of long vowels in those dialects.

2.12.2.1   Nasalisation

Vowels in the environment of a nasal consonant are nasalised to a greater or lesser degree. However, because of the loss of original voiced fricatives, the loss of earlier /ṽ/ has, in a number of dialects, given rise to apparently independent nasal vowels. However, although the topic is not discussed in these terms in the traditional dialect studies, it is possible to analyse the system as showing no independent nasal vowels, provided detailed rules are written to cover the synchronic realisations of the original voiced nasal fricatives (see, for example, Ó Cuív 1944: 54–6; de Bhaldraithe 1945: 46). It appears to be the case that in most dialects any marginally distinctive vocalic nasalisation seems to survive only among older speakers.

2.12.2.2   Glides

Because of the basic consonantal dichotomy of neutral/palatalised, clearly audible on- and off-glides are common in Irish between consonants and vowels of divergent qualities. Generally speaking, these glides are *i*-like or *u*-like, though it is also possible to find schwa-like and other vocalic transitions – see the descriptions in Ó Cuív (1944: 46–60), de Bhaldraithe (1945: 43–5) and Mhac an Fhailigh (1968: 45–7).

2.12.3   Range of vowel realisations

With a relatively small vowel system, the ranges of realisation are somewhat larger than those found, for instance, in English, with the short vowels showing greater variation than the long. One fairly systematic range of variation is triggered by the consonantal environment, where a neutral consonant has the effect of centralising a front vowel and a palatal consonant has a similar effect on a contiguous back vowel. The most variable vowel is the schwa, both long and short. The short variety is highly sensitive to the consonantal environment, being higher and fronter in the neighbourhood of a palatalised segment. The long schwa is how I have chosen to symbolise the segment which appears in the orthography as *-ao-* and which is realised variously in the dialects as [iː eː ɯː]. Figure 2.1 attempts to show some of the range of pandialectal variation of the individual vowel segments, excluding the schwa. For further details, the reader is referred to the various dialect monographs.

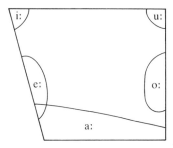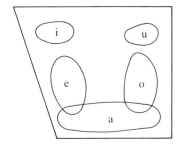

Figure 2.1   Range of vowel realisations

2.12.4   Semi-vowels

There are three phonetic semi-vowels in Irish, [w w̃ j], but it would seem preferable on the grounds of pattern congruity to interpret these as the consonants /v ṽ γ'/ – this is the approach adopted in the dialect monographs and it is followed in the descriptive framework presented here.

2.13   SYLLABLE STRUCTURE

In general, syllable structure follows the basic pattern of increasing sonority through the onset cluster to the vocalic nucleus, followed by decreasing sonority through the coda and this is only interrupted in the onset with *s*-clusters. The basic structure of the syllable can be illustrated by (220):

(220) $(C_1)(C_2)(C_3)V_1(V_2)(C_4)(C_5)$

with only the nucleus being obligatory (if a syllable consists of only a vowel, then the vowel is long). Initial and final clusters have been discussed in 2.11.1.

   Length is a function of the phonological syllable, being realised either in the vocalic nucleus or in the consonantal coda. In the historical development of Irish there appears to have been some redistribution of length away from the coda and into the nucleus, with a concomitant shortening of long consonants. The phonologically long consonants are /p t k m N ŋ L R/, together with their palatalised varieties. Of these, the liquids and nasals show most evidence of length reassignment, with a long vowel or diphthong ([u]-like or [i]-like depending on the neutral or palatalised quality, respectively, of the following consonant) appearing in the nucleus. Only in dialects of Donegal Irish, and then only among the oldest generation, are the original consonantal quantities largely retained and an examination of the process of change across the generations reveals it to be a function both of the consonantal segment involved and of the quality of the vocalic nucleus (see Ó Baoill 1980 and Ó Dochartaigh 1981 for some discussion).

Certain sequences of consonants in syllabic coda behave in a fashion very similar to the long segments. These clusters usually consist of a liquid followed by a voiced segment, liquid or stop. With these clusters, however, the possibilities for segmental length re-assignment are somewhat wider and, in addition to the development of length in the vocalic nucleus, we may also find, where the two consonants are non-homorganic, an epenthetic vowel intercalated between the two segments, giving rise to a phonetic disyllabic sequence with a schwa in the unstressed second syllable.

(221)	/am/	→	[aːm] or [aum]
	/gaL/	→	[gaːl] or [gaul]
	/baR/	→	[baːr]
	/b'iN'/	→	[ḇ ain̠] or [ḇ iːn̠]
	/karn/	→	[kaːrn]
	/ord/	→	[oːrd] or [aurd]
	/f'arg/	→	[f̡arəg]
	/arm/	→	[arəm]

2.14   STRESS

There are three degrees of phonetic stress in Irish – primary, secondary and tertiary or unstressed. Stress generally correlates with differences of loudness, vowel length and vowel quality: tertiary stress, for example, is only found with a schwa.

In northern dialects – those of most of Connacht and Ulster – stress falls on the initial syllable of non-compound words, with a few exceptions mainly in borrowed words and in a small set of adverbials. In these dialects word stress may be regarded as a demarcative prosody which serves to delineate word boundaries and this appears to reflect the historical situation in the language.

In Munster dialects stress is no longer demarcative and has generally become associated with long vowels, whether in the initial or other syllable of the word. However, this picture is complicated by the fact that under certain conditions of sentence stress and rhythm, word stress can shift back to a short initial syllable:

(222)   *cailín* /ka'l'iːn'/ but *cailín deas* /ˌkal'iːn''d'as/

where in the second case the termination *-ín* is relatively unstressed. Though exceptions are numerous, it would seem possible in a synchronic phonology of these southern dialects to write a series of rules to generate the appropriately stressed forms, in parallel to the presumed historical development of stressing.

Stress in compounds formed by means of prefixes generally takes the form of two primary stresses, one on the prefix and one on the initial syllable of the compounded noun or adjective which would normally receive it in a pausa form. In a number of derivationally opaque compounds, however, the stress pattern follows that of non-compound words.

2.14.1   Stressed and unstressed syllables

Underlying the phonetic stress system described above is a basic phonological distinction in pausa forms between stressed and unstressed syllables, with the stressed syllable having the primary word stress and the unstressed either a secondary (if it has a clear vowel) or tertiary (with schwa) stress. That unstressed non-initial syllables have been subject to various qualitative and quantitative reductions of their vowels has been a long-established feature of the language, ranging from the pre-Old Irish period to the present-day dialects which show many instances of such changes.

2.14.2   Distribution of stress

The fundamental pattern of stress in pausa forms described above may be modified, however, by the presence of varying types of stress patterns in phrases, such as combinations of verb with a subject pronoun or noun plus following adjective. Under these circumstances the stressing of the individual elements may be modified in various ways. The example of (222) shows that primary stress on a noun is lost when it appears in combination with an adjective. Instead, the adjective carries the primary phrasal stress and the stress level of the noun is no higher than a secondary stress.

2.15   PITCH

2.15.1   Syllable pitch

Pitch is non-distinctive at the level of the syllable. All syllables, stressed or unstressed, and containing monophthongs or diphthongs, tend to have a falling pitch in pausa forms (this may be modified by the exigencies of the intonation patterns – see 2.15.3) and it would appear to be the case that unstressed syllables are of somewhat lower pitch than stressed syllables.

2.15.2   Word tone

There are no phonologically distinctive word tones in the language.

2.15.3   Intonation

There exists no comprehensive study of intonation in any Irish dialect, but information on aspects of it can be obtained from a number of the dialect monographs already mentioned earlier. Blankenhorn (1983) is a useful structural analysis of the intonation patterns of a Connacht dialect and provides the best analysis available. She distinguishes various kinetic glides in the nuclear contour of an utterance: rising, falling and falling–rising, with the possibility of various starting and end points, to give high-rise, half-rise, low-fall, etc. In addition, level tones, of three levels, may appear on syllables other than those carrying the nuclear stress patterns.

The three rising glides are used chiefly to indicate incompleteness in the utterance – that is, in *yes/no* questions or statements requiring verification or to indicate a pause in the middle of a sentence. The falling glides are used in responses or in *wh*-questions, with the low-fall being the most common and relatively unmarked contour. The fall–rise contour is used for emphasis, in either questions or statements, and the low-fall–rise in particular is used in listings. At the end of a sentence it has the function of indicating that the speaker has the intention of carrying on speaking.

MORPHOPHONOLOGY

2.16 MUTATIONS

Morphophonemic mutations in Irish are of three types: initial, affecting both consonants and vowels, but mainly the former; final, affecting consonants; and medial mutation of vowels. Of these three, the medial or vowel-umlaut mutations are perhaps the simplest to deal with, being generally predictable from the phonemic environment and usually appearing in conjunction with a final consonant mutation (2.16.2). Final mutations of consonants consist of a variation between neutral and palatalised segments. The most widespread, and certainly the best studied, Irish mutations are those which appear in word-initial position and which have their origins in earlier sandhi phenomena. Around the fifth century AD a series of phonetic changes modified the Irish consonant system whereby medial single consonants were affected by their environments so that, for example, an intervocalic /-b-/ was lenited to [-w-] (for a detailed discussion of these see Jackson 1953: ch. 4). In close syntactic compounds, such as pre-verb plus verb or article plus noun plus adjective, these phonetic changes also affected the initial consonants of the members of the compounds where these appeared intervocalically. It is these initial changes which, with the subsequent loss of final syllables, have been raised to the level of synchronic morphophonemic variation.

The most satisfactory analysis of these mutations is to be found in Oftedal (1962) and his system is basically that which is followed here, with some modification of detail. Following an earlier paper by Hamp (1951), Oftedal takes the position that the initial mutations are best analysed as normally representing the effects of a preceding morpheme on a word-initial segment, and to this extent the mutation-causing morph should include in its description an indication of the type of mutation following it. The possible initial mutations are lenition or nasalisation of consonants and *h*-provection to an initial vowel and these are symbolised by the superscript letters /$^{L\ N\ H}$/, respectively, attached to the morph in question, for example:

(223)   /ə^L+kat/   → [ə xat]   'his cat'
          /ə^H+kat/   → [ə kɑt]   'her cat'
          /ə^N+kat/   → [ə gɑt]   'their cat'
          /ə^H+ahər′/ → [ə hɑhɪr]   'her father'

These types of initial mutation are referred to by Oftedal as 'projected' and are opposed to a very much smaller number of 'incorporated' mutations which appear without any preceding synchronic conditioning and no longer have any morphophonological significance, for example *cha* NEG-PT (in dialects of Ulster Irish) or *chun* 'to', where forms no longer exist with unmutated initials.

From the point of view of the triggering morph, the presence of the mutational element /ᴸ ᴺ ᴴ/ may be either intrinsic, that is, appearing in the lexicon as part of the inherent specification of the morph in question – for example, *mo*ᴸ 'my', *a*ᴸ 'his', *a*ᴴ 'her', *a*ᴺ 'their' – or extrinsic, being introduced as part of the morph at some stage in its derivation. For example, nouns marked in the lexicon as [+Feminine] take up the feature of lenition in order to allow for their effect on the initial of a following adjective. Similarly, a noun which attracts the feature [+Prepositional] in the presence of a preceding preposition will also, in a number of dialects, have the feature of lenition attached to it in the course of the derivation of its systematic phonetic form.

As was the case in the earlier language, the domain of operation of all these mutation elements only extends as far as the initial of an immediately following word in a close syntactic relationship.

2.16.1   Initial mutations

Consonantal mutations are of two types, lenition (also called aspiration) and nasalisation or eclipsis, together with a minor mutation found when an initial /s-/ follows the definite article incorporating the feature of lenition. The lenition mutation involves a weakening of the articulation of the segment in question and is usually indicated in the orthography by means of the radical consonant followed by -*h*-. However, for the consonants /L N R/, where the lenited varieties are [l n r] (in northern dialects only and usually among the older generation), there is no indication of the lenition in the orthography, with the same symbols being written for both varieties. Eclipsis affects a smaller number of consonants (see 2.16.4) and here too the radical consonant appears in the orthography, preceded by the orthographic symbol of the mutated version: for example, *a gcat* [ə gat] 'their cat', *bhur mbó* [vər moː] 'your cow'.

2.16.2   Non-initial mutations

Consonants may be mutated between neutral and palatalised qualities, with the latter being indicated in the orthography by the presence of an -*i*- preceding the mutated segment. This change can apply to all final consonants and most final clusters, though it is possible to find a variation between a final segment and its mutated counterpart where the latter has been rendered intervocalic by the addition of a final schwa, e.g. *an bhróg* 'the shoe', GEN SG *na bróige*.

Word-internal mutations of vowels, or umlaut, usually accompanies these word-final consonant mutations, with low vowels in position before a 'new' palatalised segment being themselves raised and fronted: for example, /kat/ [kɑt] 'a cat', PL /kat'/ [kɪṭ]; /muk/ [mʌk] 'a pig', GEN SG /muk'ə/ [mʷɪkə̣].

2.16.3   Prevocalic mutations

Where a word begins with a vowel, there are two possible initial mutations: eclipsis (or nasalisation) and *h*-provection. The former consists of prefixed dental nasal and appears under the same conditions as the initial eclipsis of consonants mentioned above. In the orthography it is represented by *n*-attached to the vowel, apart from before capital vowel letters when *n* appears: for example, *ár n-athair* 'our father', *i nIfreann* 'in Hell'. The mutation of *h*-provection (which derives historically from the presence of a final *-s* in the preceding morph) simply prefixes the vowel by /h/: for example, *a hathair* 'her father'.

2.16.4   Mutation classes

The chart in (224) lists the effects of the mutations on initial segments. Only the neutral consonants are given here, as the palatalised congeners generally follow the pattern shown. For a detailed discussion see Ó Dochartaigh (1979b).

(224)	Radical	/p	t	k	b	d	g	f	s	m	L	N	R	vowel/
	Lenition	[f	h	x	v	γ	γ	Ø	h	ṽ	l	n	r	−]
	Eclipsis	[b	d	g	m	N	ŋ	v	−	−	−	−	−	N]
	h-provection	[												h]

Lenition has its origins in the fact that where a preceding morph in a close grammatical relationship originally ended in a vowel, its presence was sufficient to weaken phonetically the initial segment of the following word. Similarly, eclipsis derives from an earlier nasal consonant in the coda of the preceding word (it is sometimes referred to as nasalisation). The loss of final syllables in the course of the sixth century meant that what had been a predictable sandhi phenomenon was now raised to the status of a morphophonological opposition. Quite clearly the gradation of radical–lenited–eclipsed represents a phonemic opposition in the strict sense of this term, but in a generative phonology it is possible to derive these mutated initial segments by means of rules, so that they would appear at some intermediate stage in a particular derivation – hence the use of square brackets rather than phonemic slashes in (224).

Although (224) deals only with single radical consonants, the same sets of changes affect these consonants when they are the first members of initial clusters, with the exception of /s-/ followed by a stop or /m/ which is never affected by lenition (see Ó Dochartaigh 1988 for a discussion).

The lenition of the segments /L N R/ is only found in a number of Donegal dialects and appears to be mainly confined to the speech of the oldest generation.

In general, the process of lenition appears to be one which changes the articulatory setting of the segment involved, moving a stop to its corresponding fricative and a fricative to [h] or zero. However, for the dental stops the change has gone somewhat further in so far as the lenition of /t/ is [h] and /d/ has fallen together with /g/ under lenition to give [ɣ]. However, it would seem to be the case that this treatment of the dentals is a phonetic extension of lenition, as the earlier language showed the expected dental fricatives here. Note that the lenition of /f/ is zero – this is the expected result of the opening of the articulation of a segment which at an earlier stage was most likely a frictionless continuant or approximant, rather than a simple fricative. Eclipsis has the effect of voicing a voiceless stop (and /f/) and of changing a voiced stop to a homorganic nasal. The dental fricative /s/ is not normally affected by this change but in a number of dialects one does find instances of it being eclipsed, with [z] appearing as the mutated segment.

Following the definite article, the dental stops are not affected by lenition and initial /s-/ is replaced by [t-] – e.g. *leis an duine* 'with the person' *ar an tsráid* [ər ə traːdʹ] 'on the street', compare *leis an chat* 'with the cat'.

2.16.5   Noun mutations

Instances of final consonantal and medial vocalic mutations of nouns in conjugational forms have already been dealt with in 2.6.5 and 2.6.6. Mutation of noun initials is found in a large number of instances and only some occurrences are listed here:

       1 after the article in various cases (see 2.6.7.1)
       2 after forms of the possessive adjectives (see 2.6.9)
       3 after the vocative particle
       4 after certain numerals – for example, *aon* 'one', *dhá* 'two' lenite and *seacht* 'seven', *ocht* 'eight' eclipse

5 after a number of prepositions – for example, *de* 'of', *do* 'to' and *ó* 'from' lenite and *i* 'in' eclipses
6 after a prefix
7 when an indefinite noun immediately follows a governing noun and is in the genitive case – for example, *tine mhóna* 'a peat fire'
8 in a number of compounds – see 2.9.1
9 after certain forms of the copula – for example, *ba*^L COP+PAST, *níor*^L COP+PAST+NEG

2.16.6   Adjective mutations

Final consonant mutations of adjectives have been dealt with in the section on declension (2.8), where it was noted that these generally parallel closely the final mutations of nouns. In addition, the comparative of an adjective is formed by palatalisation of a final neutral consonant and the addition of a schwa (see 2.8.2).

Initial mutation of adjectives follows the pattern for nouns within the declensions – if the initial of the noun is lenited after the article, then the initial of any following adjective is usually similarly affected – the precise rules here depend on the dialect involved. In addition, the nominative and prepositional case plurals of first-declension nouns which form their plurals by palatalising the final consonant, lenite the initial of a following adjective: for example, *na fir mhóra* 'the big men'. Adjectives are also lenited after prefixes: for example, *ró-mhór* 'too big'.

2.16.7   Verb mutations

Final consonant mutations of verbs are not common and only appear in a few verbal nouns where we find an alteration between neutral and palatalised segments: for example, *cuir* 'put', *ag cur* 'putting'.

Lenition of verbs is found:

in the imperfect and past tenses and in the conditional mood – see the paradigm in 2.7.4;
after a number of preverbal particles: for example, *ní* NEG, *a* DIRECT REL.

Eclipsis of verbs is found:

after preverbal particles: for example, *an* WH, *go* SUBORD-PT, *a* INDIRECT REL.

REFERENCES

Blankenhorn, V. 1983. Intonation in Connemara Irish: a preliminary study of kinetic glides. *Studia Celtica* 16–17: 259–79.

Bliss, A. 1984. Language and literature. In J. Lydon (ed.) *The English in medieval Ireland*, Dublin: RIA.

Breatnach, R. B. 1947. *The Irish of Ring, Co. Waterford*, Dublin: DIAS.

Carney, J. 1975. The invention of the OGOM cipher. *Ériu* 26: 53–65.

Clar 1975. *Committee on language attitudes research – report*, Dublin: Stationery Office.

Connell, J. H. 1950. *The population of Ireland 1750–1845*, Oxford: Clarendon.

de Bhaldraithe, T. 1945. *The Irish of Cois Fhairrge, Co. Galway*, Dublin: DIAS.

   1953. *Gaeilge Chois Fhairrge*, Dublin: DIAS.

   1959. *English–Irish dictionary*, Dublin: Stationery Office.

de Búrca, S. 1958. *The Irish of Tourmakeady, Co. Mayo*, Dublin: DIAS.

Dillon, M. and N. Chadwick 1973. *The Celtic realms*, London: Cardinal.

Durkacz, V. E. 1983. *The decline of the Celtic languages*, Edinburgh: John Donald.

Edwards, J. 1984. *The Irish language: an annotated bibliography of sociolinguistic publications, 1772–1982*, New York: Garland.

Fennell, D. 1981. Can a shrinking linguistic minority be saved? In E. Haugen, J. D. McClure and D. Thomson (eds.) *Minority languages today*, Edinburgh: Edinburgh University Press, pp. 32–9.

Graiméar 1960. *Graiméar Gaeilge na mBráithre Críostaí*, Dublin: Christian Brothers.

Gramadach na Gaeilge 1968. Dublin: Stationery Office.

Greene, D. 1973. The growth of palatalization in Irish. *Transactions of the Philological Society*: 127–36.

   1979. Perfects and perfectives in modern Irish. *Ériu*: 30: 122–41.

   1983. The coming of the Celts. In G. Mac Eoin (ed.) *Proceedings of sixth International Conference of Celtic Studies*, Dublin: Institute for Advanced Studies. pp. 131–7.

Hamp, E. 1951. Morphophonemics of the Keltic mutations. *Language* 27: 230–47.

Hechter, M. 1975. *Internal colonialism*, London: Routledge and Kegan Paul.

Holmer, N. M. 1962. *The dialects of Co. Clare*, Dublin: RIA.

Jackson, K. H. 1953. *Language and history in Early Britain*, Edinburgh: Edinburgh University Press.

Lewis, H. and H. Pedersen 1962. *A concise comparative Celtic grammar*, Göttingen: Vandenhoeck and Ruprecht.

Lucas, L. W. 1979. *Grammar of Ros Goill Irish, Co. Donegal*, Belfast: Institute of Irish Studies, Queen's University.

Macalister, R. A. 1945. *Corpus inscriptionem insularum Celticarum*, vol. I, Dublin: Stationery Office.

McCloskey, J. 1979. *Transformational syntax and model theoretic semantics*, Dordrecht: D. Reidel.

Mac Éinrí, F. 1970. The syntax of the sentence in modern Irish. Unpublished Ph.D. thesis, University of Georgetown, Washington, DC.

McManus, D. 1984. On final syllables in the Latin loan-words in Early Irish. *Ériu* 35: 137–62.

Mhac an Fhailigh, É. 1968. *The Irish of Erris, Co. Mayo*, Dublin: DIAS.

New Irish grammar 1980. Dublin: Christian Brothers.

Ó Baoill, D. P. 1975. Deixis in modern Irish and related problems. *Ériu* 26: 144–61.

   1980. Preaspiration, epenthesis and vowel lengthening – interrelated and of similar origin? *Celtica* 13: 79–108.

Ó Buachalla, B. 1980. The verbal-adjective formant -*iste* in Ulster Irish. *Ériu* 31: 39–45.

Ó Cuív, B. 1944. *The Irish of West Muskerry, Co. Cork*, Dublin: DIAS.

1951. *Irish dialects and Irish-speaking districts*, Dublin: DIAS.

Ó Dochartaigh, C. 1979a. Aspects of cluster modification in Irish. In Dónall Ó Baoill (ed.) *Papers in Celtic phonology*, Coleraine: New University of Ulster, pp. 124–33.

1979b. Lenition and dependency phonology. *Éigse* 17: 457–94.

1981. Vowel strengthening in Gaelic. *Scottish Gaelic Studies* 12: 219–40.

1982. Generational differences in Donegal Irish. *Belfast Working Papers in Linguistics* 6: 67–103.

1987. *Dialects of Ulster Irish*, Belfast: Institute of Irish Studies, Queen's University.

1988. Lenition of s-clusters. *Scottish Language* 7: 22–30.

Ó Dónaill, N. 1977. *Foclóir Gaeilge-Béarla*, Dublin: Stationery Office.

Oftedal, M. 1962. A morphemic evaluation of the Celtic initial mutations. *Lochlann* 2: 92–102.

Ó Muirí, D. 1982. *Coimhréir Ghaeilge Ghaoth Dobhair*, Dublin: Coiscéim.

Ó Murchú, M. 1969. Common core and underlying forms. *Ériu* 21: 42–75.

O'Rahilly, T. F. 1946. *Early Irish history and mythology*, Dublin: DIAS.

1972. *Irish dialects past and present*, Dublin: DIAS.

Ó Siadhail, M. 1989. *Modern Irish: grammatical structure and dialect variation*. Cambridge: Cambridge University Press.

Ó Siadhail, M. and A. Wigger 1975. *Córas fuaimeanna na Gaeilge*, Dublin: DIAS.

Pedersen, H. 1913. *Vegleichende Grammatik der keltischen Sprachen*, Göttingen: Vandenhoeck and Ruprecht.

Piggott, S. 1983. The coming of the Celts. In G. Mac Eoin (ed.) *Proceedings of the sixth International Conference of Celtic Studies*, Dublin: Institute for Advanced Studies, pp. 137–48.

Pokorny, J. 1969. *Altirische Grammatik*, Berlin: Walter de Gruyter.

Quiggin, E. C. 1906. *A dialect of Donegal*, Cambridge: Cambridge University Press.

Risk, H. 1968–74. French loan-words in Irish. *Etudes celtiques* 12: 585–655; 14: 67–98.

Sommerfelt, A. 1922. *The dialect of Torr, Co. Donegal*, Christiania: Jacob Dybwad.

1965. The phonemic structure of the dialect of Torr, Co. Donegal. *Lochlann* 3: 237–54.

Stenson, N. 1981. *Studies in Irish syntax*, Tübingen: Gunter Narr.

Thurneysen, R. 1946. *A grammar of Old Irish*, Dublin: DIAS.

Wagner, H. 1958. *Gaeilge Theilinn*. Dublin: DIAS.

1958–69. *Linguistic atlas and survey of Irish dialects*, 4 vols., Dublin: DIAS.

Wigger, A. 1972. Preliminaries to a generative morphology of the modern Irish verb. *Ériu* 23: 162–213.

3

The Manx language

ROBERT L. THOMSON

HISTORICAL AND SOCIAL PERSPECTIVE

3.0   EXTERNAL HISTORY OF THE LANGUAGE

Manx is the Celtic language of the Isle of Man (*Ellan Vannin*), which lies in the middle of the north Irish Sea (Old Irish *Muir Manann*). The earliest Celtic spoken in Man was probably of the Brittonic type, but Manx is a Goidelic dialect introduced by the same fifth-century expansion of Irish speakers which brought Gaelic to Scotland. Though there are signs that some kind of political connection with Brittonic areas (Cumbria, Anglesey, Gwynedd) continued for some time, evidence of a linguistic connection is tenuous. It is, however, probable that the tendency towards a more analytic form of the verb, which Manx shares with Scottish Gaelic, should be attributed to a Brittonic substratum in both.

3.0.1   During the Norse period, from the ninth to the thirteenth century, when the island became the centre of a Norse–Gaelic kingdom and of a diocese extending over all the Western Isles, Gaelic and Norse may have been locally and/or socially distributed, but the small amount of evidence from personal and early place names suggests that there was extensive bilingualism. On the cession of the island to Scotland in 1266 Gaelic became dominant again, possibly aided by migration from Galloway, and remained so until at least the end of the eighteenth century, despite the grant of the lordship by the English crown to a series of Anglo-Norman magnates ending with the Stanleys, later earls of Derby, at the beginning of the fifteenth century.

3.0.2   Apart from proper names the language remained unwritten until the translation *c.* 1610 of the Anglican *Book of Common Prayer* by John Phillips, bishop 1605–33, though the historical poem known as the *Traditionary* or *Manannan Ballad*, preserved in eighteenth-century manuscripts, may on grounds of language and content be assigned to the early sixteenth century (Thomson 1961). The spelling, both that of Phillips and that now standard, is independent of the traditional Gaelic system and based largely on the conventions of Late Middle and Early Modern English. The first external notation of Manx occurs in the material collected *c.* 1700 for Edward Lhuyd, a copy of which was recently discovered in the National Library of Wales (Ifans and Thomson 1980).

3.1   LANGUAGE STATUS

Manx has never enjoyed official status: though proceedings, civil and ecclesiastical, were conducted orally in Manx, the record of them, the statutes and all legal documents were in English, or very occasionally in Latin, from the fifteenth century, though a very few Manx legal terms have survived (Thomson 1988: 141–2).

3.1.1   The need for charitable support for publishing in Manx in the eighteenth and early nineteenth centuries meant that only works on religious subjects appeared in print, beginning with Bishop Wilson's expanded *Catechism* in 1707 and reaching a climax with the completion of the Bible translation in 1773. As the manuscript material consists mainly of collections of religious poems (*carvallyn*) and of sermons, with only a small collection of secular songs, the evidence for the classical language is heavily biased. For other areas of life we are mainly dependent on the dictionaries of John Kelly and Archibald Cregeen. Even on this evidence, however, Manx appears lexically impoverished as a result of isolation and a lack of the literary cultivation that could have kept a larger non-utilitarian vocabulary in current use.

3.1.2   From the late eighteenth century the use of Manx declined, first in the towns where business contacts and later the developing tourist industry were influential, then in the villages and lastly in the countryside. The decline was quite rapid, within three or four generations, and parents who saw Manx as an economic handicap sometimes deliberately kept it from their children. Marstrander, collecting material in the 1920s, and even Rhŷs in the 1870s, found the Manx speakers chiefly among the older generation. The last native speaker died in December 1974, but a number of people of all ages who learnt from him and his contemporaries, keep up the use of the language for social and to a limited extent for literary purposes, and by them it is also taught with varying degrees of formality to learners from school-children upwards. An O-level examination in the subject was instituted by the Northern Universities Joint Matriculation Board in 1982. In 1991 the Department of Education approved the appointment of a language officer and two peripatetic teachers to enable Manx to be offered as an official, optional subject in the curriculum from 1993.

3.1.3   The decline in the currency of Manx has, not surprisingly, been accompanied by a decline in standards compared with the 'classical' language of the eighteenth century. While to a limited extent this may be attributed to normal linguistic development the many signs of the interference of English in vocabulary and idiom make it unlikely that the limitations on syntactical and morphological variety are entirely independent of that influence; nor is there any reason to regard this late Manx as somehow more real or genuine than the classical language, for there are no grounds for regarding the latter as in any way artificial or deliberately archaic. The following account attempts to combine a description of the classical language with some notice of the changes in the late Manx of the last generation of native speakers.

SYNTAX

3.2   THE SENTENCE

Manx prefers a simple sentence structure, the one-clause sentence, the string of co-ordinate clauses or the principal clause with one subordinate. When elements normally found together are separated (e.g. by an intervening prepositional phrase or relative clause), the usual practice is to resume (e.g. a subject by a pronoun):

(1)   *yn dooinney ta   chiarn ny   cheerey, loayr   eh*
        ART man   be-PRES(-REL) lord   ART-GEN-FEM land-GEN speak-PAST he
        dy   baggyrtagh rooin
        ADV.PT threatening to-us
        'The man who is lord of the land spoke threateningly to us'

instead of the integrated sentence

(2)   *loayr y dooinney ta chiarn ny cheerey dy baggyrtagh rooin*

3.2.1   In a series of co-ordinate clauses the expressed subject of the first clause must be repeated (in pronominal form) in the succeeding clauses:

(3)   *dreggyr   e ven as   dooyrt   ee*
        answer-PAST his wife and say-PAST she
        'His wife answered and said'

but in answering a question, where the response is the affirmative or negative form of the verb of the question, the subject pronoun is not used:

(4)   *jig   eh mairagh?   hig.   cha jig.*
        come-FUT-DEP he tomorrow   come-FUT   NEG come-FUT-DEP
        'Will he come tomorrow? Yes   No'

With a verb formed by means of an auxiliary the latter alone suffices in answers:

(5)   *nagh   vel   eh creck   y   thie   shen? ta.   cha*
        NEG-INTER be-PRES-DEP he sell(ing) ART house that   be-PRES NEG
        nel.
        be-PRES+DEP
        'Isn't he selling that house? Yes / No'

3.2.2   The neutral order in the clause, that is when no element is given particular prominence, is verb, subject, object/complement, prepositional phrase; derived adverbs come either within the verbal phrase or at the end of the clause:

(6)   *ta   mee dy   kinjagh faagail   y   moddey ec y   thie*
        be-PRES I   ADV.PT constant leav(ing) ART dog   at ART house
        'I always leave the dog at home'

The verb is preceded by any negative, conjunctive or interrogative particle, all of which require it to be in the dependent form:

(7)   *hem*
        go-FUT-1SG
        'I'll go'

(8)   *cha jem*
        NEG go-FUT-DEP-1SG
        'I shan't go'

(9)   *dy   jem*
        CONJ go-FUT-DEP-1SG
        'that I (shall) go'

(10)   *nagh   jem*
        CONJ-NEG
        'that I shan't go'

(11)   (zero) *jem?*
            INT
            'Shall I go?'

(12)   *nagh   jem?*
            INT-NEG
            'Shall I not go?'

Any interrogative element precedes the verb and is followed by its independent/ relative form:

(13)   *quoi hed   er nyn   son?*
            who go-FUT for POSS-PL sake
            'Who will go for us?'

(14)   *cre   'n- fa   ta   shiu farkiaght ayns shoh?*
            what ART cause be-PRES ye   wait(ing) in   this
            'Why are you waiting here?'

3.2.2.1   When the verb is complex, that is, formed by means of auxiliary 'be' or 'do', or another auxiliary such as 'can', some variations appear. With auxiliary 'be' pronoun objects of the first and second persons singular, less commonly also of the third person plural, were formerly included in the verbal complex after *dy* (in the present series of tenses) or *er* (in the past series):

(15)   *t'   eh dy my chlashtyn*
            be-PRES he to my hear(ing)
            'He hears me'

(16)   *v'   ad   dy dty woalley*
            be-PAST they to thy beat(ing)
            'They were beating you'

(17)   *v'   ou dyn   dilgey   (ad) 'syn   aile*
            be-PAST thou to-their throw(ing) they in-ART fire
            'You were throwing them in the fire'

(18)   *ta   mee er   dt' akin*
            be-PRES I   after thy see(ing)
            'I've seen you'

3.2.2.2   Nominal objects, and increasingly in late Manx pronominal ones also, take the normal object position after the verb–noun:

(19)   *t'   eh clashtyn my choraa / mee/oo / ad*
            be-PRES he hear(ing) my voice   I   thou they
            'He hears my voice / me/you/them'

3.2.2.3   With auxiliary 'do' both pronominal objects (in the possessive form) and nominal objects are included in the verbal phrase:

(20)   *cha jean*   *eh my chlashtyn*
              NEG do-FUT-DEP he my hear(ing)
              'He won't hear me'

(21)   *ren*   *ad*   *my choraa y chlashtyn*
              do-PAST they my voice PT hear
              'They heard my voice'

As with auxiliary 'be', the pattern of nominal objects first tends to prevail with pronominal ones:

(22)   *jean-jee*   *coyrle y   dooinney creeney y chlashtyn*
              do-IMPV-2PL advice ART man   wise   PT hear

(23)   *jean-jee*   *eshyn   y chlashtyn*
              do-IMPV-2PL he-EMPH PT hear

Finally, the position at the end of the phrase becomes usual:

(24)   *jean shiu clashtyn coyrle y dooinney creeney*

(25)   *jean shiu clashtyn eh*

3.2.3   Sentences expressing the notion of 'being' divide into two classes according to whether the copula or the substantive verb is used; the latter is now generally preferred but the copula is used in the comparison of adjectives (3.8.1.2), and (sometimes in zero form) it is also normal when two items are equated, the first being a personal pronoun, a demonstrative or an interrogative:

(26)   *mish   eh*
              I-EMPH he
              'I am he'

(27)   *quoi ad?*
              who they
              'Who are they?'

(28)   *shoh 'n   dooinney*
              this   ART man
              'This is the man'

but when not affirmative the copula is expressed:

(29)   *cha nee*   *mish   eh*
              NEG COP-PRES-DEP I-EMPH he

(30)   *nee*   *shoh 'n   lioar?*
              COP-PRES-DEP this ART book
              'Is this the book?'

In tenses other than the present the substantive verb is used. The copula is used also with certain fixed predicates as the equivalent of a verb:

(31)   *shione   dou   yn boayl*
         COP-PRES-known to-me ART place
         'I know the place'

(32)   *nailt [*an + *ail +   lhiat]   goll   mârin?*
         COP-PRES-INTER + desire with-thee go(ing) with-us
         'Do you want to go with us?'

(33)   *bare   lhiam   fuirraght ec y   thie*
         COP-COND-better with-me stay(ing) at ART house
         'I'd rather stay at home'

Such sentences continue the traditional order in copula sentences, that is, copula + predicate + subject, 'Staying at home would be better in my opinion'. Similarly

(34)   *s'   feer eh*
         COP-PRES true it
         'It's true'

3.2.4   Sentences of mere existence have the predicate position filled by the pronominal preposition *ayn* 'in it', and employ the substantive verb:

(35)   *bee   fliaghey ayn*
         be-FUT rain   in-it
         'There will be rain'

(36)   *va   kiuney vooar ayn*
         be-PAST calm   great in-it
         'There was a great calm'

3.2.5   In classification sentences the class to which the member belongs is preceded by a form of the preposition 'in' and the appropriate possessive particle:

(37)   *t'   eh ny   hidoor*
         be-PRES he in-his soldier
         'He's a soldier'

(38)   *v'   ad nyn   eeasteyryn*
         be-PAST they in-their fisherman-PL
         'They were fishermen'

3.2.6   Aspect is only intermittently marked, as by the existence of the imperfect and other continuous tenses (though no such distinction is available in the present) and the distinction between preterite and perfect (3.4.2, 3.4.6), but a distinction can sometimes be made between action and state, though it is not invariably observed; so with the verbs 'sit', 'stand', and 'lie':

(39)   *ta   mee shassoo*
        be-PRES I   stand(ing)
        'I stand (up), I (come to a) stop'

(40)   *ta   mee my   hassoo*
        be-PRES I   in-my stand(ing)
        'I am standing' (cf. 3.2.4)

A few other predicates of state follow the same usage:

(41)   *v'   eh ny   host*
        be-PAST he in-his silence
        'He was silent'

(42)   *t'   ad nyn   daaue*
        be-PRES they in-their rest
        'They're idle'

3.2.7   Noun clauses

In reported speech and after verbs of asking, thinking, fearing, etc., the clause is introduced by the conjunction *dy* 'that', *nagh* 'that not', zero 'whether', all followed by dependent verb forms:

(43)   *t'   ad gra   dy   vel   mooarane skeddan ayn*
        be-PRES they say(ing) CONJ be-PRES-DEP much   herring in-it (see 3.2.4)
        'They say there's a lot of herring'

(44)   *dinsh   eh dou   nagh row   veg yn argid   echey*
        tell-PAST he to-me CONJ be-PAST-DEP any ART money at-him
        'He told me he had no money'

(45)   *dênee   ad j'ee   row   ee rieau ayns shen*
        ask-PAST they of-her be-PAST-DEP she ever in   that
        'They asked her whether she was ever there'

3.2.7.1   Alternatively, with verbs of requesting, commanding, etc., a nominal phrase construction, subject + *dy* + verb–noun, is used:

(46)   *ghuee   mee er   eh dy heet stiagh*
        beseech-PAST I   on-him he to come in-MOTION
        'I begged him to come in'

(47)   *choyrlee   shin ny   joarreeyn gyn   ad dy hannaghtyn ny sodjey*
        advise-PAST we   ART-PL stranger-PL without they to stay   longer
                                                                         (see 3.8.2)
        'We advised the strangers not to stay (any) longer'

3.2.8   Adjectival clauses

Affirmative relative clauses are introduced by a particle long reduced to zero (followed by independent or relative verb forms), with negative *nagh* (followed by dependent verb forms), and are attached directly to the antecedent; if the latter is a personal pronoun it is usually in the emphatic form, and if it is a possessive then the periphrastic construction with article and *ec* (3.3.2) is employed:

(48)   *shoh yn thie   hrog   mee*
         this   ART house raise-PAST I
         'This is the house I built'

(49)   *shen clagh nagh   drog   oo*
         that stone REL-NEG raise-FUT-DEP thou
         'That's a stone you won't lift'

(50)   *hug   eh booise dauesyn   v'   er   ghellal dy dooie rish*
         give-PAST he thanks to-them-EMPH be-PAST after deal(ing) PT kind to-him
         'He thanked those who had dealt kindly with him'

(51)   *y   chooid ocsyn   hug   nyn marrant dâ*
         ART property at-them-EMPH give-PAST their trust   to-him
         'the property of those who trusted him'

Compared adjectives used attributively are a special case of the affirmative relative with the copula (usually present, rarely past/conditional);

(52)   *y   dooinney saa*
         ART man   COP-PRES-young-COMP
         'the youngest man'

3.2.8.1   The relative with a preposition has the appropriate personal form of the preposition either before the verb of the relative clause or, more usually, at the end of it:

(53)   *shoh 'n thie   ta   shin baghey ayn*
         this ART house be-PRES we   liv(ing) in-it
         'This is the house we live in'

With the genitive of the relative the appropriate possessive appears in the relative clause:

(54)   *shen y   dooinney ta   'n   mac echey ching*
         that ART man   be-PRES ART son at-him ill
         'That's the man whose son is ill'

3.2.8.2   When the antecedent is 'that (which), what', the relative is *ny*, often *shen ny*:

(55)   *cha n'oddin   clashtyn (shen) ny   dooyrt eh*
        NEG can-COND-DEP-1ST hear   that REL say-PAST he
        'I couldn't hear what he said'

A special case is a compared adjective used predicatively or a compared adverb
derived from an adjective:

(56)   *ta   'n dooinney shoh ny   saa   na 'n   braar*
        be-PRES ART man   this REL COP-PRES-young-COMP than ART brother
        echey
        at-him
        'This man is younger than his brother'

With an antecedent qualified by 'each, all, every, any' or a superlative adjective
the affirmative relative traditionally took the form *dy* 'of those that', followed by
a dependent verb form:

(57)   *thie   erbee dy jed   shiu stiagh   ayn*
        house any   REL go-FUT-DEP ye in-MOTION in+it
        'any house you enter'

3.2.8.3   When the relative is accusative and the verb in the relative clause is
periphrastic, then with auxiliary 'be' the particle *dy* was until recently inserted
before the verb–noun, and with auxiliary 'do' the particle *y*:

(58)   *shen y   thie t'   eh dy hroggal*
        that ART house be-PRES he at-its rais(ing)
        'That's the house he's building'

(59)   *shen y   thie   ren   eh y hroggal*
        that ART house do-PAST he its raising
        'That's the house he built'

At an earlier date this construction was used with auxiliary 'be' in the past series
of tenses formed with *er* + verb–noun:

(60)   *shen y   thie t'   eh er   ny hroggal*
        that ART house be-PRES he after its raising
        'That's the house he has built'

but this fell into disuse during the eighteenth century, probably because of an
overlap with some passive forms.

3.2.8.4   The compared adverb in a relative clause appears as a compared
adjective attached to the antecedent:

(61)   *y   charvaant smoo   ta   cur   geill da goan   e vainshter*
        ART servant   greatest be-PRES giv(ing) heed to word-PL his master
        'the servant who pays most attention to his master's words'

3.2.9   Adverbial clauses

Examples are (a) time, introduced by *tra* 'when', *derrey, gys* 'until', *neayr's*
'since' (all with relative or independent verb), (*roish*) *my* 'before' (with
dependent verb, but sometimes, by confusion with *my* 'if', with relative verb);
(b) place, *raad* 'where' (relative/independent verb); (c) cause, *er-y-fa dy, son dy*
(negative *nagh*); (d) purpose and result, (*myr shen*) *dy* (negative *nagh*) 'so that',
er-aggle dy (negative *nagh*) 'in case, lest'; (e) concession, *ga* 'though' (independent), but usually *ga dy* (negative *nagh*), *er-bedy* 'were it not that, had it not
been that'; (f) condition, *my* 'if' (relative/independent), negative *mannagh*
(dependent), *dy* 'if' (with conditional only); (g) comparison, *myr* 'as' (relative/
independent), *myr dy* (negative *nagh*) 'as if' (conditional).

3.2.9.1   In the expression of purpose the preposition *dy* 'to' is used with the
verb–noun:

(62)   *hie   ad   dy chionnaghey arran*
         go-PAST they to buy(ing)   bread
         'They went to buy bread'

rather than the clause forms:

(63)   *. . . dy gionneeagh   ad   arran*
         that buy-COND-DEP they bread

(64)   *. . . dy jinnagh   ad arran y chionnaghey*
         that do-COND-DEP they bread PT buy
         '. . . that they should buy bread'

With reference to past time 'when' is also rendered by the prepositions *erreish,
lurg*, with the preposition *da* 'to' before the agent, and in the active the
verb–noun is normally preceded by *v'er* (as a quasi-perfect infinitive):

(65)   *erreish daue   v'   er   choyrt*
         after   to-them be-VN after send-VN
         'when they (had) sent'

3.2.10   Prominence

The order of the clause is variable to the extent that the subject, more usually
the object or an adverbial element, may be placed first and thereby gain
prominence:

(66)   *mish   t'   ayn*
         I-EMPH be-PRES in-it (see 3.2.4)
         'It is I'

(67)   *shoh ta   mee dy   ghra*
         this be-PRES I   at-its say(ing) (see 3.2.8.3)
         'this I say'

(68)   *fastyr Jycrean   haink   ad dy chur   shilley orrin*
         evening Wednesday come-PAST they to put-VN sight   on-us
         '(It was) Wednesday evening they came to see us'

A complementary adjective may be preceded by the present affirmative of the copula:

(69)   *s'   mooar va   nyn moggey*
         COP-PRES great   be-PAST their joy
         'Great was their joy'

For more explicit emphasis the copula, in the present tense only, and incorporating a third person singular pronoun, is used: *she*, negative *cha nee*, and with an element in a subordinate clause, *dy nee*, *dy re*, negative *nagh nee*:

(70)   *cha nee   mish dooyrt   shen*
         COP-PRES-NEG-DEP-pronoun I   say-PAST that
         'It was not I that said that'

(71)   *ta   mee credjal   dy re   ayns y   gharey hooar*
         be-PRES I   believe-VN COP-PRES-DEP+pronoun in   ART garden find-PAST
         ad   eh
         they it
         'I think they found it *in the garden*'

STRUCTURE OF THE PHRASE

3.3   THE NOMINAL PHRASE

The nominal phrase may be defined as the group of connected words looking forward or back to a noun as its centre, the elements, however many or few, occurring in a fixed order, a sequence not capable of being broken into except in limited definable circumstances and, as a unit, capable of functioning in a variety of ways in the sentence, for example as subject, as direct object, as indirect object, as complement, as adverbial phrase, as phrasal preposition, as phrasal conjunction.

3.3.1   At its fullest extent the nominal phrase consists of

(a) preposition
(b) definite article, or possessive particle, or *gach* 'each', or *dy chooilley* 'every'

(c)   numeral (ordinal and cardinal)
(d)   prefixed adjective
(e)   noun
(f)   modifier of following adjective
(g)   adjective(s)
(h)   demonstrative (requiring the article at (b))
(i)   alternative possessive (requiring article at (b)), or clarification of
       ambiguous possessive (b)

3.3.1.1   (a) Although the pre-articular forms of the Gaelic prepositions
have been generalised for use in all positions in Manx, with only occasional
exceptions, their existence (as well as the evidence of mutations) demonstrates
the closeness of the connection of this item with the noun and justifies its
inclusion in the nominal phrase.

3.3.1.2   (b) There is no indefinite article: for example, *dooinney* 'a man',
laue 'a hand'. The article, the possessives, *gach* and *dy chooilley* are mutually
exclusive. In addition to referring back to a noun already mentioned the article
is used with some abstract nouns: *y vea* 'life', *y baase* 'death', *yn irriney* 'truth', *y
dooinney* 'man(kind)'.

3.3.1.3   When one noun (in the genitive) depends on another the first is
thereby rendered definite without the use of the article: for example, *ben
dooinney* 'the wife of a man, a man's wife', *ben y dooinney* 'the wife of the man,
the man's wife'. The article may, however, be used with a noun followed by a
dependent genitive if the two nouns are felt to constitute a compound word: for
example, *y dooinney-poosee* 'the bridegroom' (lit. the man of marrying), *ny
fir-reill* 'the rulers' (lit. the persons of ruling).

3.3.1.4   The article also occurs between an interrogative adjective and a
noun: *cre'n ennym t'ort?* 'What is your name?' (lit. 'What (is) the name that is on
you?'), *quoi'n cabbyl ren oo 'reih?* 'Which horse did you choose?'; and
(ultimately by a false analysis) between *lheid* 'such' and *veg* 'any' and a noun:
lheid ny deiney 'such men', *veg yn argid* 'any money'.

3.3.1.5   The possessive particles may be followed in the demonstrative
position (h) by *hene* 'self' with the sense 'own', as *my hie hene* 'my own house'.

3.3.1.6   (c) The ordinal and cardinal numerals precede the noun when they
are single items, as *un* 'one', *daa* 'two', *three* 'three', *kiare* 'four', *queig* 'five',

shey 'six', *shiaght* 'seven', *hoght* 'eight', *nuy* 'nine', *jeih* 'ten', *feed* 'twenty', *da-eed* 'forty', *keead* 'hundred', or are inseparable, as *three feed* 'sixty', *kiare feed* 'eighty', *shey feed* '120', *shiaght feed* '140', *hoght feed* '160', *nuy feed* '180'; but in the compound numerals the noun follows the first element, as *un laa jeig* 'eleven days', *daa . . . yeig, three . . . jeig,* etc., *un . . . as feed, daa . . . as feed,* etc. Similarly with the cardinals *chied* 'first', *nah* 'second', *trass* 'third', *kiarroo* 'fourth', *queiggoo* 'fifth', *sheyoo* 'sixth', *shiaghtoo* 'seventh', *hoghtoo* 'eighth', *nuyoo* 'ninth', *jeihoo* 'tenth', *feedoo* 'twentieth', *keeadoo* 'hundredth'. When numerals are used without a noun, as in counting, the series begins *nane, jees, three, kiare* etc., and *nane* replaces *un* wherever it occurs in the compound numerals.

3.3.1.7   The noun is singular after *un, daa, feed, keead* and all compound numerals in which one of these elements precedes it, that is 1, 2, 11, 12, 20, 21, 22, 31, 32, 40, 41, 42, 51, 52, 60, 61, 62, etc. Beyond 60 or 80 the order in compound numerals changes to place the larger number first, for example *kiare-feed dooinney as shiaght* 'eight-seven men', rather than *shiaght deiney as kiare-feed.* An alternative construction with large numbers treats the numeral as a noun followed by the preposition *dy* 'of', as *three-feed as kiare dy gheiney* 'sixty-four men'; this is also used when the number of the noun would not be the same after a pair of numerals, as *ghaa ny three dy gheiney* 'two or three men' (cf. *daa ghooinney, three deiney*).

3.3.1.8   (d) The prefixed adjectives are very few: *ard-* 'principal, chief', *drogh-* 'bad', *reih-* 'choice, excellent', *shenn-* 'old'. (For (e) see 3.6.)

3.3.1.9   (f) The elements modifying adjectives are also few: *feer* 'very', *ro* 'too', *bunnys* 'almost', *lane* 'quite'. Intensives derived from other adjectives generally follow, as *mie agglagh* 'fearfully good', *mie yindyssagh* 'wonderfully good'. (For (g) see 3.3.2.1.)

3.3.1.10   (h) The article is required with a noun followed by a demonstrative: for example, *y ven shoh* 'this woman', *ny paitchyn shen* 'those children', except when the noun is a proper name, as *Yeesey shoh* 'this Jesus'.

3.3.2   (i) As an alternative to the possessive particles (b) Manx uses very freely the article in position (b) and the personal forms of the preposition *ec* 'at' in position (i): for example, *my hie* or *y thie aym* 'my house'. The forms of the prepositional pronoun are also used to explicate the ambiguous *nyn* 'our, your, their' in position (b) when necessary, particularly in phrasal prepositions (see 3.5.2).

3.3.2.1 Sentences containing more than a very few of these elements in combination are rare, and some elements are mutually exclusive, but a fairly complete example might be

(a) (b)	(c)	(d)	(e)		(f) (g)	(h)
ayns ny	*three*	*shenn*	*tholtanyn*	*feer*	*ghraney*	*shoh*
in ART-PL	three	old	ruin-PL		very ugly	this

'in these three very ugly old ruins'

As (i) *oc* 'at them' might be added, except that, though the combination of possessive and demonstrative was acceptable in early Manx, it seems not to have been so later. A nominal phrase (genitive, or introduced by a preposition) or an adjectival clause qualifying a noun, occupies position (g).

3.4   THE VERBAL PHRASE

The verbal phrase may be defined as the connected group of words that looks to a finite verb form as its core, and in Manx takes one of two forms according as the verbal element is simple or complex.

3.4.1   The simple verbal phrase consists of

(A) interrogative/negative/relative particle, or subordinating conjunction
(B) verb
(C) subject (inflection/pronoun)
(D) object pronoun

3.4.2   This type of phrase occurs only when the verb is imperative, future, conditional, or preterite, and is formed by inflection:

Imperative

(72)   *eiyr-jee*   *ad*   (i.e. B+C+D)
          drive-IMPV-2PL they
          'drive them'

Future

(73)   *tra   higmayd*   (i.e. A+B+C)
          CONJ come-FUT-1PL
          'when we come'

Conditional

(74)   *dy   vaikagh   shiu ee*   (i.e. A+B+C+D)
        CONJ see-COND-DEP ye   she
        'if you saw (were to see) her'

Preterite

(75)   *nagh   dug   oo ad?* (i.e. A+B+C+D)
        INTER-NEG send+ PAST-DEP thou they
        'didn't you send them?'

3.4.3   The complex verbal phrase consists of

(A) interrogative/negative/relative particle, or subordinating conjunction

(B) auxiliary verb

(C) subject (inflection/pronoun)

(D) (with auxiliary 'be' only) zero (*g-* before vowels) or *er(n)* for the present and perfect groups of tenses respectively

(E) provision for the inclusion of pronoun objects and, with auxiliary 'do' only, of noun objects (3.2.2–3)

(F) verb–noun

3.4.4   The complex verbal phrase is the only means of forming, with auxiliary 'be', the present, the rare continuous future, the imperfect, the perfect, the future perfect and the pluperfect. In addition, with auxiliary 'do', it provides a very commonly used alternative to the four inflected tenses, and one which in Late Manx has rendered them practically obsolete.

3.4.5   Nominal subjects in both types of phrase take the same position as pronoun subjects or inflections. In the simple verbal phrase nominal direct objects also follow the pattern of pronominal direct objects. For the nominal and pronominal objects of complex verbal phrases see 3.2.2.1–3.

3.4.6   Examples of complex verbal phrases with auxiliary 'be':

Present

(76)   *ta   mee gaase*
        be-PRES I   at-grow(ing)
        'I grow, I'm growing'

Imperfect

(77)   *v'   ad   niee*
be-PAST they (at-) wash(ing)
'they were washing, they used to wash'

Perfect

(78)   *t'   eh er n' aase*
be-PRES he after grow(ing)
'he has grown'

Future perfect

(79)   *beemayd   er   niee*
be-FUT-1PL after wash(ing)
'we shall have washed'

Pluperfect

(80)   *tra   va   shin er n' aase*
when be-PAST we   after grow(ing)
'when we had grown'

3.4.7   Complex verbal phrases with auxiliary 'do':

Imperative

(81)   *jean-jee   troggal!*
do-IMPV-2PL lift(ing)
'lift!'

Future

(82)   *nagh   jean   oo   cheet?*
INT-NEG do-FUT-DEP thou com(ing)
'Won't you come?'

Conditional

(83)   *yinnagh eh chyndaa*
do-COND he turn(ing)
'he would turn'

Preterite

(84)   *ren   ad   gee*
do-PAST they at-eat(ing)
'they ate'

Gee, verb–noun *ee*, forming as it does a kind of present participle equivalent appropriate to auxiliary 'be', is clearly out of place with auxiliary 'do'; *g-* does not occur in such contexts in Early Manx, but in the classical and later periods it has become usual.

3.5 PREPOSITIONS

Prepositions are of two kinds, simple and phrasal, though some of the simple are in origin more complex, for example *marish* 'with' (Gaelic *maille ri* 'together with'), *liorish* 'by' (probably Gaelic *láimh ri* 'at hand with, beside'). The Manx simple prepositions generally represent the form used before the article (so *ayns*, *gys*, *lesh*, *rish*) or the form with the third person singular masculine pronoun attached (so *da*, *jeh*).

3.5.1 The simple prepositions have personal endings representing the seven personal pronouns (though in Late Manx there is a tendency to resolve these inflected forms into their separate elements):

> *da* 'to':   SG 1 *dou*, 2 *dhyt*, MASC *dâ*, FEM *jee*
>   PL 1 *dooin*, 2 *diu*, 3 *daue*
> *dy*, *jeh* 'of': SG 1 *jeem*, 2 *jeed*, 3 MASC *jeh*, FEM *j'ee*
>   PL 1 *jin*, 2 *jiu*, 3 *jeu*
> *lesh* 'with': SG 1 *lhiam*, 2 *lhiat*, 3 MASC *lesh*, FEM *lhee*
>   PL 1 *lhien*, 2 *lhi(e)u*, 3 *lhieu*

The emphatic suffixes, in Early Manx freely attached to nouns and verb–nouns after a preceding possessive or objective pronoun, have since the classical period become almost entirely confined to personal pronouns, verbal inflections and these pronominal prepositions:

> *da* 'to':   SG 1 *dooys*, 2 *dhyts*, 3 MASC *dasyn*, FEM *jeeish*
>   PL 1 *dooinyn*, 2 *diuish*, 3 *dauesyn*

3.5.2 The phrasal prepositions are noun phrases of the form (a) + (e) (see 3.3.1), though when the prepositional element is Gaelic *i n-* 'in' this has been lost (except that *n-* survives before a vowel) so that they appear to consist of a noun only. When combined with a pronoun the sequence is (a) + (b) + (e), and when the preposition is Gaelic *i n-* the combination of (a) and (b) yields singular 1 *my*, 2 *dty*, 3 *ny*, plural *nyn*. Examples are *lurg* 'after' (lit. 'in the track of'), *fegooish* 'without' (lit. 'in the absence of'; the simple preposition *gyn* 'without' has no personal forms), *noi* 'against' (lit. 'in the face of'), *cour*, *gour* 'for' (lit. 'in the direction of') with first singular personal forms *my lurg*, *m'egooish*, *m'oi*, *my chour*, respectively. The ambiguity of the plural *nyn oi* 'against us, you, them' is clarified when necessary by the addition of the pronominal forms of *ec* (as with possession, 3.3.2): *nyn oi oc* 'against them', *ny(n) mast' ain* 'amongst us'. This in turn leads to a new formation without the possessive and capable of being extended to the singular: *noi oc* 'against them', *mychione oc* 'about them' (earlier *my-nyn-gione (oc)*), and *son aym* 'for me' (in place of *er my hon*) by analogy with *son ain* 'for us' from *er nyn son ain*.

MORPHOLOGY

3.6   NOUNS

Nouns may be radical or derived from other parts of speech by a limited range of suffixes, as *-aght, -id, -ys*. They vary in form only for number, except that a limited group, chiefly monosyllabic and mostly feminine, shows a separate genitive singular. The standard pattern, therefore, is two forms, a singular and a plural, the latter derived from the former either by internal change (the rarer type), or by addition. Where it occurs, the genitive singular is formed rarely by internal change, usually by addition, almost always of *-ey*. The earlier use of the nominative singular as genitive plural survives fossilised in some place names. A few nouns of plural or collective meaning are singular in form, as *cloan* 'children', *mooinjer* 'people', *sleih* 'people', *ollagh* 'cattle', and these are accompanied by a singular article but by a plural adjective (so far as these exist 3.8.1), and are referred to by plural pronouns.

3.6.1   Nouns are masculine or feminine in gender, and in animates gender generally agrees with sex. The mutational distinctions (see 3.12.2) which sustain gender have long been falling into disorder or disuse, and the gender of inanimates is poorly reflected in the third person singular pronouns; effectively some nouns are feminine, the marked class, and the remainder, the unmarked majority, are masculine.

3.6.2   The use of the two numbers, singular and plural (i.e. more than one), generally accords with the numerical facts, but traces of the dual continue in the use of the singular after *daa* 'two'; for the singular after other numbers cf. 3.3.1.6. Special rules apply to *blein* 'year' with numbers, and *laa* 'day' remains singular with all the smaller numbers.

3.6.3   Of the original oblique cases only the genitive singular, and in Early Manx a few examples of the vocative and the dative plural, are distinct in form from the nominative. Otherwise the nominative, lenited when vocative, serves for all, both singular and plural; the form of the singular is in some cases historically that of the accusative–dative.

3.6.4   The masculine genitive singular is usually distinguished from the nominative by lenition after the article; feminine nouns do not use the special genitive feminine singular form of the article unless the noun has a distinct genitive form:

caggey (MASC) 'battle'	*y caggey* 'the battle'
	er laa yn chaggey 'on the day of the battle'
sheshaght (FEM) 'society'	*y cheshaght* 'the society'
	bing y cheshaght 'the committee of the society'
bannish (FEM) 'wedding'	*y vannish* 'the wedding'
	laa ny banshey 'the day of the wedding'

Distinct genitive singular forms are largely confined to familiar phrases, as *folt e ching* 'the hair of his head', *eaghtyr y thallooin*, or *ny hooirey* 'the surface of the earth'. The freest use is in verb–nouns to form compounds, as *sheshaght-chaggee* 'army' (lit. 'company of fighting'; contrast *laa yn chaggey* above), *dooinney-poosee* 'bridegroom' (lit. 'man of marrying') (nominatives *kione*, *thalloo*, *ooir*, *caggey*, *poosey*, respectively).

3.6.5   Thus a description of declension is limited to noting distinct genitive singular forms and classifying plural formations. Internal plurals are mostly marked by palatalisation of the final consonant with consequent vowel modifications. External plurals all have the suffix -*yn*, but may have various modifications or additions before the suffix: internal plurals, *corp – kirp* 'body', *boayrd – buird* 'table', *kellagh – kellee* 'cock'; external plurals, *oyr – oyryn* 'cause', *ayr – ayraghyn* 'father', *billey – biljyn* 'tree', *briw – briwnyn* 'judge', *glion – glionteenyn* 'valley'.

3.6.6   Pronouns

Only the personal pronouns are morphologically variable, exhibiting one form for nominative–accusative: for example, *honnick mee eh* 'I saw him', *honnick eh mee* 'he saw me', with another serving as possessive–objective (see 3.2.2.1–3). Gender is distinguished only in the third person singular.

> Personal pronouns: SG 1 *mee*, 2 *oo*, 3 MASC *eh*, FEM *ee*
> PL 1 *shin*, 2 *shiu*, 3 *ad*
> Possessives: SG 1 *my* 2 *dty*, 3 MASC *e* (leniting), FEM *e*
> PL 1, 2, 3 *nyn*

When stressed, for example for contrast or as antecedent to a relative clause, the personal pronouns have reinforced forms:

> SG 1 *mish*, 2 *uss*, 3 MASC *eshyn*, FEM *ish*
> PL 1 *shinyn*, 2 *shiuish*, 3 *adsyn*

For stress on the possessive or to use it as an antecedent, recourse is had to the alternative construction described in 3.3.2.

3.6.7   The prepositional cases of the personal pronouns are represented by the combination of prepositions with personal inflections, e.g. the preposition *ec* 'at, in the possession of':

> SG 1 *aym*, 2 *ayd*, 3 MASC *echey*, FEM *eck*
> PL 1 *ain*, 2 *eu*, 3 *oc*

For fuller details cf. 3.5.1–2.

3.6.8   The demonstratives *shoh* 'this', *shen* 'that' and the rarer *shid* 'yon', are unaffected by differences of number or gender; they combine with the third-person pronouns to form demonstrative pronouns, the singular chiefly with reference to animates (while the demonstrative alone serves for inanimates), but in the plural with reference to both.

3.6.8.1   The interrogatives are *quoi* 'who(m)' (also in the selective sense 'which (one)') and *cre* 'what', as well as *c'red* lit. 'what thing' (see 3.3.1.4).

3.6.8.2   The role of indefinite pronouns is played by various special uses of nominal elements: *nhee erbee, red erbee* 'anything (at all)', *veg* 'anything', *fer*, *'nane* 'one', *dy chooilley nhee* 'everything', *dy chooilley ghooinney* 'everyone', *dagh fer* 'each (one)', *y cheilley* 'each other'.

3.6.8.3   The reflexive *hene* stands in apposition to a personal pronoun or pronominal preposition or to a possessive or to a noun: *shin hene* '(we) ourselves', *rhym pene* (*p-* after *-m*) 'to (me) myself', *my hie hene* 'my own house', *y dooinney hene* 'the man himself, even the man' (increasingly *eh-hene* latterly in the last case).

3.6.8.4   For the expression of relative pronouns see 3.2.8.3.

3.6.9   The article

The definite article has two forms, *yn* and *ny*; *yn* is the singular form except in the feminine genitive; *ny* is the feminine genitive singular (but see 3.6.4), and the plural form. Late Manx speakers tended to abandon the plural form altogether. Besides the full form *yn* two shortened forms occur, *y* and *'n*: *yn* may be used in all environments but *'n* is possible when a word ending in a vowel, typically a preposition, precedes the article, while *y* may be used before a word beginning in a consonant provided the previous word does not end in a vowel, in which case *yn* (or *'n*) is required:

y(n) dooinney 'the man'	*y(n) ven* 'the woman'
ny deiney 'the men'	*ny mraane* 'the women'
da'n dooinney 'to the man'	
mac y dooinney 'the man's son'	
laue yn dooinney 'the man's hand'	

3.7   VERBS

Verbs may be radical or derived from nouns, adjectives or verbs. Derived verbs may either have the same base as their simplex or be formed with a derivative affix, typically *-agh-*. A few verbs have verb–noun and stem identical, for example *aase* 'grow', *iu* 'drink', *tayrn* 'draw', but generally the verb–noun is a derivative from the stem, most often by adding *-ey* or some other suffix, for example *-al*, *-ail*, *-aght*, *-tyn*. In a small and decreasing number of cases the stem may be distinguished by palatalising the final consonant, for example *freayll*, *freill-* 'keep', *dooney*, *dooin-* 'shut', *cadley*, *caddil-* 'sleep'. Manx does not absolutely require the formation of any inflected tenses (see 3.4.4), and late usage avoids them all; the part played by the verb–noun is correspondingly eminent. A small number of verbs appear only as verb–nouns and form no inflected tenses.

3.7.1   As indicated above (3.4) the complete paradigm of a regular verb is a combination of inflected forms – imperative, future, conditional, preterite – and phrases utilising one of two auxiliaries which carry the tense and person, while the sense is isolated in the verb–noun. As the structure of the phrasal forms has already been illustrated (3.4.6–7) this section concentrates on the inflected forms, the auxiliaries and the irregular verbs. The verb *coayl* 'lose', stem *caill-*, will serve as a paradigm.

3.7.1.1   Imperative, second person only: 2sG the bare stem *caill*, 2PL stem + *-jee* (Late Manx *shiu*) *caill-jee*. For the first person plural, and less frequently for the third person a calque on English 'let us . . .' has been in use since Early Manx (with occasional evidence for 1PL *caillmayd*): 1PL *lhig dooin coayl*, 3sG *lhig da coayl*, 3PL *lhig daue coayl*. In this construction *lhig* (singular imperative of *lhiggey*) is invariable, in contrast to the possibility of the plural in *lhig-jee'n raad daue* 'let them go', that is, 'allow them to depart'.

3.7.1.2   The remaining inflected forms exhibit to some extent the inherited contrast between independent and dependent, indicated by inflection or mutation, and so for each a double example is given, the dependent being preceded by the negative *cha* in the future and by the conjunction *dy* 'if' in the conditional; the contrast is inoperative in regular verbs in the preterite. Future:

(85)

		Independent	Dependent
SG	1	*caillym*	*cha gaillym*
	2	*caillee oo*	*cha gaill oo*
	3	*caillee eh*	*cha gaill eh*
PL	1	*caillmayd*	*cha gaillmayd*
	2	*caillee shiu*	*cha gaill shiu*
	3	*caillee ad*	*cha gaill ad*
REL		*chaillys*	*nagh gaill*

3.7.1.3   Conditional

(86)

		Independent	Dependent
SG	1	*chaillin*	*dy gaillin*
	2	*chaillagh oo*	*dy gaillagh oo*
	3	*chaillagh eh*	*dy gaillagh eh*
PL	1	*chaillagh shin*	*dy gaillagh shin*
	2	*chaillagh shiu*	*dy gaillagh shiu*
	3	*chaillagh ad*	*dy gaillagh ad*

In Late Manx the first person singular shows a tendency to assimilate to the pattern of the other persons, *chaillagh mee*.

3.7.1.4　Preterite

(87)

	Singular	Plural
1	*chaill mee*	*chaill shin*
2	*chaill oo*	*chaill shiu*
3	*chaill eh*	*chaill ad*

3.7.1.5　The non-finite parts are the verb–noun *coayl*, and the verbal adjective or participle (passive and in transitive verbs) *caillit*, beside the older form *cailjey* used only as an adjective.

3.7.2　The auxiliaries have the same inflected tenses and, in addition, the verb 'be' has a present tense. Both function as full verbs as well as auxiliaries though there has been an increasing tendency to restrict 'do' to the status of auxiliary, as *nee eh jannoo* 'he will do' instead of earlier *nee eh*.

3.7.2.1　The substantive verb, imperative (second person): SG *bee*, PL *bee-jee, bee shiu*.

3.7.2.2　Present

(88)

		Independent	Dependent
SG	1	*ta mee*	*cha vel mee*
	2	*t'ou*	*cha vel oo*
	3	*t'eh, t'ee*	*cha vel eh, ee*
PL	1	*ta shin*	*cha vel shin*
	2	*ta shiu*	*cha vel shiu*
	3	*t'ad*	*cha vel ad*

In the negative but not the other dependent forms *nel* is found in Early Manx and has continued in the spoken language beside literary *vel*. In Early Manx and in manuscripts of the classical period *taddyr, tarrad* (INDEP 3 PL) also occur. In the independent third person singular the non-personal 'it is' is also written *te*.

3.7.2.3　Future

(89)

		Independent
SG	1	*bee'm*
	2	*bee oo, beeu*
	3	*bee eh*
PL	1	*beemayd*
	2	*bee shiu*
	3	*bee ad*
REL		*vees, vys*

Dependent 1SG *cha bee'm* etc. (the dependent is not distinct except in the relative).

3.7.2.4   Conditional

(90)

		Independent	Dependent
SG	1	*veign*	*dy beign*
	2	*veagh oo*	*dy beagh oo*
	3	*veagh eh*	*dy beagh eh*
PL	1	*veagh shin*	*dy beagh shin*
	2	*veagh shiu*	*dy beagh shiu*
	3	*veagh ad*	*dy beagh ad*

3.7.2.5   Preterite

(91)

		Independent	Dependent
SG	1	*va mee*	*cha row mee*
	2	*v'ou*	*cha r'ou*
	3	*v'eh, v'ee*	*cha row eh*
PL	1	*va shin*	*cha row shin*
	2	*va shiu*	*cha row shiu*
	3	*v'ad*	*cha row ad*

Early Manx and classical manuscript sources attest *vaddyr*, *varrad* (3PL); the non-personal third-person singular is written *ve*.

3.7.2.6   The verb–noun is permanently lenited *ve*.

3.7.3   Auxiliary 'do'

This is a member of the small class of irregular verbs in which the independent and dependent forms in part show an absence of similarity, and which generally lack the future relative.

3.7.3.1   Imperative (second person): SG. *jean*, PL *jean-jee, jean shiu*.

3.7.3.2   Future

(92)

		Independent	Dependent
SG	1	*nee'm*	*cha jeanym*
	2	*nee oo, neeu*	*cha jean oo*
	3	*nee eh*	*cha jean eh*
PL	1	*neemayd*	*cha jeanmayd*
	2	*nee shiu*	*cha jean shiu*
	3	*nee ad*	*cha jean ad*

3.7.3.3   Conditional

(93)			Independent	Dependent
	SG	1	*yinnin*	*dy jinnin*
		2	*yinnagh oo*	*dy jinnagh oo*
		3	*yinnagh eh*	*dy jinnagh eh*
	PL	1	*yinnagh shin*	*dy jinnagh shin*
		2	*yinnagh shiu*	*dy jinnagh shiu*
		3	*yinnagh ad*	*dy jinnagh ad*

3.7.3.4   Preterite
There is no distinction between independent and dependent forms.

(94)		Singular	Plural
	1	*ren mee*	*ren shin*
	2	*ren oo*	*ren shiu*
	3	*ren eh*	*ren ad*

3.7.3.5   The verb–noun is *jannoo*, and the verbal adjective *jeant*.

3.7.4   The subjunctive sense in all inflected verbs is carried by the dependent future and conditional; the optative sense by the dependent future with the conjunction *dy* 'that', except that the verb 'be' uses a form similar to the dependent preterite, *dy row* . . . (but also occasionally *dy bee* . . . on the model of other verbs). A more explicit non-indicative sense has since Early Manx been conveyed by the use of the auxiliary *foddym* 'I can' (cf. English 'may, might' in this function). This verb is defective, having no imperative and no verb–noun so that it can form no periphrastic tenses. It therefore has three forms: present–future, imperfect–conditional and preterite, but the formation of these is regular.

3.7.4.1   Present–future

(95)			Independent	Dependent
	SG	1	*foddym*	*dy voddym*
		2, 3	*foddee oo, eh*	*dy vod oo, eh*
	PL	1	*fodmayd*	*dy vodmayd*
		2, 3	*foddee shiu, ad*	*dy vod shiu, ad*
	REL		*oddys*	*nagh vod*

As in 3.7.1.2 after *cha*, *n'oddym* etc. is used in contrast to *voddym* etc. elsewhere.

3.7.4.2   Imperfect–conditional

(96)

		Independent	Dependent
SG	1	*oddin*	*dy voddin*
	2, 3	*oddagh oo, eh*	*dy voddagh oo, eh*
PL		*oddagh shin, shiu, ad*	*dy voddagh shin, shiu, ad*

3.7.4.3   Preterite

No independent–dependent contrast: SG *dod mee, oo, eh*; PL *dod shin, shiu, ad*.

3.7.5   As a specimen of the irregular verbs 'go' will serve. Verb–noun *goll*; suppletive verbal adjective *ersooyl* (active perfect participle equivalent of *shooyl* 'walk').

3.7.5.1   Imperative

Both are suppletive forms, from *goaill* 'take' and *immeeaght* 'depart'; 2SG *gow*, *immee*, 2PL *gow-jee, immee-jee*.

3.7.5.2   Future

(97)

		Independent	Dependent
SG	1	*hem*	*cha jem*
	2, 3	*hed oo, eh*	*cha jed oo, eh*
PL	1	*hemmayd*	*cha jemmayd*
	2, 3	*hed shiu, ad*	*cha jed shiu, ad*

3.7.5.3   Conditional

No independent–dependent contrast.

(98)

SG	1	*raghin*
	2, 3	*ragh oo, eh*
PL		*ragh shin, shiu, ad*

3.7.5.4   Preterite

(99)

	Independent	Dependent
SG	*hie mee, oo, eh*	*cha jagh mee, oo, eh*
PL	*hie shin, shiu, ad*	*cha jagh shin, shiu, ad*

3.7.6   There are no inflected forms for the impersonal or passive, except *ruggyr* 'is/was born'. The passive ordinarily consists of the various tenses of 'be' with either (latterly) the passive participle or (earlier) its equivalent phrase, made up of *er* + the possessive corresponding in person and number to the subject (though with a long-standing tendency to fix this in the third person singular masculine) + the verb–noun: *v'eh currit* or *v'eh er ny choyrt* 'he was sent'. There is also an idiomatic construction with the verb 'go' + *er* + the verb–noun: *hed ad er coyrt* 'they will be sent'.

3.8   ADJECTIVES

3.8.1   Adjectives may be radical or derived from nouns by a limited group of suffixes, as *-agh*, *-oil*. The only morphological variations are for number and comparison. A very few monosyllabic adjectives form a plural, when used attributively, by the addition of *-ey*: for example, *beggey* 'little', *mooarey* 'big', *aegey* 'young'; but even these are not invariably used. Some adjectives, including all those in *-agh* applicable to animates, are also used as nouns: *marroo* 'dead, a dead person', *baccagh* 'lame, a lame person', and in this function they have nominal plurals: *ny merriu* 'the dead', *ny baccee* 'the lame', *ny doail* 'the blind', *ny boghtyn* 'the poor'. Predicative adjectives are invariable.

3.8.1.1   Apart from those adjectives that are identical in form with nouns any adjective of suitable meaning can be nominalised by being associated with an 'empty' noun. If the reference is personal or animate the usual singular noun is *fer*, in the plural either *fir* or the collectives *sleih, mooinjer, feallagh*; for example, *y fer doo* 'the dark one', *sleih aegey* 'the young', *y vooinjer veggey* 'the little ones', *feallagh elley* 'others'. In Late Manx *feallagh* has acquired a plural *follee*. Impersonally, the common noun is *cooid*: for example, *cooid vooar* 'a great deal', *nee'm my chooid share* 'I'll do my best'.

3.8.1.2   Comparison is in two degrees, positive and comparative–superlative. With a few exceptions such as *chammah* 'as good, as well', *whilleen* 'as many', *wheesh* 'as much', the equative is not a morphologically distinct form but consists of *cha/cho* + the positive (followed by the preposition *rish* or the conjunction *as*). The compared form of adjectives having a positive in *-agh* generally ends in *-ee*, and there are some irregular comparisons, usually by suppletion; but in the great majority of cases the comparative is the positive preceded by the present (relative) of the copula, *s'* (rarely by the preterite *by-*) when attributive, and by *ny s'* when predicative (see 3.2.8.2). In irregular comparatives the *s* is attached without an apostrophe: *beg* 'little' – *sloo*; *mie* 'good' – *share*; *mooar* 'big' – *smoo*; *olk* 'bad' – *smessey*; *foddey* 'far' – *sodjey*;

liauyr 'long' – *slhiurey*; *ymmodee* 'many' – *sliee*; *lajer* 'strong' – *stroshey*; *shenn* 'old' – *shinney*.

(100) (a) *y dooinney s'niartal*
            'the most powerful man'
       (b) *ta'n dooinney shen ny s'niartal na mish*
            'That man is more powerful than I'
(101) (a) *y cabbyl stroshey*
            'the strongest horse'
       (b) *ta'n cabbyl shen ny shinney na'n fer aym's*
            'That horse is older than mine'

Periphrastic comparison of superiority with *smoo* 'more/most' is possible though not common; *sloo* 'less/least' provides the only means of expressing the comparison of inferiority.

3.8.2   Adverbs

Adverbs may be divided into two classes, either based on adjectives or not; some of the latter are opaque formations but many are transparent nominal phrases. The adjectival class is formed by prefixing the particle *dy* to the adjective: *dy harryltagh* 'willingly'. The equative and comparative–superlative are formed in the same way as those of adjectives and the particle *dy* is dispensed with; only the predicative form with *ny* is used: *Dreggyr eh ny s'gennal na roie* 'He answered more cheerfully than before'.

SOUND SYSTEM

3.9   CONSONANT SYSTEM

The consonant system is marked by the opposition (largely neutralised in labials) between neutral and palatal articulation. Combining this variable with the three places of articulation (labial, dental, velar), and the oppositions voiced/voiceless and stop/fricative, the system in table 3.1 emerges.

3.9.1   Some of the items in table 3.1 have a limited distribution: *f*, *v*, *ð*, *x'* and *z'* do not occur in word-final position; *ð*, *z* amd *z'* do not occur in word-initial position and *γ*, *ŋ*, *w*, *v* and *h* do so only in mutation conditions (3.12.1) or in loanwords, for example *wappin* 'weapon', *vondeish* 'advantage',

Table 3.1. *Consonant system*

labial	p	b	f	v	m
dental	t t'	d d'		ð	n n'
velar	k k'	g g'	x, x'	γ, γ'	ŋ ŋ'
liquid	l l'	r r'			
sibilant	s s'	z z'			
semi-vowel	j	w			
aspirate	h h'				

hullad 'owl'. There is a general tendency to relax the articulation of single intervocalic stops and fricatives and/or to voice them in this position, for example *cappan* ['kavan] 'cup', *cabbyl* ['kaːvəl] 'horse', *peccah* ['pɛgə] 'sin'. Hence new *z* from earlier *s*, as *poosey* ['puːzə] 'marry'; *z'* from *s'*, as *aashagh* ['ɛːz'ax] 'easy', or *d'*, as *padjer* ['paːz'ər] 'prayer'; new *ð* from *t*, as *baatey* ['bɛːða] 'boat', or *d*, as *eddin* ['ɛðən'] 'face', or *s*, as *shassoo* ['ʃaːðu] 'stand'; *γ* from *x*, as *beaghey* ['bɛːγə] 'live'; with a further tendency for *z'* and *γ* to become *j* and zero respectively, as *toshiaght* ['tɔz'ax, 'tɔjax] 'beginning', *shaghey* [ʃaː] 'past'.

3.9.2 The contrast of neutral and palatal quality is well preserved in *n* and *l* but *r'* has become less frequent so that, for example, *roo* 'to them' and *rieau* 'ever', or *roa* 'row' and *rio* 'frost', may be indistinguishable. There is no observable contrast of lenited/unlenited in these three consonants, and no orthographic evidence for it at any period. Final and preconsonantal *r* shows a weakening or loss similar to that in English, and something like the 'intrusive' *r* of English has been noted in hiatus left by the loss of *γ*, as *booaghyn* 'cows' ['buːərən], or alternatively as a case of 'quiescent' *r*, the singular *booa* being interpreted as *booa(r)*. Recent usage shows an abundance of unhistorical initial palatalisations of *k* and *g* in some or all of the recorded pronunciations of *caashey* 'cheese', *caayl* 'cabbage', *cabbag* 'docks', *cabbyl* 'horse', *cadley* 'sleep', *caggey* 'war', *cair* 'right', *cam* 'crooked', *cappan* 'cup', *casherick* 'holy', *cassey* 'twist', *karraghey* 'mend', *keayrt* 'time', *kerraghey* 'punish', *gaaue* 'smith', *garey* 'garden', *gearey* 'laugh', *geinnagh* 'sand'; and sometimes of initial and medial *l*, as recorded for *lajer* 'strong', *lane* 'full', *laue* 'hand', *moylley* 'praise'.

3.9.3 The original length in unlenited *m*, *n*, *l* and *r*, has been transferred to the preceding vowel, in monosyllables only, by way of either lengthening or diphthongisation: for example, *kione* 'head', *boayl* 'place' (diphthong or monophthong from a diphthong) *eeym* 'butter', *cam* [kɛbm] from [kɛːm] 'squint', *baare* 'tip' (Gaelic *ceann, ball, im, cam, barr*). The earlier initial clusters *kn, gn, tn, dl, tl* have fallen in with *kr, gr, tr, gl, kl*, respectively, as *knaid, craid* 'mockery', *gnwis, grooish* 'countenance', *tnw, troo* 'envy', *gloo* 'warp (in weaving)' Gaelic *dlúth*, but Early Manx *gliastyn* 'owe', later *lhiastyn*, Gaelic *dleastanas, er y klew, er y clieau* 'on the mountain', Gaelic *air an t-sléibh*. *Sr* falls in with *str*, as *strooan* 'stream', Gaelic *sruthan*; and medial *sk*, with some exceptions, with *st*, as *iesk, eeast* 'fish', *eask, eayst* 'moon', *wyskey, ushtey* 'water', *mastey* 'among', still often *maskey* in the eighteenth century, but *askaid* 'boil', *myskid* 'malice'. Final *t* after a sibilant or *x* tends to be lost, as regularly in the noun and verb–noun suffix *-aght*; after *s* in *Creest* 'Christ', *brisht* 'broken' and, reversing an earlier trend to add *-t* in this position, in *reesht* 'again', *neesht* 'also'. Final nasals in stressed monosyllables are preceded by a weak version of the corresponding voiced stop, as *trome* [troːᵇm] 'heavy', *ben* [bɛᵈn] 'woman', and with shortening *slane* [slɛᵈn] 'whole'. Dissimilation of consonants occasionally takes place, as is evidenced in *Truggan Road* = *bayr y trooan*, Gaelic *bóthar an tsrutháin* with ['truᵈn] → [truᵍn].

3.9.4   The features mentioned in 3.9.1–2 and the last two in 3.9.3 are of quite recent origin, perhaps not earlier than the late eighteenth century, and are only exceptionally reflected in the orthography.

3.10   VOWEL SYSTEM

The vowel system includes monophthongs and diphthongs, and monophthongs in stressed syllables distinguish length. The monophthongs may be represented by the following chart:

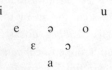

Of these *a, ɛ, i, ɔ, u, ə* may be long or short; *e* and *o* long only, except for isolated cases of shortening. The quality of the long and short vowel of each pair is not identical. Diphthongs are formed with *-i* as the second element by *a, ɛ, ɔ, ə* and *u*; and with *-u* as second element by *a, ɛ* and *ə*; *i* and *u* form diphthongs with *ə* as second element but tend to monophthongisation except before *r*.

3.10.1   In unstressed syllables the range of vowel sounds is restricted in post-tonic position to ə, *u* and *i* (the last usually long and morphologically significant), but in the noun suffix *-an*, *-ag* and the predominantly adjectival suffix *-agh*, the vowel tends to remain, though there is early evidence for *-əx* as well as *-ax*. There is widespread lengthening of *a* and ɔ in monosyllables, and in disyllables having an open stressed syllable.

3.11   STRESS

The normal position for the stress, in words capable of taking a full stress, is on the first syllable, and since pretonic elements have generally been eliminated, the presence of the stress largely coincides with the beginning of the word. However, this coincidence is modified in various ways, partly by the clustering of unstressed proclitics (3.3 and 3.4) so that the word bearing the main stress is itself in the centre or even at the end of a group of unstressed syllables, e.g. *ga dy vél mee / er jéet / dy válley / réesht* 'though I have come home again'. Partly also because originally long vowels in syllables other than the first may attract the stress to themselves, for example verb–nouns in *-ail*, *-eil*, such as *sauáil* 'save', *treigéil* 'abandon', and nouns in *-ane*, *-age/-aig*, *-eyr*, such as *farráne* 'spring', *rolláge* 'star', *moltéyr* 'deceiver'. This is also the case with long vowels created during the evolution of the language by the reduction of two syllables to one, for example *thalloo*, GEN *thallóoin* 'land' (Gaelic *tal(a)mhan*), *sheelóghe* 'generation' (Gaelic *síol(a)bhach*), *buirróogh* 'roar' (Gaelic *búirfeadhach*), *breeóil* 'effective' (Gaelic *bríoghamhail*). Doublets of some suffixes appear with a shortened vowel and so without stress, for example *-an* beside *-áne*, *-ag* beside *-áge*, *-al* beside *-óil*, as *beggan* 'a little', *soieag* 'seat', *niartal* 'powerful' (but Early Manx *niartóil*), *troggal* 'raise'. When the stress is placed elsewhere than on the long vowel of the first syllable that long vowel is liable to shortening, though this is not always reflected in the spelling if the stress may return to the first syllable in other forms of the word, for example *arráne* 'song' (Gaelic *amhran*, *óran*), but *faagáil* 'leave', stem *faag-*, participle *fáagit*, though in unconventional spelling the verb–noun appears as *fegaile* with the shortening indicated.

MORPHOPHONOLOGY

3.12   MUTATION

Many of the initial consonants are liable within the phrase to undergo changes to other, originally closely related, sounds, and these changes have been shown in the writing of all periods. As these mutations occur in particular sequences of elements, they can for the most part be described in terms of the preceding elements which 'cause' them. In some cases, however, the preceding element has now disappeared and the mutation appears spontaneous: in this category may be included the lenition of the inflected future relative, the independent conditional, and the preterite forms of the regular verb (3.7.1.2–4), such as *chaillys, chaillin, chaillagh, chaill*, and similar forms in the irregular verbs which sometimes add the whole independent future, for example *hed* 'will go' (lenited *t'*), *hee* 'will see' (lenited *k'*), *hig* 'will come' (*t'*), *yiow* 'will get' (*g'*), *ver* 'will give' (*b'*). In addition, some adverbs show the same permanent lenition, as *hannah* 'already', *har* 'east', *heear* 'west', *heese* 'below', *heose* 'above', *hoal* 'yonder', as well as the prepositions *harrish* 'over', *huggey* 'to him', the pronoun *hene* 'self' and, except in Early Manx, the adjective *cheddin* 'same'.

3.12.1   The initial consonants *p, b, f, m, t, d, k, g, s*, are liable to mutation.

There are two mutations of consonants: lenition and nasalisation. In lenition stops become the corresponding fricatives (or further developments thereof), and *m* becomes *v/w*; *s* followed by a vowel becomes *h*, but after the singular article *t*, and *f* becomes zero (though this mutation often fails). Thus

	p	b	t t'	d d'	k k'	g g'	m	s s'	f
→	f	v, w	h h'	γ γ'	x x'	γ γ'	v, w	h h'	–
written:	ph	v, w	h hi	gh y	ch chi	gh y, ghi v w		h hi	–

In nasalisation the voiceless stops become voiced, the voiced stops become the corresponding nasals, and *f* becomes *v*. Thus

	p	b	t t'	d d'	k k'	g g'	f
→	b	m	d d'	n n'	g g'	ŋ ŋ'	v

but the orthographic expression in dentals and velars is complex and confusing.

3.12.2   Mutation has almost completely disappeared from Late Manx. In

the classical period the principal occurrences of lenition in nouns and verb–nouns are:

(a) in the vocative, singular and plural: (*y*) *charrey* 'friend', *chaarjyn*;

(b) after the singular article (dentals, i.e. *t*, *d*, always excepted, and *f* frequently) in feminine nouns in the nominative: *y ven* 'the woman', *y gheay* 'the wind'; in the nominative when used as genitive (3.6.4): *ayr y ven* 'the woman's father'; in masculine nouns in the genitive: *ennym y vac* 'the son's name'; and in nouns of both genders in the sequence preposition + singular article + noun: *rish y vac* 'to the son', *lesh y voir* 'with the mother';

(c) after the possessives *my* (1SG), *dty* (2SG), *e* (3SG MASC): *my charrey* 'my friend', *dty vainshter* 'your master', *e voddey* 'his dog';

(d) after all ordinal numerals and the cardinal numerals *un* 'one' (except dentals and *s*) and *daa* 'two': *un vac* 'one son', *un charrey* 'one friend', but *un dooinney* 'one man'; *daa vac, daa charrey, daa ghooinney*;

(e) after the prepositions *dy* 'of', *dy* 'to', and in some phrases *fo* 'under': *paart dy gheiney* 'some men', *aarloo dy gholl ersooyl* 'ready to go away', *fo-harey* 'under orders', place name *Folieu* (*slieau* 'mountain');

(f) in proper names in the genitive: *braar Pherick* 'Patrick's brother', and in surnames such as *Cooil* (Gaelic *Mac Dhubhghaill*), *Kerrúish* (Gaelic *MacFhearghuis*);

(g) after the prefixes and preposed adjectives *aa-* 're-', *mee-/neu-* 'un-', *drogh-* 'bad', *ard-* 'chief', *shenn-* 'old': *aa-hroggal* 'rebuild', *mee-chairys* 'injustice', *neu-chooie* 'unfit', *drogh-haghyrt* 'accident', *ard-valley* 'city' but *ard-saggyrt* 'high-priest' (dental), *shenn-ven* 'old woman' but *shenn dooinney* 'old man' (dental).

3.12.2.1 To initial vowels the consonant *h-* may be prefixed in nouns:

(a) after the genitive feminine singular of the article: *ny hooirey* 'of the earth';

(b) after the plural article *ny*: *ny Hewnyn* 'the Jews';

(c) after the third person singular feminine possessive: *e haigney* 'her mind'.

The writing of this mutation has always been inconsistent.

3.12.2.2   Nasalisation occurs in nouns:

(a)   after the plural possessive: *nyn gaarjyn* 'our/your/their friends';
(b)   in fixed phrases and place names after the genitive plural of the article: *shooyl ny dhieyn* 'walking the houses (i.e. begging)', field name *bwoaillee ny giark* 'hens' fold'.

3.12.3   Lenition is found in adjectives:

(a)   after a feminine singular noun: *ben vie* 'a good woman';
(b)   after a noun in the vocative: *Hiarn vie* 'good Lord';
(c)   after a plural noun when the plural is formed by palatalisation: *peccee hreih* 'miserable sinners';
(d)   after the modifiers *feer* 'very' (except dentals) and *ro* 'too': *feer vie* 'very good', but *feer trome* 'very heavy', *ro vooar* 'too great'.

3.12.3.1   Prefixed *h-* is occasionally found in adjectives after *dy* forming adverbs: *dy harryltagh* 'willingly'.

3.12.4   The chief occurrences of lenition in finite verbs are:

(a)   in the future relative: *hroggys eh* 'which he will lift, which/who will lift him/it';
(b)   in the preterite: *hrog eh* 'he lifted';
(c)   in the independent conditional: *hroggagh ad* 'they would lift'.

And in the verb–noun:

(d)   after the objectives of the first and second persons singular, preceded by *dy* or *er: t'ad dy my choyrt* 'they send me', *t'ad dy dty choyrt* 'they send you', *t'ad er my choyrt* 'they have sent me', *v'ad er dty choyrt* 'they had sent you';
(e)   after the prepositions *dy* 'to' and *er(n)* 'after' (in most cases), and the particle *dy* when the object has preceded: *dob ad dy chur tastey dâ* 'They refused to pay attention to him', *v'eh er chlashtyn jeh* 'He had heard of it', *cre t'ad dy ghra?* 'What are they saying?'

3.12.4.1   Nasalisation occurs in the finite verb:

(a)   in the voiceless sounds *p, t, k, f* only, after *cha* 'not', *dy* 'that', *nagh* 'that not, who(m) not', *mannagh* 'if not, unless', *dy* 'if' (conditional only), *my* 'before': *cha n'aagym* 'I shall not leave', *dy drog eh* 'that he will lift', *nagh gionnee ad* 'that they will not buy', *mannagh gooinee shiu* 'if you do not remember', *dy gaillin* 'if I were to lose', (*roish*) *my jyndaa oo* 'before you return' (verb–nouns *faagail*, *troggal*, *kionnaghey*, *cooinaghtyn*, *coayl*, *chyndaa* respectively).

And in verb–nouns:

(b)   after the plural objective preceded by *dy* or *er*, giving *dyn* (*dy nyn*) and *er nyn*: *t'eh dyn dilgey ad 'syn aile* 'He is throwing them in the fire', *v'ad er nyn vakin ayns y traid* 'They were seen in the street';

(c)   after *er* 'after' (in some cases, but generally replaced by lenition): *ta shin er vakin* (or *er n'akin*) *yn ard-valley* 'We have seen the city', *vel ad er jeet dy valley* 'Have they come home?'

In (a) and (c) above *n'* is prefixed to an initial vowel and the mutation of *f* + vowel varies between *n'* and *v*.

REFERENCES

Cregeen, A. 1835. *A dictionary of the Manks language*, Douglas: printed and published for the author by J. Quiggin.
Ifans, D. and R. L. Thomson 1980. Edward Lhuyd's *Geirieu Manaweg*. *Studia Celtica* 14–15: 129–67.
Kelly, J. 1804. *A practical grammar of the antient Gaelic, or language of the Isle of Mann, usually called Manks*, London: Nichols.
      1866. Fockleyr Manninagh as Baarlagh, vol. XIII ed. Rev. W. Gill, Douglas: printed for the Manx Society.
Thomson, R. L. 1961. The Manx *Traditionary Ballad*. *Etudes celtiques* 9: 521–48, 10: 60–87. (Edition and commentary.)
      1988. Manx–Latin *Gilbogus* again. *Celtica* 20: 141–4.
      1991. Foreign elements in the Manx vocabulary. In *Language Contact in the British Isles: Proceedings of the Eighth International Symposium on Language Contact in Europe 1988* (Linguistische Arbeiten 238), Tübingen: Max Niemeyer 127–40.

FURTHER READING

Broderick, G. 1981. Manx stories and reminiscences of Ned Beg Hom Ruy. *Zeitschrift für celtische Philologie* 38: 113–78, 39: 117–94. (Written by a native speaker in the 1880s; text, translation, and commentary.)
      1984. *A handbook of late spoken Manx*, 2 vols. Tübingen: Max Niemeyer. (Grammar, texts and glossary.)

1991. *Some Manx Traditional Songs*, Douglas: An Cheshaght Ghailckagh. (Reprint of various articles.)

Goodwin, E. 1966. *First lessons in Manx*, 3rd revised edn, Douglas: Yn Cheshaght Ghailckagh.

Jackson, K. H. 1955. *Contributions to the study of Manx phonology*, Edinburgh: Nelson.

Kneen, J. J. 1931. *A grammar of the Manx language*. London: Oxford University Press. (To be used with considerable caution.)

Thomson, R. L. 1954. A glossary of early Manx. *Zeitschrift für celtische Philologie* 24: 272–307, 25: 100–40, 264–308, 27: 79–160. (From the Prayer Book of 1610.)

1960. Svarabhakti and some associated changes in Manx. *Celtica* 5: 116–26.

1969. The study of Manx Gaelic. *Proceedings of the British Academy* 55: 177–210. (An account of the earlier scholarship, including the dictionaries of Cregeen 1835, Kelly 1866 and the grammars of Kelly 1804, and Kneen 1931.)

1976. The stressed vowel phonemes of a Manx idiolect. *Celtica* 11: 255–63.

1981. *Lessoonyn sodjey'sy Ghailck Vanninagh*, Douglas: Yn Cheshaght Ghailckagh. (A linguistic commentary on the translations of St John's Gospel.)

1990. The Revd Dr John Kelly as a lexicographer. *Proceedings of the Isle of Man Natural History and Antiquarian Society* 9: 443–58. (Supplement to Thomson 1969.)

4

The Scottish Gaelic language

DONALD MACAULAY

HISTORICAL AND SOCIAL PERSPECTIVE

4.0 EXTERNAL HISTORY OF THE LANGUAGE

The theory concerning the origins of Scottish Gaelic that is most widely accepted nowadays – and, indeed, the one that is most strongly supported by the available evidence – is that the Gaelic language was carried to Scotland by immigrants from Ireland. Earlier 'nativist' theories have not stood the test of time. Early Celtic names in north Britain, cited, for example, in Roman sources or on Ptolemy's map, do not indicate Gaelic settlement.

It is not clear when the earliest emigrations of Gaelic speakers began, how they progressed or how they were distributed in north Britain. It is reasonable to associate them with the out-migrating impulse that saw the Irish impinging on the west coast of Roman Britain from the late fourth century, leading to considerable settlement after the decline of Roman power. The most important settlement in Scotland was that of the Dál Ríata in Argyll (the name, in Gaelic *Oirthir Gaidheal*, means 'the coastline of the Gael'). This settlement established what appears to have been a cross-channel 'kingdom'. Eventually, at some time in the second half of the fifth century, the colony became more politically important than the motherland and the centre of power moved from Dál Ríata in Antrim in north-east Ireland to Dál Ríata in Scotland. This change was the result of political re-adjustments in Ireland and, in Scotland, of settlement consolidation: there is no archaeological evidence of large-scale migration into Scotland during this period. The Dál Ríata leadership remained in the Scottish branch for around 150 years, until the connection was severed after the battle of Mag Rath (*c.* 637) (Bannerman 1974).

4.0.1   The historical position

4.0.1.1   Areal distribution

From the base of Dál Ríata the Gaels expanded their territory fairly rapidly in the west of Scotland, as the survey in the early document *Senchus Fer nAlban*, 'The history of the men of Alban' shows (Bannerman 1974: 111ff.). From there they expanded through the Great Glen northwards and through the straths to the east coast. This penetration was achieved at the expense of the earlier inhabitants, the so-called Picts – at times against formidable Pictish resistance.

The Gaels were aided in the colonisation and consolidation of their new territories by the prestige and success of the Christian church established in Iona by Colum Cille in the middle of the sixth century. The organisation of this church and the secular administrative instruments set up in the Gaelic territories operated hand in hand, following on the fruitful relationship established between Colum Cille and Aedhán mac Gabhráin, the reigning king of Dál Ríata in his time. By establishing itself in areas beyond the Gaelic hegemony it provided a common link between the Gaels and the Picts which operated to the advantage of the former. As to the Gaelic language, it benefited from the prestige of the Columban church, with its Gaelic origins. That prestige, no doubt, along with the status it derived from the dominant Gaelic institutions ensured that the Gaelic language eventually replaced the other tongues spoken in north Britain.

The Picts were united with the Scots in the middle of the ninth century under a Gaelic king who was probably of mixed ancestry. This appears to have been a rationalisation resulting from political pressures, the chief of which was probably the advent of the Norsemen. They came first as raiders, in the late eighth century, and later as settlers on the north and west mainland and in the islands of Shetland and Orkney, the Hebrides and Man, where they set up the Norse Kingdom of the Isles. The Hebrides belonged to the Kingdom of Norway until the middle of the thirteenth century and the Northern Isles until the fifteenth century. The Hebrides thereafter became Gaelic speaking but the Northern Isles and the very north-east of Caithness show no evidence of Gaelic occupation.

In the south the Brittonic territories of Strathclyde and territories in Rheged were taken over by the Gaels as were some areas earlier conquered by the Angles. By the early eleventh century, following the battle of Carham in 1018, the southern border of 'Scotland' was pretty well where it remains today. However, the eleventh century was a period of internal strife, notably the confrontation between MacBeth and Duncan, which resulted in Duncan's defeat and his family's exile in England. Duncan's son, Malcolm Canmore, married an Anglo-Norman wife and used his English supporters to win back his kingship. Once he was established on the throne he set about consolidating his power. Briefly, the instrument he used to do this was the feudalism which had been introduced to England with such conspicuous success as a system of control by William of Normandy. This system was entirely different from the Gaelic system in social, political and military organisation, and was suited to the establishment of a centralised state. Malcolm used Anglo-Norman soldiers of fortune to quell resistance and rewarded them with charters to the lands of those who opposed him.

This policy was followed by his descendants, leading to the gradual replacement of the Gaelic-speaking leadership in state and church, first in the southern areas of the kingdom and then moving inexorably northwards along the fertile eastern seaboard. This advance can be clearly traced in medieval documents, using evidence, for example, of changing place and personal names (Murison 1974). The Anglo-Norman leadership brought in their train to Scotland English-speaking followers, and their descendants replaced Gaelic speakers throughout the population. Indeed, it was their language that triumphed eventually throughout lowland Scotland, becoming particularly the language of towns and cities.

The boundaries of the *Gaeltachd*, or Gaelic-speaking area, continued to recede. The evidence for the earlier periods, before the middle of the eighteenth century, is very limited; indeed we are dependent on 'estimates' (some not very reliable) until the advent of the official population surveys of the nineteenth century. Map 4.1 delineates the boundaries as they appear at different periods (after Withers 1979).

4.0.1.2   Demographic distribution

As we have noted above of areal boundaries, hard information about populations of Gaelic speakers and their numbers is available only when we get official census reports in the nineteenth century. There are accounts before then, for example that by John Walker of the situation around 1770 (McKay 1980) and data gathered by the Earl of Selkirk (1806) as well as the Old Statistical Account of the end of the eighteenth century, but at best they enable us to make intelligent estimates (Withers 1984). The first census to take account of Gaelic speakers was that of 1881. Table 4.1 shows the demographic changes from the mid-eighteenth century to the present (after Thomson 1983: 111). These tables show the diminution of the number of speakers from an estimated *c.* 300,000 in 1800 to *c.* 80,000 in 1981. Maps 4.2 and 4.3 show the recession between 1891

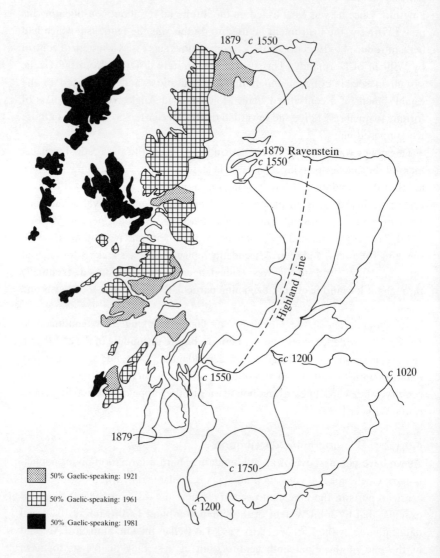

Map 4.1   Recession of Gaelic language *c*. 1020–1981 (partly after Withers 1979)

Table 4.1. *Gaelic speakers in Scotland, c. 1755–1981*

Source	Scottish population	Speakers of Gaelic only	Speakers of Gaelic and English	Speakers of Gaelic and English as % of population
c. 1755[a]	1,265,380	289,798		
c. 1800[b]	1,608,420	297,823		
1881[c]	3,735,573	231,594		
1891	4,025,647	43,738	210,677	5.2
1901	4,472,103	28,106	202,700	4.5
1911	4,760,904	18,400	183,998	3.9
1921	4,573,471	9,829	148,950	3.3
1931	4,588,909	6,716	129,419	2.8
1951	5,096,415	2,178	93,269	1.8
1961	5,179,344	974	80,004	1.5
1971	5,228,965	477	88,415	1.7
1981	5,035,315	—[d]	82,620[e]	1.6

[a] Walker (1808), using data collected by Webster c. 1755. See McKay (1983).
[b] Based on 1801 Census.
[c] 1881 and subsequent dates: census data.
[d] No data on Gaelic monoglots in 1981 Census.
[e] Specifically: 'speaks, reads or writes Gaelic'.

(the first full survey of speakers of Gaelic and English) and 1981, the latest census.

4.0.1.3   Status

Historically, the status of Gaelic has been subject to varying fortunes. Gaelic has never been the sole language of Scotland. On its arrival in north Britain it was in competition with the Brittonic languages (and whatever other languages may have been spoken there). It shared its sphere with Latin, which was the primary ecclesiastical language, and gradually gained ascendancy over the other secular languages, as the Gaels established their dominance, so that by the eleventh century it was the chief language through which political, administrative, legal and cultural meanings were mediated. Following the French and Anglo-Norman influx under Malcolm III its place in the court and in politics and its central place in religious affairs was taken over by Norman French, and as the culture of the centre spread with the feudalisation of Scotland it was displaced from a larger

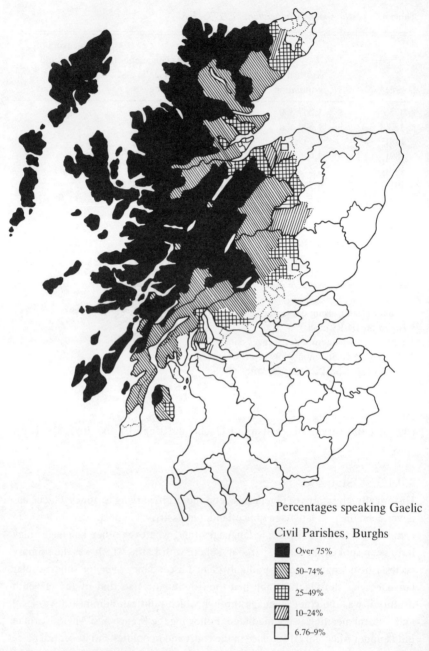

Percentages speaking Gaelic

Civil Parishes, Burghs

■ Over 75%

▨ 50–74%

▦ 25–49%

▧ 10–24%

□ 6.76–9%

Map 4.2   Proportions of local populations speaking Gaelic in 1891
         (after MacKinnon 1986)

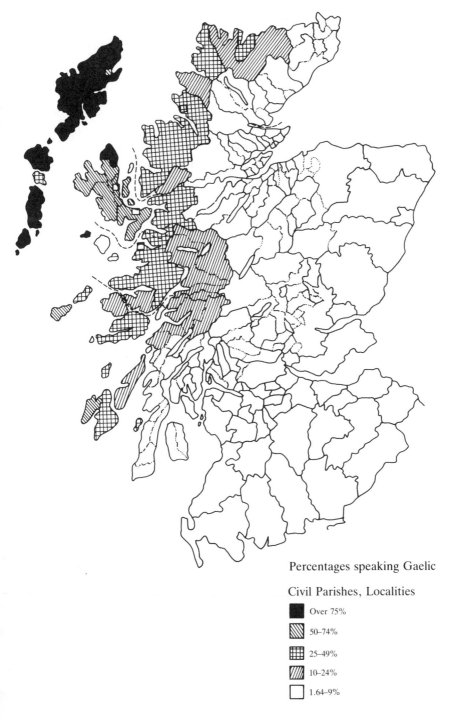

Percentages speaking Gaelic

Civil Parishes, Localities

- ■ Over 75%
- ◩ 50–74%
- ▦ 25–49%
- ▨ 10–24%
- □ 1.64–9%

Map 4.3   Proportions of local populations speaking Gaelic in 1981
(after MacKinnon 1986)

and larger set of domains over a wider and wider area. When Norman French
went into decline it was followed by 'Inglis', a form of northern English, as the
prestige tongue.

The process, however, took some time and there is evidence that the
'classical' literary form of the Gaelic language at least retained its status into the
sixteenth century, when the 'Statutes and Rules' of the Aberdeen Grammar
School say that scholars were allowed to converse in Latin, Greek, Hebrew,
French and Gaelic but not in the 'vulgar Inglis tongue'. This classical form of the
language was common to Gaelic Scotland and Ireland and its high culture status
was sustained by the bardic poetry for which it was the vehicle, particularly the
poetry of panegyric, which had an important social role in traditional sanctions
associated with kingship and the definition of leadership.

Gaelic was strongest in the west, where it retained its ties with Ireland. The
focus of this strength in the fourteenth and fifteenth centuries was the 'Lordship
of the Isles' (Bannerman 1977), which remained a Gaelic language polity until
its forfeiture in 1493.

The demise of the Lordship led to a power impasse in the area and a period of
chaos whilst it was being resolved. This coincided with the next great revolution
in Scotland after feudalism, that of the reformation, creating conditions which
enabled James VI (and I of Great Britain) to put his centralist theories of
kingship into effect. These entailed the destruction of Gaelic culture and
language. This is clearly to be read in the Statutes of Iona of 1609 with their
attack on tradition bearers, 'bards and other idlers of that class' and the
requirement of men having property to the value of sixty cattle to send their
eldest child to school to learn to speak, read and write English. These
requirements were reinforced by enactments of the Scottish Privy Council in
1616, the language requirement packaged in pious guise:

> Forsamekle as, the Kingis Majestie haveing a speciall care
> and regaird that the trew religioun be advanceit and
> establisheit in all the pairtis of this kingdome, and that all his
> Majesties subjectis, especiallie the youth, be
> exercised and trayned up in civilitie, godlines, knawledge, and
> learning, that the vulgar Inglishe toung be universallie
> plantit, and the Irish language, whilk is one of the cheif
> and principall causes of the continewance of barbaritie and
> incivilitie amongis the inhabitantis of the Isles and
> Heylandis, may be abolisheit and removit.

This established a set of negative reactions to the Gaelic language which have remained entrenched in official attitudes to some degree until the present century. As a result of it the Bible was not translated into Gaelic until 1767 (New Testament) and 1801 (Old Testament) (see Durkacz 1983: chs. 1 and 2; Withers 1988: ch. 3). When schools were set up in every parish it was decreed that these should be English schools. In 1709 the Scottish Society for the Propagation of Christian Knowledge was set up in Scotland to bring 'education' to the Highlands. Their policy declarations, as seen in the minutes of their meetings, show the same antipathy to the Gaelic language as that of the parish schools: Gaelic was excluded from the curriculum and children were forbidden to use it in the environs of the school and punished and held to ridicule if they were caught doing so. It was even maintained that it was not possible to teach children literacy in Gaelic (even when it was their own tongue). That state of affairs prevailed until the translation of the New Testament gave the language the status of a language of the scriptures: a vehicle of God's Word. It was not until the establishment of the Gaelic Schools Societies (in Edinburgh in 1811, in Glasgow in 1812 and in Inverness in 1818) that the Gaelic language found a central place in the educational system.

In spite of the success demonstrated by the societies' schools of using Gaelic as a language of instruction in the development of literacy (and its knock-on effects for literacy in English) the Nicolson Commission of 1860 did not find in its favour and the Education (Scotland) Act of 1872 ignored the existence of the language (MacLeod 1963: *passim*). The result of this was that Gaelic was once again defined out of the curriculum as a language of education. When it was introduced it was as a 'subject' like Latin or Greek (but without their prestige).

In spite of these official 'discouragements', however, the language retained a richness of expressive resource and a (restricted) range of differentiated registers associated with language arts, especially poetry, folktale and historical narrative, with crafts and with the range of community activities which require special vocabularies. The translation of the Bible provided a written corpus which both reinforced the oral language skills and conserved vocabulary. It also was the main text for the development and maintenance of literacy in the largest part of the population, though the church did not organise the formal development of 'Bible literacy' in the way that Welsh chapels did, for example.

Of secular organisations established to support the language, An Comunn Gaidhealach ('The Highland Society'), founded in 1891, is probably the most influential (see Thomson 1983: 48–9). The Gaelic Society of London, set up in 1777, is still operative (Thomson 1983: 109), as is the Gaelic Society of Glasgow,

founded in 1887, and, the most important of the learned societies, the Gaelic
Society of Inverness, founded in 1871, which has produced fifty-five volumes of
transactions. The Gaelic Texts Society, dedicated to the production of scholarly
texts of major writers in the language, was founded in 1934. These organisations
and others provided a supportive context for the language to survive, as has
Comann na Gàidhlig, established in 1984.

4.0.2   The contemporary position

As the historical statistics shown above in 4.0.1.1 and 4.0.1.2 make clear, the
Gaelic language is, as a community language, greatly diminished both in areal
spread and in the number of its speakers.

4.0.2.1   Areal distribution

Map 4.3 shows the areal distribution of Gaelic speakers in 1981. For example,
we see that now there is no enumeration district on the mainland of Scotland
which is 50 per cent Gaelic-speaking. In fact, communities having the 'survival
level' of over 70 per cent are confined to the Western Isles, some districts of
Skye and Tiree. Almost 50 per cent of the Gaelic-speaking population is not to
be found in Gaelic communities at all but in networks or as individual units,
mostly in Scottish cities, but also in other urban and non-urban populations. In
the Western Isles region there are 23,589 speakers; in Highland Region,
excluding Inverness and Nairn (3,900), there are 14,098 and in the Argyll and
Bute district of Strathclyde Region there are 6,408. The rest of Strathclyde
region accounts for 19,692, with Glasgow city having 9,472, Renfrew 1,548 and
Dumbarton 890, adding up to 11,910. Edinburgh city has 3,739, Aberdeen
1,210, Stirling 1,066, Falkirk 778 and Dundee city 769.

4.0.2.2   Demographic distribution

The figures above have demographic as well as areal implications. They reveal
centres of concentration of Gaelic speakers and are statistics of prime importance to language planners. A dimension that map 4.3 does not reveal is the age
structure of the Highland and Hebridean Gaelic-speaking communities. This is
disproportionately biased to the older age groups, as more detailed census
statistics show. This means that Gaelic-speaking young people constitute a lower
than normal proportion of these populations – which has serious implications for
future viability. Furthermore, the normal peer-group language of the 5–18 age
group is almost invariably English.

4.0.2.3   Status

Gaelic is recognised for educational and religious purposes as a using language in Scotland; it has, however, no political standing outside the Western Isles region. *Comhairle nan Eilean*, the Western Isles Council, has declared a bilingual policy in its operations, for example in educational provision, in road-signing and in council debates. This overt declaration has been of considerable support to the maintenance of the language.

4.0.2.4   Gaelic in education

The past decade has seen considerable advances for Gaelic in the educational sphere both in the Gaelic community and in the Gaelic networks. These advances benefit greatly from developments initiated in the 1960s and 1970s. Of particular importance have been the widespread establishment of *Sgoiltean Araich*, Gaelic nursery schools and, often leading on from these, Gaelic-medium units in primary schools; the spread of Gaelic-medium teaching in some secondary schools of general subjects; and some use of Gaelic as a teaching medium in those departments in universities and in education colleges that teach Gaelic or Gaelic-specific subjects.

4.0.2.5   Gaelic in religion

Gaelic has to some extent retained its place in religious practice in Gaelic-speaking areas, though with the spread of bilingualism – the only monoglots now being English-speaking incomers – the norm is for Gaelic- and English-language services to alternate. Gaelic services in the cities are largely reserved for occasions celebrating special events in the Gaelic social calendar.

4.0.2.6   Gaelic publishing

One area in which Gaelic has made considerable progress in the recent past is that of publication. The major Gaelic publisher is Gairm Publications, established in 1952, with offices in Glasgow. Its main publications have been literary works but it has covered the whole range of publication types. Catering mostly for educational publications (though it also tackles a wider range) is Acair, with offices in Stornoway. Apart from these, other smaller Gaelic publishers have made a contribution and general Scottish publishers have published Gaelic materials (Thomson 1983: 245–7). There is one periodical, *Gairm*, founded in 1951, which is entirely in Gaelic. Three newspapers publish regular weekly Gaelic features: the general Scottish daily, the *Scotsman*, in its weekend supplement and the weeklies, *The Stornoway Gazette*, published in Lewis, and the *West Highland Free Press*, published in Skye.

4.0.2.7   Gaelic broadcasting

Only the BBC participates in Gaelic radio broadcasting. There is a varied programme of news bulletins, programmes of light entertainment, schools programmes and religious programmes as well as occasional arts programmes broadcast almost exclusively on VHF and available throughout most parts of Scotland. Both BBC and independent companies provide television programmes, mostly entertainment and current affairs, but with some good programmes for younger children, and with very occasional serious arts offerings. Television programmes average about two per week at present, but government has given a grant of £9.5 million to produce 200 hours of new programming.

4.0.2.8   Gaelic literacy

There are no reliable statistics on the depth or extent of Gaelic literacy. The large majority of Gaelic speakers have some degree of reading skills, though this varies very considerably from person to person. The central position the Gaelic Bible traditionally held in Protestant areas has been the main agent leading this ability. At its most extreme it has led also to a unique set of readers who can read the Bible but claim not to be able to read anything else. The number of those who are able to write in Gaelic functionally is relatively small – English having been the official language of the school and the transactional language of business and of formal communication generally. The lasting impact of new Gaelic education policies on this situation remain to be seen. To date they appear to be reasonably effective in shifting the focus of literacy in favour of the language.

4.0.2.9   Gaelic in Nova Scotia

The Gaelic language was carried abroad to North America by emigrants from the eighteenth century on. Some of the earlier emigrants settled in the Carolinas and formed Gaelic-speaking enclaves in that territory. These, however, were of comparatively short duration, many re-emigrating to Canada after the American War of Independence.

The settlements in Nova Scotia, however, have been more lasting. Beginning in Pictou in 1773, it has been estimated that as many as 10,000 Highlanders went to Nova Scotia and Upper Canada before 1803. Emigration continued, with the Gaelic emigrants settling predominantly in the eastern counties of Pictou and Antigonish and later in Cape Breton Island. It has been estimated that there were about 80,000 Gaelic speakers in Cape Breton Island in 1880 (out of about 100,000) (see Edwards 1988). By that time, however, there were strong signs of language decline. Gaelic was a rural language, and lacked the status associated with powerful political and economic institutions. It became associated with backwardness and poverty. Because of the economic situation, out-migration from Cape Breton to Canada and the eastern United States was heavy, and depopulation, combined with the infiltration of English as the language of advantage, led to rapid Gaelic decline (Dunn 1974: 134). No provision had been made for Gaelic in the state schools (set up in 1864) and indeed, these schools could be regarded as Gaelic-hostile institutions, so that when Gaelic was allowed as an optional subject in 1921, there was no longer any strong demand for it. In fact, Gaelic appears to have been decreasing by about 50 per cent per ten-year period since 1930.

The census figures for Nova Scotia from 1931 to 1971 are as follows (estimates for Cape Breton Island from various sources are given in parentheses; see Edwards 1988):

> 1931: 25,000 (25,000–30,000)
> 1941: 12,000 (10,000)
> 1951: 6,800 (7,000)
> 1961: 3,700 (3,400)
> 1971: 1,420 (965)

It must be emphasised that the above figures are to be treated with great caution. Clearly, the questions in the census have proved difficult to interpret for some respondents. Also, there has been Gaelic under-reporting for various cultural reasons to do with the status of the language, on the one hand, and, on the other, over-estimation on the part of the language enthusiast and revivalists (Edwards 1988). Whatever position is most accurate, it is irrefutable that Gaelic in Cape Breton, unlike their blossoming revived version of 'Scottish culture', is in a precarious state.

4.0.2.10   Language contact

The Gaelic language in Scotland has never been the sole or an isolated tongue within the area. It has borrowed in different domains from all the languages from which it has been in contact. Its Latin borrowings in areas of religion and learning are mostly early and held in common with Irish. Its borrowings from the Brittonic languages are remarkably few, probably because it made its contacts in the role of ascendant language. Its borrowings of French origin appear, many of them, to have been borrowed through Scottish English (apart from those that belong to the classical Gaelic period). Borrowings from Norse belong mainly to the sphere of boats, fishing and the sea-shore and the names of topographic features, but there are also a good many core vocabulary items (see Thomson 1983: 151–5).

Contact with these languages has affected not only the vocabulary of Gaelic but also its structure and its idiom. English, however, has had the most powerful influence. This influence can be traced to the sixteenth century in religious texts (Thomson 1983: 152), and religious writings continued to be an important channel, especially the translations of the Bible in the eighteenth century and their use as school texts as well as texts to be read in church. Borrowings from other domains of vocabulary are increasingly in evidence in Gaelic writing from that period on, developing to the present situation, when vicarious borrowing in any domain may occur (see MacAulay 1982b).

4.1   SYNCHRONIC LINGUISTIC VARIATION

4.1.1   Dialect differentiation

There are considerable difficulties attendant on an attempt to give a succinct overall description of Scottish Gaelic dialects. The basic problem is one of available data. This is not so much a problem of quantity of information as of its quality. In spite of excellent published descriptions of local dialects and indeed of surveys of different areas (e.g. Robertson 1906–9; Borgstrøm 1940, 1941; Oftedal 1956; Wagner and Ó Baoill 1969: appendix 1; Ternes 1973; Dorian 1978; Ó Murchú 1989), there are serious gaps in coverage; there is a lack of systematisation, in some cases, which makes comparisons difficult, and, too often, informants for a particular point are so few and their responses so restricted that it is dangerous to base much generalisation on their output. It is hoped that with the publication of the data of the Gaelic Linguistic Survey, of which very few results have appeared since its inception in 1949, many of these problems will be solved. Meanwhile we have to proceed with many uncertainties.

4.1.1.1   There are some problems also with the interpretation of dialect groupings in Scottish Gaelic. It has become customary to speak of a 'central' group and a 'peripheral' group (Jackson 1968: 67), and this categorisation is based on sound criteria, for example the distribution of preaspiration of stop consonants. However, in moving from that position to make generalisations about focal and relic areas, centres of innovation and contact phenomena, it is wise to be cautious. The last mentioned, as an explanation of phonological phenomena, can indeed often be discarded or relegated to peripheral status by examining the developmental potential of the inherent features of the language itself. The development of preaspiration, for example, is a reasonable enough one given the presence of distinctive 'strong' stops and should be seen as a phenomenon comparable to, for example, diphthongisation before long sonants rather than an example of Norse influence (Borgstrøm 1974; Ó Dochartaigh 1981).

4.1.1.2   As well as a central vs peripheral dimension, it is also maintained that Scottish Gaelic dialects show east vs west and north vs south distinctions (Jackson 1968). The east vs west distinction appears to be little more than a restatement in different terms of the central vs peripheral hypothesis selecting those features which have a specifically east vs west orientation.

4.1.1.3   The north vs south division is more complicated and appears to be a function of the historical north to south disposition of Gaelic dialects extending over Scotland and Ireland. As we said above (4.0.1.1), there were extensive Gaelic settlements in Scotland from an early date, and although evidence for differentiation is obscured by the existence of a common literary language (Jackson 1951), clearly differentiation took place. Scottish Gaelic both retains ancient features such as Old Gaelic hiatus, for example in *biidh* the genitive singular of *biadh* 'food', Modern Irish /biː/, Scottish Gaelic /bi-i/, and shows extensive and different innovations found as fully fledged systems in the earliest Scottish Gaelic texts, for instance in the verbal system.

At the same time there is a strong continuity between northern Irish dialects and those of southern Scotland, notably Kintyre (as one would expect from the history of contact between the two areas). The evidence of Rathlin Island and of the relics of Antrim Irish reinforces this continuity (see Ó Baoill 1978). Given those conditions and the criteria on which north vs south is usually established, it is best to see that division in the overall picture of Gaelic dialects in Scotland and Ireland. Such a perspective, indeed, is a useful corrective to more parochial interpretations in both countries.

4.1.2   Lexis

The amount of sytematic information easily available about vocabulary differentiation is limited. Most studies are phonologically oriented and what lexical information we get tends to be incidental. Wagner and Ó Baoill (1969) are an exception to this and their lists give us some degree of information for the points that were investigated by them. These were (a) Arran; (b) Kintyre; (c) Argyll

(Inverary); (d) Benbecula; (e) Lewis (Carloway); (f) Wester Ross (Lochalsh); (g) Sutherland (Assynt). These yield interesting groupings for different items. For example (a) and (b) are differentiated from the rest by a number of items (the (a–b) forms are given first): 'dog', *madadh/cù*; 'neck', *muineal/amhaich*; 'women', *mnathan/boireannaich*; 'plough', *beart/crann*; 'close (door)', *druit/ dùin*; 'stars', *reultan/rionnagan*; 'hurry', *deifir/cabhaig*. This division is the most marked (for this set of vocabulary items). (a–c) are differentiated from the rest by the following: '(she is) chewing the cud', *a' cagnadh a cìr/a' cnàmh a cìr*; 'mare', *capall/làir*; 'knitting needle', *dealg/bior*; 'we get', *tha sinn a' faotainn/tha sinn a' faighinn*. (a–d) are differentiated from the rest by: 'garden', *gàradh/leas*; 'smoke', *toit/ceò*. (e–g) generally agree with each other, with (e) and (f) showing strongest agreement. Kintyre and Arran, then, exhibit strong similarities with each other and a tendency to agree with Inverary to form a southern group. Carloway, Lochalsh and Assynt show strong agreement to form a northern group. Benbecula agrees with the latter for most items, but has significant affinity with the former. Some items differentiate the points more discretely, for example, 'gable of house': (a–c) [(b) not given] *stuaigh* vs (d) *binneag* vs (e–f) *ceann* vs (g) *tulchainn*. Despite the limited extent of the sample (which must be stressed) these findings agree well with our expectations from observing other studies.

4.1.2.1   Within the more limited area of the Western Isles interesting vocabulary heteroglosses are also to be found. The major ones come between Lewis and Harris, with Harris agreeing with the islands to the south (the Lewis forms are given first): 'drinking water', *bùrn/uisge*; 'cream', *bàrr/uachdair*; 'box', *bucas/bocsa*; 'sweets', *siùcaran/suiteas*. The next most important division is between Harris and North Uist, distinguishing Lewis and Harris from the Uists, Benbecula and Barra, for example: 'floor', *làr/urlar*; 'hair of the head', *falt/gruag*; 'smoke', *ceò/toit*.

There are other less distinctive, but nevertheless substantive, vocabulary differences among the southern islands (see Borgstrøm 1940: 229–44). It should be pointed out that the above are 'first response' items. All of these forms will be known to all traditional Gaelic speakers in the islands. An interesting study of vocabulary differentiation in another dialect area is found in Grant (1987). This is centred on the island of Islay, of which a detailed description is given. Using Islay as a focus, it shows the set of linguistic relationships between the island and Kintyre and Arran, with which it is most closely connected, with the rest of Argyll and with the northern Irish coast with which there has been a continuing connection across the North Channel.

4.1.3   Syntax and morphology

By and large, it can be said that the syntax of Scottish Gaelic has been remarkably homogeneous. Such differences as appear, in peripheral dialects for example, are often consequences, direct and indirect, of contact with English. These appear also in the speech of younger members of more conservative dialects as exposure to English becomes more intense (see 4.1.5).

4.1.3.1   Some interesting independent distinctions are, however, to be found. In Wagner and Ó Baoill, for example, in two instances of the passive Arran shows constructions with the verb 'be' + past participle: 'You will be drowned' *Bithidh thusa bàithe* and 'They were killed' (*Bha iad*) *caillte*, a structure identical with that used in Ulster Irish. In another instance both Arran and Kintyre translate 'turned' by *tionntaichte*. None of the other respondents produces a past-participle construction in either case.

4.1.3.2   Morphologically, there is more differentiation, which occurs over a range of cases. Some of these are general, for example in east Perthshire (Ó Murchú 1989) there has been weakening of final syllables and their consequent loss. This occurs typically in disyllabic nouns which thus become monosyllabic, for example 'stick' *maide* > *maid*, and in the genitive singular of feminine nouns: 'hen (GEN)', *circe* > *circ*. This obviously has an effect on the noun paradigm and hence on declension paradigms of the noun phrase, for example, on adjectival agreement in ART + N + ADJ constructions, where *na circe bige* > *na circ bhig*, etc. This loss of ending appears also in the verb–noun: 'praising', *a' moladh* > *a' mol* (/mɔLəɣ/>/mɔLə/>/mɔL/). Dialects where this change has occurred clearly differ substantially in their sound distribution from those in which it did not.

4.1.3.3   Verb–nouns may also show different endings from dialect to dialect: for example 'following', *leantainn* vs *leantail* vs *leanmhainn*; 'hearing', *cluinntinn* vs *cluinnteail* vs *cluinnsinn*; 'thinking', *smaointinn* vs *smaoineachadh*, *smaoineachdainn*.

4.1.3.4   Genitive relation is expressed in two ways (a) N + N [GEN] and (b) NP [SUBJ] + *aig* + NP [LOC/POSS]: (a) 'the boy's dog', *cú a' bhalaich* and (b) *an cú aig a' bhalach*. In some dialects kin relationship cannot be expressed as in (b); in others they normally are (Ó Murchú 1989).

4.1.3.5   Noun gender differs from dialect to dialect: for example, 'sea', *a'
mhuir* (fem.) and *am muir* (masc.) and 'mist', *a' cheó* (fem.) and *an ceó* (masc.).

4.1.3.6   In finite verbs there are a small number of well-attested differential
features. Person is normally expressed analytically by means of a pronoun, not
synthetically by means of a personal ending. Exceptions to this are the first
singular and the first plural of the second indefinite form of the verb: 'I would
be', *bhithinn*, and 'we would be', *bhitheamaid. Bhithinn* is generally attested (at
least from older speakers). *Bhitheamaid*, however, is of much more restricted
distribution: it is not found in peripheral dialects and in the Western Isles it is
one of the features which serve to distinguish the Gaelic of Lewis from that of
Harris and the islands to the south.

4.1.3.7   Another verbal distinguishing features is the use of an *-s* /s/ ending,
corresponding to that of the relative form, in the third person singular
(sometimes extending to the second and even the first person) of the first
indefinite form, in place of the more familiar *-dh* /ɣ/ form. This form with *-s* is
widely dispersed, found in south-east Lewis (Oftedal 1956), Wester Ross
(Borgstrøm 1941), Easter Ross (Watson 1974), east Sutherland (Dorian 1978)
and east Perthshire (Ó Murchú 1989). It is at present not possible to draw
accurate boundaries for these different features.

4.1.4   The sound system

The sound system has figured more prominently than any other language level
in the study of Gaelic dialects. Indeed, it forms the core of most descriptions and
is the basis on which most generalisations about dialect distribution have been
based. A number of phonological criteria for dialect differentiation have
evolved, such as preaspiration of 'fortis' stops, diphthongisation of vowels
before originally long sonants, and diphthongisation of long *e* before non-palatal
consonants. We will have a brief look at these and at some additional
phenomena of distributional interest.

4.1.4.1   Preaspiration of stops

The Gaelic languages had distinctive series of 'strong' and 'weak' consonants.
This distinction is maintained in the modern tongues and shown in writing by
representing 'strong' stops as *p, t, k* and 'weak' stops as *b, d, g*. There are two
series of these, palatal(ised) and non-palatal(ised). The conditions below apply
to both. In Scottish Gaelic the strong stops *p, t, k* are realised differently in

different regions in the codae of syllables bearing stress. Several patterns of realisation and of combinations of realisations take place:

1   There may be no preaspiration
2   Preaspiration may be slight, often sounding simply like a devoicing of the vowel of the nucleus and represented as /ʰp/, /ʰt/, /ʰk/.
3   Preaspiration may be more pronounced, /hp/, /ht/, /hk/.
4   There is pronounced preaspiration of *p* and *t* and a homorganic fricative before *k*: /hp/, /ht, /xk/.
5   /x/ appears as the 'preaspiration form' of all three: /xp/, /xt/, /xk/.
6   *p* and *t* have no preaspiration, and *x* appears before *k*: /pʰ/, /tʰ/, /xk/,

The relationship of 6 to the other preaspiration types is problematic. It is as likely to have developed as a strong form *k*, contrasting in codae with *g*, in parallel with the development of earlier /xt/ → /xk/ (an unstable group, no doubt due to its non-homorganic coupling, in Scottish Gaelic). This is supported by the fact that we get the change /kʰ/ > /xk/ and /k'ʰ/ > /x'k'/ in consonant groups, e.g. 'hen', *cearc*: /k'ʰɛ rkʰ/ > /k'ʰɛ rxkʰ/, etc.

These types are distributed as shown on map 4.4. It should be pointed out that boundaries are in many cases approximate, data not being accessible for many areas.

4.1.4.2   Diphthongisation or lengthening before sonants

Gaelic possessed a 'strong' (long) and 'weak' (short) contrastive series of sonants operating in codae of stressed syllables. Each of these was distinctively palatal(ised) or non-palatal(ised). Long and short *l*, *n* and *r* were written -*ll*, *v*, -*l*, -*nn*, *v*, -*n* and -*rr*, *v*, -*r* respectively; long and short *m* were not orthographically differentiated. Syllables with long-sonant codae had short-vowel nuclei. In most Scottish Gaelic dialects those long sonants became shortened and the vowels lengthened in stressed monosyllables (or when the sonant was supported by another consonant medially (Ó Dochartaigh 1981). The lengthened vowel may be a simple segment or a diphthong, depending on dialect; some dialects retained the original long sonants. This gives us schematically (C)VC: > (C)V:C or (C)VVC, which we may exemplify as follows: 'keep (IMP)', *cum* /kʰūm:/ vs /kʰū:m/ vs /kʰo um/; 'ill', *tinn* /t'ʰī N':/ vs /t'ʰ ī:N'/ vs /t'ʰēɪ N'/; 'foreigner', *gall* /gaL:/ vs /ga:L / vs /gauL/; 'top', *barr* /baR:/ vs /ba:R/. Vowels were not diphthongised before *r*. (However, in certain areas, diphthongisation is found before *r+n* and *r+d*, giving 'craft', *ceàrd* /kʰ/ʰaurd/ and 'hammer', *òrd* /ourd/ (Robertson 1900).) Map 4.5 shows the approximate boundaries of the areas where long consonants are retained. There is insufficient evidence to indicate

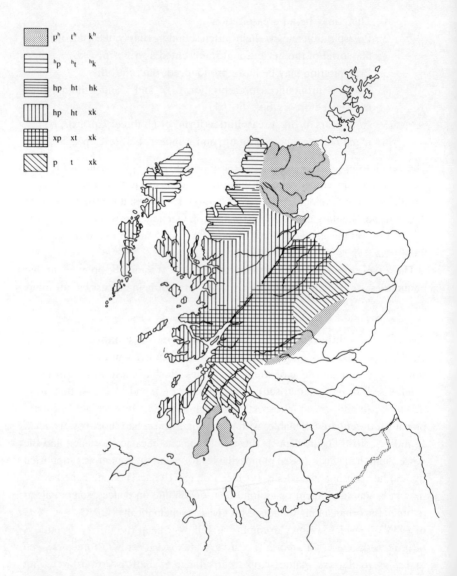

Map 4.4   Distribution of preaspiration

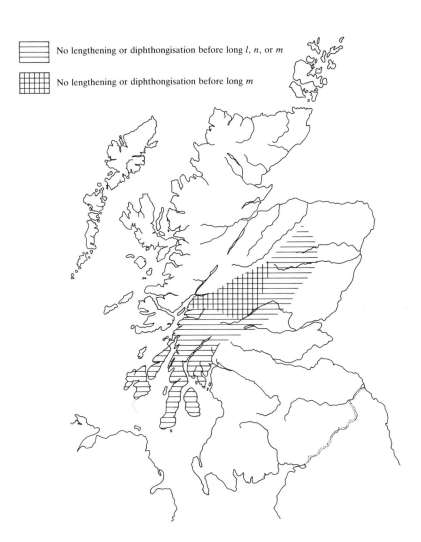

No lengthening or diphthongisation before long *l*, *n*, or *m*

No lengthening or diphthongisation before long *m*

Map 4.5   Lengthening and diphthongisation before long *l*, *n* and *m*

the boundaries between areas with simple vowel lengthening and those with diphthongisation.

4.1.4.3   Diphthongisation of long *e* before non-palatals

Gaelic 'long *e*' derives from different sources; not all of them undergo 'breaking' (Jackson 1968). Jackson selects what he takes as eight key examples and, basing his study on findings from the Gaelic Linguistic Survey archive, shows the degree of breaking which takes place over the Gaelic dialect areas from which data was available, in terms of percentages which he plots on to a dialect map (map 4.6). Needless to say, the actual percentages will almost certainly vary with the number of items that one examines. For example, in a list of 45 items only two show diphthongisation in Islay: 4.44 per cent. However, 39 out of 45 show diphthongisation in Bernera, Lewis: 86.66 per cent, which is near the 87.5 per cent of Jackson's map. It is only with very low and very high numbers that the percentages deviate. The relative picture given in Jackson's map seems to reflect, by and large, the findings with larger numbers.

4.1.4.4   Morphophonology

The most notable morphophonological feature of differentiation is the realisation of nasal mutation. This mutation occurs when a noun (for example) is preceded by an element which ends in a nasal, as in: 'the dog', *an cù*; 'the blacksmith', *an gobha*, 'the man', *am fear*; 'the summer', *an samhradh*. This junction is realised in different ways. We may get, for example, $\{ \partial^N \ k^H u{:}\} \rightarrow$ /əku:/ with the deletion of the nasal and the class change of $k \rightarrow g$. Beside this we get $\{ \partial^N \ ko{-}\partial \} \rightarrow$ /ə go–ə /, showing a neutralisation of the $k \ v \ g$ distinction under nasalisation. The same applies to all stop consonants (see Dorian 1978: 70ff., for East Sutherland). In Ternes (1973: 13) we have a version of this in Western Ross where k and g show $\{^N k\} \rightarrow [k^h]$ and $\{^N g\} \rightarrow [k]$. In other dialects a nasal segment appears before the word-initial k, which is unaspirated: [əⁿku:]. In Lewis a third type appears: $\{ \partial^N k^H u{:}\} \rightarrow [\partial \ \eta^k u{:}]$ and $\{ \partial^N \ ko{-}\partial \} \rightarrow [\partial \eta o{-}\partial]$, etc., where the stop is replaced by a homorganic nasal – k by a voiceless, postaspirated nasal and g by a voiced unaspirated nasal. f and s do not undergo nasalisation except in southeastern and eastern dialects, where we get $\{ \partial^N \ f\epsilon r \}$ $\rightarrow$ /mvɛr/ and $\{ \partial^N \ sa\tilde{u}r \} \rightarrow$ /nza\tilde{u}r/ (Ó Murchú 1989: 341 and 394, on east Perthshire).

4.1.4.5   We have looked mainly at larger dialect distinctions here. However, there are lesser dialect areas with distinctions of equal fascination which yield data of prime distributional and historical importance (see MacAulay 1978).

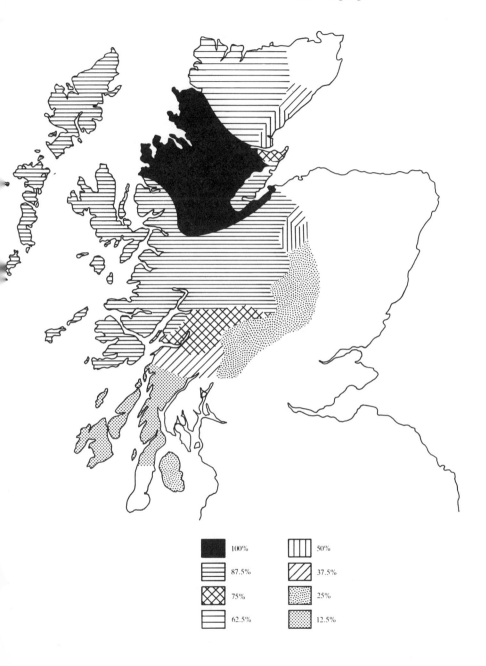

Map 4.6   The breaking of original long *e* (after Jackson 1968)

4.1.5   Other features of linguistic differentiation

4.1.5.1   Register differentiation

In Scottish Gaelic we get the normal range of register differentiation, depending (if one may paraphrase) on who is communicating what to whom, in what circumstances, for what purpose and by what means. A few examples will have to suffice here.

Status is shown by a range of 'deference markers'. For example, *Nach dean sibh suidhe?*, 'Will you not sit down?' (Will you (pl.) not make a sitting?), instead of *Dèan suidhe* (Make a sitting), which is 'polite' or 'welcoming', or simply *Suidh*, 'Sit down'. This example shows, as well as the negative question form, the use of the plural pronoun *sibh* instead of the singular *thu*, which is a crucial status indicator in discourse and an important indicator in polite discourse generally. In some subdialect areas a 'familiarity' system cuts across the status one. To put it too simply, children in a simple 'status' system always address their elders as *sibh*, in a 'familiarity' system they address their familiars, their parents, for example, as *thu* but other adults as *sibh*. The systems interact in a complex manner, with fluctuating demarcation boundaries. There are specific markers to indicate intimacy and to establish distance.

There is a range of relative formality. Religious discourse is marked by lexical choice ('the language of the Bible'), solemnity of tone of voice and shape of discourse. Extempore prayer and extempore preaching have special contours of pitch crescendo and diminution, which are otherwise found only in the declamation of poetry. General markers of formal discourse owe much to the religious sphere because of the importance of the Bible both as a prestigious written text and as a text for reading aloud. Formal written discourse has generally used it as a fundamental model. Formal spoken discourse tends to imitate the read version. A clear example of this is with prepositional phrases such as *don bhaile*, which one regularly hears in formal situations spoken as /tɔn'valə/ by speakers of all dialects most of whose normal pronunciation would be /ɣan'valə/ or /ɣanə'valə/. We see here one medium borrowing the resources of the other to establish register differentiation (see MacAulay 1982a: *passim*).

Needless to say, not all speakers have command over all varietal forms: for example, there are speakers of Gaelic who are unable to read the language; there are many who can read Gaelic but whose language for writing is English; and there are many whose command of the more restricted content-specific registers is minimal.

4.1.5.2   Age differentiation

The second major source of differentiation we mentioned is related to age: different age groups use the language differently. A good deal (but by no means all) of this difference is the result of increasing English contact and penetration. It should be borne in mind that this process has operated on different communities at different times and with varying degrees of intensity. Younger people in one community, then, may have similar degrees of deviation from a 'traditional Gaelic norm' as older people in another. There are conservative and advanced examples of this deviation, and this may be reflected in dialect areas or subdialect areas or in networks based on kin or interest (MacAulay 1978, 1982a).

English has affected the Gaelic language at different levels. In vocabulary it has replaced Gaelic terms both in restricted and in core vocabulary, more intensely in the language of young people. Many terms belonging to traditional activities have been lost as these activities have been peripheralised. But common words, also, have been replaced. In the language of buying and selling, for example, English names of fish have been substituted for Gaelic ones: 'cod' is *cod* not *trosg*, 'salmon' is *salmon* not *bradan*, etc. More centrally, 'kettle' is often *kettle* not *coire*, 'jar' is *jar* not *crogan*. Even earlier borrowings are brought up to date: 'can' is *can* not *cana*; 'tin' (container) is *tin* not *tine* (or its earlier form /tʰənə/); 'bedspread' is *bedspread* not *cuibhrig* (from 'covering') and so on.

English has also invaded the syntax of younger speakers. Syntax shows a high incidence of calquing on English structure. This is seen, for example, in the order of sentence elements: 'I have eaten the bread' is traditionally *Tha mi air an t-aran ithe* [I am after the bread eat]. This is often heard as *Tha mi air ithe an (t-)aran* [I am after eat the bread] with the English verb + object order.

Changes in the form of expression and loss of distinctions result from English interference. Gaelic has no verb 'to have', possession being expressed in a structure 'be + subject/possessed + (preposition + locative/possessor)': *Tha aran aig Iain* [Is bread at Iain] (see 4.2.8 below). In traditional Gaelic, different prepositions appear in the locative phrase, for example *Tha bial air Iain*, *Tha bial an Iain*, *Tha bial aig Iain*, 'There is a mouth *on* Iain' (for eating) and '. . . *in* Iain' (for speaking). 'There is a mouth at Iain' means 'Iain is proficient in the use of bad language'. All of these distinctions are subsumed under the one form, *Tha bial aig Iain* being simply a translation equivalent of 'Iain has a mouth', *aig* being the commonest preposition for expressing possession.

An area especially rich in English-based calquing is that of idiom. Here again an age-group difference is plain, but there seems to be an unusual degree of feedback from younger to older groups. This is also the case in (non-technological) language switching (see MacAulay 1982a, 1982b).

Changes in morphology are relatively independent of English influence, directly at least. Generationally, there has been a marked loss of distinctions of case marking in the noun phrase. If we look at the traditional paradigm of a feminine noun and a masculine noun, with definite-article and adjective modification, we get nominative, prepositional and genitive forms:

	Feminine	Masculine
Nominative	*a' chearc bheag*	*an cù beag*
Prepositional	*a' chirc bhig*	*a' chù bheag*
Genitive	*na circe bige*	*a' choin bhig*

A typical development is that in one generation the genitive form coalesces with the prepositional and in two generations this coalesces with the nominative, giving one form for all cases: *a' chearc bheag, an cù beag*. In some cases the nominative masculine coalesces with the prepositional (rather than the other way round) and we get, for all cases, *a' chearc bheag* and *a' chù bheag*, with consequent loss of grammatical gender. The paths to these outcomes are, of course, often complex, and involve a great deal of intergenerational overlap.

SYNTAX

4.2   SENTENCE STRUCTURE

4.2.1   Simple and complex sentences

Simple sentences are those that consist overtly of only one sentence or clause. Complexity comes at different points in structure: at sentence level in the simple conjoining of two sentences; in phrases consisting of conjoined elements or containing qualifying clauses, where clauses are used as noun substitutes – indeed, in the whole range of positions in which complexity occurs in English and other European languages.

4.2.2   Parataxis and hypotaxis

Hypotactic relationships are shown in (1):

(1)   *Sheas   Iain agus shuidh   Anna*
       stood-up Iain and sat-down Anna
       'Iain stood up *and* Anna sat down'

typically signalled by *agus* (often abbreviated *is*). The adversative correlate of (1) is (2):

(2)   *Sheas Iain ach shuidh Anna*
       'Iain stood up *but* Anna sat down'

Agus and *ach* are the only overt co-ordinating conjunctions.

4.2.2.1   The same relationship may be expressed by means of intonation, in paratactic structures. Each clause apart from the final one in the sequence has a distinctive non-final tone contour (see 4.15.3).

(3)   *Sheas Iain, shuidh Anna, thuit Seumas*
       'Iain stood up, Anna sat down, Seumas fell over'

4.2.2.2   From a constituency point of view, clauses with subordinating 'conjunctions' are better regarded in Gaelic as adjunctal sentence elements. These conjunctions affect the structure of their clauses in different ways, as may be demonstrated by 'temporal' clauses:

(4)   *Sheas   Iain nuair a   shuidh   Anna*
       stood-up Iain when REL sat-down Anna
       'Iain stood up *when* Anna sat down'

(5)   *Sheas   Iain an dèidh do Anna suidhe*
       stood-up Iain after   to Anna sit-VN
       'Iain stood up *after* Anna sat down'

4.2.2.3   'Contemporal' clauses, that is clauses that denote an event that coincides in time with the event of the 'main clause', are introduced by *agus*. Unlike other clauses introduced by *agus* (e.g. (1) above) these clauses are non-finite.

(6)   *Sheas   Iain agus Anna a' suidhe*
       stood-up Iain *and* Anna at sitting-down
       'Iain stood up whilst Anna was sitting down'

These sentences do not have adversative correlates with *ach*: **Sheas Iain ach Anna a' suidhe*.

4.2.2.4   It will be noted that contemporal clauses contain the progressive aspect. There are other aspectually marked clauses introduced by *agus*:

(7)   *Sheas Iain agus Anna air suidhe*
         'Iain stood up *and* Anna after sit (VN)'

This normally (but not strictly necessarily) implies consequence rather than just subsequence: 'Iain stood up consequently on Anna's sitting down'. Other 'consequence' clauses are similar in structure to (4) above; for example:

(8)   *Sheas Iain bhon a shuidh Anna*
         'Iain stood up *because* Anna sat down'

4.2.2.5   *Ach* also conjoins dependency-related structures, for example, concessive clauses of the type:

(9)   *Sheasadh   Iain ach Anna suidhe*
         stand-up−INDEF 2 Iain *but* Anna sit-VN
         'Iain would stand up provided that Anna sat down'

Similar are sentences with clauses that denote 'means of effecting something' introduced by *le*; for example:

(10)   *Shuidh Iain le stòl fhaighinn dha fhéin*
         'Iain sat down *by* getting a stool for himself'

Le is basically the instrumental preposition, and the structure which follows it here is a 'nominalisation'. *Ach* (9) has the same grammatical function.

4.2.2.6   There is the usual range of clause classes; for example 'purpose' clauses:

(11)   *Shuidh Iain gus an suidheadh Anna*
         'Iain sat down *so that* Anna would sit down'

'locational' clauses:

(12)   *Shuidh Iain far an do shuidh Anna*
         'Iain sat *where* Anna sat'

'conditional' clauses of two kinds (a) 'realised condition', for example:

(13)   *Suidhidh Iain ma shuidh Anna*
         'Iain will sit down *if* Anna sat down'

and (b) 'unrealised condition', for example:

(14)   *Shuidheadh Iain nan suidheadh Anna*
         'Iain would sit down *if* Anna would sit down'

and so on. Our examples cover a limited number of classes.

4.2.3   Obligatory and optional elements of structure

We may take as the basic elements in Gaelic sentence structure *verb*, *subject*, *complement* and *adjunct*.

4.2.3.1   Sentences, unmarked imperative for example, may consist overtly only of the verb:

(15)   *Seas!*
         'Stand up!'

(16)   *Seasaibh!* (with 2 pl. ending)
         'Stand up!'

(17)   *Seasamaid!* (with 1 pl. ending)
         'Let us stand up!'

4.2.3.2   Particularising imperatives such as (18),

(18)   *Seas thusa!*
         '*You* stand up!'

contain the singular address pronoun *thu* marked by the particularising postclitic -*sa*.

4.2.3.3   'Third-person imperatives' must contain either the pronoun: (a) particularising:

(19)   *Seasadh esan!*
         'Let *him* stand up!'

(b) given:

(20)   *Seasadh e!*
         'Let him stand up!'

or the noun:

(21)   *Seasadh Iain!*
         'Let Iain stand up!'

4.2.3.4   Identifying imperatives combine vocatives and imperatives:

(22)   *Seas, Iain!*
         'Stand up, Iain!'

(23)   *Iain, seas!*
         'Iain, stand up!'

reverses the order of elements, the initial-position vocative serving to focus the addressee's attention – as indeed it does when prefixed to any sentence.

4.2.3.5   Identifying and particularising types may be combined:

(24)   *Seas thusa, Iain!*
         'You stand up, Iain!'

(25)   *Iain, seas thusa!*
         'Iain, you stand up!'

This normally happens only with second-person imperatives.

4.2.3.6   Intransitive sentences are a well-defined class in Gaelic. They consist obligatorily of verb and subject as in the constituent sentences in (1) above, *Sheas Iain* 'Iain stood up', and *Shuidh Anna* 'Anna sat down', or in such examples as (26)–(32):

(26)   *Bhàsaich an duine*
         'The man died'

(27)   *Dh'fhalbh Iain*
         'Iain went away'

(28)   *Thàinig an latha*
         'Day came'

(29)   *Thuit an oidhche*
         'Night fell'

(30)   *Thòisich an t-uisge*
         'The rain began'

(31)   *Sguir am fuaim*
         'The noise stopped'

(32)   *Stad am bus*
         'The bus stopped'

4.2.3.7   Transitive sentences may have the special type of complement traditionally called a *direct object*, for example:

(33)   *Cheannaich Iain leabhair*
         'Iain bought a book'

(34)   *Dh'òl an cat bainne*
         'The cat drank (some) milk'

(35)   *Dh'ith an cù an t-aran*
         'The dog ate the bread'

(36)   *Chunnaic Iain an cù*
         'Iain saw the dog'

Direct objects are nominals. Our examples above are nouns, (33) and (34), and noun phrases, (35) and (36). They may also be pronouns:

(37)   *Dh'ith an cù e*
          'The dog ate it'

or 'nominalised' sentences

(38)   *Chunnaic Iain gun dh'ith an cù an t-aran*
          'Iain saw that the dog ate the bread'

4.2.3.8   Some sentences, 'transactional' ones for example, obligatorily have two complements, a *direct* [O] and an *indirect* [I] *object*, traditionally speaking:

(39)   *Thug Iain leabhar* [O] *do Anna* [I]
          'Iain gave a book to Anna'
(40)   *Fhuair Iain leabhar* [O] *bho Anna* [I]
          'Iain got a book from Anna'
(41)   *Chuir Iain leabhar* [O] *gu Anna* [I]
          'Iain sent a book to Anna'

'Indirect objects' are locative prepositional phrases containing directional prepositions denoting basically 'source' and 'goal'.

4.2.3.9   Transactional sentences raise some interesting points concerning the expression of directionality. In (39), *Thug Iain leabhar do Anna*, the indirect object is a 'goal locative', *do Anna*, 'to Anna', and *thug* is translated 'gave'; in (42),

(42)   *Thug Iain leabhar bho Anna*
          'Iain took a book from Anna'

bho Anna is a source locative, Anna is 'deprived' of a book and *thug* is translated 'took'. In (43),

(43)   *Thug Iain leabhar gu Anna*
          'Iain brought/took a book to Anna'

thug may be translated 'brought' or 'took' as the 'speaker/other'-orientation system does not operate. Example (43) admits of two prepositional phrases, 'source' and 'goal', with the status of 'indirect objects':

(44)   *Thug Iain leabhar gu Anna bho Mhàiri*
          'Iain brought/took a book to Anna from Màiri'

Thug may also take either type of the locative without, in this case, altering its sense, for example:

(45)   *Thug Iain leabhar à Dùn Eideann*
          'Iain brought a book from Edinburgh'

This interchangeability is not possible with the other examples.

Chuir also operates in sentences with source and goal locatives:

(46)   *Chuir Ian leabhar gu Anna à Dùn Eideann*
         'Iain sent a book to Anna from Edinburgh'

(47)   *Chuir Iain leabhar à Dùn Eideann*
         'Iain sent a book from Edinburgh'

However, (47) seems to belong to the elliptical class of sentence from which the goal locative has been elided (see below). Grammatically, it requires an overt goal (but not an overt source) if it is not contextually 'bound'. Further problems with this class of sentence (which are too complex for us to go into here) derive from the realisation potentiality of source and goal elements, the conflation of these categories with actor/agent categories, and the way in which grammatical constraints and different locative categories have been used in the language to express a range of 'abstract' usages; for example,

(48)   *Thug Iain leabhar bho Anna do Mhàiri*

(cf. (39) and (42)) can mean that Iain took a book from Anna (either 'with Anna willing' or 'with Anna unwilling') to/for Màiri (either 'at Màiri's instigation' or 'to Màiri's advantage').

4.2.3.10   There are other types of complement in addition to the direct-object and indirect-object types. There are, for example *locational* complements:

(49)   *Bha Iain aig an dorus*
         'Iain was at the door'

(50)   *Chaidh Iain chun an doruis*
         'Iain went to the door'

To be grammatical, sentences with the verbs *bha* and *chaidh* require complements. There are *adjectival* complements, as well as locative ones:

(51)   *Tha Iain òg*
         'Iain is young'

(52)   *Dh'fhàs Iain sean*
         'Iain became old'

Sentential complements will be dealt with below (4.2.10)

4.2.3.11   Adjuncts are grammatically optional sentence elements. They may be added appropriately to any sentence and there is no grammatical constraint on their number; for example:

(53)   *Bha Iain aig an dorus an diugh aig deich uairean*
              'Iain was at the door today at ten o'clock'

We have said that subordinate clauses are best regarded as sentential adjuncts: for example, the temporal clause in (4) above, *Sheas Iain nuair a shuidh Anna* 'Iain stood up when Anna sat down', and the contemporal clause in (6) above *Sheas Iain agus Anna a' suidhe* 'Iain stood up whilst Anna was sitting down'. In sentences such as (54) and (55),

(54)   *Chunnaic Iain Anna agus i   aig an dorus*
              saw   Iain Anna *and she at the door*
              'Iain saw Anna at the door'

(55)   *Chunnaic Iain Anna aig an dorus*
              'Iain saw Anna *at the door*'

the italicised elements in the glosses should be regarded as deriving from structures similar to the contemporal clause in (7), by appropriate rules. The primary reading of *aig an dorus* in (55) certainly relates to (54) rather than to (56):

(56)   *Chunnaic Iain Anna agus e aig an dorus*
              saw   Iain Anna and *he* at   the door
              'Iain saw Anna as he was at the door'

In sentences such as (57) and (58),

(57)   *Chunnaic Iain Anna 'na   seasamh aig an dorus*
              saw   Iain Anna in-her standing at the door
              'Iain saw Anna standing at the door'

(58)   *Chunnaic Iain Anna 'na   sheasamh aig an dorus*
              saw   Iain Anna in-his standing at the door
              'Iain saw Anna as he stood at the door'

the dependency is clear.

4.2.3.12   What we have said above applies (in the main) to full sentences – sentences from which elements have not been omitted. The elements omitted from elliptical sentences must be systematically retrievable. Such sentences are found as responses, typically (but not necessarily) in question-and-answer sequences. The answers in the following set of such sequences could all 'stand for' the full sentence in (59):

(59)   *Cheannaich Iain leabhar do Anna an de*
              'Iain bought a book for Anna yesterday'

(60)   Q: *An do cheannaich Iain labhar do Anna an dé?*
              'Did Iain buy a book for Anna yesterday?'

A: *Cheannaich*
     'Yes'
     (lit. 'Bought'. There is no single word in Gaelic for 'yes')

(61)   Q: *Cò cheannaich leabhar do Anna an dè?*
            'Who bought a book for Anna yesterday?'
       A: *(Cheannaich) Iain*
            (bought)   Iain
            'Iain (did)'

(62)   Q: *Dè cheannaich Iain do Anna an dè?*
            'What did Iain buy for Anna yesterday?'
       A: *(cheannaich) leabhar*
            (bought)   a book
            'A book'

(63)   Q: *Cò dha cheannaich Iain leabhar an dè?*
            'For whom did Iain buy a book yesterday?'
       A: *(Cheannaich) do Anna*
            (bought)   for Anna
            'For Anna'

(64)   Q: *Cuin a cheannaich Iain leabhar do Anna?*
            'When did Iain buy a book for Anna?'
       A: *(Cheannaich) an dè*
            (bought)   yesterday
            'Yesterday'

The verb is optional in those cases in which it is in parentheses. These brief examples illustrate quite clearly the principles that apply in elliptical sentences. (For question form see 4.2.5.)

4.2.4   Order of elements in structure

Generally, Gaelic is taken to be typologically a VSO language; that is to say that basically the elements are realised in the sequence verb + subject + object, as in (33), *Cheannaich Iain leabhar* (bought Iain book) 'Iain bought a book'. This order holds in simple sentences, but for some complex sentences and for some subordinate sentences, the statement must be modified.

4.2.4.1   In aspectually marked sentences we get, for example, with progressive aspect:

(65)   *Bha Iain a' ceannach an leabhair*
          was Iain at buying of the book
          'Iain was buying the book'

(For a detailed description see below 4.2.9.) Here it is the 'auxiliary' *bha* which comes in initial position and the 'lexical verb' comes after the subject. In perfective aspect, for example:

(66)   *Bha Iain air   an leabhar a cheannach*
       was Iain after the book   to buy
       'Iain had bought the book'

(see 4.2.9), both the subject and the object come before the lexical verb in sequence. What would appear to be the case in Gaelic, examining this surface sentential string, is that what we might call the pro-verb or sentence predicator comes in initial position. The pro-verb and the lexical verb may be combined or separate, and when they are combined, as they usually are in simple sentences (containing lexical verbs), then the lexical verb comes at the beginning; otherwise it does not. Pro-verbs always carry distinctions of tense. They also indicate distinctions such as those between 'state' and 'process' and between the subclasses of the latter 'event' and 'action'. The following examples illustrate these functions.

(67)   *Dh'fhalbh Iain*
       'Iain went away'

has a marked affective equivalent

(68)   *Rinn Iain falbh*
       did   Iain go-away-VN

(*rinn* being the past tense of the verb 'do/make') in which the typical dynamic-action pro-verbal element is separate from the lexical verb.

(69)   *Chaidh falbh*
       went   going-away-VN
       'There was a going away'/'People departed'

illustrates the impersonal pro-verb.

(70)   *Tha Iain a' falbh*
       is   Iain at going-away-VN
       'Iain is going away'

shows the pro-verb *tha* marking the sentence as stative, though it 'contains' a lexical verb that is normally associated with dynamic situations (see Lyons 1977: 483). (See below, 4.2.6.) Sentences with pro-verbs and lexical verbs in Gaelic are best regarded as complex sentences with the sentence containing the lexical verb embedded in that containing the pro-verb. (See MacAulay 1988.)

4.2.4.2   In non-finite subordinate clauses, for example the noun clause in (71),

(71)   *Dh'iarr Iain air Anna (i)   leabhar a cheannach*
               asked   Iain on Anna (she) a-book to buy
               'Iain asked Anna to buy a book'

the order of elements is *subject* (optional when equivalent in reference to the matrix indirect object) + *object* + *verb*; cf. (5) above and (72):

(72)   . . . *an dèidh do Iain leabhar a cheannach*
                       after   to Iain a-book to buy
               . . . after Iain had bought a book'

4.2.4.3   The unmarked sequence among complements when both are nouns or noun phrases is that the direct object precedes the indirect. When the direct object is a noun clause or when it is a noun phrase containing a relative clause the unmarked sequence is that the indirect object precedes the direct. This is also the unmarked order when either object or both objects are pronominal.

4.2.4.4   Adjuncts may intervene between any other sentence elements, but rarely intervene between verb and subject and never between verb and direct object in non-finite clauses.

4.2.5   Affirmatives and interrogatives; positives and negatives

All Gaelic sentences are either affirmative or interrogative and either positive or negative. The systems operate simultaneously. Affirmative positive sentences are the minimally marked set.

4.2.5.1   In the affirmative or interrogative set the affirmative member is formally unmarked (except in 'reported' classes; see 4.2.10).

(73)   *Bha am balach anns an sgoil*
               'The boy was in school'

(74)   *Ceannaichidh Iain an leabhar*
               'Iain will buy the book'

When the sentence proposition is questioned (*yes/no* questions) it is marked by the interrogative particle *an* which comes in sentence-initial position and by the use of the dependent version of those verbal forms (see 4.7.3), which shows the independent/dependent distinction:

(75)   *An robh am balach anns an sgoil?*
               'Was the boy in school?'

(76)   *An ceannaich Iain an leabhar?*
          'Will Iain buy the book?'

4.2.5.2   Different elements in the sentence may be questioned: that is, questions may be asked as to their identity. The simplest form of such questions inserts a question pro-form in the slot to be questioned:

(77)   *Cheannaich cò   an leabhar?*
          bought   who the book
          '*Who* (stressed) bought the book?'

The function of this (relatively uncommon) form of question, like that of its English counterpart, is to seek further information concerning the element it substitutes for, in the (usually) immediately previous piece of discourse. Any sentence element or major category within a sentence element may be questioned in this way as may the verb + complement complex:

(78)   *Cheannaich Iain dè?*
          'Iain bought what?'

(79)   *Bha an leabhar aig cò?*
          was the book at who
          '*Who* had the book?'

(80)   Q: *Rinn Iain dè?*
               'Iain did what?'
          A: *Cheannaich e   leabhar* or   *(Rinn) leabhar a cheannach*
               bought   he book   (did) a-book to buy
                        'He bought a book'

4.2.5.3   The commonest form of this type of question has the question elements in first position in the sentence (where primary sentence class markers normally occur) and the verb in relative form, indicating that the clause containing it was in origin embedded,

(81)   *Cò   a   bha anns an sgoil?*
          who REL was in   the school

(82)   *Dè   a   cheannaich Iain?*
          What REL bought   Iain
          'What did Iain buy?'

Generally, such questions follow the same structural model where nominals are concerned. The adverbial locational question pro-form *càite*, however, is followed by the dependent form of the verb:

(83)   *Càite an   robh   Iain?*
          where PART was-DEP Iain
          'Where was Iain?'

whereas all other adverbial question elements (like nominal ones) are followed by relative forms; for example:

(84)   *Cuin a   cheannaich Iain an leabhar?*
       when REL bought   Iain the book
       'When did Iain buy the book?'

4.2.5.4   Questions involving prepositional phrases reflect the complexity of highlighting involved in such structures. (See (79) above and 4.2.12 below.)

(85)   *Cò dha   a   bhitheas Iain a' toirt   an leabhair?*
       who (to-PRON-3SG-MASC) REL will-be   Iain at giving-VN the book-GEN
       'To whom will Iain be giving the book?'

means the same as

(86)(a)   *Cò do'm bi   Iain a' toirt   an lebhair?*
          who to PT will-be Iain at giving the book-GEN

In the former case the whole of the prepositional phrase is questioned: in the latter the nominal within the prepositional phrase is questioned. This is further complicated by the occurrence of a third version:

(86)(b)   *Cò a bhitheas Iain a'toirt an leabhair dha?*
          who REL will be Iain at giving the book-GEN to him

4.2.5.5   Questions such as (87) and (88)

(87)   *An e am balach a bha anns an sgoil?*
       'Was it the boy who was in school?'

(88)   *An ann anns an sgoil a bha am balach?*
       'Was it in school that the boy was?'

are question versions of topicalised sentences; for example:

(89)   *Is e am balach a bha anns an sgoil*
       'It is the boy who was in school'

(90)   *Is ann anns an sgoil a bha am balach*
       'It is in school that the boy was'

They relate to (81) above (for example) in that in (81) the lexical slot questioned is empty whereas in (87)–(90) it is not (see also 4.2.7 below on the functions of *is*).

4.2.5.6   There are four kinds of tag questions, two with reversed and two with similar polarities. Those with reversed polarities are leading questions, for example (see 4.2.5.8 for negative questions):

(91)   *Tha am balach anns an sgoil, nach eil?*
       'The boy is in school, is he not?'

(92)   *Is e am balach a tha anns an sgoil, an e?*
        'It is the boy who is in school, is it?'

(93)   *Chan eil   am balach anns an sgoil,   a   bheil?*
        NEG is-DEP the boy   in   the school, INTER.PT is-DEP
        'The boy is not in school, is he?'

(94)   *Chan e am balach a tha anns an sgoil, an e?*
        'It is not the boy who is in school, is it?'

Each of these expects agreement with the preposition of the initial sentence.
The two types with similar polarities are,

(95)   *Tha am balach anns an sgoil, a bheil?*
        'The boy is in school, is he?'

(96)   *Chan eil am balach anns an sgoil, nach eil?*
        'The boy is not in school, isn't he?'

4.2.5.7   Positive sentences are the unmarked member of the positive–
negative system. Negative sentences contain a negative particle which comes in
sentence-initial position and the verb is in the dependent form:

(97)   *Chaidh am balach don sgoil*
        'The boy went to school'

(98)   *Cha deachaidh am balach don   sgoil*
        NEG went-DEP the boy   to-the school
        'The boy did not go to school'

In (98) the sentence proposition is negated. Different elements in the sentence
may be negated using topicalising devices identical to those used for questioning
elements (see (87)–(90) above and 4.2.12 below), for example,

(99)   *Chan e am balach a chaidh don sgoil*
        'It is not the boy who went to school'

(100)   *Chan ann don sgoil a chaidh am balach*
        'It is not to school the boy went'

4.2.5.8   In questions and in finite dependent clauses the negative particle is
nach:

(101)   *Nach   deachaidh am balach don   sgoil?*
        NEG-INTER went-DEP the boy   to-the school
        'Did the boy not go to school?'

(102)   *Nach e am balach nach deachaidh don sgoil?*
        'Is it not the boy who did not go to school?'

(103)   *Thubhairt Iain nach deachaidh am balach don sgoil*
        'Iain said that the boy did not go to school'

4.2.5.9   In non-finite clauses the negative particle is realised as *gun*:

(104)   *Thubhairt Iain gun am balach a dhol don   sgoil*
          said   Iain NEG the boy   to go to-the school
          'Iain said the boy should not go to school'

(105)   *Chaidh am balach don   sgoil gun Iain a fhaicinn*
          went   the boy to-the school NEG Iain his seeing-VN
          'The boy went to school without Iain seeing him'

Gun is the form of the negative generally in nominalisations. It is in origin the privative preposition and operates as 'negative' correlate of *le*; for example:

(106)   POSITIVE: . . . *duine le   càr*
                         a-man with a-car
          NEGATIVE: . . . *duine gun   chàr*
                         a-man without a-car

Nominalisations with *gun* can occur in any appropriate position; for example:

(107)   POSITIVE: *Tha a bhith ag òl   bainne   gu   math dhuit*
                    is   to be at drinking-VN milk-GEN ADV.PT good for-you
                    'Drinking milk is good for you'

          NEGATIVE: *Tha gun a bhith ag òl   bainne   gu*
                    is   NEG to be at drinking-VN milk-GEN ADV.PT
                    math dhuit
                    good for-you
                    'Not drinking milk is good for you'

4.2.6   Active and passive sentences

There are both active and passive sentences in Gaelic. The active class is divided into personal and impersonal subclasses. Impersonal sentences are often the translation equivalents of English passives. Passive sentences are complex, involving embedding in much the same way as indicated for sentences with 'auxiliary' verbs at 4.2.4.1 above.

4.2.6.1   In the personal active sentences

(108)   *Dh'ol am balaich am bainne*
          'The boy drank the milk'

(109)   *Dh'òl e am bainne*
          'He drank the milk'

the agent *am balach* is cited lexically in the former and pronominally in the latter. In the impersonal sentence (110),

(110)   *Dh'òladh   am bainne*
          drank-IMPERS the milk
          'The milk was drunk'

neither lexical nor personal information is given, and this is marked by the impersonal ending -*adh* (see 4.7.5 below).

4.2.6.2   The same impersonal notion is also expressed in structures such as (111):

(111)   *Chaidh am bainne òl*
           went   the milk   drink-VN
           'The milk was drunk'

The verb *chaidh*, 'went' is used as an auxiliary with the sense 'happened', 'came to pass' and *am bainne òl* is the 'nominalised' sentential subject of the sentence. This version has no agentive implication. It is a common correlate of English passives, though it is somewhat difficult to find a real English equivalent for a sentence such as (112):

(112)   *Chaidh falbh*
           went   departing-VN
           'A departing was effected (?)'

(which, to say the least, is entirely the wrong register).

    Normally, in Scottish Gaelic we do not find an agent in such sentences as (110)–(112), but it is possible (especially arising as a calque on English usage):

(113)   *Dh'òladh   am bainne leis na cait*
           drank IMPERS the milk   *by the cats*
           'The milk was drunk by the cats'

(114)   *Chaidh am bainne òl   leis na cait*
           went   the milk   drink-VN *by the cats*
           'The milk was drunk by the cats'

'*Le*' is the instrumental preposition in Gaelic, not, normally, the agentive one; for example (115) but not (116):

(115)   *Mharbhadh Iain leis a'ghunna*
           'Iain was killed with the gun'

(116)   *Mharbadh Iain le Calum*
           meaning 'Iain was killed by Calum'

4.2.6.3   Genuinely passive sentences where the 'sufferer' is in sentence subject position are restricted to those that are aspectually marked; for example:

(117)   *Tha Iain ga   mharbhadh*
           is   Iain at-his killing
           'Iain is being killed'

The sentence has the sense 'Iain is killing him' when the subject and the pronoun infixed in the predicate refer to different persons (see 4.2.8 and 4.2.9 below).

The reflexive is expressed as in (118):

(118)   *Tha Iain ga   mharbhadh fhèin*
          is   Iain at-his killing-VN   self
          'Iain is killing himself'

(*fhèin* being the reflexive postclitic (see 4.3.8).

Genuine passives may take agents:

(119)   *Tha Iain ga   mharbhadh aca*
          is   Iain at-his killing-VN   at-them
          'Iain is being killed by them'

(120)   *Tha Iain air   a   mharbhadh aca*
          is   Iain after his killing-VN   at-them
          'Iain has been killed by them'

4.2.6.4   It is also possible to say (121) and (122):

(121)   *Tha Iain marbh   aca*
          is   Iain dead   at-them
          'Iain has been killed by them'

(122)   *Tha Iain leònte   aca*
          is   Iain wounded at-them
          'Iain has been wounded by them'

using the verb *tha* (*not* as an 'auxiliary') followed by a deverbal adjective and a past participle respectively.

4.2.7   'Being' sentences

There are two verbs 'to be' in Gaelic, *is* and *tha*, traditionally called the 'copula' and the 'substantive' verbs respectively (Anderson 1909; 1910). As these historical functions are no longer strictly maintained we will avoid the use of these labels here.

4.2.7.1   *Tha* is primarily the *stative* verb. It functions thus in classificatory sentences with adjectival complements such as (123):

(123)   *Tha an càr mòr*
          'The car is large'

in locative sentences such as (124):

(124)   *Tha an càr air an rathad*
          'The car is on the road'

and in aspectually marked sentences (as the stative 'auxiliary', so called);

(125)   *Tha an càr a' siubhal*
          'The car is travelling'

4.2.7.2   *Tha* is the verb used in existential sentences in conjunction with *ann*, the preposition *an*, 'in', combined with the third singular masculine pronoun (the unmarked form (see 4.6.8), which we may conveniently write as 'in-it'):

(126)   *Tha Dia ann*
         is   God in 3SG-MASC-PRON (= in-it)
         'God exists'

(127)   *Tha daoine ann a   chanas nach eil Dia ann*
         is   people in-it REL say   NEG is God in-it
         'There are people who say that God does not exist'

4.2.7.3   Not all usages of *tha . . . ann* are existential:

(128)   *Tha an t-Earrach ann*
         is   the spring   in-it

meaning 'It is spring', as well as 'There is such a thing as spring'.

(129)   *Tha an t-uisge ann*
         is   the rain   in-it
         'It is raining'

(130)   *Tha am èirigh   ann*
         is   time rising-GEN in-it
         'It is time to get up'

Examples (128)–(130) can hardly be given convincing existential senses.

4.2.7.4   *Tha* with the preposition 'in' also occurs in complex classificatory sentences:

(131)   *Tha Iain 'na   shaighdear*
         is   Iain in 3SG-MASC-PRON (*in-his*; for convenience) soldier
         'Iain is a soldier'

(132)   *Tha Anna 'na   h-oileanach*
         is   Anna in-her student
         'Anna is a student'

There is obligatory agreement between the embedded pronoun of the predicate and the subject nominal. The translation 'in-his', 'in-her' simply reflects the pronoun's position in pre-head, typically 'possessive' position. A similar structure marks the static member of static vs dynamic pairs such as (133) and (134):

(133)   *Tha an duine a' suidhe*
         is   the man at sitting-VN
         'The man is sitting down (i.e. becoming seated)'

(134)   *Tha an duine 'na   shuidhe*
         is   the man in-his sitting
         'The man is sitting down (i.e. seated)'

4.2.7.5   *Is*, too, occurs in classificatory sentences:

(135)   *Is duine Iain*
          'Iain is a man'

Such sentences commonly denote inalienable class membership, but this does not always hold:

(136)   *Is iasgair   gun   fheum am fear sin!*
          is a-fisherman without use   the one there
          'That one is a useless fisherman!'

Is occurs in sentences with adjectival complements:

(137)   *Is math sin!*
          is good that
          'That is good!'

(138)   *Is gòrach an duine Iain!*
          is foolish the man Iain
          'Iain is a foolish man!'

(139)   *Is motha Iain na   Anna*
          is taller Iain than Anna
          'Iain is taller than Anna'

In all these examples, instead of the normal order, verb + subject + complement, we get the order verb + complement + subject.

4.2.7.6   The VCS order of (136)–(138) and to some degree of (139) denotes affective usage. One of the main functions of *is* in contemporary Gaelic is in topicalisation (see 4.2.12), for example:

(140)   *Is mise   a   cheannaich an leabhar*
          is I-SPEC REL bought   the book
          'It is I who bought the book'

When the highlighted nominal element is realised lexically *is* is supported by *e* the third singular masculine pronoun:

(141)   *'S e   Iain a   cheannaich an leabhar*
          is 3SG MASC PRON Iain REL bought   the book
          'It is Iain who bought the book'

When adverbial elements are highlighted *is* is supported by *ann* (see 4.2.12.1).

4.2.7.7   *Is* occurs exclusively in equative sentences (with the normal order of elements).

(142)   *Is mise am fear a   cheannaich an leabhar*
          is I-SPEC the man REL bought   the book
          'I am the man who bought the book'

If the subject is a lexically realised nominal *is* again is supported, this time by *e* (see 4.2.7.6)

(143)   *'S e Iain am fear a   cheannaich an leabhar*
          is he Iain the man REL bought   the book
          'Iain is the man who bought the book'

The sentences in 4.2.7.6 and 4.2.7.7 appear to differ only in that the former do not contain *am fear* before the relative. It is reasonable to assume that (140) and (141) are versions of (142) and (143) respectively where *am fear* has been deleted under identity conditions, *e*, *Iain* and *am fear* all referring to the same referent. Therefore (140) and (141) are equative sentences.

4.2.8   Locative and possessive sentences

There is no possessive verb (e.g. equivalent to *have*, *avoir*, *haben*) in Gaelic. Possession is expressed sententially by structures similar to locatives, utilising the prepositions *aig*, 'at' and *le*, 'with'.

4.2.8.1   The following set of sentences demonstrates the relative operation of possessives and locatives utilising the preposition *aig*:

(144)   *Tha am balach aig a' bhòrd*
         is   the boy   at the table

(145)   *Tha am balach aig a' chù*
         is   the boy   at the dog

(146)   *Tha an cat aig a' chù*
         is   the cat at the dog

(147)   *Tha am bòrd aig a' chù*
         is   the table at the dog

(148)   *Tha an cù aig a' bhalach*
         is   the dog at the boy

(149)   *Tha am bòrd aig a' bhalach*
         is   the table at the boy

(150)   *Tha Iain aig Màiri*
         is   Iain at Màiri

(151)   *Tha am bòrd aig an dorus*
         is   the table at the door

Each of these sentences may be neutrally formulated as 'X to be located with relation to Y': that is, as a basic locative. The English translation of (144) is 'The boy is at the table', a locative sentence, as is (151) 'The table is at the door'. The equivalents of (148) and (149) 'The boy has got the dog', 'The boy has got the table' are, normally, equally clearly 'possessive'. Example (147) would have a normal 'possessive' equivalent 'The dog has got the table'. Sentences (145) and (146) could have either the 'locative' or the 'possessive' reading, with the 'locative' 'The boy is at (e.g. attending to) the dog' probably preferred for (145), but the 'possessive' 'The dog has got the boy' equally possible; and the 'possessive' 'The dog has got the cat' (it would also be true for 'The cat has got the dog', or 'The frog has got the elephant') as first reading for (146) but with the 'locative', 'The cat is at (beside) the dog', possible. What this shows is that (all things being equal) when the locative-phrase noun is of higher value, on a rising 'animacy' scale *inanimate–animate–human*, than the subject phrase noun, then the normal reading is 'possessive'. When the reverse is the case then the normal reading is 'locative'. When the values are equal and both 'inanimate' the reading is 'locative': for example, (151) 'The table is at the door'. When both nouns are 'human' the normal reading is 'possessive', as in (150) 'Màiri has got Iain', but the 'locative' reading is possible: for example, with extended meaning, 'Iain is visiting Màiri'.

4.2.8.2   The difference in usage in sentences (the rules in the noun phrase are different: see 4.3.11) with *aig* and *le* is that the former denotes 'in the possession of', the latter 'belonging to'; for example:

(152)   *Tha an cù aig Iain*
           'Iain has got the dog'

(153)   *Tha an cù le Iain*
           'The dog belongs to Iain'

In adjunctal phrases, however, *le* has the comitative sense 'with':

(154)   *Bha Iain ann le   cù*
           was Iain in-it with a-dog
           'Iain was there *with a dog*'

4.2.9   Aspectually marked sentences

There are three basic aspectual forms in Scottish Gaelic: *progressive*, *perfective* and *prospective*.

4.2.9.1   *Progressive* denotes ongoing events relative to a point in time (see 4.7.4). It is expressed in the complement of the verb *tha* by means of the preposition *ag* (*a'* before consonants; it is *aig* before nouns), dominating the 'verb(al) noun', as this element, the bare non-finite lexical verb, is traditionally referred to in Celtic grammars.

(155)   *Tha am balach a' falbh*
               is   the boy   at leaving-VN
               'The boy is leaving'

In (156a) the complement of the preposition is a more complex phrase:

(156)(a)   *Tha am balach a' ceannach an leabhair*
               is   the boy   at buying-VN the book-GEN
               'The boy is buying the book'

Here the lexical verb (or verb(al) noun) is the head of the endocentric construction, basically similar to that of the noun phrase (see 4.3), with the object of that verb in dependent genitive relationship to it. In (156b)

(156)(b)   *Tha am balach ga   cheannach*
               is   the boy   at-3SG-MASC-PRON buying-VN
               'The boy is buying it'

the object of the verb is pronominal and combines with it as a preposed dependent pronoun, similar to a possessive pronoun (see 4.3.11).

4.2.9.2   Perfective aspect is similarly expressed

(157)   *Tha am balach air   falbh*
               is   the boy   after leaving-VN
               'The boy has left'

(158)(a)   *Tha am balach air   an leabhar a cheannach*
               is   the boy   after the book   to buy-INF
               'The boy has bought the book'

(158)(b)   *Tha am balach air   a cheannach*
               is   the boy   after it-3SG-MASC-PRON buying-VN
               'The boy has bought it'

There are, however, some differences. Comparing (156a) and (158a) we see that whereas *ag* is followed by an endocentric, phrasal, construction, *air* is followed by an exocentric, clausal, construction such as we find, for example, in clausal complements of reporting verbs (see 4.2.10). When the object of the verb in these clausal constructions is pronominal, however, the expressions after *aig* and *air* are identical, that is, the pronominal object appears as a preposed 'possessive' pronoun dependent on the verb–noun as head of an endocentric construction (see (156b) and (158b)).

Should these pronominal objects be modified (by the specifying or reflexive enclitic, for example), however, different rules govern their expression after *aig* and *air*, as follows:

(159)   *Tha an duine gam mharbhadh*
               is   the man at-1SG-PRON killing-VN
               'The man is killing me'

(160)   *Tha an duine gam   mharbhadh sa*
             is   the man at-1SG-PRON killing-VN   SPEC
             'The man is killing *me*'

(161)   *Tha an duine ga   mharbhadh fhèin*
             is   the man at-3SG-MASC-PRON killing-VN   self
             'The man is killing himself'

(162)   *Tha an duine air   mo   mharbhadh*
             is   the man after 1SG-PRON killing-VN
             'The man has killed me'

(163)   *Tha an duine air   mise   a mharbhadh*
             is   the man after 1SG-PRON-SPEC to kill-INF
             'The man has killed me'

(164)   *Tha an duine air   e-fhèin   a mharbhadh*
             is   the man after 3SG-MASC-PRON-self to kill-INF
             'The man has killed himself'

With these modifications of the pronoun, *ag* allows endocentric constructions but *air* does not.

In the matter of usage, the present perfect is relatively rare in Scottish Gaelic, though its use is increasing under the influence of English. The simple past is used in many cases where English would use the present perfect.

4.2.9.3   *Prospective aspect* is expressed in constructions syntactically identical with those expressing the perfective. The preposition *gu(s)* basically meaning 'to' is used.

(165)   *Tha an duine gus falbh*
             'The man is about to leave'

(166)   *Tha an duine gus   an leabhar a cheannach*
             is   the man towards the book   to buy-INF
             'The man is about to buy the book'

(167)   *Tha an duine gus   a cheannach*
             is   the man towards 3SG-MASC-PRON to buy-VN
             'The man is about to buy it'

(168)(a)   *Tha an duine gus   e-fhèin a mharbhadh*
             is   the man towards himself to kill
             'The man is about to kill himself'

Sentences (165)–(168a) can have two senses equivalent to, to take (168a) as an example, 'The man is about to (complete) kill(ing) himself' the primary reading, and 'The man is to kill himself' a reading typically found with time adverbials denoting a time remote from the time of the action of the main verb, for example:

(168)(b)   *'Tha an duine gus e-fhèin a mharbhadh, a màireach*
         'The man is to kill himself, tomorrow'

All verbs that have a potential *completive* sense display this sense after *gus*: the translation equivalent of (169)

(169)   *Tha Iain gus   a   dhìnner ithe*
         is   Iain towards his dinner   to-eat-INF

is not 'Iain is about to eat his dinner' but 'Iain is about to finish his dinner'. The Gaelic equivalent of the former would be

(170)   *Tha Iain gus tòiseachadh air a dhìnnear*
         'Iain is about to begin his dinner'

The inceptive feature has to be given specific realisation in Gaelic and the completive in English.

4.2.9.4   These aspects can combine in the following manner:

1 *Perfective + progressive*

(171)   *Tha Iain air   a   bhith a' togail   an taighe*
         is   Iain after to be   at building the house-GEN
         'Iain has been building the house'

2 *Prospective + progressive*

(172)   *Tha Iain gus   a   bhith a' togail   an taighe*
         is   Iain towards to be   at building the house-GEN
         'Iain is about to be building the house'

3 *Perfective + prospective*

(173)   *Tha Iain air   a   bhith gus   an taigh a   thogail (o chionn bliadhna)*
         is   Iain after to be   towards the house to build . . .
         'Iain has been about to build (i.e. complete) the house (for a year)'

4 *Prospective + perfective*

(174)   *Tha Iain gus   a   bhith air   an taigh a   thogail*
         is   Iain towards to be   after the house to build
         'Iain has been about to have built the house'

5 *Perfective + prospective + progressive*

(175)   *Tha Iain air   a   bhith gus   a   bhith a' togail   an taighe*
         is   Iain after to be   towards to be   at building the house-GEN
         'Iain has been about to be building the house'

6 *Prospective + perfective + progressive*

(176)   *Tha Iain gus   a bhith air   a bhith a' togail   an taighe*
          is   Iain towards to be   after to be   at building the house-GEN
          dà   bhliadhna
          two year
          ?'Iain is about to have been building the house for two years'

Double perfectives are sometimes encountered:

(177)   *Bha e   air   a bhith air   a   dhinnear ithe   uair a thìde roimh'n sin*
          was he after to be   after his dinner   to-eat hour of time before   that

It is usually, but not exclusively, found in past perfects and appears to have the
same sense basically as the ordinary past perfect: 'He had finished his dinner an
hour before'.

4.2.9.5   Predictive aspect

Expressions such as we see in English 'Iain is going to buy the book' are
sometimes classed as aspectual (see Comrie 1986: 64–5). Gaelic has a parallel
expression:

(178)   *Tha Iain a' dol   a cheannach an   leabhair*
          is   Iain at going to buy   the book-GEN
          'Iain is going to buy the book'

This normally would denote *intention* and would therefore be better treated as a
modal usage. It may, however, operate simply as a prediction. When we
compare it with sentences such as (179) and (180):

(179)   *Tha Iain a' dol a thuiteam*
          'Iain is going to fall'

(180)   *Tha Iain a' dol a bhàsachadh*
          'Iain is going to die'

it is clear that sentences with *a' dol* can have a range of senses. *Intention* is
confined to sentences with actor/agentive subjects such as (178); (179) and (180)
have 'experiencer' subjects, the former is a simple prediction, the latter a simple
prediction or a prediction based on a universal truth. We could say, then, that *a'
dol* basically expresses *predictive* aspect, and is capable of expressing additional
senses when governed by the appropriate contexts.

4.2.9.6   Iteratives and habituals

These are dealt with below (4.7.4.4).

4.2.10   Clausal complements

Certain classes of verb take clausal complements. They are, basically, reporting verbs, request verbs, command verbs and causative verbs. Many members of these classes, apart from causitives, can take direct speech sentential complements on the model of (181):

(181)   *Thubhairt Ian, 'Tha an latha fuar'*
             'Iain said, "The day is cold"'

4.2.10.1   The basic verb of reporting is the (irregular) verb *abair*, 'say'. It takes a finite clause complement:

(182)   *Thubhairt Iain ri Anna gun robh   an latha fuar*
             said   Iain to Anna AFF was-DEP the day cold
             'Iain said to Anna that the day was cold'

The verb *innis* 'tell' takes a similar type of complement:

(183)   *Dh'innis Iain do Anna nach   do cheannaich e an leabhar*
             told   Iain to Anna NEG-DEP PT bought   he the book

4.2.10.2   The basic verb for requesting information is *faighnich* 'ask'. It operates similarly to 'abair' except that the complement clause is introduced by a question (INTER) rather than an affirmative particle:

(184)   *Dh'fhaighnich Iain do Anna an do   cheannaich i   an leabhar*
             asked   Iain to Anna INTER PT bought   she the book
             'Iain asked Anna if she bought the book'

The verb for requesting things and actions is *iarr*: it takes a non-finite clause complement:

(185)   *Dh'iarr Iain air Anna (i)   an leabhar a cheannach*
             asked   Iain on Anna (she) the book   to buy
             'Iain asked Anna to buy the book'

4.2.10.3   *Abair* is also used as a command verb. In that case it takes a non-finite clause complement (cf. (182)):

(186)   *Thubhairt Iain ri Anna (i)   an leabhar a cheannach*
             said   Iain to Anna (she) the book   to buy
             'Iain told Anna to buy the book'

4.2.10.4   The basic causative construction also takes a non-finite clause complement:

(187)   *Thug Iain air Anna (i)   an leabhar a thoirt do Mhàiri*
          gave Iain on Anna (she) the book   to give to Màiri
          'Iain made Anna give the book to Màiri'

An agentless version of this sentence is:

(188)   *Thàinig air Anna an leabhar a thoirt do Mhàiri*
          came   on Anna the book   to give to Màiri
          'Anna had to give the book to Màiri'

Here we have not a clausal complement but a clausal subject.

4.2.11   Modal sentences

The syntax of modal sentences is in some respects similar to that expounded in 4.2.10:

(189)   *Feumaidh Iain an leabhar a cheannach*
          must   Iain the book   to buy
          'Iain must buy the book'

has a modal verb with a non-finite clausal complement, as has (190):

(190)   *Faodaidh Iain an leabhar a cheannach*
          may   Iain the book   to buy
          'Iain may (is permitted) to buy the book'

The negative version of (189)

(189)(a) *Chan fheum Iain an leabhar a cheannach*
          NEG must   Iain the book   to buy

means 'Iain *need* not buy the book'. 'Iain *must not* buy the book' is translated either by the negative version of (190) in (190a) or (191):

(190)(a) *Chan fhaod Iain an leabhar a cheannach*
          NEG may   Iain the book   to buy

(191)   *Feumaidh Iain gun an leabhar a cheannach*
          must   Iain NEG the book   to buy

with the negative in the embedded sentence of the complement.

4.2.11.1   Some modal sentences are introduced by the verb *is* followed by modal complements; for example, *is fheudar* (necessity), *is còir* (obligation) and *is urrainn* (ability). These have non-finite clausal subjects, for example:

(192)   *Is còir do Iain an leabhar a cheannach*
          is right to Iain the book   to buy
          'Iain should buy the book'

4.2.11.2   Modal sentences such as (193) take finite clausal subjects:

(193)   *Is dòcha   nach do cheannaich Iain an leabhar*
          is possible NEG bought   Iain the book
          'Perhaps Iain didn't buy the book'

4.2.12   Types of topicalisation

Marked order of elements such as occur in the following type of sentence serve
to highlight such elements in discourse

(194)   *Aig an dorus chunnaic mi Iain*
          'At the door I saw Iain˙

(195)   *Iain chunnaic mi ach Anna chan fhaca*
          'Iain I saw but Anna I did not'

4.2.12.1   The most common kind of topicalised sentence, however, does not
involve the re-ordering of internal elements. It is a sentence with the verb *is*
followed by the element topicalised (if that is a pronoun or an adjective; if it is
not, *is* is re-inforced by *e* (the unmarked pronoun) if the highlighted element is
nominal and by *ann*, 'in-it', if it is not; see 4.2.7.6).

4.2.12.2   Different sentence elements may be topicalised. If we take the
unmarked sentence *Thug Iain an leabhar do Anna an dè*, 'Iain gave the book to
Anna yesterday', we get sentences which we might see as topicalisation versions
of this sentence in which

          1 the subject is topicalised:

(196)   *Is e   Iain a   thug an leabhar do Anna an dè*
          is 3SG-MASC-PRON Iain REL gave the book   to Anna yesterday
          'It is Iain who gave the book to Anna yesterday'

          2 the direct object is topicalised:

(197)   *Is e   an leabhar a   thug Iain do Anna an dè*
          is 3SG-MASC-PRON the book   REL gave Iain to Anna yesterday
          'It is the book that Iain gave to Anna yesterday'

          3 the indirect object is topicalised:

(198)   *Is ann do Anna a   thug Iain an leabhar an dè*
          is in-it to Anna REL gave Iain the book   yesterday
          'It is to Anna that Iain gave the book yesterday'

4 the adjunct is topicalised:

(199)   *Is ann an dè   a   thug Iain an leabhar do Anna*
             is in-it yesterday REL gave Iain the book   to Anna
             'It was yesterday that Iain gave the book to Anna'

4.2.12.3   The complements of aspectual sentences appear in topicalisations, for example:

(200)   *Is ann a' toirt   an leabhair   to Anna a   bha Iain*
             is in-it at giving-VN the book-GEN to Anna REL was Iain
             *'It was giving the book to Anna that Iain was'

4.2.12.4   In addition, items that are not sentence elements may feature in topicalisation, for example, the noun phrase in a prepositional phrase

(201)   *Is e   Anna do'n tug   Iain an leabhar*
             is PRON Anna to-PT gave Iain the book
             'It was Anna to whom Iain gave the book'.

STRUCTURE OF THE PHRASE

4.3   STRUCTURE OF THE NOMINAL PHRASE

The nominal phrase has an endocentric structure consisting of a *head* element around which cluster *modifier* elements:

(202)   *an dà bhàta gheal aig Iain*
             the two boats white at Iain
             'Iain's two white boats'

4.3.1   Order of elements

As (202) demonstrates, modifiers may be either pre-head or post-head. Normally, individual modifiers operate independently, but in some cases the presence of a post-head element requires the presence of a certain preceding pre-head item, for example reflexives in most instances (see 4.3.9).

4.3.1.1   Pre-head modifiers, reading right to left and beginning with the one nearest to the head, are exemplified by the following:

(203)(a)   *deagh bhàta*   '(a) good boat'
     (b)   *dà dheagh bhàta*   'two good boats'

(c)	*a' cheud dà dheagh bhàta*	'the first two good boats'
(d)	*an aon cheud dà dheagh bhàta*	'the same first two good boats'

In first position comes the *definite article*, followed by the *identifier*, followed by *ordinals* (both of these require the definite article to be present); followed by *cardinals* followed by *pre-head epithet* virtually confined to the set *deagh* 'good', *droch* 'bad', *fìor* 'real' and *sean* 'old'. The pre-head *possessive pronoun* occupies the same position as the definite article. They cannot of course co-occur. These pronouns are specified as definite (see 4.3.11).

4.3.1.2   Post-head modifiers reading left to right from the head are exemplified by the following:

(204)(a)	*bàta mòr*, 'large boat'
(b)	*bàta mòr fiodha*, 'large wooden boat'
(c)	*bàta mòr fiodha le siùil*, 'large wooden boat with sails'

leading on to a 'maximal co-occurrence' set of classes like:

(d) *am bàta mòr fiodha le   siùl sin eile   le   Iain a   chunnaic mi an dè*
the boat big wooden with sails that other with Iain REL saw   I   yester-
                                                                          day
'that other big wooden boat with sails belonging to Iain that I saw yesterday'

Immediately after the head come *adjectivals* (see 4.3.13 for subclasses), followed by epithets of *substance* followed by *non-finite clausals* (see 4.3.2.3) followed by *post-deictics* (see 4.3.6), followed by *post-possessives* (see 4.3.11), followed by finite *clausal* modifiers.

4.3.2   Embedding: phrasal and clausal modifiers

Phrasal modifiers are of two kinds: nominal and prepositional. Clausal modifiers are either finite relative clauses or non-finite clauses. All occur post-head.

4.3.2.1   Nominal-phrase modifiers are most commonly noun phrases in the genitive case, for example (205) or (206):

(205)	*seòl a' bhàta mhòir*
	sail (the boat big-GEN)
	'the sail of the big boat'
(206)	*bàta mac Chaluim*
	boat (son Calum-GEN)
	'Calum's son's boat'

These modifying phrases are open to the same modifications as occur in primary phrases:

(207)   *bàta an duine bhochd gun iasg a chunnaic sinn an dè*
           'the boat of the poor man without fish we saw yesterday'

It is also possible to have progressive embedding:

(208)   *bàta mac Iain   mac Sheumais   mac Dhomhnaill . . .*
           boat son Iain-GEN son Seumas-GEN son Donald-GEN . . .
           'the son of Iain son of Seumas son of Donald's . . .boat'

Such embedding, in contrast to English, is strictly right-branching.

4.3.2.2   Prepositional-phrase modifiers operate similarly:

(209)   *am bàta aig a' bhalach aig an nighinn aig Iain*
           the boat at the boy   at the girl   at Iain
           'Iain's daughter's boy's boat'

4.3.2.3   Non-finite clausal modifiers introduce *le* (or in some cases *is*) and their negative counterpart, *gun*:

(210)   *am bàta mòr le/is seòl geal   oirre*
           the boat large POS sail white on-it
           'the large boat with a white sail (on it)'

(211)   *bàta gun seòl idir oirre*
           boat NEG sail at-all on-it
           'a boat without a sail on it at all'

Clearly, what follows the *le/is* and *gun* is clausal rather than phrasal in structure. It might be argued that it constitutes the head of a prepositional phrase, since *le* seems to operate as a preposition elsewhere in the system. This, however, would be hard to sustain.

   Multiple (central) embedding may occur here:

(212)   *fear is bàta le seòl le dealbh faoileig   air   aige*
           man POS boat POS sail POS picture seagull-GEN on-it at-him
           'a man with a boat with a sail with a picture of a seagull on it'

4.3.2.4   Relative clauses are the rightmost elements in the noun phrase. Right embedding of the 'house that Jack built' type are theoretically infinite and do not present problems of understanding:

(213)   *am fear a chaisg an cù a bhìd an cat a mharbh an luch* etc.
           'the man that stopped the dog that bit the cat that killed the mouse' etc.

Centre-embedding sequences are limited by comprehension problems:

(214)   *am bàta a   chuala am balach a   chunnaic Iain a   chaidh fodha*
        the boat that heard the boy   that saw   Iain that went under
        'the boat that the boy Iain saw heard had gone down'

4.3.3   Submodification

Submodification occurs in a range of both pre-head and post-head positions. The submodifier *cha mhòr* 'almost' occurs ubiquitously as in English. *Fìor* occurs as an intensifier submodifier with the set of pre-head epithets; for example:

(215)   *fìor dhroch latha*
        'very bad day'

The normal post-head intensifier is *glè*; other versions *eagalach*, *uamhasach*, 'fearful', 'awful', etc., are also used as in English. They intensify adjectives:

(216)(a)   *latha glè   mhath*
           day very good
           'very good day'

    (b)   *latha uamhasach dona*
           day awful   bad
           'awfully bad day'

Perhaps the most common traditional method of adjective intensification is repetition; for example:

(217)   *latha math math*
        'a good, good day'

4.3.4   Systems of the noun phrase

It will not be possible here to deal in detail with the very complex set of intersecting systems that operate in the noun phrase. The following gives a brief account of some of the more important ones.

4.3.5   Definiteness and indefiniteness

There are two intersecting systems involving these categories in which 'indefinite' contrasts with 'definite' and with 'marked indefinite'. We would characterise these systems as [+DEF] vs [−DEF] and [+INDEF] vs [−INDEF].

4.3.5.1   The distinction between [+DEF] and [−DEF] is realised by the presence of the article in [+DEF] phrases and its absence in [−DEF] ones;

(218)(a)   *am bàta mòr*
            'the large boat'

   (b)   *bàta mòr*
            '(a) large boat'

4.3.5.2   The basic function of the article is to denote the head as 'given' rather than 'new' or 'first mention'. Contextually referring elements such as pronouns, therefore, do not co-occur with the article. Some elements such as *ordinals* (with unspecified nouns) and certain *deictics* and *post-possessives*, on the other hand, can occur only in marked definite phrases; for example:

(219)(a)   *a' cheud bhàta*
            'the first boat'

   (b)   *am bàta sa*
            the boat this
            'this boat'

   (c)   *am bàta agam*
            the boat at-me
            'my boat'

4.3.5.3   In phrases with definite noun-phrase modifiers there is a strict rule which requires definiteness to be marked only once, whatever the degree of embedding:

(220)(a)   *seòl a' bhàta mhòir*
            sail (the boat large-GEN)
            'the sail of the large boat'

   (b)   *seòl bàta mòr an   iasgair*
            sail (boat large (the fisherman-GEN))
            'the sail of the fisherman's large boat'

The definiteness is marked in the final embedded phrase. (Genitive marking often occurs only in that phrase also.)

4.3.5.4   Marked indefinites contain [+INDEF] postmodifiers such a *sam bith* or *air choreigin*, for example:

(221)(a)   *bàta sam bith*
            'any boat'

   (b)   *bàta air choreigin*
            'some boat or other'

Certain pro-formal nouns, such as *fear* 'one' (masc.), *tè* 'one' (fem.), *cuid* 'some', *rud* 'thing', *àit* 'place', *uair* 'time', etc., are converted into marked indefinites by the appending of *-eigin*; for example:

(222)(a)   *fear-eigin*
           'someone' (MASC)
    (b)   *rud-eigin*
           'something'
    (c)   *àit-eigin*
           'somewhere'

4.3.6   Deixis

There is a three-term deictic system: *seo/-sa*, *sin* and *siud/-ud* (*-sa* and *-ud* are unstressed forms). This is basically a locational/orientational system related to discourse-participant distinctions, *seo/-sa* meaning 'to be located with relation to the speaker', *sin* 'to be located with relation to the addressee' and *siud/-ud* 'to be located with relation to *neither* the speaker *nor* the addressee'. The stressed forms may appear as the head of a phrase. Unstressed forms occur in post-head position in phrases with the definite article:

(223)(a)   *am bàta sa/seo*
           the boat this
           'this boat'
    (b)   *am bàta sin*
           the boat that
           'that boat'
    (c)   *am bàta ud*
           the boat that/yon
           'that/yon boat'

(The *-sa/-seo* alternative is dialectal.)

Translation between Gaelic and standard English presents difficulties as proximate/remote implications are strictly secondary in Gaelic.

4.3.7   Selection

Selection functions of the deictic system are also secondary. In certain circumstances *am bàta sin* denotes 'that boat rather than any other', and appears to be the equivalent of (224):

(224)   *am bàta a   tha an sin*
           the boat that is in that
           'that boat'

4.3.7.1   A selective or particularising system operates with pre-head possessives.

(225)   *mo bhàta sa*, '*my* boat'   *ar bàta ne*, '*our* boat'
         do bhàta sa, '*your* (SG) boat'   *ur bàta se*, '*your* (PL) boat'
         a bhàta san, '*his* boat'
         a bàta se, '*her* boat'   *am bàta san*, '*their* boat'

4.3.8   Reference

Intralinguistic reference is a complex issue to which we can only make passing reference here (see Lyons 1977: ch. 15). We have looked at the exophoric function of deictics in 4.3.6 and we have indicated that the basic function of the article is to indicate the head as 'given' which establishes the basis for anaphoric and cataphoric reference.

4.3.8.1   We may say (briefly and to simplify the issue) that reference has also to do with *speaker*, *addressee* and *other*, but not with their spatial location but with what is assumed to be (a) in their knowledge and/or (b) in their focus of interest. For example, in (226)

(226)   *Thàinig am fear sa a-steach*
         'This man came in'

the speaker implies his own referential 'knowledge' of the 'man' but does not imply any such referential knowledge on the part of the addressee. On the other hand, in (227)

(227)   *Thàinig am fear sin a-steach*
         ?'That man came in'

such referential knowledge on the part of the addressee is implied.

(228)   *Thàinig am fear ud a-steach*

is neutral in respect of such implications.

(229)   *Am fear sa a dh'innis thu dhomh cò e*
         ?'This man you told me who he is'

Example (229) illustrates the complexity which may occur: *sa* indicates that the 'man' is the focus of the speaker's interest and this overrides (on this occasion) assumptions of the addressee's knowledge and interest.

4.3.9   Reflexives

The reflexive modifier *fhèin* combines with both noun and pronoun heads (unlike English):

(230)   *Thàinig an duine fhèin a-steach*
          came   the man self   in
          'The man himself came in'

(231)   *Thàinig e-fhèin a-steach*
          came   he-self in
          'He came in himself'

The structural equivalent of 'He came in himself', with extraposed pronoun with identical reference, occurs also:

(232)   *Thàinig e a-steach e-fhèin*
          came   he in   he-self

4.3.9.1   *Fhèin* is also used (usually with indefinite verb forms) in sentences such as (233)

(233)   *Dhèanadh amadan fhèin sin*
          do-INDEF2 fool   self that

with the sense 'Even a fool could do that'.

4.3.10   Enumeration

Cardinal numbers may appear alone, in which case they are preceded by the particle *a* (*a h-* before vowels), or as pre-head modifiers.

(234)(a)   1   *a h-aon*   6   *a sia*
           2   *a dhà*   7   *a seachd*
           3   *a trì*   8   *a h-ochd*
           4   *a ceithir*   9   *a naoi*
           5   *a' còig*   10   *a deich*

     (b)   *aon taigh* 'one house', etc.   *sia taighean*
           dà thaigh   *seachd taighean*
           trì taighean   *ochd taighean*
           ceithir taighean   *naoi taighean*
           còig taighean   *deich taighean*

4.3.10.1   We note from (234b) that marked plurality begins at 'three': *dà thaigh* vs *trì taighean*. This residual dual system gives rise to no morphological change in masculine nouns; in feminine nouns, however, it produces a form equivalent to the 'dative' or post-prepositional case (see 4.6.6):

(235)   *aon taigh, dà thaigh* vs *aon làmh, dà làimh* ('hand')

4.3.10.2   The numbers 11–19 are based on the 1–10 system with the addition of postmodifier *deug* '-teen', which operates like an indeclinable adjective:

(236)   *aon taigh deug, dà thaigh d(h)eug, trì taighean deug*, etc. 'eleven houses' etc.

4.3.10.3   'Twenty houses' is *fichead taigh*. *Fichead* and *ceud*, 'hundred', *leth-cheud*, 'fifty' ('half-hundred'), *mìle*, 'thousand', *millean*, 'million' together with their compounds, are followed by singular form of the noun and always appear in their singular form in enumeration: *dà cheud* 200, *trì mìle deug* 13,000, etc.

4.3.10.4   The numbers from 21 to 39 may be expressed in different ways:

1   We have first of all the system we have with 11–19:

(237)   *aon taigh fichead, dà thaigh f(h)ichead, trì taighean fichead* . . . *deich taighean fichead*, 'twenty-one, twenty-two, twenty-three . . . thirty houses'

This 'system' ceases to operate at 'thirty', where it would become very complicated, for example **aon taigh deug fichead*.

2   Another system operates as follows:

(238)   *taigh ar fhichead* (house over twenty), 'twenty-one houses'
               dà thaigh ar fhichead, 'twenty-two houses' . . .
               naoi taighean deug ar fhichead, 'thirty-nine houses'

3   A third system combines modifier and head numerals:

(239)   *fichead taigh agus a h-aon* (twenty houses and one), 'twenty-one houses'
               fichead taigh agus a dhà, 'twenty-two houses'
               fichead taigh agus a naoi deug, 'thirty-nine houses'

4   Related to (2) and (3) is,

(240)   *taigh is fichead* (house and twenty) 'twenty-one houses'
               dà thaigh is fichead, 'twenty-two houses'
               naoi taighean deug is fichead, 'thirty-nine houses'

4.3.10.5   Enumeration proceeds normally by twenties or scores. 'Forty', 'sixty' and 'eighty' are expressed as multiples of twenty: *dà-fhichead, trì-fichead* and *ceithir fichead*, respectively. There are no single terms in current use for 'thirty', 'seventy' or 'ninety': these are expressed as 20+10, (3×20)+10 and (4×20)+10; 'fifty' is expressed as (2×20)+10 *dá fhichead agus a deich*, or *leth-cheud* (half hundred). Score counting continues up to 399 but not beyond: that is, **fichead fichead* is not possible but *naoi fichead deug agus a naoi deug* (19 score and 19) is. 'Hundred', 200 etc. would normally be *ceud, dà cheud* etc., but 120 would traditionally be *sia fichead* 'six twenty'.

4.3.10.6   The most common way of counting items from 11–39 is by using a phrase with an enumerator head followed by a partitive phrase modifier; for 21–29 a version of (2) above is used.

(241)   *a h-aon deug de thaighean* (one teen of houses) 'eleven houses'
       a h-aon ar fhichead de thaighean (one over 20 of houses) 'twenty-one houses'
       . . . *a naoi deug ar fhichead de thaighean* (19 over 20 of houses) 'thirty-nine
       houses'

From 41 onwards the most common way is the third above:

(242)   *dà fhichead taigh agus a h-aon* (two twenty house and one)
       . . . *sia mìle   is   sia ciad   is   ceithir fiched taigh agus*
          'six thousand and six hundred and four   twenty house and
       a ceithir deug
       fourteen'

That is '6,694 houses'. The system works *ad infinitum*.

4.3.11   Possessives

There are three ways of expounding 'possessives' in the noun phrase: by means
of juxtaposition of nouns or noun phrases, by means of personal pronouns and
by means of locational prepositional phrases.

4.3.11.1   Noun phrase possessives operate in post-head position:

(243)(a)   *taigh   Chaluim*
             house Calum-GEN
             'Calum's house'

     (b)   *taigh a' bhalaich   bhig*
             house (the boy little-GEN)
             'the little boy's house'

4.3.11.2   Prepositional phrase possessives also operate in post-head position.
They are of two kinds, depending on whether the phrase is definite or not.
Definite phrases require the locational preposition *aig* and non-definite phrases
the preposition *le*:

(244)(a)   Definite: *an cù aig a'bhalach*
                          the dog at the-boy
                          'the boy's dog'/'the dog belonging to the boy'

     (b)   Non-definite: *cù leis a'bhalach*
                          dog with the-boy
                          'a dog of the boy's'/'a dog belonging to the boy'

It may be mentioned that the most common distinction between *le* and *aig* in
Scottish Gaelic is that between 'belonging to' and 'being with', as is seen in the
following pair of phrases with relative-clause modifiers:

(245)(a)   Belonging: *an cù a tha leis a'bhalach*
                          'the dog that belongs to the boy'

(b)   Accompanying: *an cù a tha aig a'bhalach*
            'the dog the boy has with him'

4.3.11.3   Pronominal possessives occur before the head and are the set of bound pronouns, viz.:

(246)   *mo chù   do chù   a chù   a cù*
            'my dog' 'your (SG) dog' 'his dog' 'her dog'
            ar cù   ur cù   an cù
            'our dog' 'your dog' 'their dog'

4.3.11.4   Pronominals also appear as the heads of possessive prepositional phrases:

(247)(a)   *an cù aige*
            the dog at-him
            'his dog'

   (b)   *an cù aca*
            the dog at-them
            'their dog'

4.3.11.5   Pre-possessive pronominals traditionally occurred obligatorily when possession was 'inalienable' (and the phrase was definite), for example with natural relationships and parts of the body, but not with contractual relationships:

(248)(a)   *mo cheann   mo bhràthair*
            'my head'   'my brother'

but

   (b)   *taigh leam   a bhean agam*
            'a house of mine' 'my wife'

and compare

            bràthair dhomh
            brother to-me
            'a brother of mine'

4.3.11.6   The different types of possessive exponent can occur in the one phrase (with appropriate embedding):

(249)   *an cù aig mac bràthar   do mo mhathair*
            the dog (at son (brother-GEN (to my mother)))
            'my mother's brother's son's dog'

4.3.12   Partitives

Partitives are normally expressed by prepositional phrases with the preposition *de*.

(250)   *pìos   den   aran*
         piece of-the bread
         'a piece of the bread'

4.3.13   Adjectivals

Adjectives occupy the position immediately following the head of the noun phrase. There are different subclasses of adjectival and these occur in a non-random order.

4.3.13.1   The main subclasses are adjectives denoting *size, quality* and *colour* and when they co-occur they come in that order:

(251)   *cù   mòr briagha   dubh*
         dog big beautiful black
         'a beautiful big black dog'

Other orders, of course, occur and are exploited for affective purposes.

4.3.13.2   Other items such as past participles of verbs (whose use in Scottish Gaelic is rare) and certain nouns, for example nouns denoting substance, are treated as adjectivals for purposes of agreement (see 4.3.14).

4.3.14   Agreement

In the noun phrase the head noun dominates its modifiers and its specifications are 'transferred' to certain of these modifiers producing 'agreement' between it and, for example, the article and adjectives, in gender, number and case. This we can exemplify with the following phrases:

(252)(a)   *an cù dubh*
            'the black dog'

     (b)   *a' chaora dhubh*
            'the black sheep'

Cù is a masculine noun and *caora* is feminine and this results in different forms of the article and different forms of the adjective co-occurring with them.

Modifier noun phrases are dominated by the head and appear in the genitive case:

(253)(a)   *ceann a'   choin dhuibh*
           head (the dog black-GEN)
           'the head of the black dog'

      (b)   *ceann na   caorach duibhe*
           head (the sheep black-GEN)
           'the head of the black sheep'

Noun phrases in prepositional phrases are governed by prepositions and appear in the post-prepositional case:

(254)(a)   *air a'   chù dhubh*
           on (the dog black-PREP)
           'on the black dog'

      (b)   *air a'   chaoraich dhuibh*
           on (the sheep   black-PREP)
           'on the black sheep'

As (253) and (254) show, there is case agreement between the noun and the adjective and the article.

There is also number agreement between them, for example:

(255)(a)   *na coin dhubha*
           'the black dogs'

      (b)   *na caoraich dhubha*
           'the black sheep (PL)'

4.3.14.1   As we have shown in 4.3.7 there is concord of person between pre-possessives and particularising deictics.

4.3.15   Pronominal phrases

As well as having noun heads, noun phrases may also have pronoun heads. These allow only two classes of modifier: selective or particularising deictics and reflexives.

4.3.15.1   The deictics are the set shown in 4.3.7 as co-occurring with modifier pronouns (their force is expressed by stress in English):

(256)   *mise*   'I'   *sinne*   'we'
           thusa   'you (SG)'   *sibhse*   'you (PL)'
           esan   'he'
           ise   'she'   *iadsan*   'they'

4.3.15.2   The form of the reflexive is *fhèin*

(257)   *mi-fhèin* 'I myself'
            thu-fhèin 'you (SG) yourself' etc.

4.3.16   Nominalisations

It is not possible in the space available to enter into this rather complex topic. A wide range of nominalisation types commonly occur as heads of noun phrases and do not normally permit of modification. The following examples must suffice:

(258)   *Leighis a bhith ag òl   an uisge bheatha e*
            cured   to be   at drink-VN the water life-GEN he
            'Drinking whisky (habitually) cured him'

(259)   *Leighis an t-uisge beatha òl   e*
            cured   the whisky   drink-VN he
            'The fact that he drank the whisky cured him'

(260)   *Leighis òl   an uisge bheatha e*
            cured   drink-VN the whisky-GEN   he
            'The drinking of the whisky cured him'

4.4   STRUCTURE OF THE VERBAL PHRASE

By verbal phrase here is meant a phrasal (as distinct from clausal) structure of the kind we have in the noun phrase, in which the head is a verb; *òl an uisge bheatha* in (260) is an example.

4.4.1   As (260) shows, verbal phrases may occur as exponents of sentence subjects, but their most common occurrence is in prepositional phrases expressing progressive aspect (see 4.2.9.1 above).

(261)(a)   *ag òl   an uisge bheatha*
            at drink-VN the whisky-GEN
            'drinking the whisky'

    (b)   *ag ithe   an arain ùir   a   fhuair e bho Mhàiri*
            at eat-VN the bread new-GEN REL got he from Mairi
            'eating the new bread he got from Mairi'

We note that the verb is the head of the phrase; its object is expressed as a noun phrase in the genitive case and is open to the normal range of modification.

4.4.2   Modification of the head itself is restricted to the direct object of the verb. Example (261) shows noun phrase objects. Pronominal objects are expressed in the same way as NP pre-possessives:

(262)(a)   *ga òl*
        at-PRON-3SG-MASC drink-VN
        'drinking it'

   (b)   *ga h-iarraidh*
        at-PRON-3SG-FEM seek-VN
        'seeking her'

4.5   STRUCTURE OF THE PREPOSITIONAL PHRASE

Prepositional phrases consist of a preposition followed by a nominal or pronominal or verbal phrase.

4.5.1   With noun phrases and pronominals there is no restriction on the range of prepositions which may be used or on the complexity of the phrase, beyond that which obtain in free position.

(263)(a)   *aig uinneag*
        'at (a) window'

   (b)   *don uinneig mhòir   air taigh Iain*
        into (window large-PREP) on house Iain-GEN
        'into the large window in Iain's house'

4.5.1.1   Prepositions govern noun phrases in the prepositional (traditionally called 'dative') case. This case is marked in definite phrases but not in non-definite phrases, as (263a,b) illustrate. Exceptions are fossilised phrases such as *air làimh*, 'by (the) hand'; *an cois* (lit. 'in foot') 'accompanying'.

4.5.1.2   Some prepositions derived from phrases govern nouns in the genitive case:

(264)(a)   *an cois   a'choin*
        in foot-PREP (the dog-GEN)
        'along with the dog'

   (b)   *an dèidh   a'choin*
        in 'behind' (the dog-GEN)
        'after the dog'

Most compound prepositions have such origins.

4.5.2   Prepositions with pronominals

When prepositions govern pronominal phrases the two elements combine into single items sometimes referred to as conjugated prepositions (see 4.10).

4.5.3   Prepositions with verb phrases

The prepositions *ag* 'at' and *an* 'in' are used in verb phrases in aspectual sentences (see (265) below). In clausal nominalisations no such restrictions occur.

4.5.3.1   *Ag* is normally found in 'dynamic' verbal contexts. There is a 'stative' correlate found with *suidhe* 'sit', *seasamh* 'stand', *laighe* 'lie down', *cadal* 'sleep' and a number of others. This gives us pairs like:

(265)(a)   *Tha Iain a' cadal*
              is   Iain at sleep-VN
              'Iain is falling asleep'

   (b)   *Tha Iain 'na   chadal*
              is   Iain in-PRON-3SG-MASC sleep-VN
              'Iain is asleep'

4.5.4   Prepositional systems

Preposition systems and their implications are complex. They operate in spatial and temporal and abstract dimensions. We will look at some of their basic features.

4.5.4.1   The spatial system is the base from which the others derive. It is locative and directional. It refers to an 'object' which may be *locus* or *goal* or *source*. If the object is *bocsa* 'a box' then we may list the four basic locative prepositions 'at', 'in', 'on', 'under' in column (a) and their corresponding directional goal (petal) and source (fugal) equivalents in columns (b) and (c); the pronominal form is shown in parentheses (see 4.10; *bocsa* is a masculine noun).

(266)	(a)	(b)	(c)
(i)	*aig bocsa* (*aige*)	*gu bocsa* (*thuige*)	*bho bhocsa* (*bhuaidhe*)
	'at (a) box'	'to-at (a) box'	'from (a) box'
(ii)	*am bocsa* (*ann*)	*do bhocsa* (*ann*)	*à bocsa*
	'in (a) box'	'into (a) box'	'out of (a) box'

(iii)	*air bocsa* (*air*)	*gu/air bocsa*	*bho/de/far bocsa* (*dheth*)
	'on (a) box'	(*thuige/air*)	'off (a) box'
		'onto (a) box'	
(iv)	*fo bhocsa* (*fodha*)	*fo bhocsa* (*fodha*)	*fo bhocsa* (*fodha*)
	'under (a) box'	'to under (a) box'	'from under (a) box'

4.5.4.2 It will be noted that normally the three categories are represented by three different prepositions. *Fo*, however, is the same form for all three. That is also the case, normally, with compound prepositions which cover all three categories.

4.5.4.3 It will be seen also that the preposition in the noun phrase is not always the same one as in the pronominal: *do bhocsa* 'into a box', but *ann* 'into it', as well as 'in it'.

4.5.4.4 Some prepositions combine with nouns denoting objects that are moving only (they may also be used with expressions of time):

(267)(a)	*an dèidh a'chàr*	but	*air cùl an taighe*
	'behind/after the car'		'behind the house'
(b)	*roimh 'n chàr*	but	*air bialabh an taighe*
	'in front of/before the car'		'in front of the house'

4.5.4.5 When compound prepositions combine with pronouns we get, for example:

(268)(a)	with noun:	*air cùl an taighe*
		on back (the house-GEN)
		'behind the house'
(b)	with pronoun:	*air a chùl*
		on PRON-3SG-MASC back
		'behind it'

4.5.4.6 We have seen above (e.g. in 4.3.11) that prepositions may be used abstractly to denote possession. That is only one of a rich range of such uses: *le* has a wide range of 'instrumental' denotations; *aig* denotes 'agency'; *air* denotes 'disadvantage'; *do* often marks 'actor' and so on.

MORPHOLOGY

Scottish Gaelic morphology, unlike syntax, has been dealt with in various degrees by many writers of 'grammar books' from Shaw (1778) to Calder (1923). It also figures with various degrees of coverage and reliability in the monographs on different dialects: Borgstrøm (1937, 1940, 1941), Holmer (1957, 1962), Oftedal (1956), Mac Gill-Fhinnein (1966), Dorian (1978), O'Murchú (1989).

4.6   NOUNS

Nouns exhibit systems of inherent and contextual features such as countability, animacy, gender, number, case and person, combining to form a fairly complex inflectional system.

4.6.1   Structure: stems and endings

Noun stems may be simple or complex. Complex stems are formed typically by noun–noun or noun–adjective combination or by the addition of affixes (see 4.9), examples being respectively:

(269)(a)   *teangeòlachd* (*teanga*, 'tongue' + *eòlachd*, 'science'), 'linguistics'
    (b)   *mòrchuid* (*mòr* 'large' + *cuid* 'portion'), 'majority'
    (c)   *ainneart* ((PREF-NEG) *an−* + *neart* 'strength'), 'tyranny'
        ceannas (*ceann* 'head' + *−as* (SUFF-ABST)), 'leadership'
        cuairteag (*cuairt*, 'circle' + *ag* (SUFF-DIM-FEM)), 'eddy'.

4.6.2   Countability

Nouns may be *uncountable* or *countable*. Uncountable nouns do not appear in plural forms:

(270)   *bainne*, 'milk': *?*bainneachan* (cf. *gloinne/gloinneachan* 'glass'/'glasses'); *min*, 'meal': *?*minean*.

4.6.2.1   Uncountables may be either *mass* nouns as in (270) or *collective* nouns as in *crodh* 'cattle', which is singular only in form, but has plural reference.

4.6.2.2   Some uncountables have singulative correlates:

(271)   *gràn* 'grain'/*gràinne*, 'a grain'; *falt* 'hair'/*fuiltean* 'a hair'. The singulative suffix *-ne* is no longer productive and *gràinne*, for example, often appears as

gràinnean with what corresponds to the diminutive masculine suffix *-an* (cf. *fuiltean*).

4.6.2.3   It should be noted that many mass nouns have no derived singulative correlate. There is a set of words that denote something like 'the least quantity of' which have quasi-singulative force, for example: *sil/boinne(ag) uisge/bainne/leanna* 'a drop of water/milk/beer'; *gràinne/griodhan mine/siùcair/ salainn* etc. 'a grain/speck of meal/sugar/salt, etc.'; *leogan/sgolb cloiche* 'a pebble/splinter (depending on context) of stone'; *beathach cruidh* 'an "animal" of cattle' (used also of other (singular) generic animal terms: *beathach eich*, 'an "animal" of horse', i.e. 'a horse').

4.6.3   Animacy

There are no morphologically marked distinctions of 'animacy' in Scottish Gaelic (see 4.3.11 above for distinctions with locatives/possessives).

4.6.4   Gender

There are two categories of gender in Gaelic: all nouns are either masculine or feminine. Normally, grammatical gender follows natural gender, but there are some striking exceptions: *boireannach*, 'female/woman' is masculine in gender but has feminine reference: *bha i . . .* 'she was'.

4.6.4.1   Gender is realised in noun declension (4.6.7) and in adjective and article concord (4.16). Pronominally, it is manifested only in third person singular (4.6.8).

4.6.5   Number

There are two categories of number, singular and plural, with residual features of a dual system.

4.6.5.1   As we said above some nouns show singular forms only. It does not seem to be the case that there are plural forms without a corresponding singular. Some plural forms are suppletive; for example, normally:

(272)   *bò*, 'cow' : *crodh* 'cows'

However *crodh* in 4.6.2.1 is a singular noun; *bò* has a specific plural form *ba* which is used for counting purposes *sia ba* 'six cows'.

4.6.5.2   Dual is only marked after the numeral *dà* 'two' and only in feminine nouns that have marked forms of the prepositional/dative case with which it coincides:

(273)   *dà làimh (làmh)* 'two hands'; *dà chois (cas)*, 'two feet'; but *dà cheann (ceann)*, 'two heads'.

Làmh and *cas* are feminine and *ceann* masculine unmarked forms.

4.6.5.3   Plurals are formed in a number of ways: by suppletion (272), by suffixing, by mutation in the class of the final consonant of the stem, by mutation of stem vowel and by combinations of these (with or without syncope in polysyllabic words):

    1 Simple suffixing:

       (a) in *-an*:

(274)   *cuileag* 'fly' : *cuileagan*
          cuilean 'puppy' : *cuileanan* (see 2 below)
          ite 'feather' : *itean*
          loch 'loch' : *lochan*

       (b) in *-ichean/-achan* (non-principled alternatives):

(275)   *balla* 'wall' : *ballachan/ballaichean*
          bata 'stick' : *bataichean*
          àite 'place' : *àiteachan*
          ogha 'grandson' : *oghaichean*

       (c) in *-(an)nan*:

(276)   *ainm* 'name' : *ainmnean*
          oidhche 'night' : *oidhcheannan*
          nàbaidh 'neighbour' : *nàbannan*

       (d) in *-tean*:

(277)   *cùil* 'nook' : *cùiltean*
          sgoil 'school' : *sgoiltean*

    2 With stem-consonant mutation (and concomitant stem vowel affection):

(278)   *balach* 'boy' : *balaich* (/paLəx/~/paLix′/)
          cuilean 'puppy' : *cuilein* (/kʰulan/~/kʰul/ɛN′) (see 1(a) for alternative plural)
          ceann 'head' : *cinn* (/k′ʰauN/ ~ / k′ʰeiN′/)
          cùl 'back' : *cùil* (/kʰu:L/~/kʰu:ʎ/)

    3 (a) With *-an* plus syncope: *doras* 'door' : *dorsan*.
       (b) With *-an* + syncope + lengthening of root vowel: *caraid* 'friend' : *càirdean*.
       (c) With *-an* +shortening of root vowel: *bàrr* 'top' : *barran* (/pa:R/~/paRən/)

    4   With *−(an)nan* + shortening of root vowel:

(279)   *ceum* 'step': *ceumannan* (/kʹʰeːm/~/kʹʰeməNən/)
             am 'time': *amannan* (/aum/~/aməNən/)

    5   (a) With *-tean* + dropping of final vowel + lengthening of root vowel, *coille* 'wood' : *coilltean* (/kʰəLʹə/~/kʰəiLʹtʹən/).

         (b) With *-tean* + dropping of final vowel + lengthening of root vowel + palatalisation of final stem consonant (which always occurs unless it already has palatal quality) *teine* 'fire' : *teintean* (/tʹʰɛnə/~/tʹʰɛiNʹtʹən/).

4.6.5.4   Some plurals, mostly those in item 1 of section 4.6.5.3, are based on the stem of the unmarked or nominative form. Others, for example those in item 4 of the same section, are based on the stem of the genitive case (see 4.6.7.6, example (286)).

4.6.6   Case

There are three cases: unmarked/'nominative', genitive and prepositional/ 'dative'. These are not realised in all cases.

4.6.6.1   In non-definite phrases prepositional case is not normally differentiated in the modern language (except in the feminine in '"correct" style' or in fossilised phrases); in definite phrases these forms are overtly marked, for example:

(280)(a)   Non-definite:

	Masculine	Feminine
NOM	*balach* 'a boy'	*caileag* 'a girl'
GEN	*ainm balaich* 'a boy's name'	*ainm caileige* 'a girl's name'
PREP	*air balach* 'on a boy'	*air caileag*/*air caileig* 'on a girl'

      (b)   Definite:

	Masculine	Feminine
NOM	*am balach* 'the boy'	*a' chaileag* 'the girl'
GEN	*ainm a' bhalaich*	*ainm na caileige*
	'the boy's name'	'the girl's name'
PREP	*air a' bhalach* 'on the boy'	*air a' chaileig* 'on the girl'

It will be seen that in (280b) nominative and prepositional in the masculine are differentiated by the forms of initial noun mutation, and in the feminine by the forms of the endings.

4.6.6.2   In the plural in both masculine and feminine both definite and non-definite the nominative and prepositional cases are undifferentiated.

(281)(a)   Non-definite:

	Masculine	Feminine
NOM	*balaich* 'boys'	*caileagan* 'girls'
GEN	*ainm bhalach* 'boys' name'	*ainm chaileag(an)* 'girls' name'
PREP	*air balaich* 'on boys'	*air caileagan* 'on girls'

(b)   Definite:

	Masculine	Feminine
NOM	*na balaich* 'the boys'	*na caileagan* 'the girls'
GEN	*ainm nam balach* 'the boys' name'	*ainm nan caileag(an)* 'the girls' name'
PREP	*air na balaich* 'on the boys'	*air na caileagan* 'on the girls'

Nouns with suffix plurals may have genitive form the same as nominative singular or plural.

4.6.6.3   Vestiges of an older 'dative' case in *-ibh* remain in certain phrases, for example *mo làmh do na fearaibh* (instead of . . . *do na fir* (from *fear* 'man')) meaning 'congratulations to the fellows' (literally: 'my hand to the men').

4.6.7   Declensional classes

There is a class of undeclinable nouns in Gaelic as well as a number of other declensional classes that exhibit different patterns of case differentiation and plural formation. We have dealt with plural formations in 4.6.5. These formations are not in many cases predictable from the singular and so can only be used, normally, as a secondary marker of declension class. The basic criteria are supplied by the pattern of case differentiation in the singular.

4.6.7.1   Type I

The major set of indeclinable nouns are polysyllables ending in the derivational suffixes *-achd*, *-air*, *-iche* and many disyllabic nouns ending in a vowel *-a/-e* including all English borrowings of that structure:

(282)   *seòltachd* 'cunning', *iasgair* 'fisher', *lighiche* 'healer', *bainne* 'milk', *gunna* 'gun'

Nouns in *-achd* are normally abstract uncountables; those in *-air* and *-iche* take *-an* plurals.

4.6.7.2   Types II and III

The nouns *balach* and *caileag* declined in 4.6.6 are examples of well-defined masculine and feminine declension classes. For example, all masculine diminutives belong to the *balach* class and all feminine diminutives belong to the *caileag* class. The *balach* class forms the nominative plural the same as the genitive singular and the genitive plural the same as the nominative singular. The *caileag* class has a nominative plural in *-an* and genitive plural either as nominative singular or with *-an* suffix (4.6.6.2).

4.6.7.3   Type IV

This is a class of feminine disyllabic nouns ending in *-air* and having *-ichean* plurals, exemplified by *cathair* 'city', which forms its genitive by depalatalisation of the final *r*, syncope of the unstressed syllable and the suffixing of *-ach*:

(283)		Singular	Plural
	NOM/PREP	*caithair*	*cathraichean*
	GEN	*cathrach*	*cathraichean/cathair*

4.6.7.4   Type V

Another set of nouns ending in *air* express family relationships.

(284)	Nominative/prepositional	Genitive
	athair, 'father'	*athar*
	màthair, 'mother'	*màthar*
	bràthair, 'brother'	*bràthar*
	piuthar, 'sister'	*peathar*
	seanair, 'grandfather'	*seanar*
	seanmhair, 'grandmother'	*seanmhar*

Some of these have syncopated plurals in *-ichean* based on the genitive, some have plurals in *-an* based on the genitive and some in *-an* based on the nominative: *athraichean*, *màthraichean*, *bràthran*, *peathraichean*, *seanairean*, *seanmhairean*.

4.6.7.5   Type VI

This type of noun forms its genitive singular by adding a vowel to the stem of the nominative. This might be a simple addition to the stem or it may entail various manipulations of the stem such as palatalisation of the final consonant, depalatalisation of the final consonant, change of quality in stem vowel, syncope in polysyllables and combinations of these. Some examples are:

(285)		Nominative/prepositional	Genitive
(a)		*fiodh*, 'wood'	*fiodha*
(b)		*agh*, 'heifer'	*aighe*

(c)	*bàrr*, 'top'	*barra* (/paːR/~/paRə/)
(d)	*fuil*, 'blood'	*fola*
(e)	*muir*, 'sea'	*mara*
	abhainn, 'river'	*aibhne*

4.6.7.6   Type VII

Similar to (285c), but sufficiently well defined to be regarded as a class in themselves, are a set of monosyllabic nouns ending in *-m* forming their genitive by shortening the vowel of the stem and adding a vowel (historically, the vowel was short and the *-m* was long). Examples are:

(286)	Nominative/prepositional	Genitive
	ceum, 'step'	*ceuma* (/kʰeːmʲ/~/kʰemʲə/)
	leum, 'leap'	*leuma* (/Lʲeːmʲ/~/Lʲemʲə/)
	am, 'time'	*ama* (/aum/~/amə/)

These are all masculine nouns and have plurals in *-annan*: *ceumannan*, *amannan*, etc.

4.6.7.7   Type VIII

This is a small class of feminine nouns which form their genitive singular in *-adh* and their prepositional, where they survive, form in *-idh* (i.e. /-ɣ/ and /-ij/):

(287)	NOM	*criadh*, 'clay' (/kʰrʲia/); *ceò*, 'mist' (/kʰ ɔː/)
	GEN	*criadhadh* (/kʰrʲia-əɣ/); *ceothadh* (/kʰɔ-əɣ/)
	PREP	*criadhaidh* (/kʰrʲia-ij/); *ceothaidh* (/kʰɔ-ij/)

4.6.7.8   There are many irregular nouns that we are unable to examine here. Indeed, we have been able to deal with only a small sample of the noun inventory. Oftedal (1956) has a good range of examples for the dialect he is concerned with.

4.6.8   Pronouns

The following set of free pronouns occur:

(288)		Singular	Plural
	1	*mi*	*sinn*
	2	*thu/tu*	*sibh*
	3 MASC	*e*	*iad*
	FEM	*i*	

4.6.8.1   They have stressed and unstressed forms, the former occurring only under contrastive stress and realised as vowel length. Unstressed forms are short.

4.6.8.2   There is a corresponding set of bound pronouns which occur in post-head position in noun and verb phrases (see 4.3.11 and 4.4 above):

(289)		Singular	Plural
	1	*mo*	*ar*
	2	*do*	*ur*
	3 MASC	a^L	
			an
	FEM	*a*	

(Masculine *a* causes lenition in the following word; hence superscript ^{L} to differentiate it from feminine *a*, which does not.)

4.6.8.3   On the items co-occurring with pronouns see 4.3.6, 4.3.7, 4.3.9, 4.3.11 and 4.3.15 above.

4.6.9   Person

The system of person, denoted by 1, 2 and 3 in 4.6.8, for example, is discourse-based and refers to *speaker* (first person), *addressee* (second person) and *other* (third person); *mi* refers to the speaker, *thu* to a single addressee; *sibh* refers to *addressee*, obligatorily, and optionally can include additional *addressee(s)*, *other(s)* or both, but excludes *speaker*; *sinn* refers to *speaker* obligatorily, and optionally can include *speaker(s)*, *addressee(s)*, *other(s)*; *e, i, iad* exclude *speaker* and *addressee*.

4.6.9.1   Nouns as well as pronouns are governed by the category of person. Nouns are normally in the third person; the so-called 'vocative case' form is, in fact, a noun marked for the second person. The marking takes the form of an unstressed particle *a* preceding the noun and causing lenition together with palatalisation of the final consonant of masculine, but not feminine, nouns; there is adjective concord:

(290)(a)   MASC *a bhalaich bhig* 'little boy!'
     (b)   FEM *a chaileag bheag* 'little girl!'

4.6.9.2   Plural vocatives are normally marked only by the preceding leniting particle, but there are vestiges of suffix-marked forms; for example:

(291)   *a chàirdean* 'friends!' (PL *càirdean*)
     but *a fhearaibh* 'men!' (PL *fir*)
     a chonaibh 'you dogs!' (PL *coin*)

4.6.10   There is a set of proformal nouns, for example: *neach* 'person', *fear* 'one' (MASC); *tè* 'one' (FEM); *feadhainn* ('ones' = plural of *fear* and *tè*); *rud* 'thing'; *cuid* 'some' (partitive).

4.7   VERBS

Gaelic verbs are complex in several ways, both in structural and systemic terms. We can only look at these matters briefly. Exemplification of the verb paradigm is well set out in the various grammar books but both the categorisation and the implication tend to be misleading. We will look briefly at only the basic points.

4.7.1   Stems and endings

Stems may be simple or complex. Complex stems may be composed of prefix + stem or stem + formational suffix or prefix + stem + suffix:

(292)(a)   *ceartaich* 'correct' from adjective *ceart*, 'correct' + verbalising suffix
  (b)   *ath-fhosgail* 're-open' from *ath-*, 're-' and verb *fosgail*, 'open'
  (c)   *ath-cheartaich* 're-correct'.

4.7.1.1   Apart from the imperative, only one personal ending, that of the first person singular of the second indefinite (past conditional, traditionally), is to be found regularly in the modern language. The first person plural is also found, but its distribution is restricted.

(293)(a)   *bhithinn* 'I would be'
  (b)   *bhitheamaid* 'we would be' (alternative: *bhitheadh sinn*)

4.7.1.2   In commands we have, for example, the singular and plural imperative forms: *fosgail* 'open!' and *fosgailibh* 'open! (PL)'. The singular imperative is the minimal stem form of the verb; the plural is marked by the ending *-ibh*. There is also a 'first plural imperative', *fosglamaid* 'let us open', with the same ending as in (293).

4.7.1.3   There are vestiges of first-person marking in verbs of perception: *faicim* 'let me see'; *chithim* 'I see'.

4.7.1.4   Impersonals are morphologically marked (see 4.7.5.1).

4.7.2   Verb classes

Some verbs such as *ith* 'eat', *òl* 'drink' are (unlike English) *completive* rather than *inceptive* in mode. This can be tested in sentences with *prospective* aspect:

(294)(a)   *Tha e gus a bhiadh ithe*
            'He is about to finish eating his food'
     (b)   *Tha e gus falbh*
            'He is about to leave'

English 'He is about to eat his food' is translated *Tha e gus tòiseachadh air a bhiadh ithe*, 'He is about to *begin* to eat his food'.

4.7.2.1   Verbs are either inherently stative or dynamic (see 4.5.3.1).

4.7.3   Finite/non-finite

There are two non-finite forms of the verb, the so-called verbal noun and the infinitive. The verbal noun is marked by a small set of suffixes added to the stem:

(295)(a)   *till* 'return' (IMP SG)
            tilleadh 'returning' (VN)
            a thilleadh 'to return' (INF)
     (b)   *cum* 'keep' (IMP SG)
            cumail 'keeping' (VN)
            a chumail 'to keep' (INF)
     (c)   *lean* 'follow' (IMP SG)
            leantainn 'following' (VN)
            a leantainn 'to follow' (INF)

All other verb forms are finite.

4.7.3.1   Dependent/independent

There are two classes of verb traditionally called 'strong' and 'weak' verbs. Weak verbs operate with one stem only under all conditions. Strong verbs have differentiated stems: *independent* when not dominated by overt sentence class markers; and *dependent* when so dominated:

(296)   PRES *tha*, 'is' ~ *chan eil*, 'is not' and *am   bheil*, 'is?'
                    NEG is   INTER is
         PAST *bha*, 'was' ~ *cha robh*, 'was not' and *an   robh*, 'was?'
                    NEG was   INTER was

The verb *tha* which is a strong verb contrasts with the weak verb *seall* 'to look' (only the verb *tha* has a present tense):

(297)   *seall*   ~   *cha do sheall*
         look-PAST   NEG PT look-PAST
         'looked'   'did not look'
                           an   do sheall
                           INTER PT look-PAST
                           'did . . . look?'

4.7.3.2   Definite/indefinite

As well as utilising different stems for independent and dependent forms, strong verbs differentiate between 'definite' and 'indefinite' forms. Weak verbs do not distinguish in terms of stems but do so in terms of endings.

(298)(a)   *sheall e* 'he looked'
            shealladh e 'he would look'
    (b)   *bha e* 'he was'
            bhitheadh e 'he would be'

We see that the same endings are suffixed to differentiated and undifferentiated stems.

4.7.4   Tense

If we take *tense* to apply strictly to 'time of action' (relative to 'time of speaking') then there are only two tenses in Gaelic: *present*, referring to the 'time of speaking', and *past*. Furthermore, these are to be found only in the verbs 'be', *tha* and *is* (and not unambiguously in the latter, which has only two forms: *is* which has copular and deictic functions and is [−PAST] and [−INDEF]; and *bu* which may be either [+PAST] or [+INDEF 2]):

(299)   PRES *tha* 'is'; *is* 'is'
         PAST *bha* 'was'; *bu* 'was' (and 'would be')

No other verb has a present-tense form in the strict sense. Reference to action occurring at the time of speaking is carried periphrastically by a sentence with the verb *tha* (denoting the present reference) and with the lexical verb embedded in its complement.

(300)   *Tha Iain a' leughadh*
         is   Iain at read-VN
         'Iain is reading'

4.7.4.1   We noted above the distinction between *definite* and *indefinite* stems and endings. The terms 'definite' and 'indefinite' are used deliberately to avoid the value loading of traditional nomenclature which can be misleading and irrelevant. The distinction is similar to that between *realis* and *irrealis* (see Comrie 1985: 50ff.; the functional range, however, is different from that cited there). If we take (a) the verb *tha*, (b) *chì*, a strong verb, and (c) *seall*, a weak verb, they exhibit the following form sets:

(301)(a)

DEFINITE	PRES	INDEP	*tha*	'is'
		DEP	*bheil*	
	PAST	INDEP	*bha*	'was'
		DEP	*robh*	
INDEFINITE	FIRST	INDEP	*bithidh*	'is', 'will be'
		DEP	*b(h)i*	
	SECOND	INDEP	*bhitheadh*	'would be',
		DEP		'used to be'

(b)

DEFINITE	PRES	INDEP	–	
		DEP	–	
	PAST	INDEP	*chunnaic*	'saw'
		DEP	*faca*	
INDEFINITE	FIRST	INDEP	*chì*	'sees', 'will see'
		DEP	*faic*	('can see')
	SECOND	INDEP	*chitheadh*	'would see'
		DEP	*faiceadh*	'used to see' ('could see')

(c)

DEFINITE	PRES	INDEP	–	
		DEP	–	
	PAST	INDEP	*sheall*	'looked'
		DEP		
INDEFINITE	FIRST	INDEP	*seallaidh*	'looks' 'will look'
		DEP		
	SECOND	INDEP	*shealladh*	'would look' 'used to look'
		DEP		

4.7.4.2   These diagrams show the different spread of forms in these different classes with *tha* alone showing [+PRES] and *chì* alone showing both independent and dependent forms throughout the indefinite mode. All verbs show the distinction definite ~ indefinite. As we have seen, *tha* operates as an 'auxiliary' verb. All forms of *tha* participate in this function to create a complex network of expressions of tense, aspect and mode.

4.7.4.3   The uses of the different verb forms is a complex issue which has not been investigated to the degree which would enable us to make definitive statements about it. The translation equivalents in the above examples give a basic indication. There are no difficulties with the definite mode. We will demonstrate some of the uses of the indefinite, from the verb *tha* only (to conserve space). What we have called 'first indefinite' (INDEF 1) is often called 'present/future' in grammar books. It, however, is marked neither [+PRES] nor [+FUT]. In fact (302a) is multiply ambiguous:

(302)(a)   *Bithidh*   *Iain tinn*
             be [+INDEF 1] Iain ill

Bithidh is simply a form which is compatible with a range of contexts (in which *tha* will not normally do). We can have:

   (b)   *Bithidh Iain tinn am màireach*
             'Iain will be ill tomorrow'
   (c)   *Bithidh Iain tinn a h-uile latha*
             'Iain is ill every day'
   (d)   *Bithidh Iain tinn, 's dòcha*
             'Iain is/will be ill, perhaps'

(b) is *future*, (c) is *reiterative*, (d) is *speculative modal*, but these features are carried by the adjuncts not by the verb. As far as time reference is concerned all that we can say is that none of these sentences have past reference. It should be said that through contact with English *bithidh* is acquiring a 'first reading' of [+FUT] and *tha* is used more and more with reiterative adjuncts. This makes for an alternative and complicating 'shadow' system which causes great problems to learners of the language (and to linguists!) but which does potentially enrich the system.

    If we take sentence (303a) with the 'second indefinite' (INDEF 2),

(303)(a)   *Bhitheadh*   *Iain tinn*
             be [+INDEF 2] Iain ill

it is similarly compatible with a range of contexts, some similar to (302) and some different:

   (b)   *Bhitheadh Iain tinn a h-uile latha*
             'Iain used to be ill every day'
   (c)   *Bhitheadh Iain tinn am màireach nan itheadh e sin*
             'Iain would be ill tomorrow if he ate that'

Clearly (302b) and (303b) invite comparison, and it is tempting to assign [−PAST] to the former and [+PAST] to the latter and to assign these as distinctive features of the verb form. For reasons we have no space to go into here, it is safer to say that verbs in the 'indefinite' mode are always tenseless, and 'time of action' is contextually supplied.

Example (303c) shows the use of INDEF 2 in conditional sentences where that mode appears in the matrix and subordinate clause. INDEF 1 appears in the matrix when the verb in the conditional clause is marked relative (see 4.7.4.5):

(304)   *Bithidh Iain tinn ma dh'itheas e sin*
          'Iain will be ill if he eats that'

4.7.4.4   If we take a verb other than *tha* we see that in addition to the contexts we have illustrated above indefinite forms can occur without co-textual or contextual supplementation:

(305)   *Ithidh Iain aran*
          'Iain eats bread' (i.e. 'is a bread-eater')

In these cases it has 'generic' denotation. This reinforces the 'tenseless' interpretation. The following sentence illustrates different functions, 'generic' and 'habitual' (which coincides in operation with 'reiterative'):

(306)   *Ithidh   Iain aran ach cha bhi   e   ga   ithe*
          eat-INDEF 1 Iain bread but NEG be-INDEF 1 he at-it eat-VN
          'Iain eats bread but he does not eat it (usually)'

4.7.4.5   Verbs in relative clauses, except for strong verbs, are morphologically marked in the indefinite 1, dependent form by the ending *-as*. Both *tha* and *is* have relative forms.

(307)(a)   *am fear as   oige*
             the one is-REL younger
             'the younger one'

     (b)   *am fear a   bhitheas ann*
             the one REL be-REL in-it
             'the one who "will be" there'

     (c)   *am fear a   dh'itheas an t-aran*
             the one REL PT eat-REL   the bread
             'the one who eats the bread'

4.7.5   Passive/impersonal

There are no morphologically marked passive forms in Gaelic. There are passive sentences which are discussed in 4.2.6.

4.7.5.1   There is a set of impersonal endings which are added to all forms of the verb. The ending for all indefinite 1 forms and for present (in *tha* only) is in *-ar*. All indefinite 2 forms have the ending *-te* (or the alternative *-ist(e)*). Past forms of weak verbs have the ending *-adh* and of strong verbs the ending *-as*. The following show impersonal forms together with forms of the third singular masculine (verb + pronoun).

(308)(a) 3SG MASC: *tha e   a bheil e   bithidh e   am bi e*
          IMPERS: *thathar a bheilear bithear   am bithear*

          3SG MASC: *bha e   an robh e   bhitheadh e   am bitheadh e*
          IMPERS: *bhathas an robhas   bhite   am bite*

Strong verbs, *mutatis mutandis*, follow the pattern of *tha*. Weak verbs show the following pattern. (They do not distinguish INDEP ~ DEP or DEF ~ INDEF stems: see (301).)

(b) 3SG MASC: *sheall e* (PRET)   *seallaidh e* (INDEF 1)   *shealladh e* (INDEF 2)
     IMPERS: *shealladh*   *seallar*   *sheallte*

4.8   ADJECTIVES

4.8.1   Structure

Adjectives may be simple, consisting of a single stem, or complex, consisting of a stem with prefixes and suffixes, for example:

(309)(a) *mòr* 'big'
   (b) *duineil* 'manly' (*duine* 'man' + adjectival suffix *-ail*); *gruamach* 'sad' (*gruaim* 'melancholy' + adjectival suffix *-ach*)
   (c) *neo-ghruamach* 'happy' (negative prefix + *gruaim* + adjectival suffix *-ach*)

4.8.2   Comparison

Comparison may be illustrated in the following way:

(310) *Predicative:*
  (a) BASE: *Tha an t-eun glas*
          is   the bird grey
          'The bird is grey'
  (b) COMP: *Tha an t-eun nas   glaise*
          is   the bird be-REL grey [+COMP]
          'The bird is greyer'

(c)   SUP: *Is e an t-eun as   glaise*
                is it the bird be-REL grey [+ COMP]
                'The bird is greyest'

The difference between comparative and superlative is carried by the different sentence structures in which *tha* and *is* operate. What is *morphologically* marked is the difference between *base* and *non-base* and entails palatalisation of the final consonant of the stem and the suffixing of *-e*: *glas* → *glaise*.

(311) *Attributive:*

		(a) non-definite	(b) definite
(i)	BASE:	*eun glas*	*an t-eun glas*
		'a grey bird'	'the grey bird'
(ii)	COMP:	*eun nas glaise*	*an t-eun as glaise*
		'a greyer bird'	'the greyer bird'
(iii)	SUP:	–	*an t-eun as glaise*
			'the greyest bird'

There is, of course, no non-definite superlative. In our examples there is no distinction between comparative and superlative as that distinction is not morphologically marked.

4.8.2.1   If we add a comparator to the sentences in (310) we get (310b′) and (310c′):

(310)(b′)   *Tha an t-eun nas glaise na 'n cat*
               'The bird is greyer than the cat'

(310)(c′)   *Is e an t-eun as glaise na 'n cat*
               'It is the bird that is greyer than the cat'

The latter is a topicalised version of the former (comparative) and not a superlative form at all. Superlatives then are 'uncompared comparatives'.

4.8.2.2   Similarly, if we add a comparator to (311)(b)(ii/iii):

(311)(b)(ii′/iii′)   *an t-eun as glaise na 'n cat*
                     'the bird that is greyer than the cat'

we get a marked comparative. Only the 'uncompared comparative' is potentially 'superlative'.

4.8.2.3   Equatives

Equative constructions are exemplified in constructions such as:

(312)   *Tha an t-eun cho glas ris a' chat*
           is   the bird EQ grey with the cat
           'The bird is as grey as the cat'

It is not morphologically marked.

4.8.2.4   Historically, there was a 'second comparative' denoting 'degree', formed by adding *-de* to the stem of the comparative. It survives in expressions such as the following (see (314) for the base and first comparative forms of the adjectives involved):

(313)(a)   *Is feàirrde*   *Iain sin*
             is better [+ COMP 2] Iain that
             'Iain is the better for that'

      (b)   *Is misde*   *Iain sin*
             is worse [+ COMP 2] Iain that
             'Iain is the worse for that'

4.8.3   Adjective classes

Glas belongs to the regular class of ajdectives which form their comparatives by palatalisation and suffixing, and sometimes mutation of stem vowel; for example, *glas*: *glaise*, *geal* 'white': *gile*, etc. Many common adjectives, however, belong to the irregular class, where automatic rules cannot be applied:

(314)   BASE: *mòr* 'big' *beag* 'small' *math* 'good' *dona* 'bad'
          COMP 1:   *motha*   *lugha*   *feàrr*   *miosa*
          COMP 2:   *mòide*   *lughde*   *feàrrde*   *misde*

4.8.3.1   Distributional subclasses are discussed in 4.3.13 above.

4.8.4   Adverbs

Adverbs may be simple or compound. The commonest adverbial structure consists of the adverbial particle *gu* combined with a form which operates (normally) as an adjective; for example, *math* 'good': *gu math* 'well'; *cinnteach*, *gu cinnteach* 'sure', 'surely'.

4.8.4.1   Adverbs are modified by the same set of intensifiers as modify adjectives, viz.: *glè*, *fìor*, *ro-*, etc.

4.8.5   Adverb classes

The same range of adverb classes operate in Gaelic as in other European languages. Basically denoting *place*, *time*, *manner*, etc., of state or action, their pro-formals are found in questions such as *càite* (INTER place), 'where?', *cuin* (INTER time), 'when?', etc.

4.8.5.1   Locational/directional systems are of considerable interest in that they are basically 'speaker-oriented' systems. For example, where the speaker is located is always *a bhos* a marked locative version of *an seo*, 'here'. It enters into a set of contrasts:

(315)(a)   LOC: '*at* speaker'   '*not at* speaker'
                 a bhos   *thall*
           DIR: '*to* speaker'   '*from* speaker'
                 a nall   *a null*

(b)   LOC: '*up at* speaker'   '*up not at* speaker'
                 a bhos   *shuas*
           DIR: '*up to* speaker'   '*up not to* speaker'
                 a nìos (from down)   *suas* (to up)

(c)   LOC: '*down at* speaker'   '*down not at* speaker'
                 a bhos   *shìos*
           DIR: '*down to* speaker'   '*down from* speaker'
                 a nuas (from up)   *sìos* (to down)

4.8.5.2   In many dialects *a nìos* and *a nuas* have fallen together, usually under *a nuas*. In many mainland dialects *a bhàn* is used for 'downwards'.

4.9   COMPOUND WORDS

Compounds words have been dealt with briefly in the sections dealing with the structure of different word classes.

4.9.1   Derivational compounds

We can give only brief examples of this extensive topic here. Word compounds are derived by joining together two lexical stems or by adding derivational prefixes or suffixes.

4.9.2   Lexical combination

(316)(a)   With the accent on the first element:
           cís-mhaor 'tax officer', *mart-fheòil* 'beef', *mòr-thìr* 'mainland', *brù-dhearg* 'red-breast(ed)', *bàn-dhearg* 'pale red' ('pink'), *dùbh-ghorm* 'dark blue'
(b)   With the accent on the second element:
           muileann-gaoithe 'windmill', *glas-ghuib* 'gag',
           crith-thalmhain 'earthquake', *àite-còmhnaidh* 'residence'

4.9.3   Compounds with prefixes

(317)(a) negative: *neo-, mi-, an-*:
ainmeil 'famous': *neo-ainmeil* 'unfamous': *mì-ainmeil* 'infamous'; *iochdmhar* 'kind': *an-iochdmhar* 'pitiless'

(b) *so-* and *do-* as positive/negative:
sothuigse 'comprehensible': *dothuigse* 'incomprehensible':
soirbh 'easy': *doirbh* 'difficult'

4.9.4   Compounds with suffixes

4.9.4.1   Nouns
There are a number of noun suffixes:

(318)(a) *-ach*: *boireannach* 'woman' (*boireann* 'female'); *fireannach* 'man' (*fireann* 'male')

(b) *-achd*: *rìoghachd* 'kingdom' (*rìgh* 'king'); *fialachd* 'generosity' (*fial* 'generous')

(c) *-ad* (abstract nouns formed by addition of the suffix to the first comparative stem):
gilead 'whiteness' (*gile* 'whiter'), *giorrad* 'shortness' (*giorra* 'shorter') *boidhchead* 'beauty' (*boidhche* 'more beautiful')

(d) *-adair* (many deverbal, some denominal):
seinneadair 'singer' (*seinn* 'sing')' *eunadair* 'fowler' (*eun*, 'bird')

(e) *-(a)iche*: *maraiche*, 'seaman' (*mara*(GEN) 'sea'); *searmonaiche*, 'preacher' (*searmon*, 'sermon')

(f) *-air*: *iasgair* 'fisherman' (*iasg* 'fish'), *dannsair* 'dancer' (*danns(a)* 'dance')

(g) the diminutive endings *-an* (masc.) and *-ag* (fem.): *cuilean* 'puppy' (from *cù* 'dog'), *searbhan* 'sour one' (*searbh* 'sour'), *guileag* 'whimper' (*gul* 'weeping'), *gionag* 'greedy one' (*gion* 'greed')

(h) *-as* (abstracts): *ceartas* 'justice' (*ceart* 'right'), *grinneas* 'neatness' (*grinn* 'neat').

4.9.4.2   Adjectives
The main adjectival suffixes are *-ach* and *a/eil* (see 4.8.1).

4.9.4.3   Verbs
For non-finite form suffixes see (295).
   The most common verbal derivational suffix is *-(a)ich*: *ceartaich* 'correct' (*ceart* 'right'), *cuairtich* 'encircle' (*cuairt* 'circuit'), *falmhaich* 'empty' (*falamh* 'empty').

4.10   CONJUGATED PREPOSITIONS

Prepositions as they function in phrases are generally dealt with in 4.5 above.
When prepositions combine with pronouns they are amalgamated into word
structures consisting of the preposition as stem to which are suffixed a set of
personal endings, singular and plural, corresponding to the range of personal
pronouns in the language. A selection of these is exemplified below:

(319)

			aig 'at'	*an* 'in'	*do* 'to'	*de* 'of'	*le* 'with'	*air* 'on'	*fo* 'under'
SG	1		agam	annam	dhomh	dhiom	leam	orm	fodham
	2		agad	annad	dhuit	dhiot	leat	ort	fodhad
	3	MASC	aige	ann	dha	dheth	leis	air	fodha
		FEM	aice	innte	dhith	dhith	leatha	oirre	foidhpe
PL	1		againn	annainn	dhuinn	dhinn	leinn	oirnn	fodhainn
	2		agaibh	annaibh	dhuibh	dhibh	leibh	oirbh	fodhaibh
	3		aca	annta	dhaibh	dhiubh	leotha	orra	fodhpa

SOUND SYSTEM

The Gaelic sound system is by far the most widely investigated area of the
language. There are several dialect monographs: Borgstrøm (1937, 1940, 1941),
Holmer (1957, 1962), Oftedal (1956), MacGill-Fhinnein (1966), Dorian (1978),
Ternes (1973; with extensive discussion), Ó Murchú (1989), Grant (1987), as
well as Wagner and Ó Baoill (1969) and a good range of articles on the subject,
from Robertson (1906–9) to Watson (1974).

4.11   THE CONSONANT SYSTEM

There is no 'standard dialect' of spoken Scottish Gaelic. An inventory of single
consonants operating contrastively in the language dialects would be as shown in
table 4.2. Such an inventory does not, of course, represent the consonant *system*
for any single dialect (and, possibly, it is not exhaustive). For example, the
quaternary set of contrastive stops represented by $b–b^h–p–p^h$ etc. is rare. Ternes
(1973) finds it operative for a subset of Applecross speakers. The contrastive set
$b–p–p^h$ showing the feature marking [+VOICE] – [−VOICE, − ASPIR] – [+ASPIR] is
more common but probably less common than a binary contrast which is usually
[+ASPIR] – [−ASPIR] but may be [+VOICE] – [−VOICE]. As both of these contrasts
are often represented by /b/~/p/, confusion can sometimes arise, especially if the
phonetic specification provided is inadequate.

Table 4.2. *Consonant system*

	+VOICE −ASPIRATION	+VOICE +ASPIRATION	−VOICE −ASPIRATION	−VOICE +ASPIRATION
Stops	b	(b^h)	p	p^h
−PALATAL	d	(d^h)	t	t^h
	g	(g^h)	k	k^h
+PALATAL	b′	(b'^h)	p′	p'^h
	d′	(d'^h)	t′	t'^h
	g′	(g'^h)	k′	k'^h

Fricatives	+VOICE		−VOICE	
−PALATAL	v, ṽ		f	
	γ		x	
+PALATAL	v′ ṽ′		f′	
	γ′		x′	

Continuants
Nasals

−PALATAL	m (m^h)	N (N^h) ŋ $(ŋ^h)$		n
+PALATAL	m′ (m'^h)	N′ (N'^h) ŋ′ $(ŋ'^h)$		n′

Laterals

−PALATAL	L	l
+PALATAL	L′	l′

Vibrants

−PALATAL	R	r
+PALATAL		r′

Sibilants	−VOICE	+VOICE
−PALATAL	s	(z)
+PALATAL	s′	(z′)

Semi-consonants	−VOICE	+VOICE
−PALATAL	h	
+PALATAL	h′	j

　　The commonest contrast in (non-labial) nasals and in laterals is a ternary one, usually *N–N′–n* and *L–L′–l* with the [±PALATAL] distinction being lost in the 'weak' set. This can further be reduced to *L–l′* and *N–N′* with *N* and *n*, and *L′* and *l′* falling together, probably by processes such as the following:

(320)   (a)   N – n – N′ – n′   *and*   (a)   L – l – L′ – l′

     (b)   N – n – N′   (b)   L –   L′ – l′

     (c)   N – N′   (c)   L –   l′

4.11.1   Single consonants, consonant clusters and consonant length

It is unrealistic to deal here *in extenso* with an inventory such as we have in Table 4.2. It is equally unrealistic to deal with a range of dialectal realisations (but see 4.1.1 and 4.16.1). For these reasons exemplification in this section on the sound system and in the following section on morphophonology will be from a sample dialect, that of Bernera, Lewis (see Borgstrøm 1940: 11–86) which is the writer's native dialect; supplementary notes on alternative realisations are included where appropriate. This is a conservative dialect (in Ternes' (1973) terms).

4.11.1.1   Single consonants
The system of single consonants in the sample dialect is as shown in table 4.3.

4.11.1.2   Positional distribution

    1 All the consonants in table 4.3 occur in word-initial position.
    2 All except those in parentheses occur medially and finally (/ŋ/ and /ŋ′/ occur medially and finally in some dialects).

4.11.1.3   Consonant clusters

    1 Initial clusters

(321)   pL-   pl′-   pʰL-   pʰl-   tL-   tl′-   tʰL-
           pr-   pr′-   pʰr-   pʰr′-   tr-   tʰr-

           kL-   kl′-   kʰL-   kʰl′-   fL-   fl′-
           kr-   kr′-   kʰr-   kʰr′-   fr-   fr′-
           sN-   s′N′-   sL-   s′L′-

(*v*, *v′*, *ṽ*, *ṽ′*, *γ*, *γ′*, *x*, *x′*, and those consonants in parentheses in table 4.2, occur in initial clusters only as morphophonemic alternants of their radicals, whose patterns they follow (see 4.16 below).)

(322)   sp-   sp′-   st-   s′t′-   sk-   sk′-
           spL-   spl′-   spr-   spr′-   str-
           skL-   skl′-   skr-   skr′-

Table 4.3. *Single consonants*

Stops						
−PALATAL	p	p^h	t	t^h	k	k^h
−PALATAL	p′	p′^{h}	t′	t′^{h}	k′	k′^{h}
Fricatives						
−PALATAL	v ṽ f				γ	x
+PALATAL	v′ ṽ′ f′				γ′	x′
Nasals						
−PALATAL	m (m^h)		N (N^h) n		(ŋ) (ŋ^h)	
+PALATAL	m′ (m′^{h})		N′ (N′h)		(ŋ′) (ŋ′^{h})	
Laterals						
−PALATAL	L					
+PALATAL	L′	l′				
Vibrants						
−PALATAL	R	r				
+PALATAL		r′				
Sibilants						
−PALATAL	s					
+PALATAL	s′					
Semi-consonants						
−PALATAL	h					
+PALATAL	h′	j				

2 Final clusters

(323)   -Nt^h -N′t′^{h} -Lp^h -l′p^h -Lt^h -L′t′^{h} -rp^h -r′p′^{h} -Rt -Rt^h -st -s′t′
-nk^h -n′k′^{h} -Lk^h -l′k′^{h} -rk^h -r′k′^{h} -rN   -sk -s′k′
-xk

3 Medial clusters

(a) All initial clusters (conditioned and unconditioned) and all final clusters may appear as medial clusters.

(b) Potentially (for example in noun+noun compounds) all combinations of final consonants or consonant clusters with initial consonants or consonant clusters can occur. Oftedal (1956), Dorian (1978) and Ó Murchú (1989) give useful lists of the combinations that occur in their material.

230   *Donald MacAulay*

4.11.1.4   Consonant length

Consonants are normally short. There is, however, a contrast of length in nasals, laterals and vibrants in some dialect areas. For example, in the words *lann* 'blade', *am* 'time', *gall* 'foreigner', *barr* 'top' – /LaN:/, /am:/, /kaL:/, /paR:/ respectively – we have long continuants as against *glan* 'clean', *màm* 'peak', *gal* 'weeping', *car* 'turn' – /kLan/, /ma:m/, /kaL/, /kʰar/ – in the same dialects – or /LauN/; /aum/; /kauL/; /pa:R/ in those dialects which do not show consonant length.

Length in these consonants is historical. If we compare the two types of dialect we see that where consonant length is lost the length is redistributed from the coda to the nucleus of the syllable to maintain syllable length in monosyll-ables – CVC: → CV:C. In disyllables this length is usually lost (unless it is protected by a following suffix consonant); for example, /paR:/ and /pa:R/ but /paRan/ for plural *barran* (see Ó Dochartaigh 1981).

4.11.1.5

Some dialects (including our sample dialect) have developed secondary length, under certain conditions of syncope, in these same conso-nants. The clearest case of this is in the plural of *-an* diminutives. Alongside the palatalised plural in *-ain* there is a suffixed plural in *-an* (as for *-ag* diminutives). If we take the example *cuilean* 'puppy' we get, generally, plurals *cuilein* or *cuileanan*. The normal realisation of the latter in this dialect is (beside /kʰul'anən/) /kʰul'an:/ giving the contrast /kʰul'an/ singular vs /kʰul'an:/ plural. (For further examples see MacAulay 1990.)

4.11.2   Consonant classes

Consonant classes are shown in tables 4.2 and 4.3 and examples (320)–(323). There is, along with the other less pervasive contrasts, a systemic distinction throughout between segments with the features [−PALATAL] and [+PALATAL]. This distinction is sometimes neutralised in labials with the palatal feature redistributed to the syllabic nucleus. In the stops and fricatives there is also a distinction most commonly expressed by the features [−ASPIRATION] and [+ASPIRATION] (but sometimes [−VOICE] and [+VOICE]) in the stops and [−VOICE] and [+VOICE] in the fricatives. This distinction is found also in the semi-consonants, which can indeed be said to be pro-formal realisations of members of the two feature systems:

(324)
$$\begin{bmatrix} +\text{ASPIR} \\ -\text{VOICE} \\ -\text{PALATAL} \\ h \end{bmatrix} \quad \begin{bmatrix} +\text{ASPIR} \\ -\text{VOICE} \\ +\text{PALATAL} \\ h' \end{bmatrix} \quad \begin{bmatrix} -\text{ASPIR} \\ +\text{VOICE} \\ +\text{PALATAL} \\ j' \end{bmatrix}$$

This demonstrates clearly how [+ASPIRATION] and [−VOICE], and [−ASPIRATION] and [+VOICE] are associate categories. The other members of the system have zero realization (cf. the lenition of f → Ø below, 4.16); w, which occurs in some dialects (and in all dialects in English borrowings, of course) is positively marked [+LABIAL].

4.11.3   Range of consonant realisations

The range of consonant realisation is considerable. The realisations for different dialects may be seen in the sources cited at the beginning of this section, and more completely when the findings of the Gaelic Linguistic Survey are published in the near future. Meantime, we can set down in table 4.4 the phonetic realisations of the consonants in our sample dialect, see table 4.3.

Table 4.4. *Consonant realisations*

p	pʰ	t	tʰ	k		kʰ
p	pʰ	ṭ	ṭʰ	ɟ		c
v ṽ	f			γ		x
v ṽ	f			j		ç
m	mʰ	n̪	n̪ʰ	n	ŋ	ŋʰ
m̥	m̥ʰ	ɲ	ɲʰ		ɳ	ɳʰ
ɫ	l̥	R	ɾ			
ʎ		ð				
s		h				
ʃ		h̩	i̩			

4.11.3.1   In this dialect /R/ is realised as a retroflected vibrant: /Rn/ is realised as [ɳ] and /Rt/ as [ṭ] retroflected *n* and *t* respectively. /Rtʰ/ is realised as [ṣṭ]; this cluster has a range of dialectal realisation from [ṛṭʰ] to [ṣṭʰ]. As we said above (4.11.1.4), /m/ /N/, /L/, /R/ are in some dialects realised as long segments [mː], [n̪ː], [ɫː], [Rː] as are their palatal counterparts. /t'/ and /t'ʰ/ are realised as front palatal or palatalised alveolar stops, and /L'/ as prepalatal or palatalised alveolar lateral. /L/ is [ɫ], a velarised dental lateral in our dialect, except for one subdialect area where it is [ɫ] a velarised alveolar. The [ɫ] realisation is the general one throughout Scotland, but [wɫ], [γɫ] and [tɫ], with lateral tongue position, appear as alternatives. Final and medial /pʰ/, /tʰ/ and /kʰ/ (and their palatal(ised) counterparts) have a range of realisations. They may simply be voiceless stops with some aspiration, or they may be preaspirated. Preaspiration takes a number of forms: it may be weak [ʰp], [ʰt], [ʰk] or strong [hp], [ht], [hk], or it may appear as a fricative [xp], [xt], [xk] (see 4.11.1 above).

4.12   THE VOWEL SYSTEM

The set of simple short vocalic nuclei in stressed syllables for our sample dialect is the following:

(325)   i   ɯ   u
        e   ə   o
            ɛ   a   ɔ

This system seems to be pretty consistent throughout the Gaelic area.

4.12.1   Monophthongs, diphthongs and vowel length

Monophthongs may be either short as in (325) or long. The set of long and short monophthongs in stressed syllables coincide.

(326)   i   i: ɯ ɯ: u   u:
        e   e: ə ə: o   o:
            ɛ   ɛ: ɔ   ɔ:
                    a   a:

4.12.1.1   Diphthongs are long nuclei. The set of diphthongs in our dialect are: (a) /ei, əi, ai, oi/; (b) /ou, au/; (c) /iə, ia, ua, ua/. (a) and (b) consist of peripheralising closing diphthongs, (a) fronting and (b) backing; (c) consists of centralising diphthongs with different degrees of opening movement.

4.12.1.2   Vowel length

In this dialect only two degrees of vowel length are observed. However, in other dialects different degrees of length are postulated: Ternes (1973) postulates three degrees of length and Ó Murchú (1989) has an important chapter (pp. 83ff.) on complex nuclei.

4.12.2   Vowel classes

The classification of vowels in terms of front ~ back and open ~ close is implicit in the diagrams in (325) and (326). The opposition long ~ short is shown in (326). Monophthongs, short or long, and diphthongs may be oral or nasal.

4.12.3   Range of vowel realisations

As we said above, the system of short and long monophthong oppositions in (326) holds for most dialects. Sometimes the /ɯ(:)/ ~/ə(:)/ distinction is absent.

There is an extensive range of realisations for each unit. For example, /i/ may be realised as [i] or [ɪ] or [ɨ]; /u/ as [u] or [ʉ]; /uː/ as [uː] or [ʉː] or even [yː]. /aː/ ranges from [ɒ̃ː] to [ɛ̃ː]. Realisations of diphthongs vary similarly. In addition, the range of complex nuclei differs greatly from area to area. For example the diphthongs in (a) and (b) of 4.12.1.1 above derive from the redistribution of length in the coda of syllables originally ending in long continuants to their nuclei (4.11.1.4). Those dialects that have retained long continuants do not have these classes of diphthong. At the same time other complex nuclei have been developed (un-uniformly), from the loss of intervocalic fricatives, for example (see Ó Murchú 1989: ch. 4).

4.12.4   Semi-vowels

In Gaelic so-called 'semi-vowels' are best regarded as semi-consonants, since they operate in the consonant system (see tables 4.3 and 4.4).

4.13   SYLLABLE STRUCTURE

The syllable consists of a nucleus, an onset and nucleus, a nucleus and coda, or an onset, nucleus and coda. The onset may consist of one consonant, two consonants or three consonants; the nucleus of a short or long monophthong or a vocalic complex; and the coda of one or two consonants. This may be expressed in the formula:

(327) $(C_1)(C_2)(C_3) \ V_1(V_2) \ (C_4)(C_5)$

The realisation of C_1 is always /s/ and C_2 /p/, /t/ or /k/. (See table 4.3 and examples (325) and (326) above.)

4.13.1   Syllable length

Length is a syllable feature rather than one simply of the nucleus. In (C)VC structure when the coda is long then the nucleus is short; for example, dialects with long continuants have [kʰaLː], as against [kʰauL] in those that do not, for *call* 'loss' etc.

4.13.2   Syllabification

In our sample dialect (other claims have been made for other varieties) syllabification in CVCVCV strings is of the kind (C)V|CV|CV. . ., unless the (non-string-initial) C is a stop, in which case the closure seems to function as coda and the release as onset: CVC|C. . .

4.13.3   Hiatus

Syllable sequences of the structure (C)V + V(C) sometimes collapse into monosyllabic structures. If we take, for example, *taigh* [t̪ʰəh] 'house' and *agh* [əɣ], 'heifer' we get (328a) and (328b):

(328)(a)   [t̪ʰəh] + GEN → [t̪ʰɛhə]
    (b)   [əɣ] + GEN → [ɛ − ə]

In certain circumstances (normally in our dialect) [ɛ − ə] becomes [ɛɛ] or [ɛː] with falling pitch (see 4.15.2.1) whereas [t̪ʰɛhə] either remains a disyllable or is shortened to [t̪ʰɛ(h)] (see Ternes 1973: sec. 2.1).

4.14   STRESS

Stress is realised at syllable level. There are basically two classes of syllable: stressed and unstressed. Stressed syllables fall into at least two subclasses, primary stress and secondary stress (see Ó Murchú (1989: ch. 2) for a more elaborate system). Emphatic stress is a special case of primary stress.

4.14.1   Discourse function

Stress has a discourse function. Each unit of discourse has at least one primary stress correlating normally with primary 'information point' (see 4.15.3).

4.14.2   Distribution of stress

Uncompounded words have stress on the first syllable, compound words on the root syllable (normally):

(329)(a)   *dealachadh* 'parting' /ˈtˈaLəxəɣ/
    (b)   *eadardhealachadh* 'difference'/ˌatərˈɣˈaLəxəɣ/

In phrases, the placement of stress reflects the discourse function of the phrase elements; for example, in noun phrases primary stress goes on lexical modifiers rather than on the head, that is on the category 'new' rather than 'given':

(330)   *cuilean* 'a puppy' /ˈkʰulˈan/
    cuilean mòr 'a big puppy' /ˌkʰulˈanˈmoːr/

Normally the primary stress comes on the last lexical item in the phrase:

(331)   *cuilean mòr salach dubh* 'a dirty, big, black puppy' /ˌkʰulˈanˌmoːrˌsaLəxˈtu/

Articles, pre-possessives, pronouns, particles and simple prepositions are normally unstressed. In certain contexts, however, for example in assertive or explicatory responses, these items may take stress. Also, in contrastive contexts, the normal distribution of stress in utterances (and in phrases) may be overruled (see 4.15.3.4).

4.15   PITCH

4.15.1   Syllable pitch

Unstressed and short stressed syllables have no inherent independent pitch contour associated with them. Long syllables, however, may have either a maintained level pitch or a falling pitch contour and this difference is, in some dialects at least (including our sample dialect), distinctive.

4.15.2   Word tone

Long monosyllabic words (as follows from 4.15.1) have an inherent pitch contour. This applies both to words with long nucleus and words with long continuant coda. The nature of the pitch contour is that the pitch level is maintained (relatively) throughout the word. This contrasts with disyllabic words where we have a falling pitch contour:

(332)(a)   *màl* 'rent'   /ma:L/
         mall 'slow', (i) /mauL/
            or (ii) /maL:/

   (b)   *mala* 'brow'   /maLə/
        maille 'delay' /maL'ə/

4.15.2.1   In the section on hiatus above (4.13.3) we showed that in hiatus conditions disyllabic sequences can collapse into monosyllabic ones. Disyllabic words, then, of the structure (C)V + V(C) (where '+' merely indicates the V-to-V transition) may become monosyllabic words of the structure CVVC. This long nucleus maintains the pitch contour of its origin. Thus we may have original long monosyllables and derived long monosyllables which are identical in segmental constituency, but are distinguished by pitch contour; for example:

(333)   *bò* 'cow'   /po:/   *duan* 'ditty'   /tuan/
      bogha 'reef' /po:/   *dubhan* 'hook' /tuan/

4.15.2.2   Svarabhakti

In the list of non-initial consonant clusters (4.11.1.3 above) certain gaps are apparent. Some gaps are due to neutralisation, for example, between [+ ASPI-

RATED] and [−ASPIRATED] in stops in the sequences *L* or *N* before dental stop and *L′* or *N′* before a prepalatal stop, and some are due to historical 'accident'. In one class of cases the gap is due to the development of an epenthetic vowel between the consonants of what were, indeed, clusters historically. Such vowels developed between (orthographic) *l, n, r* and *b, g* (but not normally *p, d, t* or *k*), *bh, mh, ch, gh* and *m* (in both the non-palatal and palatal series). (See Oftedal (1956: 142–3) for extensive set of examples.) We may exemplify with the following:

(334)(a)   *dearg* 'red'   /t′arak/
             deirge 'redness'   /t′er′ek′ə/
             borb 'wild'   /pɔrɔp/
             tilg 'throw'   /t′^{h}il′ik′/
             tulg 'dent'   /t^{h}uLuk′/
             ainm 'name'   /anam/; etc.

but not

(b)   *tearc* 'rare'   /t′^{h}ark^h/
             teirce 'scarcity'   /t′^{h}er′k′^{h}ə/
             corp 'body'   /k^{h}ɔrp^h/

In the same way as long syllables derived from disyllables (example (333)) keep the falling pitch contour of their origin, so svarabhakti strings deriving from original long monosyllables keep the typical non-falling contours of such syllables:

(335)   *ainm* 'name' /anam̅/ ~ *anam* 'soul' /ana̅m/

               balg 'bulge' /pa̅Lak/ ~ *ballag* 'garment' /paLa̅k/

The difference is the same as that between the monosyllables /po̅:/ and /po̅:/ in (333).

It will be noted that the epenthetic vowel in the dialect exemplified here is a replica of that in the original monosyllable. This is not the case for all dialects; nor do all dialects have pitch differentiation at this level.

4.15.3   Intonation

The study of intonation in Scottish Gaelic has been very limited, consisting in most cases of tentative diagrams of 'sentence tunes'. The following remarks apply, strictly, only to our sample dialect, but my experience is that the distinctions carried by the basic tones, and the distribution of tones, have wide application.

4.15.3.1   Nuclear tone

In discussing stress, above, we said that it was a function of discourse and that all discourse units have at least one primary stress. The same may be said of intonational distinctions: each discourse unit has at least one nuclear tone and that coincides distributionally with primary stress. By nuclear tone is meant a pitch movement normally distinctive within a vocalic nucleus (though its domain may extend onwards over a number of nuclei).

4.15.3.2   Primary tone types

There are four primary tone types each with its distinctive pitch configuration (MacAulay 1979: 27ff.). We may exemplify with the utterance, *Cheannaich Iain an leabhar* 'Iain bought the book' and some discourse responses to it.

> *Tone I: falling pitch*

(336)   *Cheannaich Iain an | leabhar*

The vertical cut denotes the beginning of the tonic element separating it from the pretonic (which we cannot deal with here). The fall is distinctive in the first (stressed) syllable of *leabhar* but extends to the end of the utterance. This tone is associated with statements, primarily, though not necessarily, with affirmation. For example, questions with overt Q-elements can also have tone I, as in:

(337)   *An do cheannaich Iain an | leabhar?*

> *Tone II: rising pitch*

(338)   *Cheannaich Iain an | leabhar?*
  'Iain bought the book?'

This tone is associated with interrogation.

> *Tone III: rising–falling*

(339)   *Cheannaich Iain an leabhar.*

  An do | cheannaich?
  Q PT bought
  'Did he?'

This tone denotes surprise (but not dissent).

> *Tone IV: falling–rising*

(340)   *Cheannaich Iain an leabhar.*

  |Cheannaich?
  Bought
  'He did?!'

This tone denotes disbelief (or 'pseudo-disbelief').

4.15.3.3   Secondary tone types

Each of the four primary tones has (a) unmarked, (b) high and (c) low subtypes. The marked forms denote the speaker's attitude to the message rather than modify the message.

Tones may combine to give tonally complex utterances. These combinations are distinct from tones III and IV.

4.15.3.4   Distribution of tones

Tones may occur on any normally stressed syllable or on any syllable acquiring contrastive stress.

(341)(a)   *Cheannaich e an | leabhar*

    (b)   *|Cheannaich e an leabhar*

                   unmarked
    (c)   *Cheannaich | e an leabhar*   'He *bought* the book'
                                     'He *did* buy the book' (refutation)
    (d)   *Cheannaich e | an leabhar*   'He bought *the* book' (not *a* book)

(For further examples and explication see MacAulay 1979.)

MORPHOPHONOLOGY

4.16   NOUN MUTATIONS

The morphophonology of Scottish Gaelic, as of other Celtic languages, is a complex phenomenon. (The general statements made in 2.16 concerning Irish apply, *mutatis mutandis*, to Scottish Gaelic also.) Nouns show mutations of consonants and vowels in initial and non-initial position.

4.16.1   Initial mutations of consonants

Initial mutations occur in noun-initial (and other category-initial) position when that noun is preceded by a mutation-causing feature. This feature may be intrinsic to the preceding element, for example those associated with third person pre-possessive pronouns. If we take the example *cù* 'dog' we get:

(342)   Unmarked   /kʰuː/ 'dog'
          3SG FEM   /ə'kʰuː/ 'her dog'
          3SG MASC   /ə'xuː/ 'his dog'
          3PL   /ə'ŋʰuː/ 'their dog'

4.16.1.1   The feature, on the other hand, may be acquired from a dominating element. The article, for example, takes its specifications of number, gender and case from the head noun in its noun phrase, so that

(343) $\text{ART} + \text{N} \begin{bmatrix} +\text{SG} \\ +\text{MASC} \\ +\text{NOM} \end{bmatrix} \rightarrow \text{ART} \begin{bmatrix} +\text{SG} \\ +\text{MASC} \\ +\text{NOM} \end{bmatrix} + \text{N} \begin{bmatrix} +\text{SG} \\ +\text{MASC} \\ +\text{NOM} \end{bmatrix} \text{etc.}$

Let us take the examples *cù* /kʰuː/ which is masculine and *cuileag* 'fly' /kʰulʲak/, which is feminine, in the nominative singular with the article:

(344)(a)   {ART[+MASC] + kʰuː:[+MASC]} → {əᴺkʰuː:} ⇒/əˈŋʰuː/
   (b)   {ART[+FEM] + kʰulʲak [+FEM]} → {əᴸ kʰulʲak} ⇒/əˈxulʲak/

(In normal orthography these are *an cù* and *a' chuileag*, respectively.) In these cases we have marked the prepossessive elements and the article with the appropriate mutation feature ᴺ for nasal mutation and ᴸ for lenition (see 4.16.3).

4.16.1.2   As well as the article and the pre-possessive pronouns other elements cause mutation of nouns.

   1 Other pre-head elements in the noun phrase cause lenition (regardless of gender):
      (a) the cardinal numbers 'one' and 'two': *aon chù, dà chù*;
      (b) *aon* meaning 'same': *an aon fhear* 'the same man';
      (c) the set of pre-head qualitative adjectivals and intensifiers: for example, *droch chù* 'bad dog', *fìor chù* 'a "real" dog'.
   2 In noun + noun phrases
      (a) The second, modified, noun is in the genitive case; when it is plural it lenites:

(345)   *biadh chon*
      food   dogs-GEN
      'dogs' food'

      (b) Nouns modifying feminine nouns lenite: for example:

(346)(a)   *ciste fhiodha*
      chest wood-GEN
      'wooden chest'
   (b)   *ciste mhine*
      chest meal-GEN
      'meal chest'

      (These are subject to the same rules that apply to adjectives (4.16.6).)

(c) Names of male persons in the genitive case (and in some dialects names of female persons) lenite: for example, *cù Sheumais* 'Seumas's dog'.

(d) Nouns lenite after the vocative particle: *a choin!* '(you) dog!'

3 Preposition + noun phrases:

(a) Some prepositions cause lenition: *do chù* 'to a dog'; *gun chù* 'without a dog': /tə'xu:/, /kən'xu:/.

(b) Some cause nasal mutation: *an cù* /ə'ŋʰu:/ 'in a dog'.

(c) Some do not cause mutation: *le cù* /l'ɛ'kʰu:/ 'with a dog'.

4.16.2   Non-initial mutations of consonants

4.16.2.1   Non-contrastive non-initial mutations

Non-initial mutation occurs internally in compounds. Prefixes ending in vowels cause lenition:

(347)   *ceartas*, 'justice' : *mì-cheartas*, /'m'i:x'aRtʰas/

If they end in a nasal (a) they cause nasal mutation:

(348)   *duine*, 'man' : *anduine* / 'aNənə/ 'non-man'

or (b) they develop a svarabhakti sequence (4.13):

(349)   *ceartas*, 'justice': *an(a)ceartas* /'anak'ʰaRtʰəs/

Nouns, as non-initial elements in compounds, where the preceding element is a lexical item, of whatever class, and bears stress, normally lenite. This might be further modified by the class of the consonant in contact at internal word junction, for example

(350)   *geal* 'white' + *cas* 'foot' *geal* + *chas* /'kʰ'aLaxas/ 'white-foot'

4.16.2.2   Contrastive non-initial mutations

The commonest place of occurrence of contrastive non-initial mutations is in the final consonants of noun stems (or suffixes). This set of mutations is different in kind from the above since the contrast involved is that between [−PALATAL] and [+PALATAL].

Normally, the change is from [−PALATAL] to [+PALATAL]; for example:

(351)   *màl* 'rent' (MASC) NOM SG = /ma:L/ → GEN SG and NOM PL / ma:l'/
          cat 'cat' (MASC) NOM SG = /kʰatʰ/ → GEN SG and NOM PL /kʰɛt'ʰ/
          cas 'foot' (FEM) NOM SG = /kʰas/ → PREP SG / kʰɔs'/

However, the mutation may involve [+PALATAL] → [−PALATAL]

(352)   *athair*, 'father' (MASC) NOM SG = /ahər'/ → GEN SG /ahər/
          màthair, 'mother' (FEM) NOM SG = /ma:hər'/ → GEN SG /ma:hər/

All final consonants and consonant clusters that have [−PALATAL] ~ [+PALATAL] correlates can potentially be involved in this mutation. It is interesting that the alternants categorise *l* as [+PALATAL] and *n* as [−PALATAL] (see diagram in (320) above):

(353)(a)   *cuilean* 'puppy': /kʰul'an/ ~ /kʰul'εN'/, i.e. *n*~*N'*
     (b)   *geal* 'white': /k'aL/ ~ /k'il'/, i.e. *L*~*l'*, as well as *geall* 'bet': /k'auL/ ~ /k'eiL'/, i.e. *L*~*L'*.

Svarabhakti sequences undergo this mutation as well as consonant clusters:

(354)(a)   *tarbh* 'bull': /tʰarav/~/tʰεr'εv'/
     (b)   *dealg* 'dart': /t'ʰaLak/~/t'ʰel'ek'/

Non-initial mutation occurs, similarly, in adjectives and verbs.

4.16.3   Consonant mutation classes

There are three classes of mutations. The first two, lenition and nasal mutation, are exemplified in 4.16.1 (342) and the third, the palatal mutation, in 4.16.2.2ff.

4.16.3.1   Example (355) shows the effect of lenition and nasalisation on the initial consonants and consonant clusters of nouns in our sample dialect. (Post-article mutations are described below, 4.16.5.)

    1 *Single consonants*

(355)   Radical: p p' pʰ p'ʰ t t' tʰ t'ʰ k k' kʰ k'ʰ f f' m m' N N' L L' R s s'
          Lenited: v v' f f' γ γ' h h' γ γ'x x' øø ṽ ṽ' n n L l' r hh'
          Nasalised: m m' mʰ m'ʰ N N' Nʰ N'ʰ ŋ ŋ' ŋʰ ŋ'ʰ f f' m m' N N' L L' R s s'

    2 *Consonant clusters*
    In clusters with initial *p*, *pʰ*, *t*, *tʰ*, *k*, *kʰ*, *f* (palatal and non-palatal) these consonants undergo the same mutations as they do in (355) and only the initial consonants are affected. All other clusters have *s*-initial consonants and mutate as follows:

(356)   Radical: sN   s'N'   sL   sL'   str
          Lenited: n   n   L   l'   r
          Nasalised: sN   s'N'   sL   s'L' str

    str- appears in some dialects as *sr*-; this also lenites to *r*-.

4.16.3.2   The realisation of lenition is pretty uniform throughout the dialects. There are, of course, gaps where oppositions have become inoperative, for example in the nasals and laterals, and in less conservative dialects, also, the incidence of occurrence of lenition is reduced. The realisation of nasalisation is a good deal more varied, in particular the nasalisation of stops and *f* which ranges from the situation shown in (355), where unaspirated stops are replaced by (voiced) unaspirated homorganic nasals, and aspirated sto₉s are replaced by voiceless postaspirated homorganic nasals, to prenasalised homorganic clusters (Ó Murchú 1989), or to simple replacement by the unaspirated variety (Dorian 1978). For example:

(357)   (a)   (b)

$$p \rightarrow m \qquad\qquad\qquad\qquad p^h \rightarrow m^h$$
$$\rightarrow mb \quad \Big/ \quad \underline{\quad N\quad} \qquad \rightarrow mb \quad \Big/ \quad \underline{\quad N\quad}$$
$$\rightarrow b \qquad\qquad\qquad\qquad \rightarrow b$$

4.16.4   Prevocalic mutations

The effect of mutating elements on following noun-initial vowels may be conveniently illustrated by showing them in contact with pre-possessive pronouns (see (342) above); *athair* /ahər'/, 'father' gives us:

(358)   PRON 3SG MASC {ə^L + ahər'}⇒ /'ahər'/
         PRON 3SG FEM: {ə^H + ahər'} ⇒ /ə'hahər'/
         PRON 3PL: {ə^N + ahər'} ⇒ /ə'Nahər'/

Before back vowels the preposed elements are [−PALATAL], before front vowels they are [+PALATAL]; for example, *each* /ɛx/ 'horse' gives /ə'h'ɛx/ and /ə'N'ɛx/.

4.16.5   Mutation after the article

Post-article mutations, though they may be classed generally as lenition, nasalisation and *h*-provection, are more complex than those found after those elements with intrinsic mutating features (4.16.1). As we said above, the mutation-causing features of the article are acquired (4.16.1.1) and so they are governed by noun-associated features such as gender, number and case. The simplest way of illustrating this phenomenon is by giving an example of the article with a masculine noun, *cat* /kʰatʰ/ 'cat' and a feminine noun *cearc* /K'ʰarkʰ/ 'hen'.

(359)

		Masculine	Feminine
SG	NOM	*an cat* /ə'ŋʰatʰ/	*a' chearc* /ə 'x'arkʰ/
	GEN	*a' chait* /ə'xɛt'ʰ/	*na circe* /nə 'k'ʰir'k'ʰə/
	PREP	*a' chat* /ə'xatʰ/	*a' chirc* /ə 'x'ir'k'ʰ/

PL	NOM and PREP	MASC	*na cait* /nə 'kʰɛt'ʰ/
		FEM	*na cearcan* /nə 'k'ʰarkʰən/
	GEN	MASC	*nan cat* /nə 'ŋʰatʰ/
		FEM	*nan cearc(an)* /nə 'ŋ'ʰarkʰ(ən)/

We see that nominative singular masculine and genitive plural masculine and feminine undergo nasal mutation; nominative and prepositional singular feminine and genitive and prepositional singular masculine undergo lenition. Genitive singular feminine and nominative and prepositional plural masculine and feminine do not undergo mutation. That pattern is stable for the consonants p, p^h, k, k^h and m. For all consonants [−PALATAL] and [+PALATAL] sets follow the same mutation rules.

4.16.5.1 t, t^h, t' and t'^h undergo nasal mutation in *all* the mutation environments shown in (359); for example, *doras* 'door' /tɔrəs/ → /Nɔrəs/ after the article in all singular forms and in the genitive plural; nom. and prep. pl. *dorsan* /tɔRsən/.

4.16.5.2   After the article the following consonants and clusters mutate as shown:

(360)   Base forms f f' s s' fr f'r'fL f'l' sN s'N' sL s'L' str (sr)
(a) Singular masculine
NOM   f f' s s' fr f'r'fL f'l' sN s'N' sL s'L' str
GEN   N N' Nʰ N'ʰ R R L L' Nʰr Nʰr NʰL Nʰl' Nʰr
PREP   N N' Nʰ N'ʰ R R L L' Nʰr Nʰr NʰL Nʰl' Nʰr
(b) Singular feminine
NOM   N N' Nʰ N'ʰ R R L L' Nʰr Nʰr NʰL Nʰl' Nʰr
GEN   f f' s s' fr f'r'fL f'L'sN s'N' sL s'L' str
PREP   N N' Nʰ N'ʰ R R L L' Nʰr Nʰr NʰL Nʰl' Nʰr

None of these mutate in the plural.

4.16.5.3   Initial clusters beginning with stops mutate like single stops. The mutation does not go beyond the stop. N, N', L, L', R do not mutate after the article.

4.16.5.4   Vowel-initial words mutate as follows: *àl* 'brood' (masc.); *ite* 'feather' (fem.)

(361)

	Singular masculine	Singular feminine
NOM	*an t-àl* /ə'Nʰa:L/	*an ite* /ə'N'it'ʰ/
GEN	*an àil* /ə'Na:l'/	*na h-ite* /nə'h'it'ʰ/
PREP	*an àl* /ə'Na:L/	*an ite* /ə'N'it'ʰ/

Plural masculine and feminine

NOM/PREP *na h-àil* /nə'ha:l'/; *na h-itean* /nə'h'it'ʰən/

GEN   *nan àl* /nə'Na:L/; *nan itean* /nə'N'it'ʰən/

The preposed *N* and *h* are palatal before front vowels and non-palatal before back vowels.

4.16.5.5   There is considerable dialect variation in the realisation of the post-article mutations.

4.16.6   Vocalic mutations

There are basically two kinds of vocalic mutation: mutations of quality and mutations of quantity. Sometimes these combine.

4.16.6.1   Vocalic mutations of quality

These are to be found with both monophthongs and diphthongs. They mostly co-occur with mutations of quality in the following consonant segment of the kind we have looked at above (4.16.2.2 (351)–(353)). There are many subclasses of vocalic quality mutations (Oftedal (1956: 173) finds twenty-eight). We can only give some examples; it will be noted that the change is from open to close or back to front or both. We may illustrate with /a/ long and short and the diphthong /au/.

(362)

a →ɛ	/kʰatʰ/ → /kʰɛt'ʰ/ (*cat* 'cat')
ã →ĩ	/mãkʰ/ → /mĩk'ʰ/ (*mac* 'son')
a(<ɔ) →ɔ	/kʰas/ → /kʰɔs'/ (*cas* 'foot')
a: →ɛ:	/Rãṽ/ → /Rɛ:ṽ'/ (*ràmh* 'oar')
a: → ai	/Lã:ṽ/ → /Lãiṽ'/ (*làmh* 'hand')
a: →ɔ:	/fa:t/ → /fɔ:t'/ (*fàd* 'peat')
au → ei	/k'auL/ → /k'eiL'/ (*geall* 'bet')
au → əi	/bauL/ → /bəiL'/ (*ball* 'member')

4.16.6.2   Mutations of quantity

These may be changes (a) from short to long or (b) from long to short ('long' may be monophthong or diphthong). Group (a) usually derives from syncope either with loss of consonant or across hiatus; (b) is almost always the product of the shortening of lengthened originally short vowels:

(363)(a)   /āṽiN'/ → /ẽīnə/ (*abhainn/aibhne* 'river (NOM ~ GEN)')
            /Rɔ–ət'/ → /Rɔ:t'ən/ (*rathaid/ròidean* 'road (GEN SG ~ PL)')
      (b)   /pa:R/ → /paRən/ (*barr/barran* 'top/tops')
            /pauL/ → /paLan/ (*ball/ballan* 'spot/spots (+ DIMIN)')
            /peiN'/ → /peN'ə/ (*beinn/beinne* 'mountain (NOM ~ GEN)')

4.17   ADJECTIVE MUTATIONS

Adjectives undergo initial and non-initial consonant mutations and vowel mutations. These mutations correspond to some of those found in nouns: that is, initial lenition and non-initial palatalisation and qualitative and quantitative vocalic mutation. Neither nasalisation nor prevocalic mutation normally occurs.

4.17.1   Adjectives acquire their specifications of gender, number and case from the nouns they modify. The manner in which these are marked by mutation is illustrated in the following article + noun + adjective sequences (*an cù donn* 'the brown dog', *a' chas dhonn* 'the brown foot'; *cù* is an irregular masculine noun and *cas* is a regular feminine noun):

(364)

		Masculine	Feminine
SG	NOM	/ə ŋʰu: touN/	/ə xas γouN/
	GEN	/ə xɔN' γəiN'/	/nə kʰɔs'ə təN'ə/
	PREP	/ə xu: γouN/	/ə xɔs' γəiN'/
PL	NOM/PREP	/nə kʰɔN γoNə/	/nə kʰasən toNə/
	GEN	/nə ŋʰɔn toNə/	/nə ŋʰasən toNə/

4.17.2   In the singular the initial consonant mutations of the masculine and feminine adjective follow those of nouns in initial *p* and *p*ʰ (except for the nominative singular masculine which never undergoes mutation). Final consonant mutation of adjectives follow those of nouns of declension type I when they modify masculine nouns and nouns of declension type II when they follow feminine nouns. The vocalic mutations also follow those of these two classes with the regular alternants for the radical vowels being realised: ou → əi/__ C^Y; ou → o/__C^W+V; əi → ə/__C^Y+V (C^Y and C^W are convenient symbols for palatal(ised) and non-palatal(ised) consonants respectively (see MacAulay 1962)).

4.17.3   Plural adjective mutations are phonologically conditioned. If the noun ends in a palatal consonant then the following adjective lenites. Otherwise there is no mutation.

4.17.4   Adjectives are also lenited by adjective modifiers such as *glé* 'very' and *ro* 'too'.

4.18   VERB MUTATIONS

Verb-initial segments are mutated by preceding preverbal particles or sentence class markers.

4.18.1   Preverbal particles

A preverbal particle occurs before past-tense and second-indefinite forms. (The dependent forms of strong verbs are an exception.) Originally, this particle was *do* followed by lenition. The particle itself normally disappears where it is not preceded by a sentence class marker; the lenition, however, remains; for example, *tog* 'raise' gives:

(365)   PAST   *thog* /hok/
             INDEF 2   *thogadh* /hokəγ/

Before vowels and *f* a vestige /d/ or /γ/ of the preposition is preposed or substituted; for example *òl* 'drink' and *fàg* 'leave' give, in different dialects:

(366)   PAST (a) *dh'òl* /d'òl* /γɔːL//tɔːL/
                  (b) *dh'fhàg* /d'fhàg* /γaːk//taːk/

When preceded by a sentence marker such as the negatives *cha* or *nach* the *do* remains in the past but not in the indefinite 2: *cha*/*nach do thog* /xa(nax)tə'hok/. Before vowel and *f* we get either (367a) or (367b):

(367)(a)   *nach d'òl*/*d'fhag* /nax 'tɔːL//nax 'taːK/
      (b)   *nach do dh'òl*/*do dh'fhag* /nax tə'γɔːL//nach tə'γaːk/

In the (b) version the γ-appears to have become fixed before vowels and as an alternant for *f*- (owing to the latter's Ø realisation when lenited). The relative particle *a* causes lenition generally, but again γ- appears before vowels and as the alternant for *f*-.

4.18.2   Sentence and clause particles

The sentence interrogative particle *an*, {əN}, causes nasal mutation following the pattern in (355) above, as does *gun* {gəN} the affirmative marker in dependent clauses.

The negative particle has two forms: (a) *cha*, in free clauses, which causes lenition of *p*, *pʰ*, *m*, *N*, *N'*, *L'*, *R*, *s*, nasalisation of vowels and *f*-, and no lenition of *t*, *tʰ*; and (b) *nach*, in bound clauses, which does not cause mutation.

There are two conditional particles (a) *ma*, in definite mode, is followed by a relative form of the verb which it normally lenites, but preposes γ- to vowels and substitutes γ- for *f*-; and (b) *nan* {na^N}, which occurs with indefinite 2, nasalises. The negative conditional, *mana* /manə/ or *mur(a)* /mər(ə)/, according to dialect, does not cause mutation generally but the /manə/ form preposes *h*- to vowels and substitutes *h*- for *f*-.

REFERENCES

Anderson, A. O. 1909. The syntax of the copula *is* in modern Scottish Gaelic. *Zeitschrift für celtische Philologie* 7: 439–49.
  1910. The syntax of the substantive verb *tha* in modern Scottish Gaelic. *Zeitschrift für celtische Philologie* 8: 236–41.
Bannerman, J. W. M. 1974. *Studies in the history of Dalriada*, Edinburgh: Scottish Academic Press.
  The Lordship of the Isles. In J. M. Brown (ed.), *Scottish society in the fifteenth century*, London: Arnold, 209–40.
Borgstrøm, C. Hj. 1937. The dialect of Barra in the Outer Hebrides. *Norsk Tidsskrift for Sprogvidenskap* 8: 71–242.
  1940. *The dialects of the Outer Hebrides* (Norsk Tidsskrift for Sprogvidenskap, Suppl. bind 1), Oslo: Aschenhoug.
  1941. *The Dialects of Skye and Ross-shire* (Norsk Tidsskrift for Sprogvidenskap, Suppl. bind 2), Oslo: Aschenhoug.
  1974. On the influence of Norse on Scottish Gaelic. *Lochlann* 6: 91–103.
Calder, G. 1923. *A Gaelic grammar*, Glasgow: MacLaren.
Comrie, B. 1985. *Tense*, Cambridge: Cambridge University Press.
Dorian, N. 1978. *East Sutherland Gaelic*, Dublin: Dublin Institute for Advanced Studies.
Dunn, C. W. 1974. *Highland settler*. Toronto: Toronto University Press.
Durkacz, V. E. 1983. *The decline of the Celtic languages*, Edinburgh: John Donald.
Edwards, J. 1988. Gaelic in Nova Scotia. In C. H. Williams (ed.) *Geolinguistic essays*, Clevedon, Avon: Multilingual Matters, 86–102.
Grant, J. H. 1987. The Gaelic of Islay: phonology, lexicon and linguistic context. PhD thesis, Aberdeen University.
Holmer, N. M. 1957. *The Gaelic of Arran*, Dublin: Dublin Institute for Advanced Studies.
  1962. *The Gaelic of Kintyre*, Dublin: Dublin Institute for Advanced Studies.
Jackson, K. H. 1951. *Common Gaelic: the evolution of the Goedelic languages* (Rhŷs Memorial Lecture). London: Oxford University Press.
  1968. The breaking of original long *é* in Scottish Gaelic. In J. Carney and D. Greene (eds.) *Celtic studies: essays in memory of Angus Matheson 1912–1962*. London: Routledge and Kegan Paul, 65–71.
Lyons, J. 1977. *Semantics*, vol. 2, Cambridge: Cambridge University Press.
MacAulay, D. 1962. Notes on some noun-initial mutations in a dialect of Scottish Gaelic. *Scottish Gaelic Studies* 9: 146–75.
  1978. Intra-dialectal variation as an area of Gaelic linguistic research. *Scottish Gaelic Studies* 13, 1: 81–97.
  1979. Some functional and distributional aspects of intonation in Scottish Gaelic. In D. P. Ó Baoill (ed.) *Papers in Celtic phonology* (occasional papers in linguistics and language learning no. 6), Coleraine: The New University of Ulster, 27–38.

248   *Donald MacAulay*

1982a. Register range and choice in Scottish Gaelic. *International Journal of the Sociology of Language* 35: 25–48.

1982b. Borrow, calque and switch: the law of the English frontier. In J. Anderson (ed.) *Papers dedicated to Angus McIntosh* (Current issues in linguistic theory, 15) Amsterdam: John Benjamins, 205–37.

1988. On the order of elements in Scottish Gaelic clause structure and some related linguistic problems. In G. W. MacLennan (ed.) *Proceedings of the First North American Congress of Celtic Studies*, Ottawa: Ottawa University Chair of Celtic, 397–407.

1990. The development of long consonants in a dialect of Scottish Gaelic. In D. S. Thomson (ed.) *Gaelic and Scots in harmony: proceedings of the second International Conference on the Languages of Scotland*, Glasgow: Glasgow University Celtic Department, 72–7.

MacGill-Fhinnein, G. 1966. *Gàidhlig Uibhist a Deas*. Dublin: Dublin Institute of Advanced Studies.

McKay, Margaret M. (ed.) 1980. *Rev. John Walker's report on the Hebrides of 1764 and 1771*, Edinburgh: John Donald.

MacKinnon, K. M. 1986. The Scottish Gaelic speech community: some social perspectives. *Scottish Language* 5: 65–84.

MacLeod, M. 1963. Gaelic in Highland education. *Transactions of the Gaelic Society of Inverness* 43: 305–34.

Murison, D. 1974. Linguistic relationships in medieval Scotland. In G. W. S. Barrow (ed.) *The Scottish tradition: essays in honour of R. G. Cant*, Edinburgh: Scottish Academic Press, 71–83.

Ó Baoill, C. 1978. *Contributions to a comparative study of Ulster Irish and Scottish Gaelic*, Belfast: Institute of Irish Studies.

Ó Dochartaigh, C. 1981. Vowel strengthening in Gaelic. *Scottish Gaelic Studies* 12: 219–40.

Ó Murchú, M. 1989. *East Perthshire Gaelic*, Dublin: Dublin Institute for Advanced Studies.

Oftedal, M. 1956. *The Gaelic of Leurbost* (Norsk Tidsskrift for Sprogvidenskap, Suppl. bind 4), Oslo: Aschenhoug.

Robertson, C. M. 1900. The Gaelic of Perthshire. *Transactions of the Gaelic Society of Inverness* 22: 4–42.

1906–9. Scottish Gaelic dialects. *Celtic Review* 3: 95f.; 4: 69f.; 5: 79f.

Shaw, W. 1778. *An analysis of the Gaelic language*, London; repr. 1972: Menston Scolar Press.

Ternes, E. 1973. *The phonemic analysis of Scottish Gaelic* (forum phoneticum 1), Hamburg: Helmut Buske.

Thomson, D. S. (ed.) 1983. *The companion to Gaelic Scotland*, Oxford: Blackwell.

Wagner, H. and C. Ó Baoill. 1969. *Linguistic atlas and survey of Irish dialects*, vol. IV, Dublin: Dublin Institute for Advanced Studies.

Walker, J. 1808. *An economical history of the Hebrides and Highlands*, Edinburgh.

Watson, J. 1974. A Gaelic dialect of N. E. Ross-shire. *Lochlann* 6: 9–90.

Withers, C. W. J. 1979. The language geography of Scottish Gaelic. *Scottish Literary Journal (Language Supplement)*, 41–54.

1984. *Gaelic in Scotland 1698–1981*, Edinburgh: John Donald.

1988. *Gaelic Scotland: the transformation of a culture region*, London: Routledge.

PART II
The Brittonic languages

5

The Welsh language

ALAN R. THOMAS

HISTORICAL AND SOCIAL PERSPECTIVE

5.0   EXTERNAL HISTORY OF THE LANGUAGE

5.0.1   Areal distribution

Before the Saxon incursions into the western parts of mainland Britain, the
Welsh language – or its precursor, British or Brittonic – had been spoken from
the Firth of Forth in the north to what is now known as the West of England,
and in the seventh century the Saxons were still confined to the eastern half of
what is now England itself. Thus, at this early time, there was land contact
between all those areas in which the indigenous British tongue was the dominant
language, though there is little evidence of sustained contact between Cumbria,
Northumbria in the far north, Rheged east of the Pennines and the southern
regions in today's Wales, Cornwall, Devon and Dorset. What little evidence
there is suggests that the language spoken in all these areas was relatively
uniform in structure: Cornish is strikingly like Welsh – particularly the southern
dialects of Welsh – in its phonology and in the broader aspects of its syntax and
morphology (though the data is stylistically very restricted); and what fragments
of evidence remain of the language of Cumbria can be interpreted through
correspondence with similar forms in Welsh – Gregor (1980), for instance,
quotes the three surviving forms

> *galnys*, cf. Welsh *galanas* (blood-money due for homicide)
> *mercheta*, cf. Welsh *merch* (girl or daughter)
> *kelchyn*, cf. Welsh *cylch* (circuit)

Within living memory, shepherds in Cumbria have been recorded as using a
counting system which is clearly Brittonic in origin, and children at play use a
counting system which is probably derived from it: Gregor, again, quotes from

I. and P. Opie (*The Times Literary Supplement*, 14 July 1979, p. 799), who say that children, counting aloud, use 'twenty' as a unit, and there is some likeness between many of the numerals from 'one' to 'ten' and those of Welsh; he quotes *yau, tau, tethera, methera, pimp, sethera, lethera, nothera, dothera, dick* though *sethera* (if correspondent with *saith*) is not optimally ordered for the correspondences with Welsh, which are *un, dau, tri, pedwar, pump, chwech, saith, wyth, naw, deg*. During the sixth and seventh centuries, however, the Saxons advanced westwards to the Severn and the Dee, thus severing the land link between what is now Wales and the British territories north and south of it. From about this time onward, the dialects of Cornwall and Wales began to develop independently of each other, and that of the northern kingdoms languished and disappeared.

5.0.2   Demographic distribution

Until the arrival of the Normans in the eleventh century, and the warring which led ultimately to the subjugation of Llywelyn, the last indigenous prince of Wales, in the thirteenth century, there is no reason to believe but that the Welsh language was uniformly distributed throughout the population. During the medieval period, however, the establishment of walled and fortified towns – particularly along the border with England and on the northern coast, and notably by Edward I – led to a separation of rural and urban communities, in which the indigenous Welsh population was frequently excluded from the townships (and from involvement in the commercial services which they provided). This relegation of the indigenous population to non-urban activities was exacerbated with the ascent of the Tudors to the throne of England, when many of the native Welsh aristocracy – usually the most ambitious in politics and business matters – migrated to London, attendance at court and all the material advantages that that would bring. In this way, the most vigorous and forward-looking of the aristocracy were largely anglicised.

The anglicisation of the most influential strata in society continued after the Acts of Union of 1536 and 1542 excluded the Welsh language from use in the courts and functions of government and administration. And, after the industrial revolution, it was disseminated into yet other social strata, when the linguistic division between managers and workers came to reflect that between landowners (largely the anglicised gentry) and tenant farmers (the Welsh-speaking 'gwerin').

Nevertheless, Southall (1892) was able to show that the whole of Wales excepting Pembrokeshire south of the 'landsker', the Gower peninsula, and the extreme eastern borders in Flint, Radnor and Monmouth, had more than 60 per cent of its adult population able to understand or speak Welsh (see map 5.1). Of course, in the western enclaves where the language was (and is yet) at its strongest, the situation was even more encouraging than Southall's map would suggest: even today, according to the 1981 Census, those same western districts have over 50 per cent of their population able to speak Welsh. In the intervening period – largely because of rural depopulation which bled off the younger generations – the proportion of Welsh speakers in the western areas rose to over 74 per cent in what is present-day Gwynedd, and to over 63 per cent in present-day Dyfed, according to the Census report for 1951. The picture since then has been one of gradual decline, persistent but undramatic in purely numerical terms.

In the mid nineteenth century, a Welsh settlement was established in Patagonia (for which, see R. Bryn Williams 1962 and G. Williams 1975). There are still some there who speak the language regularly, and a description of some of its distinctive phonological features, and of contextual variation within it, can be found in R. O. Jones 1984.

5.0.3   Status and institutionalisation

Until the fall of Llywelyn in 1288, the Welsh language clearly had status in administration and government. The Laws of Hywel Dda, codified in the tenth century, set out the duties and obligations of the various officers of the princely court, setting out a terminology for professional functions and legal and administrative procedures which were obviously of long standing. The Acts of Union, on the other hand, removed the Welsh language from all prestigious public and administrative functions: the act of 1536 states 'all justices . . . shall proclaim and keep . . . all . . . courts in the English tongue; . . . no person or persons that use the Welsh speech or language shall have . . . any office . . . within this realm of England, Wales or other the King's Dominion . . . unless he or they use and exercise the English speech or Language' (quoted in Williams 1950).

It is probable that the language would not have survived but for the translation of the Bible into Welsh in 1588, providing both a symbol of prestige and a model for standard written and public oratorical usage which persisted until the second half of the present century, latterly alongside the conservative literary standard established by the publication of Morris-Jones (1913). The non-conformist chapels with their Sunday Schools were the principal vehicles of language maintenance in Wales until the second half of the twentieth century;

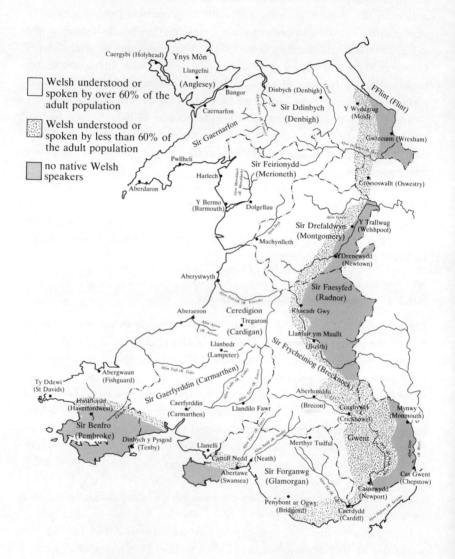

Map 5.1   Southall's linguistic map of Wales (after Southall 1892)

and, in teaching the language, they produced a literate working class which inspired the journalistic expansion of the nineteenth century (see Lloyd 1973).

The educational system, on the other hand, was a positive hindrance to the propagation of the language until the second half of the present century. The *Reports of the commissioners of inquiry into the state of education in Wales* (1848) was unequivocal in its view of the value of the Welsh language: 'The Welsh language is a vast drawback to Wales, and a manifold barrier to the moral progress and commercial prosperity of the people. It is not easy to overestimate its evil effects . . . It dissevers the people from intercourse which would greatly advance their civilisation, and bars the access of improving knowledge to their minds' (p. 309). The Welsh people themselves, however, did not respond to such views in a combative way. Williams (1973) perceptively points out that 'the people of Wales wanted their children to acquire a knowledge of the English language and they were prepared to see their own language persecuted and devalued if they believed that it hindered the development of competence in English' (p. 97). In this way, the people of Wales acquiesced in the subjugation of their language; the Education Act of 1870 brought education within the reach of every child in Wales – through the medium of English. And when secondary education became generally available in the 1890s, only minimal provision was made for the teaching of Welsh as an academic subject.

5.0.3.1   Functional range, literacy

There is a long and continuing literary tradition which reaches back, in poetry, to the early 'northern' works of the sixth century associated with Taliesin, Llywarch Hen and Aneirin's *Gododdin* (the oldest 'Scottish' poem); it spans the strict metres of 'cynghanedd', and from the sixteenth century onwards free verse in a more vernacular vein. The prose tradition goes back to Laws of Hywel Dda, a few medieval romances and the tales known as the Mabinogi; though they clearly preserve a much older tradition, the oldest substantial prose manuscripts (like those of the poems) date from around the thirteenth century. The prose tradition is less varied and rich than that of the poetry, but it revived after the translation of the Bible in the sixteenth century gave rise to a considerable amount of religious and theological writing, though much of it was translation.

Although the nineteenth century had seen a proliferation of Welsh-language journalism, from straightforward reportage to philosophical, political and theological publications (Lloyd 1973), the growth of literacy was generally retarded by its exclusion from the educational system. At the same time, its use in the non-conformist Sunday Schools ensured its reproduction in a substantial proportion of the population. Those who learned to read and write in Welsh did so despite the established educational system.

5.0.4   Contemporary position

5.0.4.1   Areal distribution

The Welsh language is indigenous to all areas except the District of Radnor and most of Brecknock and Monmouth; the southern parts of Preseli and south Pembrokeshire, and the Gower peninsula (the District of Swansea) have been anglicised for many generations. The density of Welsh speakers varies from 61.2 per cent in Gwynedd to 2.5 per cent in Gwent: map 5.2 shows the distribution of speakers by county, noting the total number in each case and the percentage which the Welsh speakers form of the total population of the county. Although there are over 120,000 speakers in the three industrial and urbanised counties of Mid, South and West Glamorgan, they comprise, on average, only about 10 per cent of the population of the area.

5.0.4.2   Demographic distribution

The figures in table 5.1 reveal the decline in the number of Welsh speakers during the past fifty years. It is not, in essence, dramatic, but less than a fifth of the population overall now speak the language; and, even in the heartlands of Gwynedd and Dyfed, there has been a substantial decline in the last thirty years.

Yet more revealing are the figures in table 5.2, which detail the decline within age groups. The overall tendency has been for speakers of the language to be concentrated increasingly in the older age groups, with regular increments in the proportion of Welsh speakers in each higher age group. In the figures from the last two censuses, however, the pattern has changed, so that by 1981 children of school age (from five to fourteen) show a higher percentage of Welsh speakers than do their immediate seniors. This suggests that educational policy may be enjoying some success in teaching the language at the primary level.

The census form now asks about the individual's reading and writing habits in regard to the Welsh language, as well as their ability to speak it. It is significant, in view of the educational deprivation suffered by the language until the middle of this century, that there is a considerable disparity between the overall number of speakers and the number who record themselves as being readers and writers as well: almost a fifth of the half million speakers of the language register themselves as being neither readers nor writers of it.

5.0.4.3   Status

As a consequence of recommendations made in the *Hughes Parry Report on the Legal Status of the Welsh Language*, the Welsh Language Act of 1967 granted the language equal validity with English in legal proceedings in the courts of

Table 5.1. *Proportion of Welsh speakers at successive census counts (after Census 1981)*

Area	1921	1931	1951	1961	1971	1981
Wales	37.1	36.8	28.9	26.0	20.8	18.9
Counties						
Clwyd	41.7	41.3	30.2	27.3	21.4	18.7
Dyfed	67.8	69.1	63.3	60.1	52.5	46.3
Gwent	5.0	4.7	2.8	2.9	1.9	2.5
Gwynedd	78.7	82.5	74.2	71.4	64.7	61.2
Mid Glamorgan	38.4	37.1	22.8	18.5	10.5	8.4
Powys	35.1	34.6	29.6	27.8	23.7	20.2
South Glamorgan	6.3	6.1	4.7	5.2	5.0	5.8
West Glamorgan	41.3	40.5	31.6	27.5	20.3	16.4

Wales. A considerable number of government forms are now available in Welsh, and cheques written in Welsh are accepted by all the major banks: the extent to which correspondence on legal, technical and financial matters can be conducted in Welsh varies tremendously, depending frequently on the whims of individuals as much as their ability to do so or on the availability of appropriate linguistic terminology and accepted and familiar formulae.

5.0.4.4   Institutionalisation
The language was orthographically fluid until the early years of this century. With the publication of *Orgraff yr Iaith Gymraeg* (1928) the orthography was codified, roughly on phonemic principles. The publication of Morris-Jones' grammars (1913, 1921) had already done the same for its syntax and morphology, although on very conservative grounds. Until the end of the nineteenth century, grammars such as Anwyl (1899) had provided realistic synchronic descriptions of the language as it was used at the time: Morris-Jones' aim was different, as he states (1913: iii): 'the object which I had in view was the practical one of determining the traditional forms of the literary language'. Although Morris-Jones' study developed into a historico-descriptive work, it was this variety which became the authoritative standard for both literary and formal spoken usage in this century.

Despite the existence of a prestigious model of usage, the language continued to decline. Its recognition in the field of education was very patchy until the second half of the century, when the provision of bilingual schools, at both primary and secondary levels, made available a tool for language planning and maintenance. Such schools are in existence in all parts of Wales, and they are

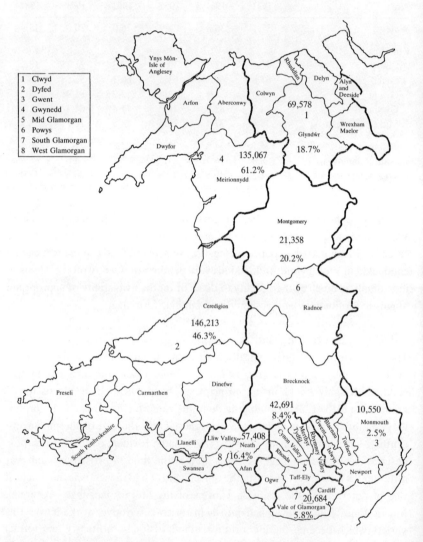

1 Clwyd
2 Dyfed
3 Gwent
4 Gwynedd
5 Mid Glamorgan
6 Powys
7 South Glamorgan
8 West Glamorgan

Ynys Môn-
Isle of
Anglesey

Rhuddlan

Delyn

Alyn
and
Deeside

Arfon   Aberconwy   Colwyn   69,578
1

Wrexham
Maelor

Glyndŵr
18.7%

Dwyfor   4 135,067
61.2%

Meirionnydd

Montgomery

21,358
20.2%

6

Ceredigion   Radnor

146,213
46.3%

2

Brecknock

Preseli   Carmarthen   Dinefwr   42,691
8.4%

10,550

Monmouth
2.5%
3

Llanelli   Lliw Valley 57,408
Neath

Cynon Valley

Merthyr
Tydfil

Rhymney Valley

Blaenau
Gwent

Islwyn

Torfaen

8 16.4%
Rhondda
5

Swansea   Afan   Ogwr   Taff-Ely   Newport

Cardiff
7 20,684
Vale of Glamorgan
5.8%

Map 5.2   Counties and districts of Wales showing totals of Welsh speakers in each
county, and the percentage they represent of the populations of the counties
(after Census 1981)

Table 5.2. *Proportion of Welsh speakers at successive census counts, by age (after Census 1981)*

Age last birthday	1921	1931	1951	1961	1971	1981
All ages 3 and over	37.1	36.8	28.9	26.0	20.8	18.9
3–4	26.7	22.1	14.5	13.1	11.3	13.3
5–9	29.4	26.6	20.1	16.8	14.5	17.8
10–14	32.2	30.4	22.2	19.5	17.0	18.5
15–24	34.5	33.4	22.8	20.8	15.9	14.9
25–44	36.9	37.4	27.4	23.2	18.3	15.5
45–64	44.9	44.1	35.4	32.6	24.8	20.7
65 and over	51.9	49.9	40.7	37.2	31.0	27.4

becoming, increasingly, the focus of efforts to safeguard the language. Provision for study through the medium of Welsh at tertiary level is still rare – except for Welsh-language studies themselves. A number of factors have rendered the traditional agencies of reproduction of the language ineffectual: the decline of religious observance has removed both an institution of prestigious association and an instrument of instruction; as mixed language marriages become more common, the family becomes a less frequent source of transmission of the language; the same process of anglicisation renders the workplace and the peer group less effective as agents of reinforcement; and frequently, particularly in the urbanised areas of the south, there is no identifiable 'community' of Welsh speakers in the traditional sense, but simply loose networks of people linked by such factors as occupation, workplace and membership of public institutions and places of worship.

5.0.4.5 Functional range

Apart from beginning the establishment of a comprehensive system of bilingual education, the single most significant development for maintaining the language has been the expansion of its use in the broadcast media. At one and the same time, this furnishes the language with public exposure in prestigious circumstances, and provides a set of contexts which can foster the development of a range of registers, from newscasting to comedy to children's programmes, and many others besides. Welsh-language radio is well established and well regarded; Welsh-language television has not yet developed the same degree of virtuosity, and so the recent decision to concentrate all Welsh-language programmes on one channel (Sianel Pedwar Cymru) is controversial since it requires a decision to 'switch into' a channel and thus loses the 'inertial' factor in much media viewing – we can only await the outcome. There are, of course, well-established formal registers which are associated with the contexts of religion, academic writing and discussion, weekly newspapers and topical journals. The University of Wales has been active, over the past thirty years or so, in coining specialised vocabularies for teaching scientific and technical subjects, and publishes a scientific journal, *Y Gwyddonydd*, aimed primarily at the upper school. There is an ever-widening range of contexts in which the language can be used, and technical servicing of those who wish so to do. And there is a wide range of literary genres in both poetry and prose.

5.0.4.6   Literacy

It was mentioned earlier that almost a fifth of Welsh speakers neither read nor write the language. This reflects the 'literacy gap' which derives from the long-term exclusion of the language from prestigious public usage, and from the educational process. A large proportion of non-professional Welsh speakers choose not to be literate in the language.

5.1   SYNCHRONIC LINGUISTIC VARIATION

5.1.1   Dialect variation

Dialect variation in the Welsh language is most profusely exemplified at the lexical level, and it is only this level which has been substantially investigated (Thomas 1973, 1980). Phonological variants tend to coincide with the boundaries of major and minor lexical speech areas, while there is no reliable information on the geographical provenance of syntactic variants.

5.1.2   Lexis

Lexical variation defines two dialect continua, north and south. Each of these is further divided, mainly into eastern and western sub-areas. The information we have is based on a survey of lexical variation which is reported in Thomas (1973, 1980). Older-generation usage was recorded at 175 enquiry sites spread throughout the Welsh-speaking areas. The responses to some 390 items in the questionnaire form the basis for published analyses, and in all comprise 996 distinct responses.

Areal clustering procedures reveal the internal structure of these continua. As map 5.3 shows, there is an extensive transition belt between the northern and southern continua, the northern penetrating to the southern sea-coast, and the

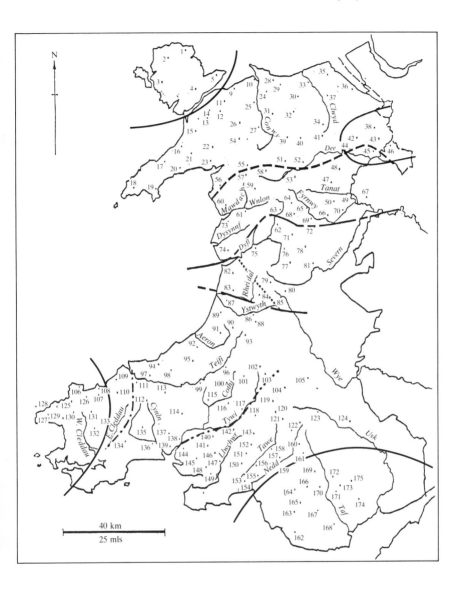

· · · · · · · · · · Line of strongest north–south differentiation

– – – – – Northern limits of southern continuum

·—·—·— Southern limits of northern continuum

———— – - Core-area boundaries, with transition belt between them

———— Dialect nuclei

Map 5.3 Lexical variation

southern extending to the southern banks of the river Dee. The major northern and southern areas are defined, respectively, by the distributions of 158 and 145 lexical items. The following are instances of words which distinguish these two major areas:

North		South
taid	'grandfather'	*tadcu*
nain	'grandmother'	*mamgu*
rw̄an	'now'	*nawr*
allan	'out'	*mās*

The sub-areas have their nuclei at the peripheries of the continua (see Thomas 1980 for discussion of this):

the north-west in Anglesey, which is distinguished by such forms as

chwiw	'gnat'
rarȳd	'rickyard'
ffunan	'handkerchief'
torth	'bar (of salt)'

the north-east in the region of the lower Dee, marked by such forms as

ymadael	'to move house'
hws	'a hiding'
derfa	'wheelbarrow'
mochyn daear	'mole'

the south-west in the tip of the district of Preseli (roughly the old county of Pembroke), marked by such forms as

cuch	'sty (on the eye)'
pendduÿn	'a boil'
troglwyth	'litter (of pigs)'
costen wenyn	'bee-hive'

the south-east in the eastern part of the old county of Glamorgan, marked by forms such as

mān	'bakestone'
erw	'acre'
twtan lawr	'crouch'
cwarel	'pane (of glass)'

However, the south-eastern nucleus is most often distinguished by the *absence* of a consistent response; migration to this urban and industrial area from all parts of Wales, and from the beginning of the industrial revolution to this day, has ensured that its dialects are extremely mixed, frequently recording forms which are typical of other parts of the country.

It is instructive to compare the relative distinctiveness of the nuclei of the sub-areas; the distributions of lexical items which define these geographically restricted nuclei are, of course, superimposed on the distributions of forms which pervade the whole continuum of which they form a part. We can measure the degree to which any one nucleus stands out from its continuum by totalling the number of forms in the nucleus which are of general distribution within the continuum and those which are restricted to the sub-branch, and then expressing the forms of restricted distribution as a proportion of the grand total. The results are as follows:

North-west	29%
North-east	14%
South-west	40%
South-east	39%

The two southern nuclei stand out from their environments much more dramatically than do the northern ones – and the north-east is seen to be particularly weakly distinguished. This is an indication of the homogeneity of the northern continuum, and the relative fragmentation of the southern one.

It is interesting, too, that the dominance of the north–south division of the dialect areas – long intuitively felt – is clearly shown by the numbers of forms which coincide in their distributions to define the various clusters of enquiry sites which, in their turn, combine to form the major areas and the components of their sub-areas. Whereas the north and south respectively attract 158 and 145 distributions, the next 'strongest' cluster of sites achieves only 30 (see Thomas, 1980).

This dominance of the north–south divide is further evidenced in an examination of the boundaries of dialect forms, rather than of their territorial extent. In plotting isoglosses for the 996 dialect items on a predrawn grid, it was found that a climactic break occurred along a line which runs inland from the mouth of the Dyfi to the sources of the Severn and Wye (see map 5.3). Along this line, there is an isolated set of isogloss counts which rise as high as 238, dissecting the country within the transition belt between the two major continua.

5.1.3   Syntax and morphology

There are no differences between the dialects in syntactic or morphological categories, but only in their realisations. Differences of these kinds are also relatively few and superficial. Examples of syntactic variation involve two aspects of negation and word order in a prepositional phrase:

1   The standard negative sentence

> *Nid yw ef yn mynd*
> NEG is he in go
> 'He is not going'

can occur in the dialects as

> northern: *dydi   o   ddim yn mynd*
> NEG-is he not   in go

> southern: *nag yw e'n   mynd*
> NEG is he-in go

or

> *swmo fe'n   mynd*
> ?of   him-in go

2   In standard usage, and in northern dialects, the notion 'never' is expressed as *byth* when non-perfective, and as *erioed* when perfective, as in

> *Oedd ef byth   yn mynd*
> was he never in go
> 'He never went/used to go'

> *Oedd ef erioed wedi mynd*
> was he never after go
> 'He had never gone'

Southern dialects, however, express both sentence types with the item *byth*.

3   In normal order a preposition precedes its object pronoun, but in parts of the north-east (notably in the old county of Flint), the order is reversed, as in

> standard: *Mae car ganddo ef*
> is   car with   him
> 'He has a car'

> dialect: *mae o gan gar*
> is   he with car

There are some salient examples of variation in morphemic realisation:

1   The third person singular future-tense form of the verb has a suffix in -*ith* in the north, and in -*iff* in the south, as in

North		South
canith	'will sing'	*caniff*
gwelith	'will see'	*gweliff*

2   The south-east has a third person singular past-tense form in the suffix *-ws*, as opposed to other dialect forms in *-odd*, as in

North		South
canodd	'sang'	*canws*
gwelodd	'saw'	*gwelws*

3   Various suffixes have alternate forms, with or without a /j/ onset (orthographically 'i'); the northern forms have 'i', the southern ones do not, as in

North		South
tanio	'to fire'	*tano* (verb–noun)
gweithiwr	'worker'	*gweithwr* (noun)
beichiog	'pregnant'	*beichog* (adjective)
crafiad	'scratch'	*crafad* (noun)

4   The form of the third singular personal pronoun is *fo* in northern dialects, and *fe* in southern ones. In some south-western varieties, the second person singular personal pronoun has an intimate form which is homophonous with that of the third singular personal pronoun in the same dialect, namely *fe*, as in

> *Shwd i fe?*
> how is you
> 'How are you?'

5.1.4   Sound system

There are a few major phonological variants:

1   The more northerly parts of the northern dialect (what we may call, for the purposes of this section, the 'north proper') has the 'high mixed' vowel /ɨ/, which has merged with /i/ in all south and 'midland' dialects (i.e. those which lie within the southern section of the northern area), as in northern /dɨːn/ '*dyn*', southern /diːn/. This represents a difference of inventory.

2   In absolute initial before /w/, northern dialects have /x/, where the south-west has /h/, and the south-east /Ø/, as in northern /xweːx/, south-western

/hwe:x/, south-eastern /we:x/ *chwech* 'six'. For the north and south-west this is a difference in distribution of /x/, and /h/; the south-east differs from the north in terms of inventory (lacking /h/), and distribution (/x/).

3   Long diphthongs in monosyllables have been retained in northern dialects, where southern dialects have tended to monophthongise them, as in northern /maːɨn/ *maen* 'stone', southern /maːn/. Here again we have a difference in inventory.

4   The south-east, unlike all other areas, has no prevocalic /h/, another inventorial difference: south-eastern /eːn/ *hen* 'old', others /heːn/.

5   An interesting realisational variant is that of the long vowel /aː/ in a fronted position approximate to [æ], in a midland area roughly coextensive with the district of Meirionydd, and again in the south-east, as in [tæːd] as opposed to [taːd], *tad* 'father'. This is an interesting phenomenon, as it represents a split distribution: originally, this feature ran from the midlands along the eastern half of the country, but by today the two areas of its distribution are separated by anglicised areas of Radnor and Brecknock.

6   There are instances of differences in the incidence of phonemes which involve the lax fricatives in final position. They tend to be lost in all dialects, but in northern dialects /v/ and /ð/ are regularly lost where, in selected words, southern ones retain them:

North		South
/goː/	*gof*, 'blacksmith'	/goːv/
/koː/	*cof*, 'memory'	/koːv/
/bar/	*barf*, 'beard'	/barv/
/gar/	*gardd*, 'garden'	/garð/

7   In monosyllables which terminate in sequences of /v/ + /r/ or /l/, southern dialects frequently make them disyllabic by inserting an epenthetic vowel into the cluster:

North		South
/sovl/	*sofl*, 'stubble'	/soːvol/
/ɬivr/	*llyfr*, 'book'	/ɬivir/
/gavr/	*gafr*, 'goat'	/gavar/

5.1.5   Other features of linguistic differentiation

One of the most significant features of variation in present-day Welsh is the disparity between the written standard and vernacular usage. The vernacular language has undergone a process of massive relexification from English which has been only marginally recognised by the written standard: forms like *jwmpo*, *bilifo*, *drimo* occur alongside the indigenous *neidio* ('jump'), *credu* ('believe'), *breuddwydio* ('dream') with depressing frequency. Equally pervasive are loan-translations of English particle–verb constructions, such as *gwneud i fyny am* 'make up for', *galw lan* 'call up', *torri lawr* 'break down', which regularly attract the wrath of the literary establishment as being 'corruptions' of Welsh usage. They are, however, a fact of life for the Welsh language, and must in some way be accommodated if the language is to survive as other than an elitist phenomenon.

But there are other respects in which the language has innovated by its own momentum, and which have led to a similar separation of standard written and general vernacular usage. These will be described in the body of the description which follows, and will only be listed here, for convenience:

> tense marking and time reference (see 5.7.3.3)
> impersonal verb forms (see 5.7.3.4)
> sentence-initial and preverbal particles (see 5.2.3. and 5.2.5)
> third person singular 'present' tense verbal suffix (see 5.1.3 and 5.7.3.3)

There is one other significant development in the spoken language – the clear signs of the emergence of a standard model for pronunciation in the media and other public contexts. The model is not to be identified with any regional accent – it rejects (for southerners) the northern sound /ɨ/, and for all speakers the final-syllable monophthong (north-western /a/, otherwise /e/) for orthographic 'ai', 'ae', 'au', preferring the orthographic diphthongs themselves as models. Thus

Vernacular		Target	Orthography
North	South		
/peθe/	/peθe/	/peθaɨ, peθai/	*pethau*, 'things'
/tamad/	/tamed/	/tamaid/	*tamaid*, 'piece'
/xwara/	/ware/	/xwaraɨ, xwarai/	*chwarae*, 'to play'

Thus the model for pronunciation is an abstract one, based on the orthography, which specifies the distribution of structural units like vowel and diphthong, but allows dialectal latitude in sound quality or accent (see Thomas 1978).

SYNTAX

The description of the grammar of Welsh will take account both of contemporary written usage and of speech; the spoken variety which is described is that spoken in public contexts by people of a northern dialectal background. It differs from that of southern speakers only in details of realisation.

5.2 SENTENCE STRUCTURE

5.2.1 Simple and complex sentences

Since this section is devoted to developing a detailed account of the structure of simple and complex sentences, we note only some general facts here, for which there is no clear slot elsewhere.

1 Simple sentences may be verbal or copula types (as described below) or nominal. The nominal type occurs principally in proverbial sayings,

(1)   *Cyfaill blaidd bugail   diog*
            friend wolf shepherd lazy
            'A lazy shepherd is the wolf's friend'

or in exclamatory contexts in which the sentence can be interpreted as an ellipsis involving a verb of movement like *mynd* 'go',

(2)   *Allan a   fo!*
            out   with him
            'Out with him!'

2 Complex sentences can involve clausal adverbial modification, of a variety of kinds, with associated conjunctions: we can exemplify (with conjunctions in bold type) from

    Time

(3)   *Bydd pawb   yn barod* **pan** *ddaw'r   galwad*
            will-be everyone in ready when will-come-the call
            'Everyone will be ready when the call comes'

    Place

(4)   *Mae e'n mynd* **lle**   *mae e'n   mynnu*
            is   he-in go   where is   he-in want
            'He goes where he wants'

Cause

(5)   *Daw   neb   heddiw **am***   *ei bod hi'n hwyr*
will-come no-one today   because its be it-in late
'No-one will come today because it is late'

Purpose

(6)   *Gwaeddwch yn uchel **er** mwyn imi   glywed*
shout-you   in loud for sake to-me hear
'Shout loud so that I can hear'

Result

(7)   *Darllenodd y llythyr **fel** bod pawb   yn deall*
read-he   the letter so that everyone in understand
'He read the letter so that everyone understood'

Condition

(8)   *Ateb   fi **os** elli di*
answer-you me if can you
'Answer me if you can'

5.2.2   Parataxis and hypotaxis

Co-ordination can be either hypotactic, with a linking conjunction,

(9)   *Aeth   at y drws **a**   chanu'r gloch*
went-he to the door and ring-the bell
'He went to the door and rang the bell'

or paratactic, with simple juxtaposition of two clauses,

(10) *Cododd ar ei draed; siaradodd yn eglur*
rose-he on his feet   spoke-he in clear
'He rose to his feet; he spoke clearly'

Paratactic juxtaposition of clauses also occurs when one of them is parenthetic,

(11) *Mae hyn, mae'n siwr, yn arwydd o dywydd da*
is   this, is-in sure in sign   of weather good
'This is, for sure, a sign of good weather'

or in apposition,

(12) *Daeth yr athro, un da   yn ei dydd, i roi cyngor*
came the teacher one good in his day   to give advice
'The teacher, a good one in his day, came to give advice'

5.2.3   Obligatory and optional elements of structure

Items which occur at complement and adjunct positions in the sentence are optional extensions of the basal 'verb plus subject' structure; additionally, because of the inflectional system, personal pronouns can be deleted when they function as subject of a verb or as object of a preposition (in both cases, the tendency is for the written language to favour deletion, and for speech to favour their retention). The following sentence illustrates all cases noted,

(13)   *Canodd (ef)   (gān)   (iddi (hi))*
            sang   (he) (song)   (to   (her))
            'He sang (a song) (to her)'

5.2.3.1   Elliptical sentences

Stylistic ellipsis can involve the sentence-initial inflected copula, together with its subject pronoun and the progressive-aspect marker which attaches to it, in allegro speech;

(14)   *('Dw i'n) meddwl ei fod ef*
            (am I-in) think   his be him
            '(I) think he is'

The perfective aspect marker cannot be elided,

(15)   *(Mae ef) 'di   mynd*
            (is   he) after go
            '(He's) gone'

A type of stylistic ellipsis which differentiates even consultative-style speech from writing involves particle deletion, as in the following examples, in which the particles are normally deleted in speech;

(16)   *(Ni) welodd y   bachgen ddim*
            (NEG) saw   the boy   nothing
            'The boy did not see anything'

(17)   *(A)   welodd ef rywbeth?*
            (INTER) saw   he anything
            'Did he see anything?'

(18)   *(Yr) oedd y   bachgen yna*
            (PT) was the boy   there
            'The boy was there'

(19)   *Hwn yw'r un (a)   welodd ef*
            this is-the one (who) saw   it
            'This is the one who saw it'

and this one, in which written varieties normally reject the particle which the vernacular employs before inflected lexical verbs and paradigms of the verb *bod* 'to be' with a consonant initial,

(20)   *(Mi)ddaw   ef yfory*
            (PT) will-come he tomorrow
            'He will come tomorrow'

In this latter case, the southern dialects have a variant form *fe* for the preverbal particle.

Grammatical ellipsis can involve (in addition to the positive and negative responses of 5.2.6) a number of auxiliary verbs as responses. We can exemplify with positive sentences:

    1 the copula,

(21)   *A   wyt ti'n dōd? Ydwyf*
           INTER are you-in come am-I
           'Are you coming?' 'Yes'

    2 modal auxiliaries,

(22)   *A   elli di fynd? Gallaf*
           INTER can you go?   can-I
           'Can you go?' 'Yes'

    3 the carrier auxiliaries, which mark tense in a periphrastic construction (see 5.7.3.3):

(23)   *A   wnei di ganu? Gwnaf*
           INTER will-do you sing   will-do-I
           'Will you sing?' 'Yes'

Traditionally, this possibility of response by repetition of a verbal form extended to the lexical verb as well. In current usage, however, it is restricted to verbs of the senses and a few others like *mynd* ('go'), *dod* ('come'), and in speech mainly to the verbs *gweld* ('see'), and *clywed* ('hear'), but see Jones and Thomas (1977: 299–302).

(24)   *A   weli di hyn? Gwelaf*
           INTER see you this   see-I
           'Can you see this?' 'Yes'

(25)   *A   glywi di'r   gog? Clywaf*
           INTER hear you-the cuckoo hear-I
           'Can you hear the cuckoo?' 'Yes'

These, too, are the only lexical verbs in which the so-called 'future' tense can register a meaning other than prediction (see 5.7.3.3); note that they do not denote a simple present, but contain an implication of ability to see or hear something.

5.2.4   Order of elements

Welsh is a VSO language, so that the surface-structure order of elements in the sentence is verb + subject + complement + adjunct: for example:

(26)   *Gwelodd y   bachgen ddyn ddoe*
            saw   the boy   man yesterday
            'The boy saw a man yesterday'

The range of complement types will be illustrated in 5.4.

5.2.5   Affirmatives

All non-topicalised sentences have the order of 5.2.4. In written form, all paradigms of the verb *bod* 'to be' which typically have a vocalic initial can be preceded by the sentential particle *yr* (*y* before the exceptional consonant in the third person singular present-tense *mae*),

(27)   *Yr oedd pawb   yn gwybod hynny*
            PT was everyone in know   that
            'Everyone knew that'

In less formal writing, and in oratorical style (which is the only spoken context in which the particle occurs regularly), it is frequently contracted to *'r*,

(28)   *'Roedd pawb yn gwybod hynny*

For vernacular usage, see 5.2.3.

5.2.6   Interrogatives

'Yes/no' interrogatives are introduced by the particle *a*,

(29)   *A   welodd ef y   gath?*
            INTER saw   he the cat
            'Did he see the cat?'

Answer words to *yes/no* questions in the future and conditional tenses are the appropriate tense forms of the verb *gwneud* 'do',

(30)   *A   ddarllenith ef y   llyfr? Gwneith/ Na wneith*
            INTER will-read   he the book   will-do-he not will-do-he
            'Will he read the book?'   'Yes'/'No'

But, for past perfective forms of the verb, the answer words are *do* 'yes', *naddo* 'no',

(31)   *A welodd ef y gath? Do/Naddo*
                                  yes/not-yes
                                  'Yes'/'No'

See also 5.2.3 for responses to the verb *bod* 'to be', and some lexical verbs which behave untypically.

Yes/no interrogatives which have a built-in expectation as to the polarity of the answer have the interrogative element in one of two tag types, both involving negative particles followed by the expected answer word (which corresponds to the distribution of answer words already given). Thus, expecting 'yes', with the future tense:

(32)   *Darllennith ef y   llyfr, oni   wneith?   Gwneith*
          will-read   he the book NEGQ will-do-he will-do-he
          'He will read the book, won't he?'   'Yes'

The particle selected here is the negative interrogative particle *oni(d)*: see below, 5.2.7. Expecting 'no', the negator *na(c)* precedes the expected answer form,

(33)   *Ni   ddarllennith ef y   llyfr, na   wneith?   Na   wneith*
          NEG will-read   he the book NEG will-do-he   NEG will-do-he
          'He won't read the book, will he?'   'No'

For the past tense, the appropriate positive or negative answer form functions as the tag,

(34)   *Ni   welodd ef y   gath, naddo?   Naddo*
          NEG saw   he the cat   not-yes not-yes
          'He didn't see the cat, did he?'   'No'

Note that the polarity of the initial declarative sentence matches that of the expected answer.

Whenever a constituent of the sentence is topicalised, the interrogative particle is *ai*, and the topicalised constituent is linked to the remainder of the sentence by a relative particle *a*; the answer words, in this case, are *ie* 'yes', *nage* 'no',

(35)   *Ai   ef a   welodd y   gath?   Ie/Nage*
          INTER he REL saw-he the cat   yes/no
          'Was it he who saw the cat?' 'Yes'/'No'

When subject or object noun phrases, verb or verb phrases, or adjunct or other postverbal constituents are interrogated, the interrogative particles are the pronominal set *pwy* 'who', *beth* 'what', *pryd* 'when', *pa* 'which' (see Jones and Thomas 1977: 305–16). We can give these the generalised mnemonic QP, after their initial labial consonant,

(36)   *Pwy   a   welodd y   gath?* (subject-NP interrogative)
          INTER.PT REL saw-he the cat
          'Who saw the cat?'

(37)   *Beth   a   welodd ef?*   (object-NP interrogative)
          INTER.PT REL saw   he
          'What did he see?'

Again, the fronted interrogated constituent is followed by a relative clause. When it is governed by a preposition, the form of the relative particle is *y*:

(38)   *Gan bwy   y   gwelwyd y   gath?*
            by   INTER.PT REL was-seen the cat
            'By whom was the cat seen?'

5.2.7   Negation

The favoured convention for negation in the written language is by sentence-initial particle *ni(d)*:

(39)   *Ni   welodd ef yr haul*
            NEG saw   he the sun
            'He didn't see the sun'

The lexical items *dim* 'anything' and *neb* 'anyone' can collocate with the negative particle, as in

(40)   *Ni welodd ef ddim*
            'He didn't see anything'

(41)   *Ni welodd ef neb*
            'He didn't see anyone'

In vernacular usage, these lexical items have themselves acquired a sense of negation with ellipsis of the sentence-initial particles (see 5.2.3), and *dim* has attained the full sense of a negator in conjunction with the preposition *mo* 'of':

(42)   *'Welodd ef ddim   mo'r haul*
            saw   he nothing of-the sun
            'He didn't see the sun'

This development follows the pattern of the 'lexicalised' negators *byth* and *erioed* 'ever' and *heb* 'without'. *Byth* and *erioed* (which are in complementary distribution, the former being used in non-perfective contexts, and the latter in perfective ones) have developed full negator status with ellipsis of the particle in speech:

(43)   *(Ni) fyddaf i byth yn mynd*
            (NEG) am   I ever in go
            'I never go'

(44)   *(Nid) oeddwn i erioed wedi canu*
            (NEG) was   I ever   after sing
            'I had never sung'

Heb is inherently negative, and occurs in a positive construction which is syntactically identical to the negative-derived ones described above:

(45)   *Oeddwn i heb   ganu*
            was   I without sing
            'I had not sung'

For *heb*, see also 5.2.13. Thus, the written variety's system of initial negation has transformed, in the vernacular, into one of medial negation.

The negative interrogative particle *oni(d)*, described above as a feature of tag questions, can introduce an independent question as well,

(46)   *Onid oedd ef yna?*
          NEGQ was he there
          'Wasn't he there?'

with the same negative connotations as before.

When any sentence constituent is topicalised in a negative context, the form of the negator is *nid* or *oni(d)* in writing and in formal speech,

(47)   *Nid canu yr   oedd ef*
          NEG sing REL was he
          'It was not singing that he was doing'

(48)   *Onid canu yr   oedd ef?*
          NEGQ sing REL was he
          'Wasn't it singing that he was doing?'

and *dim* in the vernacular,

(49)   *Dim canu (yr) oedd ef*

(50)   *Dim canu (yr) oedd ef?*

The vernacular form for northern dialects is frequently *nid* . . . in both contexts.

The use of the negator *na(c)* before the imperative is now frozen usage seen almost exclusively in public address,

(51)   *Nac oedwch!*
          NEG delay-IMP
          'Do not delay!'

This usage has been lexicalised, through the verb *peidio* 'cease', which itself adopts the imperative mood:

(52)   *Peidiwch ag   oedi!*
          cease-IMP with delay
          'Do not delay!'

See further 5.2.14 for *peidio* as negator.

5.2.8   Active sentences

Active sentences have been amply illustrated in previous sections, and the order of elements in them in 5.2.4. They can be composed, in the main, of either of the following:

1 an inflected lexical verb + subject + . . .

(53)   *Cafodd y   dyn baned o goffi*
       had   the man cup   of coffee
       'The man had a cup of coffee'

2 an inflected auxiliary verb + subject + aspect marker + uninflected
lexical verb + . . .

(54)   *Oedd y   dyn yn cael paned o goffi*
       was the man in have cup   of coffee
       'The man was having a cup of coffee'

There are, of course, other types of sentence in Welsh, and they will be
described in 5.2.15 and 5.7.3.3, in so far as they have to do with tense and
modality contrasts. For our present purposes, the verb *cael* 'have' exemplifies
the inflected lexical-verb construction, and also that of an inflected auxiliary +
lexical verb–noun.

5.2.9   Impersonal sentences

The impersonal construction is a morphological category in Welsh, and will be
discussed in 5.7.3.4.

5.2.10   Passive sentences

The passive construction in Welsh is lexically marked. It is expressed through an
active construction which parallels either of the active constructions described
above, with the verb *cael* as its semantic marker. It differs from the active
constructions above in that the syntactic object is a verb–noun, preceded by a
possessive adjective which is co-referential with the syntactic subject:

(55)   *Cafodd y   dyn ei ladd*
       had   the man his kill
       'The man was killed'

When the inflected verb is an auxiliary, the perfective aspect marker *wedi* 'after'
is obligatorily selected as well,

(56)   *Oedd y   dyn wedi cael ei ladd*
       was the man after have his kill
       'The man had been killed'

and it can be negated by selection of the perfective negator *heb* instead:

(57)   *Oedd y dyn heb gael ei ladd*
         'The man had not been killed'

Negation of the passive with inflected lexical verb *cael* follows normal procedure for active sentences (see 5.2.7).

Perfect and progressive aspect can co-occur,

(58)   *Oedd y   mater wedi bod yn cael ei drafod cyn   hynny*
         was   the matter after be   in have its discuss before then
         'The matter had been being discussed before then'

The verb–noun of the passive construction must be transitive, and so either an agent or an instrument (or both) can be expressed:

         Agent

(59)   *Cafodd ef ei ladd gan filwr*
         had   he his kill by soldier
         'He was killed by a soldier'

         Instrument

(60)   *Cafodd ef ei ladd ā   chyllell*
         had   he his kill with knife
         'He was killed with a knife'

In Welsh, an underlying indirect object cannot be passivised.

5.2.11   'Being' sentences

5.2.11.1   Classificatory sentences
Classificatory sentences typically have the structure copula + subject NP + *yn* + predicate NP or ADJ:

(61)   *Mae Mair yn athrawes*
         is   Mair in teacher
         'Mair is a teacher'

(62)   *Mae Mair yn ddel*
         is   Mair in attractive
         'Mair is attractive'

The predicate particle *yn* is distinguished from the progressive aspectual *yn* by the fact that it governs soft mutation of the initial consonant of the following noun or adjective. In this type of copula sentence, the predicate noun is always indefinite, and its function is to describe the subject or to predicate something of it.

5.2.11.2   Equative sentences

Equative or identificatory sentences have the structure NP_1 + copula + NP_2:

(63)   *Mair yw yr athrawes*
        Mair is the teacher
        'Mair is the teacher'

In sentences of this type, NP_1 is directly equated with NP_2. Since NP_1 precedes the inflected verb, this sentence must be interpreted as a topicalised one: however, since NP_2 is required to be invariably definite in this type of sentence, there is no occurring non-topicalised variant to which it can be related – both **Mae Mair (yn) yr athrawes* and **Mae yr athrawes (yn) Mair* are not possible sentences in Welsh. The verb form may provide a clue. When copula sentences in the third person singular present tense are topicalised, the verb form changes from *mae* to *sydd* for subject topicalisation, and to *yw* for predicate topicalisation (see 5.2.16). We argue, therefore, that NP_1 here is a predicate and NP_2 a subject (see further Jones and Thomas, 1977: 42–9).

For existential sentences, see 5.2.12.

5.2.12   Locative and possessive sentences

Locatival copula sentences can be illustrated by the following:

(64)   *Mae llyfr ar y silff*
        is   book on the shelf
        'There is a book on the shelf/A book is on the shelf'

(65)   *Mae'r llyfr ar y silff*
        is-the book on the shelf
        'The book is on the shelf'

These sentences are syntactically undifferentiated, and are composed of copula + NP + prepositional phrase. The NP may be either definite (65) or indefinite (64), and the indefinite type has a variant with unstressed *yna* 'there' following the copula,

(66)   *Mae yna lyfr ar y silff*
        is   there book on the shelf
        'There's a book on the shelf'

In all the sentences exemplified, a wide range of prepositions can occur, and the prepositional phrase cannot be deleted; **Mae llyfr* etc. are impossible.

In all the examples quoted, too, the progressive aspect cannot occur; thus (67) is impossible:

(67)   *Mae llyfr yn bod ar y   silff*
         is   book in be on the shelf
         *The book is being/exists on the shelf'

These sentences are properly locatival, allowing no expression of duration.

Those with an indefinite NP, however, can also accommodate the progressive aspect, and can dispense with the locative,

(68)   *Mae (yna)   fleiddiau (yn Romania)*   (−loc.)
         is   (there) wolves   (in Romania)
         'There are wolves (in Romania)'

(69)   *Mae (yna) fleiddiau yn bod (yn Romania)*   (+prog.)
         is (there) wolves   in be (in Romania)
         'Wolves exist (in Romania)'

As the translation indicates, the occurrence of *bod* 'to be' in this example is best interpreted as existential usage.

The preposition *gan* 'with' occurs freely in the same sentential contexts to indicate location:

(70)   *Mae prēs   gan y   bachgen*
         is   money with the boy
         'Money is with the boy/ There is money with the boy'

In the case of this preposition, however, the order of noun phrase and prepositional phrase can be reversed: copula + prep. phrase + NP.

(71)   *Mae gan y bachgen brēs*
         is   with the boy   money
         'The boy has money'

This is a construction for expressing possession, the possessor being the noun of the prepositional phrase, and the possessum that of the noun phrase.

5.2.13   Aspectually marked sentences

Contrasts of aspect are inherent components of periphrastic constructions with the primary auxiliary *bod* 'be' as their inflected verb. The principal items involved are the progressive marker *yn* 'in' and the perfective *wedi* 'after':

(72)   *Mae Mair yn canu*
         is   Mair in sing
         'Mair is singing'

(73)   *   *Mae Mair wedi canu*
         is   Mair after sing
         'Mair has sung'

With the modal auxiliaries like *dylai* 'should', however, the aspect marker is accompanied by the verb–noun form of the copula (primary auxiliary) *bod*. The following are instances of a modal unmarked for aspect and marked for it:

Unmarked

(74)   *Dylai   Mair ganu*
           should Mair sing
           'Mair should sing'

Marked progressive

(75)   *Dylai   Mair fod yn canu*
           should Mair be in sing
           'Mair should be singing'

Furthermore, when both aspectual markers co-occur, the perfective comes first and the progressive is 'led' by the uninflected copula:

(76)   *Mae Mair wedi bod yn canu*
           is   Mair after be in sing
           'Mair has been singing'

(77)   *Dylai   Mair fod wedi bod yn canu*
           should Mair be after be in sing
           'Mair should have been singing'

These facts suggest that the aspect markers may best be seen as complex items *bod yn*, *bod wedi*, with the first-occurring *bod* being fronted to sentence-initial position in periphrastic constructions, to carry the tense features which would in other contexts be carried by a lexical verb or modal in that position. This requires that we view the fundamental structure of the Welsh sentence in this way:

        auxiliary features + subject NP + (aspect)   + lexical verb . . .
        (modal), tense   (perf., prog.)

Thus a sentence which contains a lexical verb alone would have the structure

        auxiliary   + subject   + verb
        tense: future: *-ith*   *Mair*   *canu*

Since there is no item other than the lexical verb to carry the tense feature, *canu* is fronted:

(78)   *Canith   Mair*
           will-sing Mair
           'Mair will sing'

Where a sentence has modality, the structure would be

auxiliary	+	subject	+	verb
modal: *dylu*		*Mair*		*canu*
tense: conditional: *-ai*				

(See 5.7.3.3 for tense contrasts.) The modal adopts the tense feature, giving

(79) *Dylai Mair ganu*
      should Mair sing
      'Mair should sing'

Adding in aspect features, we have the periphrastic construction

auxiliary	+	subject	+	aspect	+	verb
present		*Mair*		progressive		*canu*
				bod yn		

The first 'verbal' item *bod* is fronted to carry the Aux feature 'present' (and no longer has an independent verbal source at sentence-initial),

(80) *Mae Mair yn canu*
      is   Mair in sing
      'Mair is singing'

Where a modal is involved, the complex aspectual form is left undivided, as the modal adopts the tense feature at sentence initial, as in

auxiliary	+	subject	+	aspect	+	verb
modal: *dylu*		*Mair*		*bod yn*		*canu*
tense: tentative						

(81) *Dylai Mair fod yn canu*
      should Mair be in sing
      'Mair should be singing'

Analysis in these terms accounts for the distribution of inflected and uninflected verbal forms in a systematic way. (A further advantage which accrues from this analysis is that the predicate can be represented as an undivided entity 'underlyingly', thus facilitating statements about the 'logical' relationships between subject and predicate and within the predicate – see Jones and Thomas, 1977: 15–60.)

Conventional syntactic analyses see the aspectual items *wedi* and *yn* as independent realisations of aspect contrasts and interpret them as prepositional elements governing verb–nouns in nominal guise, either conjuring up the uninflected form *bod* where it is needed, without explanation (Anwyl, 1899) or simply ignoring its occurrence with modals and in the complex aspect marker *wedi bod yn* (Richards 1938; Watkins 1961; S. J. Williams 1959, 1980). There is an excellent formalised presentation of this position in Awbery (1976). Awbery does not, however, consider the persuasive evidence of aspectual modification of modals, with which the whole aspectual complexes *bod yn*, *bod wedi* remain undivided.

There are three other items which function in the aspectual system: *ar* 'on', which marks imminence; *newydd* 'new', which marks immediacy in the past; and *heb* 'without', which is a perfective negator, the negative correspondent of *wedi*:

(82)   *Mae mair ar fynd*
      is   Mair on go
      'Mair is about to go'

(83)   *Mae Mair newydd fynd*
      is   Mair new   go
      'Mair has just gone'

(84)   *Mae Mair heb   fynd*
      is   Mair without go
      'Mair has not gone'

Ar can collocate with *wedi*, and *newydd* with *yn*, with the positional restrictions already noted.

5.2.14   Types of complementation

5.2.14.1   Indirect questions
Indirect questions may complement a verb or an adjective, and the clause is introduced by the range of question words illustrated in 5.2.6; we illustrate with *a*,

(85)   *Gofynnodd Mair a oedd hi am fynd*
      asked   Mair Q was she for go
      'Mair asked whether she wanted to go'

(86)   *Mae'n amheus a ddaw hi*
      is-it-in doubtful Q come she
      'It's doubtful if she will come'

5.2.14.2   Noun clauses
Noun clauses can complement verbs, adjectives or nouns, and the noun clause itself may have either an inflected verb, or a verb–noun with aspectual modification. In the latter case, the NP subject of the noun clause is inverted with the copula *bod* of the (first) aspect marker (see 5.2.13), so that *bod* essentially functions as a complementising particle:

VERB

(87)   *Mae'n ymddangos bod Mair wedi clywed*
         is-it-in appear   be Mair after hear
         'It appears that Mair has heard'

ADJECTIVE

(88)   *Mae'n amlwg bod Mair yn deall*
         is-it-in obvious be Mair in understand
         'It is obvious that Mair understands'

NOUN

(89)   *Y gwir yw bod Mair yn cytuno*
         the truth is be Mair in agree
         'The truth is that Mair agrees'

When the complement is a topicalised sentence (see 5.2.16) the complementising particle is *mai* (southern, *taw*):

(90)   *Mae'n ymddangos mai Mair a oedd yna*
         is-in   appear   PT mair REL was there
         'It appears that it was Mair who was there'

The complement with inflected verb can be illustrated thus, again with inversion of subject NP and lexical verb (see 5.2.13):

NOUN

(91)   *Y diffyg yw y daw   pawb   yr un   pryd*
         the difficulty is PT will-come everyone the same time
         'The difficulty is that everyone will come at the same time'

The noun clause is introduced by the complementising particle *y* when it contains an inflected verb.

The examples discussed so far involve factive noun clauses; there are also infinitival complement clauses, which can also complement verb, adjective or noun:

VERB

(92)   *Oedd Mair yn cofio   gweld ei brawd*
         was Mair in remember see   her brother
         'Mair remembered seeing her brother'

ADJECTIVE

(93)   *Mae'n hawdd siarad*
         is-it-in easy   talk
         'Talking is easy'

NOUN

(94)   *Yr ateb   oedd dechrau o'r   newydd*
         the answer was start   from-the new
         'The answer was to start anew'

When the complement clause has an overt subject, it is introduced by the
complementiser *i* 'for':

NOUN

(95)   *Yr ateb   oedd i   Mair fynd adref*
         the answer was for Mair go   home
         'The answer was for Mair to go home'

With this independent complementiser, there is no inverting of NP subject with
any verbal form in the subordinate clause, even when it is aspectually modified:

(96)   *Yr ateb   oedd i   Mair fod wedi gorffen*
         the answer was for Mair be   after finish
         'The answer was for Mair to have finished'

Thus (assuming the analysis of underlying constituent structure of 5.2.13),
inversion of the subject NP with a following verbal form occurs only in
noun-clause complements.

   Negation of factive noun clauses involves selection of the clause-initial
negative particle *na(d)*, in place of the positive complementiser,

(97)   *Mae'n amlwg   nad yw Mair yn deall*
         is-it-in obvious NEG is Mair in understand
         'It is obvious that Mair does not understand'

(98)   *Y diffyg   yw na ddaw   neb*
         the difficulty is NEG will-come anyone
         'The difficulty is that no-one will come'

and of infinitival clauses the lexical negator *peidio ā* 'cease with' (see 5.2.17),
which precedes the lexical verb of the complement clause:

(99)   *Yr ateb   oedd i   Mair beidio ā   mynd*
         the answer was for Mair cease with go
         'The answer was for Mair not to go'

Reported speech follows the pattern for the noun-clause complement in all
respects.

5.2.15   Modal sentences

The modal auxiliaries are the verbs *cael* 'have', *gallu* and *medru* 'be able' and
dylu 'ought'. They share with the primary auxiliary *bod* 'to be' the ability to take
aspectual modification (as described in 5.2.13), and they are distinguished from

it in that they have only the three tense contrasts of the lexical verb, as opposed to the five of *bod* (see 5.7.3.3). It is thus useful to label them secondary auxilaries: because of their lexical content (as compared with the purely structural function of the primary auxiliary *bod*) they are sometimes called lexical auxiliaries as well. We will henceforth refer to them as modals. *Dylu* 'ought' has only one tense form, *dylai* – formally a conditional (see 5.7.3.3), and semantically a marker of tentativity. The range of meanings conveyed by the modals can be illustrated thus:

1   *Cael* 'have', 'receive'

(a) *permission*

(100)   *Cei   di fynd yfory*
         will-have you go   tomorrow
         'You can go tomorrow'

(b) *obtainment*

(101)   *Cei   di wybod yfory*
         will-have you know tomorrow
         'You'll (get to) know tomorrow'

(c) *suggestion*

(102)   *Cei di ddechrau ar y paentio*
         have you start   on the painting
         'You can start on the painting'

2   *Medru* (northern), *Gallu* 'be able'

(a) *ability*

(103)   *Medr/gall Mair ganu*
         is-able   Mair sing
         'Mair can sing'

(b) *physical possibility*

(104)   *Medri/gelli di dyfu tatws*
         are-able   you grow potatoes
         'You can grow potatoes'

(c) *disposition*

(105)   *A fedri   di basio'r halen?*
         Q are-able you pass-the salt
         'Can you pass the salt?'

Additionally, *gallu* is used to convey

(d) *permission*

(106)   *Gelli di   fynd adref am dri*
           can you go   home at   three
           'You can go home at three'

(e) *perception*, when it co-occurs with verbs of perception:

(107)   *Gelli di   glywed y   gwynt dan   y   tō*
           can you hear   the wind under the roof
           'You can hear the wind under the roof'

    3 *Dylu* 'ought, should'
    (a) *likelihood*

(108)   *Dylai hi   fwrw yfory*
           ought her rain   tomorrow
           'It should rain tomorrow'

    (b) *unfulfilment*

(109)   *Dylai Mair ymddiheuro*
           ought Mair apologise
           'Mair ought to apologise'

This latter use is distinguished by the fact that it contains an implied refusal to perform the action referred to.

In appropriate contexts, models may have epistemic, alethic or deontic force.

5.2.16   Types of topicalisation

Any of the constituents of a sentence can be topicalised by fronting of that constituent to precede the inflected verb; the fronted constituent is accompanied by emphatic stress. When the subject NP is fronted, it is followed by a relative clause which is introduced by the relative particle *a*; thus fronting of the subject NP of (110) gives (111):

(110)   *Oedd Mair yn adrodd stori wrth y   plant*
           was   Mair in tell   story to   the children
           'Mair was telling a story to the children'

(111)   *Mair a   oedd yn adrodd stori wrth y   plant*
           Mair REL was in tell   story to   the children
           'It was Mair who was telling a story to the children'

Verb phrase and adjunct can be fronted together,

(112)   *Adrodd stori wrth y   plant   yr   oedd Mair*
         tell   story to   the children REL was Mair
         'What Mair was doing was to tell a story to the children'

In all cases except fronting of the subject NP, the form of the relative particle is
the 'oblique' form *y(r)*. The same is true for fronting of the adjunct,

(113)   *Wrth y   plant   yr   oedd Mair yn adrodd stori*
         to   the children REL was Mair in tell   story
         'It was to the children that Mair was telling a story'

and for other constituents (see Jones and Thomas 1977: 289–95). Negation of
any topicalised sentence requires the negator *nid* in sentence-initial position, as
in

(114)   *Nid Mair a   oedd yn adrodd . . .*
         NEG Mair REL was   in tell
         'It was not Mair who was telling . . .'

and *yes/no* interrogation of a topicalised sentence requires the question word *ai*
instead of *a*, as in

(115)   *Ai   Mair a   oedd yn adrodd . . . ?*
         INTER Mair REL was   in tell
         'Was it Mair who was telling . . .?'

5.2.16.1   The 'abnormal' sentence

The type of sentence which the Welsh grammatical tradition calls the 'abnormal'
sentence is syntactically topicalised, most frequently by fronting of the subject
NP:

(116)   *Mair a   fwrodd ef*
         Mair REL hit-she him
         'Mair hit him'

It is different from topicalised sentences, however, in that there is no emphatic
stress on the fronted constituent: there is equal sentence stress on the headwords
of both the subject NP and the verb phrase, and in this the sentence type is
unusual. In my experience, the sentence type occurs only as a response to a
question 'What happened?', and may best be interpreted as a complement to an
'understood' lead clause

(117)   *Beth ddigwyddodd oedd . . . 'Mair . . .'*
         what happened-it was
         'What happened was . . . "Mair . . ."'

with the response offered as direct quotation, both subject and verb being
stressed because both items are of high informational value.

5.2.17   Imperative

Second-person singular and plural imperative forms of the verb occur regularly:

(118)   *Gwranda!* (2SG)
          'Listen!'

(119)   *Gwrandwch!*(2PL)
          'Listen!'

Formal written usage allows negation by a sentence-initial negating particle *na(d)*, as in

(120)   *Na wranda!*
          NEG listen
          'Do not listen!'

Spoken usage, however, requires the lexical negator *peidio ā* 'cease with', itself in imperative form:

(121)   *Paid ā   gwrando!*
          cease with listen (2SG)
          'Do not listen!'

Similarly, the impersonal imperative is markedly formal,

(122)   *Coded y   gynulleidfa!*
          let-rise the congregation
          'Let the congregation rise!'

STRUCTURE OF THE PHRASE

5.3   STRUCTURE OF THE NOMINAL PHRASE

5.3.1   Order of elements (see also 5.3.2, 5.3.4.2, 5.3.4.8)

The head noun may be preceded by the definite article *y(r)* in determiner position,

(123)   *y dyn*
          'the man'

and an enumerator can follow the determiner,

(124)(a)   *y   ddau ddyn*
             the two   men
             'The two men'

(b)   *yr unig beth*
       the only thing
       'the only thing'

This complex can be preceded by a quantifier as predeterminer,

(125)   *bron yr unig ddyn*
       almost the only man
       'almost the only man'

Some quantifiers are linked to the determiner by the preposition *o* 'of':

(126)(a)   *rhai o'r dynion*
       some of-the men
       'some of the men'
  (b)   *peth o'r baich*
       some of-the burden
       'some of the burden'

Adjectival, nominal and verb–noun modification follows the head noun:

       Adjective
(127)   *dyn da*
       man good
       'a good man'

       Noun
(128)   *wal frics*
       wall bricks
       'a brick wall'

       Verb–noun
(129)   *dyn coluro*
       man colour
       'Make-up man'

All items can co-occur:

(130)   *bron yr unig wal frics*
       'almost the only brick wall'

A small number of adjectives can exceptionally precede the head noun, as in

(131)   *hen ddyn*
       man old
       'old man'

(132)   *annwyl gyfaill*
       dear friend
       'dear sir' (direct address)

5.3.2   Embedding: phrasal and clausal modifiers

Clausal modification involves postmodification by means of a relative clause
introduced by the relative particle *a* (with a correlate negative particle *ni, na*).

(133)   *dyn a   oedd yn gwisgo het*
          man REL was in wear   hat
          'a man who was wearing a hat'

When a subject or object noun phrase in the relative clause contains a possessive
adjective which is co-referential with the antecedent of the relative particle, or
where the relative clause contains a preposition which is co-referential with the
antecedent, the relative particle takes the oblique form *y(r)*:

          Possessive adjective

(134)   *y   ferch yr   oedd ei   gwallt wedi ei liwio*
          the girl REL was her hair   after its dye
          'the girl whose hair was dyed'

          Prepositional

(135)   *y   gadair yr   oedd Mair yn eistedd arni*
          the chair REL was Mair in sit   on her
          'the chair that Mair was sitting on/the chair on which Mair was sitting'

Phrasal postmodification may be by prepositional phrase, itself derived from a
relative clause,

(136)   *dyn o'r   dref*
          man from-the town
          'a man from the town'

There is also a construction derived from a passive relative clause, and
introduced by the perfective particle *wedi* (see 5.2.10, 5.2.13), which has the
force of a passive participle,

(137)   *gwaith wedi ei orffen*
          work   after its finish
          'finished work'

and one derived from an active relative clause with the force of a present
participle, introduced by the progressive particle *yn* (see 5.2.13):

(138)   *merch yn crio*
          girl in cry
          'a crying girl'

(139)   *dyn yn gwisgo het*
          'A man wearing a hat' (cf. (133) above)

There is a type of non-finite clausal postmodification which has the verb–noun
preceded by the preposition *i* 'to':

(140)   *yr unig un i orffen*
          the only one to finish
          'the only one to finish'

There is also a type of postmodification which can be derived from a prepositional phrase introduced by the preposition *ar gyfer* 'for', and which may consist of a verb–noun with or without an objective:

(141)   *pric mesur*
          rod measure
          'measuring rod'

(142)   *Jac cario baw*
          Jack carry dirt
          earth-carrying vehicle (from the makers' initials, JCB)

5.3.3   Submodification

See 5.3.2.

5.3.4   Systems of the nominal phrase

5.3.4.1   Definiteness and indefiniteness

The indefinite noun phrase is unmarked; the form of the definite article (the determiner of 5.3.1) is *y* 'the' before consonants except *h*, and *yr*, before *h* and all vowels. Before the semi-vowel /j/, its form is *yr*, but before /w/ it is *y*.

(143)   *y gath*   'the cat'
          yr afon   'the river'
          yr haf   'the summer'
          yr iaith   'the language'
          y watsh   'the watch'

Definiteness is a property of other types of noun phrases than these; for instance, proper nouns and pronouns are by definition definite, as are all nouns qualified by a demonstrative adjective.

5.3.4.2   Deixis

Physical proximity is expressed, in the written language, by the demonstrative adjectives, which are formed of discontinuous morphs comprising the definite article *y* and the demonstrative element, with the featured nominal form interposed between them. Thus,

	Singular	Plural
MASC	*y.....hwn*	*y....hyn*
FEM	*y.....hon*	*y....hyn*
	'this'	'these'

(144)(a)   *y   dyn hwn*
the man this
'this man'

(b)   *y   ferch hon*
the girl   this
'this girl'

y   dynion/merched hyn
the men/girls   these
'these men/girls'

In the spoken language, and in less formal varieties of writing, this function is taken by the adverbs *yma* 'here', *yna* 'there', which are undifferentiated for gender, though they still form a discontinuous morph with the definite article,

(145)(a)   *y dyn/ferch yma*
the man/girl here
'this man/girl'

(b)   *y dynion/merched yna*
the men/girls there
'these men/girls'

Physical distance is expressed by a set of demonstrative adjectives morphologically related to the first set mentioned above,

	Singular	Plural
MASC	*y.....hwnnw*	*y....hynny*
FEM	*y.....honno*	
	'that'	'those'

(146)(a)   *Y dyn hwnnw*
the man that
'that man'

(b)   *Y ferch honno*
the girl that
'that girl'

Y dynion/merched hynny
the men/girls those
'those men/girls'

The demonstrative pronouns corresponding to both sets of demonstrative adjectives discussed above can also function in parallel pronominal contexts, in the singular: *hwn/hon* 'this', *hwnnw/honno* 'that'. There are also neuter forms, *hyn* 'this', *hynny* 'that', which have cataphoric function (see 5.3.4.5), which derives from the deictic senses of these sets of demonstratives.

In the plural, these pronominal forms are represented in deictic function by the recent developments:

(147)   *rhain* < *y rhai hyn*   'these'
    the ones these
  rheini < *y rhai hynny*   'those'
    the ones those

Location in time is conveyed by adverbials, like *rẅan* (southern *nawr*) 'now', *yna* 'then':

(148)   *Mae Mair yn canu rẅan, ac yna'n gadael y llwyfan*
  is   Mair in sing now   and then-in leave the stage
  'Mair is singing now, and then leaving the stage'

5.3.4.3   Selection
Not relevant.

5.3.4.4   Reflexives
The phrasal reflexive is composed of the appropriate possessive adjective plus the lexical item *hun(an)*, plural *hunain*.

(149)   *Mae Mair wedi lladd ei   hun(an)*
  is   Mair in   kill   her self
  'Mair has killed herself'

As well as functioning as NP object co-referential with the NP subject, the reflexive can have emphatic force, in parenthetic relationship with its co-referent:

(150)   *Mae'r gweinidog ei hun wedi galw*
  is-the minister   his self after call
  'The minister himself has called'

In the possessive construction (see 5.3.4.7), the reflexive has similar emphatic force, emphasising its possessor co-referent:

(151)   *Mae Mair wedi malu ei   char ei hun*
  is   Mair after smash her car her self (i.e. 'of her self')
  'Mair has smashed her own car'

5.3.4.5   Reference
Some means of expressing exophoric reference were illustrated in 5.3.4.2. Amongst those used for anaphoric reference are (with anaphoric items and their referents in bold print):

   1 Personal pronoun

(152)   *Gwelais i **Mair** heddiw. Mae **hi** wedi cael damwain.*
  saw   I Mair today   is   she after have accident
  'I saw Mair today. She's had an accident'

2 Demonstrative pronoun, *hynny* 'that', expressing distance:

(153)   **Oedd gwerthu'r car yn beth ffôl   i'w wneud.** Mae **hynny**'n amlwg rŵan.
was sell-the   car in thing foolish to-its do   is   that-in obvious now
'Selling the car was a foolish thing to do. That's obvious now'

Here we have back-reference to extended text, as in

3 Adverb, *dyna* 'yonder', expressing distance:

(154)   **Rhoi'r gorau i chwarae sboncyn.** Dyna'r   ateb   iti.
give-the best to play   squash   there-the answer for-you
'Give up playing squash. That's the answer for you'

4 Lexical, as with the prop-word *un* 'one',

(155)   O   bryd i'w   gilydd, daw   **chwyldro** i fydd addysg.
from time to-its other, comes revolution to world education
Gwelwyd **un** *heddiw*
was-seen one today
'From time to time, revolution comes to the world of education. One was
seen today'

Cataphoric reference (also marked by bold print) is mainly of two kinds:

1 Demonstrative pronoun, *hyn* 'this', expressing proximity:

(156)   *Mae* **hyn** *yn amlwg.* **Mair** *a*   **fydd**   *ar* *y*   **blaen**.
is   this in obvious. Mair REL will-be on the front
'This is obvious. It's Mair who will be ahead'

2 Adverb, *dyma* 'here', expressing proximity:

(157)   **Dyma'r ffordd orau.** Mynd yn syth   at yr athro.
here-the way   best. go   in straight to the teacher
'This is the best way. Go straight to the teacher'

3 Lexical, as with nominalised adjectival *y canlynol* 'the following':

(158)   *Ystyriwch* **y   canlynol.** *Mae'r byd   ar frig   rhyfel niwclear.*
consider the following. is-the world on verge war   nuclear
'Consider the following. The world is on the verge of nuclear war'

Cataphora is exclusively extended text reference.

5.3.4.6   Enumeration

From one to ten the numerals run in series, with gender contrasts in some cases:

1 *un*
2 *dau* (masc.), *dwy* (fem.)
3 *tri* (masc.), *tair* (fem.)
4 *pedwar* (masc.), *pedair* (fem.)

5 *pump*
6 *chwech*
7 *saith*
8 *wyth*
9 *naw*
10 *deg*

From 'eleven' to 'fourteen', *deg* is taken as a base to which the appropriate 'additive' numeral is prefixed, with the preposition *ar* 'on': 11 *un ar ddeg*; 13 *tri ar ddeg*; 14 *pedwar ar ddeg*. 'Twelve' is exceptional, having the additive numeral compounded with the base, *deuddeg*. 'Fifteen' is a compound of additive numeral and base, like 'twelve', *pymtheg*; 16 *un ar bymtheg*; 17 *dau ar bumtheg*; 19 *pedwar ar bymtheg* are again additive types, while 'eighteen' is a compound of two and 'nine', *deunaw*. 'Twenty' is *ugain*, which again forms the base for counting from 21 *un ar hugain* to 39 *pedwar ar bymtheg ar hugain*, using the whole of the 1–19 series in the regular additive pattern.

Subsequent units of twenty are compounds of the numerals 'two', 'three' and 'four' with *ugain*, giving 40 *deugain*; 60 *trigain*; 80 *pedwar ugain*.

The pattern within each series of twenty follows that of 21–39, but with the preposition *ā(g)* 'with': 76 *un ar bymtheg ā thrigain*; 93 *tri ar ddeg a phedwar ugain*.

'Hundred' is *cant*, to which is suffixed, for 101–199, the whole series 1–99, via the preposition *ā(g)* 'with', as in 136 *cant ag un ar bymtheg or hugain*.

From 100 to 900 the hundred points prefix the appropriate numeral, 200 *dau gant*; 300 *tri chant* etc., and intervening figures are suffixed as described for 101–199.

'Thousand' is *mil*, with succeeding unit points being prefixed with the appropriate numeral, as 2,000 *dwy fil*; 3,000 *tair mil*. Intermediate points incorporate the units 1–999, directly suffixed to the unit item: 2,566 *dwy fil pum cant ag un ar bymtheg a thrigain*.

'Million' is *miliwn*.

The predominant pattern for formation of ordinals is by suffixation with −(f)ed: 1 *unfed* (in additive types, but *cyntaf* when it stands alone); 5 *pumed*; 6 *chweched*; 7 *seithfed*; 8 *wythfed*; 9 *nawfed*; 10 *degfed*. Exceptions are 2 *ail*; 3 *trydydd* (masc.), *trydedd* (fem.); 4 *pedwerydd* (masc.), *pedwaredd* (fem.). Compound types follow the predominant pattern: 'twelfth' *deuddegfed*; 'fifteenth' *pymthegfed*; 'eighteenth' *deunawfed*; and additive types (up to 39) use the ordinal form of the first occurring number: 'eleventh' *unfed ar ddeg*; 'twenty-fifth' *pumed ar hugain*; 'thirty-sixth' *unfed ar bymtheg ar hugain*.

Beyond the first series based on 'twenty', the ordinal system becomes very unwieldy for all affixed or suffixed forms, and is generally replaced in speech by the borrowed English system. The same is true of the numeral system to a large extent, particularly amongst the higher numbers, where the indigenous additive system gets increasingly complex.

In recognition of the unsuitability of the additive system for mathematical instruction, the educational system has adopted a new one devised on the base of ten: successive 'ten' points are prefixed with the numerals from 'one' to 'nine': 10 *deg*; 20 *dau ddeg*; 30 *tri deg* etc.; intervening points are suffixed with the appropriate numeral: 11 *un deg un*; 21 *dau ddeg un*; 33 *tri deg tri*. As far as I know, there has been no attempt to grapple with the problem of devising an ordinal system to correspond with this decimal numeral system.

5.3.4.7   Possession

The order of elements in the possessive construction is possessum + possessor:

(159)(a)　　*car Mair*
　　　　　　car Mair
　　　　　　'Mair's car'
　　　(b)　　*car y   doctor*
　　　　　　car the doctor
　　　　　　'the doctor's car'
　　　(c)　　*het plismon*
　　　　　　hat policeman
　　　　　　'a policeman's hat'

The possessor may be either definite or indefinite, as the examples show; the possessum, on the other hand, is inherently definite by reason of being possessed, and cannot be marked for definiteness.

The possessive construction provides nominal compounds like (160):

(160)　　　*het plismon*
　　　　　　'policeman's hat'

definable as compounds by having primary stress on the second element (see 5.9); such compounds can be preceded by the definite article,

(161)　　　*yr het 'plismon*
　　　　　　the hat policeman
　　　　　　'the policeman's hat'

but, in this case, there is no possibility of the definite article occurring before the possessor noun.

5.3.4.8 Partitives

The partitive construction consists of a noun followed by a prepositional phrase consisting of the preposition *o* 'of', the definite article and another noun. The first noun represents 'part of' the second:

(162)(a) *rhan o'r llyfr*
        part of-the book
        'part of the book'

    (b) *llawer o'r dynion*
        many of-the men
        'many of the men'

    (c) *dau o'r bechgyn*
        two of-the boys
        'two of the boys'

They are distinctive in that they are sources for constructions like the following relative clause, in which we need sources for both the antecedent noun *bechgyn* and for its co-referential pronominal inflection (on the preposition) and pronoun in the relative clause (items in bold type):

(163) *Oedd y **bechgyn**, y bu dau ohonynt **hwy** yn y carchar,...*
       was the boys REL was two of them in the prison
       'The boys, two of whom had been in prison, were...

5.3.4.9 Adjectivals

Adjectivals include the possessive adjectives (5.6.8), demonstrative adjectives (5.3.4.2) and a range of postmodifying prepositional phrases derived from relative clauses (5.3.2).

5.3.4.10 Agreement

Agreement involves the gender and number systems of the noun. The demonstrative adjectives agree with the noun,

FEM   *y ferch hon*
          the girl this
          'this girl'

MASC   *y dyn hwn*
          the man this
          'this man'

as do the demonstrative pronouns,

FEM   *Hon yw'r ferch*
          this is-the girl
          'This is the girl'

MASC   *Hwn yw'r dyn*
            this is-the man
            'This is the man'

and numerals and ordinals in appropriate cases,

FEM   *dwy ferch/ y   drydedd ferch*
            two girl/ the third   girl
            'two girls'/'the third girl'
MASC   *dau ddyn/ y   trydydd dyn*
            two man/ the third   man
            'two men'/'the third man'

Also, a postmodifying adjective, noun or verb–noun undergoes soft mutation of its initial consonant following a feminine head noun:

ADJECTIVE   *merch dal*   (< *tal*)
            girl   tall
            'a tall girl'
NOUN   *wal frics*   (< *brics*)
            wall bricks
            'a brick wall'
VERB–NOUN   *ffon daflu*   (< *taflu*)
            stick throw
            'a throwing stick'

Agreement of feminine noun and formally marked feminine adjectival form is increasingly rare, and is restricted to a very small number of adjectival forms:

FEM   *cath wen*
            cat white
            'white cat'
            pel gron
            ball round
            'round ball'
MASC   *ci   gwyn*
            dog white
            'white dog'
            twll crwn
            hole round
            'round hole'

The system of agreement in number between noun and adjective is similarly breaking down, as plural forms of adjectives slip out of use. Picking up the gender examples described above, we can exemplify their corresponding plurals:

(164)   *peli crynion* 'round balls'
            cathod gwynion 'white cats'

On the other hand, number agreement between noun and demonstrative adjective is common:

(165)   *y merched/dynion hyn*
          the girls/men these
          'these girls/men'

as is that between noun and demonstrative pronoun,

(166)   *Y rhain yw'r dynion/merched*
          the these are-the men/girls
          'These are the men/girls'

5.3.4.11   Pronominal phrases

In so far as this category is relevant to Welsh (e.g. in terms of demonstrative adjectives, reflexives and such items as reciprocal pronouns (*ei gilydd*) see 5.3.4.2, 5.3.4.4, 5.6.10.

5.3.4.12   Nominalisations

There is only one non-finite form of the verb in Welsh, the verb–noun. It has both verb-like properties, being modified by an adverb,

(167)   *Gweithio'n galed*
          work-in   hard
          'working hard'

and noun-like ones, being postmodified by an adjective,

(168)   *canu da*
          sing good
          'good singing'

Grammars, both traditional (Williams 1959) and modern (Awbery 1976; Jones and Thomas 1977), treat it as a simple element, mainly nominal in function. They may be right. But I suspect that it is one area of the structure of the language which – like the functions of the definite article – would reward extensive study.

Adjectives can function as nouns, for instance when taking the definite article,

(169)(a)   *y tlawd* 'the poor'
     (b)   *y cyfoethog* 'the rich'

5.4   STRUCTURE OF THE VERBAL PHRASE

The various structures of the verbal phrase are fully described in appropriate sections. They are listed here for convenience (strictly verbal items are in bold type):

1 Inflected lexical verb, with or without various kinds of complement, for example *inflected verb* (+ subject) (+ complement) (see 5.7.2):

(170)   **Gwelodd** *Mair ei   chwaer*
        saw   Mair her sister
        'Mair saw her sister'

2 *Carrier auxiliary* (inflected tense-carrier) (+ subject) + *verb–noun* (+ complement) (see 5.7.3.3):

(171)   **Gwnaeth** *Mair* **dorri** *addewid*
        did   Mair break promise
        'Mair broke a promise'

3 The periphrastic construction, which marks aspectual modification. It comprises an *inflected form of the primary auxiliary bod* 'be' (+ subject) + *aspect marker(s)* + *verb–noun* (+ complement) (see 5.2.13):

(172)   **Mae** *Mair* **wedi bod yn canu**
        is   Mair after be in sing
        'Mair has been singing'

4 The modal construction, in which an *inflected modal* (+ subject) is followed by an optional *aspect marker* + *verb–noun* (+ complement) (see 5.2.15)

(173)   **Gall** *Mair* **fod yn chwarae** *tenis*
        can Mair be in play   tennis
        'Mair can be playing tennis'

5 The catenative construction, in which a lexical verb can 'take a verb–noun as object'; it comprises an *inflected lexical verb* (+ subject) +*verb–noun* (+ complement),

(174)   **Mynnodd** *Mair* **ganu** *pennill*
        insisted Mair sing verse
        'Mair insisted on singing a verse'

5.5   STRUCTURE OF PREPOSITIONAL PHRASE

5.5.1   Prepositions occur freely with noun phrases (briefly exemplified in 5.5.4).

5.5.2   With pronominals (see 5.10) prepositions occur freely when they can be inflected for person.

5.5.3 For prepositions with verb phrases, see details of aspectual modification in 5.2.13.

5.5.4 Prepositional systems

The prepositional systems are not in any way unusual for Indo-European languages, and need only brief exemplification:

    1 *spatial*: *at* 'to'

(175)   *Oedd Mair yn agosháu **at** y   dref*
            was Mair in approach the town
            'Mair was approaching the town'

    2 *temporal*: *erbyn* 'by'

(176)   *Daeth Mair adref **erbyn** Y   Pasg*
            came Mair home by   the Easter
            'Mair came home by Easter'

    3 *abstract*: *dros* 'for'

(177)   *Dyma reswm **dros** beidio ā   mynd*
            here   reason for cease with go
            'Here is a reason for not going'

MORPHOLOGY

5.6 NOUNS

5.6.1 Structure: stems and endings

In addition to a large number of simple noun forms, there are derived nouns which are formed by attaching a wide range of suffixes to a verbal, adjectival or nominal stem (references in 5.9.1). There is no paradigmatic classification of stems according to their phonological characteristics, and no contrasts of case.

5.6.2 Inherent classes

Mass nouns have only singular concord, as is illustrated by the tag in the following question (noun *prēs*),

(178)   *Mae'r prēs   wedi ei wario,   onid ydyw?*
        is-the money after its spending NEGQ is
        'The money is spent, isn't it?'

while collective nouns, although they may have plural forms, typically have plural concord with their singular forms. These are words which represent plural membership, like *pobl* (pl. *pobloedd*),

(179)   *Bydd y   bobl   yn penderfynu, oni   fyddant?*
        will   the people in decide   NEGQ will-they?
        'The people will decide, won't they?'

Count nouns have singular concord with their singular forms, plural with plural:

        Singular

(180)   *Bydd y   dyn yn penderfynu, oni   fydd?*
        will   the man in decide   NEGQ will-he?
        'The man will decide, won't he?'

        Plural

(181)   *Bydd y   dynion yn penderfynu, oni   fyddant?*
        will   the men   in decide   NEGQ will-they?
        'The men will decide, won't they?'

5.6.3   Semantic features

Nouns can be either proper (*Mair*) or common. Common nouns can be either abstract (*cyngor* 'advice') or concrete. Concrete nouns can be either inanimate (*wal* 'wall') or animate. Animate nouns can be either human (*merch* 'girl') or non-human (*gwydd* 'goose').

5.6.4   Gender

Nouns in Welsh can be either masculine (*dyn* 'man') or feminine (*merch* 'girl'), and this has implications for rules of agreement (see 5.3.4.10). The gender of a noun is evident from its form in relatively few cases, where there are distinctive suffixes; for example:

Masculine -*yn*, -*wr*   *hogyn* 'boy'   *cenhadwr* 'missionary'
Feminine -*en*, -*es*   *hogen* 'girl'   *cenhades* 'missionary'

There are cases in which the gender of a noun varies according to context: *math* 'kind' selects the masculine form of the demonstrative adjective,

(182)   *y   math hwn*
       the kind this-MASC
       'this kind'

but mutates like a feminine noun after the definite article,

(183)   *y fath* 'the kind'

The cataphoric pronoun replacement for an extraposed subject clause is the feminine *hi* 'she',

(184)   *Mae **hi**'n   amlwg bod Mair wedi anghofio*
       is   she-in obvious be   Mair after forget
       'It is obvious that Mair has forgotten'

as is the case for statements about the weather, which require a similar cataphoric subject pronoun:

(185)   *Mae hi'n   bwrw*
       is   she-in rain
       'It is raining'

5.6.5   Number

As noted in 5.6.2, count nouns contrast singular and plural forms. The principal means of forming plurals from singulars are addition of suffix: sg. *arf* 'weapon' pl. *arfau*; loss of singular suffix: sg. *mochyn* 'pig' pl. *moch*; vowel change: sg. *sant* 'saint' pl. *saint*.

The processes of suffixation and suffix loss can combine with internal vowel change:

+suffix, +V-change: sg. *gwraig* 'wife', pl. *gwragedd*
−suffix, +V-change: sg. *dalen* 'leaf', pl. *dail*

In other instances, morphophonological vowel alternations accompany suffixation, as in the following, in which vowel mutation occurs on adding a syllable (see 5.22): sg. *cwm* 'valley', pl. *cymoedd*. Also, a vowel change in the final syllable to signal pluralising (in this case $e > y$) can trigger a further vowel alternation (in this case the vowel affection $a > e$ – see 5.22) in the previous syllable: sg. *bachgen* 'boy', pl. (**bachgyn*) *bechgyn*.

5.6.6   Case

Not relevant to Welsh.

5.6.7   Declensional classes

Not relevant to Welsh.

5.6.8   Pronouns

There are two major pronominal systems – independent and dependent. We will briefly exemplify both.

In the independent system, there are three types of pronoun. The one with the widest range of syntactic functions is the simple pronoun,

	1	2	3
Singular	*mi*	*ti*	m. *ef*, f. *hi*
Plural	*ni*	*chwi*	hwy

which occurs, for instance, as object of a verb,

(186)   *Gwelodd Mair ef*
       saw   Mair him
       'Mair saw him'

or of a non-inflecting preposition,

(187)   *gydag ef*
       'with him'

There is also a reduplicative type,

	1	2	3
Singular	*myfi*	*tydi*	m. *efe*, f. *hyhi*
Plural	*nyni*	*chwychwi*	*hwynthwy*

which can occur as a fronted constituent, under emphatic stress,

(188)   *Efe   sy'n gwybod*
       he-RED is-in know
       'It's he who knows'

The conjunctive type,

	1	2	3
Singular	*minnau*	*tithau*	m. *yntau*, f. *hithau*
Plural	*ninnau*	*chwithau*	*hwythau*

has the meaning 'I too' etc., as in (189):

(189)   *Oedd hi a minnau ar fin mynd*
       was she and I-too on point go
       'Both she and I were about to go'

The dependent pronoun is an auxiliary type which is virtually identical with the independent simple pronoun in form, and occurs after inflected forms of verbs and prepositions,

(190)   *Gwelodd ef Mair*
          saw   he Mair
          'He saw Mair'

(191)   *ato ef*
          'to him'

The remaining pronominal form is the possessive adjective, which is a discontinuous morph; it encloses a nominal form between a possessive adjectival prefix and a personal pronominal suffix:

	1	2	3
Singular	*fy...i*	*dy...di*	m. *ei...ef*, f. *ei...hi*
Plural	*ein...ni*	*eich...chwi*	*eu...hwy*

(192)   *ei het ef*
          his hat he
          'his hat'

There is an infixed form of the possessive adjective (which also has objective force with only minimal variance in form in the third person – see Watkins 1977a for an exhaustive treatment of the pronouns), which occurs after a final vowel:

	1	2	3
Singular	*'m*	*'th*	*'i, 'w*
Plural	*'n*	*'ch*	*'u, 'w*

(193)   *Aeth Mair â'i   het ef*
          went Mair with-his hat he
          'Mair took his hat'

In spoken usage, these forms retain their prefixed forms after a final consonant, but contract after a final vowel. In each case, they contract to the consonant of the prefixed form where there is one, and to its final vowel where there is not; in the vernacular, first person singular is *yn* (rather than *fy*). Thus, the contracted forms are:

	1	2	3
Singular	*'n*		*'i*
Plural	*'n*	*'ch*	*'i*

Second person singular *dy* is exceptional, in that it contracts before a *following* vowel to *d'*. The *'w* forms in the third person singular and plural occur only after the preposition *i* 'to', and represent dissimilation of **i'i* to *i'w*.

Structurally, the possessive adjective is a secondary development: as was shown in 5.3.4.7, the order of elements in the possessive construction is possessum + possessor – thus *het ef* (hat his) 'his hat' can be seen as the source of the possessive adjective construction *ei het ef*, which copies a possessive form as prefix to the possessum.

Literary usage allows regular deletion of the suffixed pronominal, in both possessive and objective functions (this prefixed pronominal can also be copied from the pronoun object of a verb–noun, as in *ei lladd hi* 'to kill her').

(194)   *Collodd Mair ei   het (ef)*
         lost   Mair his hat (he)
         'Mair lost his hat'

In vernacular usage, however, this is possible only when the suffixed pronoun is co-referential with the syntactic subject of the sentence, when it is obligatorily deleted in writing as well:

         Possessive

(195)   *Mae Mair yn golchi ei   gwallt (*hi)*
         is   Mair in wash   her hair   (she)
         'Mair is washing her hair'

         Passive

(196)   *Cafodd Mair ei   lladd (*hi)*
         had   Mair her kill   (she)
         'Mair was killed'

The primacy of the suffixed pronoun in these forms is shown by the fact that when the pronominal possessor takes emphatic stress, it falls on the suffixed pronoun (and never the prefixed copy adjective) in all varieties,

(197)   *Ei het ef a   gollodd Mair*
         his hat he REL lost   Mair
         'It was his hat that Mair lost'

In those instances where it is otherwise obligatorily deleted, and is co-referential with the subject, its emphatic form is the reflexive (see 5.3.4.4):

(198)   *Mae Mair wedi golchi ei   gwallt ei   **hun***
         is   Mair after wash her hair her self
         'Mair has washed her own hair'

This regular weak stress pattern on the possessive adjective further justifies treating the so-called 'infixed' forms as contractions in the vernacular.

The demonstrative pronoun (see also 5.3.4.2) provides the only instance where gender contrasts extend to a regular contrast between masculine/

feminine/neuter. The singular forms are masc. *hwn*/fem. *hon*/nt. *hyn* 'this'; masc. *hwnnw*/fem. *honno*/nt. *hynny* 'that'. They can be exemplified:

> Masculine/feminine

(199)   *Hwn/hon yw'r   dyn/ferch*
         this/this   is-the man/girl
         'This is the man/girl'

> Neuter

(200)   *Hyn sy'n poeni pawb*
         this is-in worry everyone
         'This is what worries everyone'

In the plural, there is no gender differentiation, and the current forms are late coinings from related demonstrative adjective phrases:

> *rhain* 'these'   < *y   rhai   hyn*
>   the ones these
> *rheini* 'those'   < *y   rhai   hynny*
>   the ones those

The singular forms of the demonstrative adjectives are illustrated in 5.3.4.2: as indicated by the derivations above of the plural forms of the demonstrative pronouns, the demonstrative adjective plural forms are *y...hyn* 'these'; *y...hynny* 'those', undifferentiated as to gender.

5.6.9   Person

Person contrasts are as described in 5.6.8.

5.6.10   Other pronominals

These are only exemplified here – see Williams (1980: 59–72) for a full description.

Un 'one', *rhai* 'some' function as propwords for singular and plural nouns respectively:

(201)   *Mae'r tŷ   yn **un** mawr*
         is-the house in one big
         'The house is a big one'

(202)   *Yr afalau coch yw'r   rhai gorau*
         the apples red are-the ones best
         'The red apples are the best ones'

Rhai 'some' and *peth* 'some' (lit. 'thing') refer to plural and mass nouns respectively, in this usage linked to the definite article by the preposition *o* 'of' where the head noun is definite,

(203)   *Cefais i **rai** (o'r) afalau*
        had I some (of-the) apples
        'I had some (of the) apples'

(204)   *Cefais i **beth** (o'r) bai*
        'I had some (of the) blame'

Alternatives are expressed in the construction *y naill* 'the one' . . . *y llall* (pl. *lleill*) 'the other':

(205)   *Ni welaf i'r naill na'r **llall** ohonynt*
        NEG see I-the one nor-the other of-them
        'I don't see the one or the other of them/I don't see either of them'

For reflexives, see 5.3.4.4; for negative items *dim* and *neb*, see 5.2.7.

   Ei gilydd 'each other' is a reciprocal pronominal,

(206)   *Mae Wil a   Mair yn caru **ei gilydd***
        is   Wil and Mair in love his other
        'Wil and Mair love each other'

Welsh has no possessive pronoun, but expresses the notion with the possessive-adjective construction already described and the numeral *un* 'one' in its propword function,

(207)   *ei un ef*
        his one he
        'his'

5.7   VERBS

5.7.1   Structure: stems and endings

The verb stem can be suffixed to show its function as verb–noun (see 5.9.1), and to mark tense, mood and person (see below). There are no phonologically marked paradigms.

5.7.2   Verb classes

5.7.2.1   Intransitive

There are a small number of intransitive verbs, which cannot take an object, as *cysgu* 'sleep',

(208)   *Mae Mair yn cysgu*
          is   Mair in sleep
          'Mair is sleeping'

and two subtypes:

      1 *Reflexive*: sometimes marked morphologically with the reflexive prefix *ym-*:

(209)   *Mae Mair yn ymolchi*
          is   Mair in REFLEX-wash
          'Mair is washing (herself)'

      2 *Inchoative*: in which the verb incorporates an inherent sense of 'change of state', as in *tywyllu* 'darken':

(210)   *Mae hi'n   tywyllu*
          is   she-in darken
          'It is darkening'

5.7.2.2   Transitive

A transitive verb takes a direct object, as *hoffi* 'like',

(211)   *Mae Mair yn hoffi tenis*
          is   Mair in like tennis
          'Mair likes tennis'

In many cases, the verb may require a following preposition to introduce the object, as in *blino ar* 'tire of'; we may label these *oblique transitives* (see Jones and Thomas 1977: 36–7):

(212)   *Mae Mair yn blino ar redeg*
          is   Mair in tire on run
          'Mair is tiring of running'

Direct and oblique transitivity can be combined in the verb which takes both a direct and an indirect object, as *dweud NP wrth NP* 'tell NP to NP':

(213)   *Mae Mair yn dweud stori wrth Wil*
          is   Mair in tell   story to Wil
          'Mair is telling a story to Wil'

There are also verbs which take a quantifying complement, as *cerdded* 'walk':

(214)   *Mae Mair wedi cerdded milltir*
          is   Mair after walk   mile
          'Mair has walked a mile'

5.7.3   Verb systems

All verb forms are finite (see 5.2.13, 5.7.3.4) except for the verb–noun, which is a dependent form, functioning in a variety of verbal contexts (see particularly 5.2.13, 5.2.15).

5.7.3.1   Aspect
See 5.2.13.

5.7.3.2   Mood
Mood contrasts involve indicative, imperative and subjunctive – see 5.7.3.3.

5.7.3.3   Tense
The tense and mood systems of the written language are as set out in table 5.3 (after Williams 1980: 80–1), for the regular lexical verb. Spoken usage is considerably different:

1 The subjunctive mood is no longer productive, and occurs only in fossilised sayings, for example *doed a ddelo* 'come what may'; 3 SG–IMP–*dod*+REL+3 SG–PRES–SUBJUNCT–*dod*.
2 Imperative forms are restricted to the second person singular and plural, both being marked by suffixation, sg. *cana!*, pl. *canwch!*.
3 In the indicative mood, either the imperfect or pluperfect tense has been lost in all varieties, and the surviving paradigm has the force of a conditional:

(215)   *Can(as)ai   Mair*
          would-sing Mair
          'Mair would sing'

In northern dialects, the imperfect does sometimes retain its traditional sense.

(216)   *Canai Mair*
          'Mair used to sing'

In spoken varieties, the traditional present has future reference (but see 5.2.3.1) and will be so labelled henceforth. The third person singular form is marked by inflection (see 5.13) in all dialects.

The lexical verb in the vernacular thus has a three-term tense system; future *canith* 'will sing', past *canodd* 'sang', conditional *canai/canasai* 'would sing' (all 3 sg.), and this has parallel realisation in an analytic pattern in casual usage. The verb *gwneud* 'do' can function as a tense marker when sentence-initial, with the lexical verb retaining its verb–noun form; thus:

Table 5.3. *The regular verb: Canu* 'to sing'

<table>
<tr><td colspan="5" align="center">*Indicative mood*</td></tr>
<tr><td colspan="2" align="center">*Present tense*</td><td></td><td colspan="2" align="center">*Imperfect tense*</td></tr>
<tr><td>*Singular*</td><td>*Plural*</td><td></td><td>*Singular*</td><td>*Plural*</td></tr>
<tr><td>1 canaf</td><td>canwn</td><td></td><td>canwn</td><td>canem</td></tr>
<tr><td>2 ceni</td><td>cenwch</td><td></td><td>canit</td><td>canech</td></tr>
<tr><td>3 cân</td><td>canant</td><td></td><td>canai</td><td>canent</td></tr>
<tr><td colspan="2" align="center">*Impersonal* cenir</td><td></td><td colspan="2" align="center">*Impersonal* cenid</td></tr>
</table>

<table>
<tr><td colspan="2" align="center">*Past tense*</td><td></td><td colspan="2" align="center">*Pluperfect tense*</td></tr>
<tr><td>*Singular*</td><td>*Plural*</td><td></td><td>*Singular*</td><td>*Plural*</td></tr>
<tr><td>1 cenais</td><td>canasom</td><td></td><td>canaswn</td><td>canasem</td></tr>
<tr><td>2 cenaist</td><td>canasoch</td><td></td><td>canasit</td><td>canasech</td></tr>
<tr><td>3 canodd</td><td>canasant</td><td></td><td>canasai</td><td>canasent</td></tr>
<tr><td colspan="2" align="center">*Impersonal* canwyd</td><td></td><td colspan="2" align="center">*Impersonal* canasid (canesid)</td></tr>
</table>

<table>
<tr><td colspan="5" align="center">*Subjunctive mood*</td></tr>
<tr><td colspan="2" align="center">*Present tense*</td><td></td><td colspan="2" align="center">*Imperfect tense*</td></tr>
<tr><td>*Singular*</td><td>*Plural*</td><td></td><td>*Singular*</td><td>*Plural*</td></tr>
<tr><td>1 canwyf</td><td>canom</td><td></td><td>canwn</td><td>canem</td></tr>
<tr><td>2 cenych</td><td>canoch</td><td></td><td>canit</td><td>canech</td></tr>
<tr><td>3 cano</td><td>canont</td><td></td><td>canai</td><td>canent</td></tr>
<tr><td colspan="2" align="center">*Impersonal* caner</td><td></td><td colspan="2" align="center">*Impersonal* cenid</td></tr>
</table>

<table>
<tr><td colspan="2" align="center">*Imperative mood*</td></tr>
<tr><td>*Singular*</td><td>*Plural*</td></tr>
<tr><td>1 —</td><td>canwn</td></tr>
<tr><td>2 cân</td><td>cenwch</td></tr>
<tr><td>3 caned</td><td>canent</td></tr>
</table>

Verb–noun: canu

Future

(217)   *Gwneith Mair ganu*
         will-do   Mair sing
         'Mair will sing'

Past

(218)   *Gwnaeth Mair ganu*
         did-do   Mair sing
         'Mair sang'

Conditional

(219)   *Gwnai   Mair ganu*
         would-do Mair sing
         'Mair would sing'

For past tense only the invariant verb *ddaru* 'happened' (< *darfu*) also functions
as a carrier auxiliary for northern dialects,

(220)   *Ddaru   Mair ganu*
          happened Mair sing
          'Mair sang'

The range of tense contrasts is considerably extended for the primary auxiliary
bod 'be', the inflected verb of the periphrastic pattern which allows aspectual
modification (see 5.2.13). Table 5.4 has the forms of the written language, again
after Williams (1980: 92–3). The spoken language has reduced the paradigms in
much the same way as for the lexical verb, the subjunctive is similarly
constrained, and the imperfect and pluperfect have been reduced to a single
conditional tense. For the spoken language, we have a five-term tense system:
present *mae* 'is', future *bydd* 'will', past *oedd* 'was', past perfect *bu* 'was' (being
inherently perfect, this form cannot collocate with the perfective aspect marker
wedi), conditional *byddai/buasai* 'would sing'.

Time reference of tense forms

Conditionals can refer, with few restrictions, to past, present and future. All
past-tense forms, in the lexical verb and in the primary auxiliary, refer explicitly
to past time. Primary auxiliary present, on the one hand, and future in both
primary auxiliary and lexical verb on the other, do not, in fact, simply refer to
present and future time as their labels suggest. Rather, all three have non-past
time reference, which is not distinguished as to present and future, but as to the
certainty (or not) at the time of speaking of the information being conveyed. It
has often been said that, whereas future forms always have future time
reference, present ones may refer to either present or future time. Thus, while it
is said that the reference of *bydd* in this sentence is future,

(221)   *Bydd   Caerdydd yn chwarae Abertawe*
          will-be Cardiff   in play   Swansea
          'Cardiff will (be) play(ing) Swansea'

that of *mae* in the same context is ambiguous as between present and future,

(222)   *Mae Caerdydd yn chwarae Abertawe*
          is   Cardiff   in play   Swansea
          'Cardiff are playing/will play Swansea'

The distinction between the two forms can be illustrated by the possibility of the
sentence

(223)   *Bydd hi'n bwrw glaw yfory*
          will-be she-in throw rain tomorrow
          'It will be raining tomorrow'

as opposed to the impossibility of (223′)

(223′)   *Mae hi'n bwrw glaw yfory

Bydd is predictive in function, and so is used of events which are not yet definite: a consequence of this is that it refers to events in the future (prediction in past and present time is a function of the conditional – see Jones and Thomas 1977: 126–52). *Mae*, however, refers only to events that are certain to occur, and so is neutral to the present/future distinction. In written and formal spoken varieties, *bydd* also has a present continuous function which has been absorbed by *mae* in the vernacular.

Of the four realisations of the third person singular present-tense form of *bod*, *mae* (as exemplified above) is the unmarked one. When the complement of a copula sentence is fronted, the form is *yw*; thus, (224) gives (225):

(224)   *Mae Mair yn athrawes*
            is   Mair in teacher
            'Mair is a teacher'

(225)   *Athrawes yw Mair*
            teacher   is Mair
            'What Mair is is a teacher'

In a relative clause, the form selected is *sy*

(226)   *Gwelodd Mair y   dyn sy'n   canu yn y   côr*
            saw   Mair the man REL-is-in sing in the choir
            'Mair saw the man who is singing in the choir'

as in a sentence with fronted subject,

(227)   *Mair sy'n   canu yn y   côr*
            Mair REL-is-in sing in the choir
            'It is Mair who is singing in the choir'

In interrogatives after *a* with indefinite subject we get *oes*:

(228)   *A oes rhywun yn canu?*
            Q is anyone in sing
            'Is there anyone singing?'

A full account of the contexts of use of these variants can be found in Williams (1980: 94–9).

5.7.3.4   Impersonal

The impersonal is an inflectional category and the forms for the written language are shown in tables 5.3 and 5.4. It is an active construction, in which the 'apparent object', which follows the inflected verb, remains unmutated like any subject NP:

Table 5.4. *The verb* bod

Indicative mood

Present tense

Singular	Plural
1 wyf, ydwyf	ŷm, ydym
2 wyt, ydwyt	ych, ydych
3 yw, ydyw, y mae, mae, oes	ŷnt, ydych

Relatival form: y sydd, sydd, y sy, sy
Impersonal form: ys, ydys
Conjunctive forms: mai, taw

Future and consuetudinal present tense

Singular	Plural
1 byddaf	byddwn
2 byddi	byddwch
3 bydd	byddant

Impersonal byddir

Imperfect tense

Singular	Plural
1 oeddwn	oeddem
2 oeddit	oeddech
3 oedd, ydoedd	oeddynt (oeddent)

Impersonal oeddid

Consuetudinal imperfect tense

Singular	Plural
1 byddwn	byddem
2 byddit	byddech
3 byddai	byddent

Impersonal byddid

Past tense

Singular	Plural
1 bûm	buom
2 buost	buoch
3 bu	buant, buont

Impersonal buwyd

Pluperfect tense

Singular	Plural
1 buaswn	buasem
2 buasit	buasech
3 buasai	buasent

Impers. buasid

Subjunctive mood
Present tense

Singular	*Plural*
1 bwyf, byddwyf	bôm, byddom
2 bych, byddych, -ech	boch, byddoch
3 bo, byddo	bônt, byddont

Impersonal bydder

Imperfect tense

Singular	*Plural*
1 bawn, byddwn	baem, byddem
2 bait, byddit	baech, byddech
3 bai, byddai	baent, byddent

Impersonal byddid

Imperative mood

Singular	*Plural*
1 —	byddwn
2 bydd	byddwch
3 bydded, boed, bid	byddent

Impersonal bydder

Verb–noun: bod

(229)   *Codwyd   cofeb   iddo*
was-raised memorial to-him
'A memorial was raised to him'

The distinction between the impersonal and notions of the passive is shown by the fact that intransitive verbs can occur in the impersonal – note the difficulty of translating the following intransitive impersonal,

(230)   *Aethpwyd trwy   Gaerdydd*
was-gone through Cardiff
'They went through Cardiff'

The impersonal survives in the spoken language only in a handful of verbs like *magwyd* 'was brought up'; *ganwyd* 'was born'; *ystyrrir* 'is considered'.

5.7.4   Concord

Subject nouns, whether singular or plural, take the third person singular form of the verb:

(231)   *Canodd y   dyn/dynion*
sang   the man/men
'The man/men sang'

There is regular concord between the inflected verb and a following pronominal subject, as in the future tense *canu* 'sing':

	Singular	Plural
1	can*af* i	can*wn* ni
2	cen*i* di	can*wch* chwi
3	can*ith* ef	can*ant* hwy

For spoken realisations of all forms inflected for person, see Jones and Thomas (1977: 399–411).

5.8   ADJECTIVES

5.8.1   Structure: stems and endings

The stems of some adjectives have feminine forms for the singular, and some inflect for number (for both, see 5.3.4.10). For derivational suffixes, see 5.9.1.

5.8.2   Comparison

In addition to the radical form of the adjective, there are three degrees of comparison – equative, comparative and superlative. Adjectives of one or two syllables register comparison by inflection, the equative being enclosed within the affixes *cyn...ā(g)* 'as...as', and the comparative being suffixed by *na(g)* 'than':

Radical	*Equative*	*Comparative*	*Superlative*
oer	*cyn oered a*	*oerach na*	*oeraf*
cold	as cold as	colder than	coldest

Adjectives of more than two syllables adopt an analytic pattern, in which the radical form is enclosed within the affixes *mor...ā* 'as...as' (equative); *mwy/ llai...na* 'more/less...than' (comparative); and prefixed by *mwyaf/lleiaf* 'most/ least' (superlative):

cyfoethog	*mor gyfoethog ā*	*mwy/llai cyfoethog na*
rich	as rich as	more/less rich than
		mwyaf/lleiaf cyfoethog
		most/least rich

5.8.3   Adjectival classes

There are no differentiated adjectival classes.

5.8.4   Adverbs

Adverbs consist, in the main, of combinations of a preposition and an adjective,

(232)(a)   *yn gyflym*
        in quick
        'quickly'
   (b)   *yn sydyn*
        in sudden
        'suddenly'

though there are one-word adverbs, too,

(233)   *ddoe* 'yesterday'
      echnos 'the night before last'

and there are a number of disyllabic adverbs which have final-syllable stress, composed of a preposition and a noun or adjective (see Thomas 1979):

(234)(a)   *ymlaen*
        in-front
        'onwards'
   (b)   *ymhell*
        in-far
        'far'

5.8.4.1   Adverb classes

There are no differentiated adverbial classes.

5.9   COMPOUND WORDS

Compounds fall into two major classes: 'proper' compounds, in which the compound is the same part of speech as its second element (i.e. the headword, normal syntactic order being reversed),

(235)(a)   *gwinllan*
        wine-yard
        'vineyard'
   (b)   *gweithdy*
        work-house
        'workshop'

and so-called 'improper' compounds, in which a sequence of words in normal syntactic order is accented as one word,

(236)(a)   *pompren*
        bridge-wood
        'wooden bridge'

   (b)   *canpunt*
        hundred-pound
        'a hundred pounds'

5.9.1   Derivational word classes

There is a large number of suffixes for derivation of words in all major classes, and a wide variety of structural bases on which they can be formed in all cases. Watkins (1961) has an excellent discussion of productive and non-productive suffixes, and Williams (1980) a thorough overview of derivational processes in general, under appropriate word-class headings.

5.10   PREPOSITIONS WITH PRONOMINALS

There are invariant prepositions which are followed by the appropriate personal pronoun: *gyda mi* 'with me', *fel mi* 'like'; and three classes of conjugated prepositions formed by suffixation: first, second and third persons are contrasted in singular and plural, with a gender contrast at third person singular.

5.10.1   Class I

For these prepositions, the stem has the same form throughout the conjugation:

      1 It may be identical with the root, as with *at* 'to':

(237)	Singular		Plural
	1	ataf	atom
	2	atat	atoch
	3 MASC	ato	atynt
	FEM	ati	

      2 Some have a derived stem form throughout the paradigm, involving a stem-final alveolar nasal consonant, as with *ar* 'on':

(238)	Singular		Plural
	1	arnaf	arnom
	2	arnat	arnoch
	3 MASC	arno	arnynt
	FEM	arni	

5.10.2 Class II

This type has a stem variant for third person singular and plural only; these forms have a stem-final alveolar consonant, *t* or *dd*, as in *dros* 'over':

(239)

	Singular	Plural
1	drosof	drosom
2	drosot	drosoch
3 MASC	drosto	drostynt
FEM	drosti	

For all prepositions, the vowel of the suffix for the third person singular masculine is *o* and for the third person singular feminine is *i*, and of the third person plural *y*. For class II it is otherwise *o* throughout the paradigm. For class I, the vowel of the variable suffixes is *o* in first and second persons plural, but *a* in first and second persons singular, with the exception of the preposition *o* 'of', which has *o* throughout (conjugated on the stem *ohon-*).

5.10.3 Class III

This class has two members, *gan* 'with' and *wrth* 'by'. The vowels of the third person singular and plural are regular, as described above, but all other persons have *y*. *Gan* also has a stem variant with final *dd* in the third person singular:

(240)

	Singular	Plural
1	gennyf	gennym
2	gennyt	gennych
3 MASC	ganddo	ganddynt
FEM	ganddi	

5.10.4 The preposition *i* 'to'

This preposition forms the third person singular and plural in the regular manner, with suffixes and suffix vowels as described above, and a third-person stem variant with final *dd* after the manner of class II. However, first and second persons, singular and plural, are formed by suffixation of the appropriate personal pronoun to the root form:

(241)

	Singular	Plural
1	imi	inni
2	iti	ichwi
3 MASC	iddo	iddynt
FEM	iddi	

PHONOLOGY

5.11   CONSONANT SYSTEM

5.11.1   Single consonants, clusters and consonant length

Single consonants occur initially, medially and finally; clusters of two consonants are frequent in all positions while clusters of three occur initially and
medially.

Single consonants are phonetically long following a short stressed vowel, thus
[tɔn:] *ton* 'wave' as opposed to [to:n] *tôn* 'tune', and [kʊm:ul] *cwmwl* 'cloud', as
opposed to [ku:ru] *cŵrw* 'beer'.

5.11.2   Consonant classes

There are four main consonant classes by manner of articulation – plosives,
fricatives, affricates and nasals – distributed over three points of articulation –
labial, alveolar and velar. There is an extended fricative series reaching to the
palato-alveolar and the glottal regions, a resonant alveolar lateral and an
alveolar tap. There is a pervasive contrast between tense and lax consonants
(see 5.11.4 for this distinction), though there are structural gaps, mainly among
the lenes in the fricative series, and the nasals.

Restrictions on the occurrence of single consonants may be summarised thus:

1 /p t k/ are rare finally, though recent borrowing has significantly
increased their incidence:

(242)   /sup/ *swp* 'heap', /tap/ *tap* 'tap'
/ko:t/ *côt* 'coat', /siut/ *siwt* 'suit'
/luk/ *lwc*, 'luck', /ʃok/ *sioc* 'shock'

2 Except as mutated forms, the fricatives /x θ v ð/ occur initially very
rarely and then as the result of the reduction of the pre-stress
syllable (stress being regularly on the penultimate syllable):

(243)   /vori/ *yfory* 'tomorrow' < /əvori/; /ðauoð/ < /aðauoð/ *addawodd* 'he
promised'; /θəlɨ/ *erthylu* 'abort' < /erθəlɨ/; /xevn/ *trachefn* 'then' < /traxevn/

3 /l r ʃ/ are similarly rare as radical initials, occurring only in loans:

(244)   /lori/   *lori*   'lorry'
/ra:s/   *râs*   'race'
/ʃop/   *siop*   'shop'

Table 5.5. *Consonant classes, with examples*

	Tense	Lax
Plosives		
Labial	/p/ /pɨːs/ *pys* 'peas'	/b/ /bɨːs/ *bys* 'finger'
Alveolar	/t/ /tail/ *tail* 'dung'	/d/ /dail/ *dail* 'leaves'
Velar	/k/ /koːv/ *cof* 'memory'	/g/ /goːv/ *gof* 'smith'
Fricatives		
Labial	/f/ /fon/ *ffon* 'stick'	/v/ /van/ *fan* 'van'
Alveolar	/θ/ /uːɨθ/ *wyth* 'eight'	/ð/ /guːɨð/ *gwydd* 'goose'
	/s/ /sɨːr/ *sur* 'sour'	
Alveo-palatal	/ʃ/ /ʃiːr/ *sir* 'county'	
Lateral	/ɬ/ /ɬaːu/ *llaw* 'hand'	
Velar	/x/ /xwɨn/ *chwyn* 'weeds'	
Glottal	/h/ /haːv/ *haf* 'summer'	
Affricates		
	/tʃ/ /watʃ/ *wats* 'watch'	/dʒ/ /wedʒ/ *wedj* 'wedge'
Nasals		
Labial		/m/ /mam/ *mam* 'mother'
Alveolar		/n/ /nam/ *nam* 'blemish'
Velar		/ŋ/ /muŋ/ *mwng* 'mane'
Lateral		
Alveolar		/l/ /loːn/ *lôn* 'road'
Tap		
Alveolar	/rh/ /rhaːd/ *rhad* 'cheap'	/r/ /raːs/ *râs* 'race'

4 /h/ occurs only at stressed syllable initial:

(245)   /haːv/   *haf*   'summer'
        /parˈhaɨ/   *parhau*   'continue'

5 affricates occur only in loanwords:

(246)   /tʃips/   'chips'
        /dʒ/   'jam'

5.11.3   Clusters

5.11.3.1   Initial clusters
The most frequent initial cluster type is a two-place sequence of plosive +/r l/:

(247)(a)   /priːs/   *pris*   'price'
           /brɨːs/   *brys*   'haste'

(b)	/plaːs/	*plas*	'mansion'
	/blɨːs/	*blys*	'desire'
(c)	/triː/	*tri*	'three'
	/drɨːd/	*drud*	'costly'
(d)	/tluːs/	*tlws*	'pretty'
(e)	/krɨːs/	*crys*	'shirt'
	/griːs/	*gris*	'stair'
(f)	/klɨːsd/	*clust*	'ear'
	/glɨːd/	*glud*	'glue'

/k/ alone can precede a nasal, /n/ in an initial cluster in radical forms, for example /knoi/ *cnoi* 'to bite'.

The sibilant /s/ may precede a single plosive or a sequence of plosive +/r l/: in these cases, the contrast between the pairs /p ~ b, t ~ d, k ~ g/ is neutralised:

(248)
	/sbaːr/	*sbâr*	'spare'
	/sbriŋ/	*spring*	'spring'
	/sblendid/	*splendid*	'splendid'
	/sdoːr/	*stôr*	'store'
	/sdrap/	*strap*	'strap'

There is no attested example of /sdl-/.

(249)
	/sgoːr/	*sgor*	'score'
	/sgrubjo/	*sgrwbio*	'to scrub'
	/sgləin/	*sglein*	'shine'

These are all instances of borrowing, though evidently long established.

Initial sequences of /s/ + plosive (+ /r l/) can come about through reduction of a pre-stress syllable, particularly when the vowel of that syllable is (at least historically) /ə/:

(250)
/sbeiljo/ < */əsbəiljo/, *ysbeilio* 'to despoil'
/sbrədjon/ < */əsbrədjon/, *ysbrydion* 'spirits'

There is no attested example of /sbl- <*əsbl-/.

(251)
/sderon/ < */əsdəron/ *ystyron* 'meanings'
/sdriuja/ < */əsdriuja/ *ystrywiau* 'tricks'

There is no attested example of /sdl- < əsdl-/.

(252)
/sgɨbo/ < /*əsgɨbo/ *ysgubo*, 'to sweep'
/sgraveɬ/ < /*əsgraveɬ/ *ysgrafell*, 'curry-comb'
/sgləvaθ/ < /*əsgləvaθ/ *ysglyfaeth*, 'prey'

In all cases other than (251) and (252), there are morphologically related forms with a stressed /ə/, namely:

(253)
	/əsbail/	*ysbail*	'spoils'
	/əsbrɨd/	*ysbryd*	'spirit'
	/əsdɨr/	*ystyr*	'meaning'

/əsdrɨu/   *ystryw*   'trick'
/əsgɨb/   *ysgub*   'sheaf, broom'

The nasals /m n/ may follow an initial /s/, as in (254):

(254)   /smaljo/   *smalio*   'to care'
           /snaːm/   *snâm*   'surname'

/l/ may follow /s f/, as in (255):

(255)   /sləi/   *slei*   'sly'
           /fliːo/   *fflio*   'to fly'

while /r/ may follow /f ʃ/, as in (256):

(256)   /frɨːo/   *ffraeo*   'to quarrel'
           /ʃrɨŋkjo/   *srincio*   'to shrink'

Yet again, such sequences occur in loanwords from English, many of them long established. Reduction of the pre-stress syllable by elision of an interconsonantal vowel in allegro speech produces further examples of initial consonant-cluster types like those described, frequently extending the range of sequences, filling out the combinatory gaps. Instances which fill out such gaps are given in (257):

(257)   /kməlɨ/ < /kəməlɨ/ *cymylu* 'to cloud over'
           /pnaun/ < /prənhaun/ *prynhawn* 'afternoon'
           /tnɨːo/ < /tenɨːo/ *teneuo* 'to thin'
           /tmereð/ < /təmhereð/ *tymheredd* 'temperature'

Reduction of the pre-stress syllable can also produce untypical initial consonant clusters, as in the plosive + fricative +/r/ sequence in /kvranɨ/ < /kəvranɨ/ *cyfrannu* 'to contribute'.

The regularity and predictability of the occurrence of such clusters has, however, not been investigated, to the best of my knowledge.

5.11.3.2   Final clusters

Plosives in final position may be preceded by a homorganic nasal: the clusters which occur are /-mp, -nt, -ŋk, -nd/:

(258)   /pɨmp/   *pump*   'five'
           /kant/   *cant*   'hundred'
           /ɬuŋk/   *llwne*   'throat'
           /ɬond/   *llond*   'full'

Plosives may also be preceded by /r l/, the range of occurrences being

(259)   /karp/   *carp*   rag
           /talp/   *talp*   'lump'
           /xwart/   *chwart*   'quart'

/belt/	*belt*	'belt'
/mustard/	*mwstard*	'mustard'
/fald/	*ffald*	'sheepfold'

A final plosive may be preceded by a fricative, the examples being;

(260)
/ʃafd/	*siafft*	'shaft'
/draxd/	*dracht*	'draught (of water)'
/haːɫd/	*hallt*	'salty'
/koːsb/	*cosb*	'penalty'
/koːsd/	*côst*	'cost'
/gwiːsg/	*gwisg*	'clothing'

Fricatives in final position may be preceded by /r,l/; the range of possibilities can be exemplified thus:

(261)
/ʃilf/	*silff*	'shelf'
/sarf/	*sarff*	'serpent'
/serθ/	*serth*	'steep'
/kalx/	*calch*	'lime'
/serx/	*serch*	'love'
/ʃars/	*siars*	'charge'
/jarɫ/	*iarll*	'earl'
/barv/	*barf*	'beard'
/palv/	*palf*	'palm'
/garð/	*gardd*	'garden'

/l/ may precede a final /m/, as in /salm/, *salm* 'psalm'; while /r/ may precede a final /m n l/ as in (262):

(262)
/farm/	*ffarm*	'farm'
/karn/	*carn*	'hoof'
/perl/	*perl*	'pearl'

A final /r l n/ may be preceded by /v/, as in (263):

(263)
/gavr/	*tgafr*	'goat'
/gwevl/	*gwefl*	'lip'
/ovn/	*ofn*	'fear'

The affricate /tʃ/ in final position may be preceded by /r/ in loanwords, as in /lartʃ/ *larts* 'larch'.

Borrowing from English extends the range of final consonant clusters, notably through the adoption of noun plural forms, which introduce a range of clusters with a final /s/, as in (264):

(264)
| /kloks/ | *clocs* | 'clogs' |
| /pips/ | *pips* | 'pips' |

5.11.3.3   Medial clusters

Medial clusters can very largely be described in terms of combinations of the single consonants and clusters found at final and initial positions. Because of that, the discussion here will be exemplificatory and not exhaustive. Syllable division (marked /–/) is located immediately before or after the point of greatest obstruction to the breath-flow within the cluster.

Medial clusters may consist of the following sequences of consonant types:

    1   plosive + plosive:

(265)	/dik-der/	*dicter*	'anger'
	/at-gas/	*atgas*	'hateful'

    2   fricative + plosive:

(266)	/ɬix-der/	*uchter*	'height'
	/miɬ-dir/	*milltir*	'mile'
	/kax-gi/	*cachgi*	'coward'
	/gwaɬ-gov/	*gwallgof*	'mad'
	/əið-gar/	*eiddgar*	'ardent'

    3   plosive + fricative:

(267)	/mod-veð/	*modfedd*	'inch'
	/hebðo/	*hebddo*	'without him'

    4   plosive or fricative + /r l N/:

(268)	/ad-roð/	*adrodd*	'recite'
	/heb-ruŋ/	*hebrwng*	'accompany'
	/ad-lais/	*adlais*	'echo'
	/ad-nod/	*adnod*	'verse'
	/div-las/	*diflas*	'miserable'
	/div-rod/	*difrod*	'damage'
	/kəv-nod/	*cyfnod*	'period'
	/ox-ri/	*ochri*	'side'

    5   /r l N/ + plosive, affricate or fricative:

(269)	/xwar-ter/	*chwarter*	'quarter'
	/tel-pɨn/	*telpyn*	'lump'
	/ləŋ-kɨ/	*llyncu*	'swallow'
	/per-xen/	*perchen*	'owner'
	/per-sain/	*persain*	'melodious'
	/sil-foɨð/	*silffoedd*	'shelves'
	/kən-fon/	*cynffon*	'tail'

    6   /r l N s/ + plosive or fricative + /r l/:

(270)	/gwer-gloð/	*gwerglodd*	'meadow'
	/xwɨl-dro/	*chwyldro*	'revolution'
	/pen-dro/	*pendro*	'dizziness'
	/sərθ-ni/	*syrthni*	'apathy'
	/gwərð-ni/	*gwyrddni*	'green-ness'

7 combinations of /r l N/:

(271)	/kor-lan/	*corlan*	'sheepfold'
	/vel-na/	*fel(y)na*	'like that'
	/kor-nuɨd/	*cornwyd*	'abscess'

8 fricative + fricative:

(272)	/ɨð-ved/	*aeddfed*	'mature'
	/uɨθ-ved/	*wythfed*	'eighth'
	/kloð-va/	*cloddfa*	'quarry'

9 /r n/ + /h/:

(273)	/kən-'hesɨ/	*cynhesu*	'warm'
	/ar-'holjad/	*arholiad*	'examination'

5.11.4   Range of consonant realisations

The main articulatory features are deducible from the labelled classification given in 5.11.2. The tense/lax contrast has to do with energy of articulation: tense consonants are released with greater energy, and are invariably voiceless. Lax consonants are released with less energy and are voiced between voiced sounds and partially voiced in absolute initial or final and immediately before or after a voiceless consonant; the voicing variants may be represented thus:

(274)	[sədɨn] *sydyn* 'sudden'	[akddor] *actor* 'actor'
	[ddoːv] *dof* 'tame'	[noːdd] *nod* 'aim'

Partially voiced segments may be completely devoiced, so that the contrast becomes one of energy alone, which is realised as presence of strong versus weak aspiration for plosives and /rh/, /r/ and strong versus weak local friction for other consonants. It is not uncommon, in all dialects, for the lax fricatives /v/ and /ð/ to be lost in final position:

(275)	/treː/ *tref* 'town' < /treːv/
	/for/ *ffordd* 'road' < /forð/

After voiceless fricatives, the contrast between tense and lax plosives is neutralised, and the segments are phonetically weakly aspirated and voiceless:

(276)	[koːsb]	*cosb*	'penalty'
	[haːɬd]	*hallt*	'salty'
	[kuːsg]	*cwsg*	'sleep'

Sequences of two plosives in medial position are realised as a sequence of tense + lax, as in /dikder/ *dicter* 'annoyance'. Where the lax plosive is derived from a tense one, however, the tenseness may re-appear in careful speech, as in /dikter/: in such sequences as these, the first plosive is weakly released. The same is true of plosives following a tense fricative in medial position, giving:

allegro speech: /ɨxder/ *uchter* 'height' against
careful speech: /ɨxter/

Some consonants need a more precise label: amongst the fricatives, /f/ and /v/ are labio-dental; /θ/ and /ð/ are interdental; /s/ is alveolar and /x/ is uvular. Both /ɬ/ and /l/ are laterals, and, for most speakers, unilateral. /l/ is always dark, /rh/ (which occurs only initially) is a tap, while /r/ is a tap initially and finally, and a trill medially.

/l/, /m/, /n/ can be syllabic, as in:

(277)   [handl̩]   *handel*   'handle'
         [m̩a]   *yma*   'here'
         [n̩a]   *yna*   'there'

5.12   VOWEL SYSTEM

5.12.1   Monophthongs, diphthongs and vowel length

Syllable nuclei, in all positions, may be composed of either a monophthong or a diphthong. Long vowels, whether alone or as the first elements of diphthongs, can occur in a stressed monosyllable only, as in (278):

(278)   /toːn/ *tôn* 'tune'   ʃ   /ton/ *ton* 'wave'
         /kaːɨ/ *cae* 'field'   ʃ   /kaɨ/ (*nac*)*cau* 'refuse'

Length /ː/ is thus phonological in this position alone.

5.12.2   Vowel classes

The vowels can be classed according to three degrees of height and according to whether the front, centre or back of the tongue is the articulator. The phonemes form a 3–3–1 system, as illustrated:

	Front	*Central*	*Back*
High	i	ɨ	u
Mid	e	ə	o
Low		a	

All vowels except /ə/ have long and short variants, as is shown:

(279)   /iː/ /kiːg/ *cig* 'meat'   /i/ /kik/ *cic* 'kick'
         /eː/ /ɬeːn/ *llen* 'literature'   /e/ /ɬen/ *llen* 'curtain'
         /aː/ /taːl/ *tâl* 'payment'   /a/ /tal/ *tal* 'tall'
         /oː/ /toːn/ *tôn* 'tune'   /o/ /ton/ *ton* 'wave'
         /uː/ /suːn/ *swn* 'noise'   /u/ /pun/ *pwn* 'burden'
         /ɨː/ /ɬɨːn/ *llun* 'picture'   /ɨ/ /ɬɨn/ *llyn* 'lake'

There are three series of diphthongs, closing to all three high positions of articulation, though not all vowels can combine with all three final elements (see figure 5.1). The following diphthongs occur:

Closing to /-i/

/ai/ /bai/ *bai* 'fault'   /plastai/ *plastai* 'mansions'
/oi/ /troi/ *troi* 'turn'   /para'toi/ *paratoi* 'prepare'
(/oi/ occurs only in stressed monosyllables and in the stressed final syllable of a polysyllabic word)
/əi/ /pəirjant/ *peiriant* 'machine' /pəirjanwaiθ/ *peirianwaith* 'machinery'

Closing to /-ɨ/

/aːɨ/ /kaːɨ/ *cae* 'field'   /maːɨn/ *maen* 'stone'
/aːɨ/ occurs only in stressed monosyllables.
/aɨ/ /kaɨ/ *(nac)cau* 'refuse'   /peθaɨ/ *pethau* 'things'
/oɨ/ /doɨθ/ *doeth* 'wise'   /doɨθineb/ *doethineb* 'wisdom'
/uɨ/ /ɬuɨn/ *llwyn* 'bush'   /kəvruɨ/ *cyfrwy* 'saddle'
/əɨ/ /ɬəɨad/ *lleuad* 'moon'   /bəɨnəðjol/ *beunyddiol* 'daily'

Closing to /-u/

/iu/ /ɬiu/ *lliw* 'colour'   /amrəliu/ *amryliw* 'many-coloured'
/eu/ /teu/ *tew* 'fat'   /teuəxɨ/ *tewychu* 'thicken'
/au/ /ɬau/ *llaw* 'hand'   /əsgau/ *ysgaw* 'elder(tree)'
/ɨu/ /bɨu/ *byw* 'live'   /benɨu/ *benyw* 'female'
/əu/ /bəuɨd/ *bywyd* 'life'   /bəuadaɨ/ *bywydau* 'lives'

The major restriction on vowel distributions is that /ə/ can never occur in a word-final syllable in indigenous words: see further 5.17. It does occur in this context, however, in a growing number of loanwords; for example:

(280)   /bəs/ *bys* 'bus'   /fər/ *ffyr* 'fur'
         /fəind/ *ffeind* 'fine'   /təi/ *tei* 'tie'
         /brəun/ *brown* 'brown'   /rəund/ *rownd* 'round'

Before /-i/, /ə/ in such forms is realised in some southern dialects as /e/, and before /-u/ as /o/. We will regard these forms as representing an innovative subsystem.

5.12.3   Range of vowel realisations

/iː/ is a high front vowel, phonetically [iː], while /i/ is slightly lowered and retracted, phonetically [ɪ]. /eː/ is a half-close front vowel [eː], while /e/ is

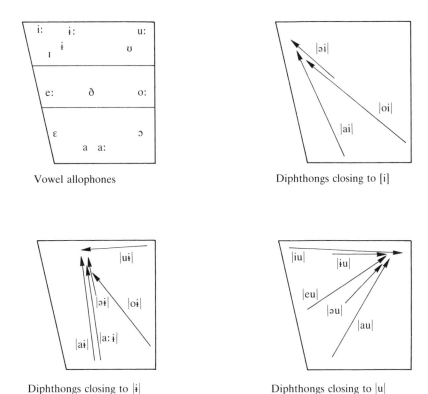

Vowel allophones

Diphthongs closing to [i]

Diphthongs closing to |ɨ|

Diphthongs closing to |u|

Figure 5.1   Typical vowel and diphthong charts for a north Welsh speaker

articulated in the half-open position [ɛ]. /aː/ is fully open and central [aː], while /a/ is slightly raised and fronted [a]. /oː/ is half-close [oː], while /o/ is half-open [ɔ]. /uː/ is close back [uː], while /u/ is slightly lowered and fronted [ʊ]. [ə] is a central vowel [ə], close to the half-close position.

The central vowel /ɨː/ is articulated with spread lips, just front of the mid position [ɨː]; the short variant /ɨ/ is slightly fronted and lowered [ɨ].

For /a(ː)/ and /ə/ the lips are neutral; for back vowels, rounding increases with the closeness of the vowel, and for front vowels the lips are increasingly spread.

Length is phonemic for all monophthongs except (ə) in stressed monosyllables, but only for the diphthongs /aːɨ/, /aɨ/; all other diphthongs are unmarked for length: the length of the first element of all is either invariable or phonetically determined: /ai/, /oi/ and /əi/ are always phonetically short [ai], [ɔi] and [əi]; /aːɨ/ is [aːɨ] and /aɨ/ the short [aɨ]; /oɨ/ and /uɨ/ are phonetically long [oːɨ], [uːɨ] in monosyllables, short [ɔɨ], [uɨ] elsewhere; /əɨ/ is always short [əɨ];

/iu/ is always short, though closer to [iu] than to [ɪu]; /eu/ and /au/ are phonetically long [e:u], [a:u] in open monosyllables, short [ɛu] and [au] in closed monosyllables and elsewhere, thus:

(281)   [te:u] *tew* 'fat'   but   [dɛur] *dewr* 'brave'
          [ɫa:u] *llaw* 'hand'   but   [baud] *bawd* 'thumb'

/ɨu/ and /əu/ are short [ɨu] and [əu] in all positions.

The closing point of the diphthong series in /-i/ is very close to that of [i:]; for phonetically short diphthongs, those in /-ɨ/ and /-u/ also approximate to the positions of the corresponding long vowels [ɨ:] and [u:], but for long diphthongs, the closing point is close to the position of the short variants [ɨ] and [ʊ].

In a final unstressed syllable, the diphthongs /ai/ and /aɨ/ are fairly regularly monophthongised to /e/, as in (282):

(282)   /peθe/   /peθaɨ/   *pethau* 'things'
          /dime/   /dimai/   *dimai* 'halfpenny'

5.12.4   Semi-vowels

There are two semi-vowels, the palatal /j/ and labial–velar /w/. They occur prevocalically, always at syllable onset, either alone or following a consonant. Phonetically, they are rapid vocalic glides moving towards the position of the following vowel, starting respectively from the positions of [i:] (with spread lips) and [u:] (with lips rounded). Examples are:

(283)   /jaiθ/ *iaith* 'language'   /gjas/ *gias* 'gas'
          /watʃ/ *wats* 'watch'   /Xwa:ɨθ/ *chwaeth* 'taste'

The consonants which can precede the semi-vowels (leaving aside instances of syllable elision in allegro speech, which can produce examples like /twelɨ/ < /tauelɨ/ *tawelu* 'quieten') are /k, g/ in the case of /j/ and /x, g/ in the case of /w/.

5.13   SYLLABLE STRUCTURE

A vowel may stand alone, as in /a/ *a* 'and', /i/ *i* 'to'. Monosyllables may have an onset of up to three consonants in a cluster; thus:

(284)   #C   /pam/   *pam*   'why'
          #CC   /pla:s/   *plas*   'mansion'
          #CCC   /sgləin/   *sglein* 'polish'

Final syllables may be closed by a single C or a cluster of two:

(285)   C # #   /pa:s/   *pas*   'whooping cough'
          CC # #   /pa:sg/   *Pasg*   'Easter'

A single consonant in medial position between a stressed syllable and a following weakly stressed one forms an interlude between two syllables: in the case of obstruents, the closure phase in the articulation of the segment closes the first syllable and its release is onset to the second; for continuants, which always follow a short vowel in this position, the stricture is held, so that again approach and release respectively close and open the two syllables; we can represent the syllable division by doubling the consonant:

(286)   /kap-pel/ : /kapel/   *capel*   'chapel'
          /kan-nɨ/ : /kanɨ/   *canu*   'sing'

For clusters of two consonants in this position, the syllable division comes between them, as it does for clusters which precede the primary stressed syllable; thus:

(287)   /bas-ged/   *basged*   'basket'
          /bas-gedi/   *basgedi*   'baskets'

and, in a cluster of three consonants in these two positions, the syllable division immediately precedes or follows the point of greatest closure, to give a CC-C or C-CC pattern; for example:

(288)   /kas-glɨ/   *casglu*   'gather'
          /gwɔrð-ni/   *gwyrddni*   'green-ness'
          /pel-droɨdjur/ *peldroediwr*   'footballer'

Where a single consonant forms the boundary between two syllables ahead of the primary stressed one, the first remains open and the consonant forms the onset to the second; thus /pre-geθur/ *pregethwr* 'preacher'.

5.14   STRESS

5.14.1   Stressed and unstressed syllables

There are four degrees of phonetic word stress in Welsh, though it is the practice to recognise only three phonologically.

5.14.2   Distribution of stress

Primary stress, in indigenous Welsh words, falls normally on the penultimate syllable, but in some cases on the ultimate. Given the location of primary stress, the secondary, tertiary and fourth degrees are assigned mechanically to syllables in almost all cases, in this pattern:

(289)   /²pre⁴ge¹θu³rol/   *pregethwrol*   'ministerial'
           /²pa⁴rat¹toi/   *paratoi*   'prepare'
           /⁴əm¹laːɨn/   *ymlaen*   'onwards'

I follow Griffen (1979) by classing secondary and tertiary together for phonological purposes, so that:

(290)   phonetic   →   phonological
           1   1
           2⎫
           3⎬   2
           4⎭
                                3

5.15   PITCH

5.15.1   Syllable pitch

Following Watkins (1961) we recognise three distinctive pitch levels: 1 (high), 2 (mid), 3 (low). In polysyllabic words with the regular stress pattern, high pitch falls on the final unstressed syllable, mid on the stressed syllable and low on the pre-stress syllable:

(291)   /²dar¹ɬen/   *darllen*   'read'
           /³dar²ɬen¹ɨð/   *darllenydd*   'reader'
           /³pre³ge²θur¹ol/   *pregethwrol*   'ministerial'

In final syllable stressed words, the pattern is low-high,

(292)   /³əm¹laːɨn/   *ymlaen*   'onwards'

5.15.2   Word tone

It is not generally considered that Welsh has word tones, but see Oftedal (1969a) for a stimulating proposal.

5.15.3   Intonation (utterance pitch contour)

In sequences of noun + adjective or of verb + complement, the basic pattern is 1–2, as in the following patterns:

(293)   /¹diːn ²teːu/   *dyn tew*   'fat man'
           /³dən¹jon ²teːu/   *dynion tew*   'fat men'
           /³ko¹ɬi ²kuːsg/   *colli cwsg*   'lose sleep'
           /³mɨnd ¹ən ²oːl/   *mynd yn ôl*   'going back'

   Marking a single pitch level for rhythmic units within the sentence, and ignoring the details of their realisations (but bearing in mind the tendency for the highest pitch in a polysyllabic unit to be realised on its post-stress syllable), we can summarise the main sentence intonation contours:

Declaratives and imperatives have a 1–2–3 pattern:

(294)(a)   ¹*Torrodd* ²*John* ³*y ffenest(r)*
'John broke the window'

(b)   ¹*Tyrd* ²*yma* ³*ar unwaith*
'Come here at once'

Particle-led questions have 3–2–1:

(295)   ³*A welaist* ²*ti'r* ¹*bachgen?*
'Did you see the boy?'

And, with the particle deleted,

(296)   ³*Welaist* ²*ti'r* ¹*bachgen?*

Inverted sentences, in which a constituent is fronted, have the pitch level 1 on the first rhythmic grouping. Thus, emphatic sentences:

(297)   ¹*Dweud ei hanes wrth yr athrawes* ³*yr oedd* ²*Mair*
'Telling her experience to the teacher was Mair'

and subject and object noun phrase interrogatives,

(298)(a)   ¹*Pwy* ²*oedd* ³*yn gweiddi?*
'Who was shouting?'

(b)   ¹*Beth wyt ti* ²*wedi* ³*ei balu?*
'What have you dug?'

The 'abnormal' sentence (see 5.2.16.1) has the pattern 1–2–3:

(299)   ¹*Mair a* ²*fwrodd* ³*ef*
'Mair hit him'

MORPHOPHONOLOGY

5.16   CONSONANT MUTATIONS

5.16.1   Initial mutations of consonants

There are three types of initial consonant mutation – soft, nasal and spirant. Their phonology is described in this section, and the contexts in which they apply in sections 5.18, 5.19, 5.20 and 5.21.

Soft mutation involves two phonological processes:

> *laxing* of the tense stops /p t k tʃ/ > / b dg dʒ/, of the tense fricative
> /ɬ/ > /l/ and of the tense liquid /rh/ > /r/ (the lax stop /dʒ/ has no
> soft-mutated variant);
> *frictionalisation* of the lax stops /b m/ > /v/, /d/ > /ð/ and of /g/ > /Ø/
> through a historical */ɣ/.

Nasal mutation involves nasalisation of all plosives, to give two corresponding
series of tense and lax nasals. Thus, /p t k/ > /mh nh ŋh/ and /b d g/ > /m n ŋ/. In
some northern dialects, this rule extends to include all stops with oral release, so
that in loanwords /tʃ dʒ/>/nhʃ nʒ/ (see Jones 1967).

Although we have two nasal series in phonological terms – one tense (and
hence voiceless), the other lax – the phonetic realisation of the mutated forms is
different from this. In almost all cases, nasal mutation is governed by a form
which itself has a final nasal (see Thomas 1966), as in the preposition /ən/ *yn* 'in'.
We can illustrate both series with the following forms:

(300)(a)   /aŋ nhar'dɨːð/ < /ən + kar'dɨːð/
            'in Cardiff'
    (b)   /əm mangor/ < /ən + bangor/
            'in Bangor'

The problematic form is the tense consonant in the first example. We begin with
a consonant sequence /-n k-/; nasalisation of the initial plosive gives /-n ŋh-/;
then we have assimilation of the final /-n/ to the place of articulation of the new
initial velar nasal, /-ŋ ŋh-/; finally, simplification of the two velar nasals leaves
the preposition with a final /-ŋ/ and the following noun with an initial /h-/; the
phonetic shape of the nasalised complex is [əŋ har'dɨːð]. Velarity and nasality is
registered in the final consonant [-ŋ] of the preposition, and tenseness (and
voicelessness) in the initial [h] of the noun.

In vernacular usage, the nasal mutation after the preposition /ən/ *yn*, 'in' (and
after the first person singular possessive adjective *fy* 'my' which similarly has the
form /ən/ in most forms of spoken Welsh) is frequently replaced by soft
mutation, accompanied by assimilation of the final nasal of /ən/ to the position
of articulation of the following consonant. Thus the examples above could be
realised as:

(301)(a)   /əŋ gar'dɨːð/
    (b)   /əm vangor/

and the possessive phrase (302) as (303):

(302)   /ən ŋha:θ i/
          fy   nghath i
          my cat   me
          'my cat'

(303)   /ən ga:θ i/</ka:θ/.

The spirant mutation, in standard usage, involves frictionalisation of the tense plosives /p t k/>/f θ x/. In southern dialects, this mutation is no longer operative, the radical consonant being normally retained.

5.16.2   Non-initial mutation of consonants

All three mutation types occur in medial or final position. *Soft mutation* occurs in the initial consonant of the second element of a proper compound (i.e. one in which the second element is the head), as in

(304)   /gwaiθ + ti:/ > /gweiθdɨ/ *gweithdy* 'workshop'
          work   + house

and after certain prefixes, e.g.

(305)   /di-/ +   /gwerθ/ > /diwerθ/ *diwerth* 'worthless'
          neg. prefix /di/ + worth

Nasal mutation can occur medially in inflected and derived forms, in which the stem has a final consonant cluster of nasal + homorganic tense plosive; for example:

(306)(a) /dant + eð/ > /daneð/ *dannedd* 'teeth'
          tooth + pl. suffix /eð/
     (b) /pɨmp + ed/ >/pɨmed/ *pumed* 'fifth'
          five +   ordinal suffix /ed/

or where the final alveolar nasal consonant of a prefix assimilates to the position of articulation of a tense initial plosive in the stem, as in

(307)   /an +   /ko:v/>/aŋov/ *angof* 'oblivion'
          neg. prefix /an/ + memory

Spirant mutation can occur in compounds formed from a numeral and a noun, when the numeral requires spirant mutation in a following noun in syntactic environments, as in (308):

(308)   /tri +   /pu ɨs/ > /trifuɨs/ *triphwys* 'three pounds'
          three + pound

5.16.3   Consonant-mutation classes

The basic system has three classes of consonants, assigned according to the
extent to which they enter into the initial mutation system. The most extensive
participation is by the tense plosives, the next by the lax plosives and the least by
a phonologically mixed set of consonants which are restricted to soft mutation.
The classes are summarised in table 5.5 (dialectal departures from the basic
system have been noted in 5.1.4).

5.16.4   Prevocalic mutation

Following some pronominal forms, an initial vowel is aspirated, as after the
third person singular copy pronoun /i/ *ei* 'her', in possessive or objective
function; for example:

(309)(a)   /i   haval hi/ < /aval/; *ei hafal hi* 'her apple'
              her apple her
     (b)   /i   hovni hi/ < /ovni/; *ei hofni hi* 'to fear her'
              her fear   her

In northern dialects, this has extended to the class of resonant consonants, so
that nasals and the lax lateral /l/ are similarly aspirated, as in (310):

(310)(a)   /i   mham hi/ < /mam/; *ei mham hi* 'her mother'
              her mother her
     (b)   /i   lhamp hi/ < /lamp/; *ei lhamp hi* 'her lamp'
              her lamp   her
     (c)   /i   mhaḷi hi/ < /maḷi/; *ei mhalu hi* 'to smash it'
              her smash her

The velar nasal /ŋ/ never occurs in absolute initial as a radical consonant, and /l/
is initial only in loan words.

5.17   VOCALIC MUTATIONS

For vocalic alternations, see 5.22.

5.18   NOUN MUTATIONS

5.18.1   Soft mutation

The contexts of soft mutation in the noun are as follows (the contextual
restrictions noted in sections 5.16.5 to 5.21 reflect current conservative usage,

Table 5.6. *Consonant mutation classes*

Class	Radical	Soft	Nasal	Spirant
I Tense plosives	/p/	/b/	/mh/	/f/
	/t/	/d/	/nh/	/θ/
	/k/	/g/	/nh/	/x/
II Lax plosives	/b/	/v/	/m/	
	/d/	/ð/	/n/	
	/g/	/Ø/	/n/	
III Mixed consonants	/m/	/v/		
	/ɬ/	/l/		
	/rh/	/r/		
	/tʃ/	/dʒ/		

though acknowledged archaisms have been omitted; the major contexts of mutation are illustrated, but see Williams (1980: 174–7) for a slightly fuller list):

> In a feminine noun following the definite article /ə/ *y* 'the':

(311)   /ə gaːθ/ 'the cat' < /kaːθ/

> and in the numeral /daɨ, duɨ/ (*dau* masc., *dwy* fem.) after the article, as in (312):

(312)   /ə ðaɨ vaxgen/ *y ddau fachgen* 'the two boys' < /baxgen/

> In a noun qualifying the feminine head noun of a nominal phrase:

(313)   /koːt lau/ *cot law* 'raincoat' < /glau/
         coat rain

> After the predicate particle /ən/ *yn*, 'in':

(314)   /mai X ən ganur/, 'X is a singer' < /kanur/
         is X in singer

> A noun in apposition to another noun:

(315)   /diu daːd/ *Duw Dad* 'God the Father', < /taːd/
         God Father

> A noun following the numerals, /daɨ/ *dau* (masc.), /duɨ/ *dwy* (fem.) 'two':

(316)(a)   /daɨ ðiːn/ *dau ddyn* 'two men' < /diːn/
    (b)   /duɨ verx/ *dwy ferch* 'two girls' < /merx/

> and a feminine noun following /ɨːn/ *un* 'one':

(317)   /iːn verx/ *un ferch* 'one girl' < /merx/

Feminine nouns after all ordinals:

(318)   /ə drədeð verx/ *y drydedd ferch* 'the third girl' < /merx/

except /ail/ *ail* 'second' which mutates all nouns:

(319)   /ər ail ðiːn/ *yr ail ddyn* 'the second man' < / diːn/

A noun after copy pronouns (in possessive or objective function):

(320)(a)   /də/ *dy* (2 sg.) 'your': /də gaːθ/ *dy gath* 'your cat' < /kaːθ/
     (b)   /i/ *ei* (3 sg. masc.), 'his': /i gaːθ/ *ei gath* 'his cat' < /kaːθ/

A noun after expletive /dəma/ *dyma* 'here', /dəna/ *dyna* 'there':

(321)   /dəma, dəna ðiːn/ *dyma, dyna ddyn* 'here's, there's a man' < /diːn/

A noun after the interrogative particle /pa/ *pa* 'what':

(322)   /pa verx/ *pa ferch?* 'what girl?' < /merx/

A noun following /naiɬ/, as in the idiom /ə naiɬ...aːr ɬaɬ/ *y naill....a'r llall* 'the one...and the other', /ə nail ðiːn aːr ɬaɬ/ *y naill ddyn a'r llall* '(both) the one man and the other' < /diːn/.

A noun after the pronominal /rhɨu/ *rhyw* 'some', and its derivatives /amrɨu/ *amryw* 'several', /kəvrɨu/ *cyfryw* 'such', /ɨnrhɨu/ *unrhyw* 'any', as in /rhiu ðiːn/ *rhyw ddyn*, 'some man' < /diːn/.

An object noun after an inflected form of the active verb:

(323)   /kanoð gaːn/ *canodd gân* 'he sang a song' < /kaːn/
     sang-he song

The subject noun, and the object noun of a verb–noun, mutate only when they are separated from their respective verbal forms by an interpolation; for example, expletive /əna/ *yna* 'there' in the following example of a subject noun:

(324)   /oːɪð əna   ðiːn/ *oedd yna ddyn* 'there was a man' < /diːn/;
     was there man

Most prepositions govern soft mutation in an object noun, as with /ar/ *ar* 'on':

(325)   /ar ben/ *ar ben* 'on top' < /pen/

5.18.2   Nasal mutation

Nasal mutation after the preposition /ən/ *yn* 'in' and the first person singular copy pronoun /ən/ *fy* 'my' (see section 5.6.8) was illustrated in 5.16.1.

The nouns /blui̇ð/ *blwydd* 'year of age' and /bləneð/ *blynedd* 'years in time' (a form which co-occurs only with numerals) mutate after the numerals /pɨm/ *pum* 'five', /saiθ/ *saith* 'seven', /uɨθ/ *wyth* 'eight', /nau/ *naw* 'nine' and /deːg/ *deg* 'ten' and its derivatives /dəɨðeg/ *deuddeg* 'twelve' and /pəmθeg/ *pymtheg* 'fifteen'; for example:

(326)   /pɨm mləneð/ *pum mlynedd* 'five years' < / bləneð/

In the case of /deːg/ and its derivatives, the initial mutation is accompanied by nasal assimilation of the final consonant of the numeral:

(327)   /deŋ mluɨð/ *deng mlwydd* 'ten years old' < /deg + bluɨð/

Nasal mutation after *saith* and *wyth* is rare in speech.

5.18.3 Spirant mutation

After the third person singular feminine copy pronoun /i/ *ei* 'her', in possessive function (see section 5.6.8); for example:

(328)   /i   xaːθ hi/ *ei chath hi* 'her cat' < /kaːθ/
          her cat her

After the numerals /tri/ *tri* 'three' and /xweː/ *chwe* 'six', as in (329):

(329)   /tri xiː/ *tri chi* 'three dogs' < /kiː/

After the conjunctions /na/ *na* 'than, nor' and /aː/ *a* 'as'; for example:

(330)   /gweɬ na   xəvoɨθ/ *gwell na chyfoeth* 'better than wealth' < /kəvoɨθ/
          better than wealth

5.19   ADJECTIVE MUTATIONS

5.19.1 Soft mutation

In an adjective following a feminine noun:

(331)   /merx vaːx/ *merch fach* 'little girl' < /baːx/

In an adjective following the predicating particle /ən/ *yn* 'in':

(332)   /maːɨr dɨːn ən dal/ *mae'r dyn yn dal* 'the man is tall' < /tal/
          is-the man in tall

In the superlative form of the adjective following the comparative particle /po/ *po* 'so much':

(333)   /goraɨ po   gənta/ *gorau po gyntaf* 'the sooner the better' < /kəntav/
          best   so-much soonest

After the adverbial intensifier /traː/ *tra* 'very':

(334)   /tra xrɨːv/ *tra chryf* 'very strong' < /krɨːv/

5.20   VERB MUTATIONS

5.20.1   Soft mutation

After the relative particle /a/ *a* 'who, which':

(335)   /ər iːn a   ðaːiθ/ *yr un a ddaeth* 'the one who came' < /daːiθ/;
the one who came

After the copy pronouns /də/ *dy* (2 sg.) 'your' and /i/ *ei* (3 sg. masc.),
'his' in objective function (see section 5.6.8); for example:

(336)   /də weld ti/   *dy weld ti* 'to see you' < / gweld/
your see   you

After the affirmative verbal particles /mi/ *mi*, /ve/ *fe* (see 5.2.3):

(337)   /mi weli   di/   *mi weli di* 'you will see' < /gweli/
PT   will-see you

the negative particle /ni/ *ni* (/na/ *na* in subordinate clause) (see
5.2.7, 5.3.2):

(338)   /ni ðau   neːb/ *ni ddaw neb* 'no-one will come' < /dau/
NEG will-come any-one

and the interrogative particles /a/ *a* (affirmative), /oni/ *oni* (neg.)
(see section 5.2.7, 5.2.14.2):

(339)   /a ðau   rhɨuin/ *A ddaw rhywun?* 'Will someone come?' < /dau/
Q will-come someone

5.20.2   Spirant mutation

After the copy pronoun /i/ *ei* (3 sg. fem.) 'her', in objective function
(see section 5.6.8):

(340)   /i xarɨ hi/ *ei charu hi* 'to love her' < /kari/
her love her

After the negative relative particle /ni/ *ni*, /na/ *na*
(see section 5.3.2):

(341)   /ə saul   na   ał.../ *y sawl na all...* 'the person who cannot...' < /gał/
the person NEG REL is-able

After the negative particle /ni/ *ni* (/na/ *na* in subordinate clauses)
(see section 5.2.7):

(342)   /ni xavoð gəvle/ *ni chafodd gyfle* 'he didn't get a chance' < /kavoð/
NEG got-he chance

After the conjunction /aː/ *a* 'and':

(343) /bara a   xaus/ *bara a chaws* 'bread and cheese' < /kaus/
bread and cheese

and some prepositions, for example /gəda/ *gyda* 'with':

(344) /gəda xəvaiɬ/ *gyda chyfaill* 'with a friend' < /kəvaiɬ/
with friend

After the negative interrogative particle /oni/ *oni* (see section 5.2.6):

(345) /oni xləusox xi/ *Oni chlywsoch chwi?* 'Didn't you hear?' < /kləusox/
NEGQ heard you

and the conjunction /oni/ *oni*, 'until, unless':

(346) /oni xləuav rɨubeθ/ *oni chlywaf rywbeth* 'unless I hear something'< /kləuav/
unless hear-I something

5.21   ADVERB MUTATIONS

5.21.1   Soft mutation

In an adjective after the adverbial particle /ən/ *yn* 'in'. In an adverbial phrase:

(347) /rhedeg ən gəvlɨm/ *rhedeg yn gyflym*, 'running quickly' < /kəvlɨm/
run   in quick

In a nominal functioning as an adverbial:

(348) /arhosoð viːs/ *arhosodd fis* 'he stayed a month' < /miːs/
stayed-he month

5.22   OTHER MORPHOPHONOLOGICAL ALTERNATIONS

5.22.1   Before a close front vowel in the final syllable, /a/>/e/ in the penult:

(349) /gwlaːd/ *gwlad* 'country' > /gwledig/ *gwledig* 'rural'

Also when the final syllable has the semi-vowel /j/, /a/>/ei/ in the penult

(350) /maːb/ *mab* 'son' > /meibjon/ *meibion* 'sons'

This alternation is known as vowel affection, and is not a general rule, so that forms which undergo it have to be marked. See Thomas (1966).

5.22.2   Another rule for which words have to be marked is that by which some vowels, notably /ɨ/ and /u/, alternate with /ə/, in non-final syllables:

(351)(a)   /diːn/ *dyn* 'man'   > /dənjon/ *dynion* 'men'
   (b)   /kum/ *cwm* 'valley' > /kəmoɨð/ *cymoedd* 'valleys'

For a fuller description of this alternation, see Thomas (1979) and its modified versions in Fowkes (1977) and Ball and Jones (1984).

5.22.3   /h/ in stressed syllables can alternate with /∅/ in unstressed ones, after nasals and /r/:

(352)   /brenin/ *brenin* 'king', but /brenˈhinoɨð/ *brenhinoedd* 'kings'

Williams (1980: 177–80) gives a full account of vowel alternants and the contexts in which they occur.

REFERENCES

In order to provide a broad guide to the standard literature, the bibliography contains some additional references to those in the text. The Board of Celtic Studies of the University of Wales is preparing for publication a full bibliography on Welsh language studies.

Anwyl, E. 1899. *A Welsh grammar for schools*, parts I and II (Parallel Grammar Series), London: Swann Sonnerschein.
Awbery, G. M. 1976. *The syntax of Welsh: a transformational study of the passive* (Cambridge Studies in Linguistics 18), Cambridge: Cambridge University Press.
Census 1981, *Welsh language in Wales*, London: HMSO.
Committee of Council on Education 1847. *Reports on Wales*. London: HMSO.
Gregor, D. B. 1980. *Celtic: a comparative study*, Cambridge: Oleander Press.
Griffen, T. D. 1979. On phonological stress in Welsh. *Bulletin of the Board of Celtic Studies* 28, 2: 206–12.
Jones, M. and Alan R. Thomas 1977. *The Welsh language: studies in its syntax and semantics*, Cardiff: University of Wales Press for the Schools Council.
Jones, R. O. 1967. A structural phonological analysis and comparison of three Welsh dialects. Unpublished MA thesis, University of Wales.
   1984. Amrywiaeth tafodieithol a phatrwm newid ieithyddol yng Nghymraeg y Wladfa. *Studia Celtica* 17/19: 253–67.
Lloyd, T. M. 1973. The Welsh language in journalism. In M. Stephens (ed.) *The Welsh language today*, Llandysul: Gomer Press.
Morris-Jones, J. 1913. *A Welsh Grammar*, Oxford University Press.
   1921. *An elementary Welsh grammar*, Oxford University Press.
Orgraff yr iaith Gymraeg, 1928, Adroddiad Pwyllgor Llên Bwrdd Gwybodau Celtaidd Prifysgol Cymru, Gwasg Prifysgol Cymru.
Richards, M. 1938. *Cystrawen y frawddeg Gymraeg*, Cardiff: Gwasg Prifysgol Cymru.
Southall, J. E. 1892. *Wales and her language*, Newport: J. E. Southall: London: E. Hicks.

Thomas, Alan R. 1966. Systems in Welsh phonology. *Studia Celtica* 1: 93–127.

1973. *The linguistic geography of Wales: a contribution to Welsh dialectology*, Cardiff: University of Wales Press.

1978. Dialect mapping. In J. E. Alatis (ed.) *International dimensions of bilingualism* (Georgetown University Round Table on Languages and Linguistics 1978), Washington D.C.: Georgetown University Press.

1979. A lowering rule for vowels and its ramifications, in a dialect of North Welsh. In D. P. O'Baoill (ed.) *Papers in Celtic phonology* (Occasional papers in Linguistics and Language Learning, no. 6), Coleraine: The New University of Uslter; also (with modifications) in R. A. Fowkes (ed.) 1977, 166–86, and (with further modifications) in Ball, and Jones (eds.) 1984.

1980. *Areul analysis of dialect data by computer: A Welsh example*, Cardiff: University of Wales Press.

Watkins, T. A. 1961. *Ieithyddiaeth*, Cardiff: Gwasg Prifysgol Cymru.

1977a. The Welsh personal pronoun, in R. A. Fowkes (ed.) *Celtic Linguistics 1976, Word* 28: 1 and 2.

1977b. Cyfnewidiadau seinegol sy'n gysylltiedig â'r 'acen' Gymraeg. *Bulletin of the Board of Celtic Studies*, 26, 4: 399–405.

Williams, D. 1950. *A history of modern Wales*, London: John Murray.

Williams G. 1975. *The desert and the dream: a study of Welsh colonisation in Chubut, 1865–1915*, Cardiff: University of Wales Press.

Williams Jac L. 1973. The Welsh language in education. In M. Stephens (ed.) *The Welsh language today*, Llandysul: Gomer Press.

Williams, R. Bryn 1962. *Y Wladfa*, Cardiff: Gwasg Prifysgol Cymru.

Williams, S. J. 1959. *Elfennau gramadeg Cymraeg*, Cardiff: Gwasg Prifysgol Cymru.

1980, *A Welsh grammar*, Cardiff: University of Wales Press.

Willis, P. 1987. A reply to T. D. Griffen 'Early Welsh aspiration'. *Word* 38, 1: 47–55.

FURTHER READING

Adler, M. K. 1977. *Welsh and the other dying languages in Europe: a sociolinguistic study*, Hamburg: Helmut Buske.

Albrow, K. H. 1966. Mutation in 'Spoken North Welsh'. In C. E. Bazell, J. C. Catford, M. A. K. Halliday and R. H. Robins (eds.), *In memory of J. R. Firth*, London: Longman, Green.

Awbery, G. M. 1975. Welsh mutations: syntax or phonology? *Archivum Linguisticum* 6: 14–25.

1977. A transformational view of Welsh relative clauses. *Bulletin of the Board of Celtic Studies* 2: 155–206.

1984a. Welsh. In P. Trudgill (ed.), *Language in the British Isles*, Cambridge University Press.

1984b. Sentence particles in spoken Welsh. *Bulletin of the Board of Celtic Studies* 31: 17–30.

1987. *Pembrokeshire Welsh: a phonological study*, Cardiff: Welsh Folk Museum.

Ball, M. J. and G. E. Jones (eds.) 1984. *Welsh phonology: selected readings*, Cardiff: University of Wales Press.

Bellin, Wynford 1984. Welsh and English in Wales. In P. Trudgill, (ed.) *Language in the British Isles*, Cambridge: Cambridge University Press.

Council for the Welsh Language 1978. *A future for the Welsh language*, London: HMSO.
Council for Wales and Monmouthshire 1963. *Report on the Welsh language today*, London: HMSO.
Davies, W. B. 1952. Ffin dwy dafodiaith. *Bulletin of the Board of Celtic Studies* 14, 3: 273–83.
Evans, J. J. 1946. *Gramadeg Cymraeg*, Aberystwyth: Aberystwyth Press.
Fife, J. 1986. Literary vs. colloquial Welsh: problems of definition. *Word* 37, 3: 141–51.
Fowkes, R. A. (ed.) 1977. *Celtic Linguistics 1976, Word* 28: 1 and 2.
Geiriadur Prifysgol Cymru, vols. I–, 1950–, Cardiff: Gwasg Prifysgol Cymru.
Griffen, T. D. 1980. The Passive in Welsh: a relational analysis. *Bulletin of the Board of Celtic Studies* 28, 4: 558–78.
   1985. *Early Welsh aspiration: a dynamic perspective. Word* 36, 3: 211–35.
Hughes Parry, D. 1965. *Report on the legal status of the Welsh language*, London: HMSO.
Jones, D. M. 1948. The accent in modern Welsh. *Bulletin of the Board of Celtic Studies*, 13, 2: 63–4.
Jones, G. E. 1971. Hyd llafariaid yn yn Gymraeg – y llafariaid hirion. *Studia Celtica* 6: 175–88.
   1972. Hyd llafariaid yn y Gymraeg – y llafariaid byrion. *Studia Celtica* 7:120–9.
Jones, M. 1973. The present condition of the Welsh language. In M. Stephens (ed.), *The Welsh language today*, Llandysul: Gomer Press.
Jones, R. Brinley 1970. *The old British tongue: the vernacular in Wales, 1540–1640*, Cardiff: Avalon Books.
Jones, R. O. 1969. The status of the glottal fricative in the Dyffryn Nantlle dialect of Welsh. *Studia Celtica* 4: 99–109.
   1984. Change and variation in the Welsh of Gaiman, Chuput. In M. J. Ball and G. E. Jones (eds.) *Welsh phonology: selected readings*, Cardiff: University of Wales Press.
Jones, S. 1926. *A Welsh phonetic reader*, London: University of London Press.
Jones, T. J. Rhys 1977. *Living Welsh: a complete working course*, London: Hodder and Stoughton (Teach Yourself Books).
Lewis, E. G. 1978. Migration and the decline of the Welsh language. In J. Fishman (ed.), *Advances in the study of societal multilingualism*, The Hague: Mouton.
Mac Cana, P. 1980. Notes on the 'abnormal sentence'. *Studia Celtica* 24/25: 174–87.
Morgan, T. J. 1952. *Y treigladau a'u cystrawen*, Cardiff: Gwasg Prifysgol Cymru.
Oftedal, M. 1969a. 'Word tones' in Welsh? *Tilegnet Carl HJ Borgstrøm et Festskrift* PÅ 60-Årsdagen, Oslo: Universitetsforlaget Oslo.
   1969b. A new approach to North Welsh vowels. *Lochlann* 4: 243–69
Palmer, F. R. 1964. Grammatical categories and their phonetic exponents. In Horace G. Lunt (ed.), *Proceedings of the ninth international congress of linguists*, The Hague, Mouton.
Pilch, H. 1975. Advanced Welsh phonemics. *Zeitschrift für Celtische Philologie* 34: 60–102.
   1984. The structure of Welsh tonality. *Studia Celtica*, 28/29: 234–52.
Pryce, W. T. R. 1978. Welsh and English in Wales, 1750–1971: a spatial analysis based on the linguistic affiliation of parochial communities. *Bulletin of the Board of Celtic Studies*, 28, 1: 1–36.
Rhys, John 1879. *Lectures on Welsh philology*, London: Trubner.
Rowlands, E. I. 1977. Y frawddeg gymysg a'r frawddeg dro. *Bulletin of the Board of Celtic Studies*, 28, 2: 218–22.
   1981. Dosbarthu'r rhagenwau personol. *Bulletin of the Board of Celtic Studies*, 29, 3: 419–31.

1982. Sylwadau pellach ar gystrawennau'r frawddeg gymysg a'r frawddeg dro. *Bulletin of the Board of Celtic Studies* 4, 4: 674–80.

Sadler, L. 1987. *Welsh syntax: a government–binding approach*, London: Croom Helm.

Sommerfelt, A. 1925. *Studies in Cyfeiliog Welsh: a contribution to Welsh dialectology*, Oslo: I Kommission hos Jacob Dybwald.

Stephens, M. (ed.) 1973. *The Welsh language today*, Llandysul: Gomer Press.

1976. *Linguistic minorities in Western Europe*, Llandysul: Gomer Press.

Sweet, H. 1884. Spoken North Welsh. *Transactions of the Philological Society*, 1882–4. Reprinted in C. H. Wyld (ed.) *Collected papers of Henry Sweet*, Oxford: Oxford University Press, 1913.

Thomas, Beth 1980. Cymrêg, Cymraeg: cyweiriau iaith siaradwraig o Ddyffryn Afan. *Bulletin of the Board of Celtic Studies*, 28, 4: 579–92.

Thomas, C. H. 1974. Y tafodieithegydd a 'Chymraeg Cyfoes'. *Llên Cymru*, 13: 113–52.

1982. Registers in Welsh. *International Journal of the Sociology of Language*, 35: 87–115.

Thorne D. A. 1984. Sylwadau ar rai treigladau. *Bulletin of the Board of Celtic Studies* 31: 74–86.

1985. *Cyflwyniad i astudio'r Gymraeg*, Cardiff: Gwasg Prifysgol Cymru.

Watkins, T. A. 1953. The accent in Cwm Tawe Welsh. *Zeitschrift für Celtische Philologie*, 24: 6–9.

1978. Y rhagenw ategol. *Studia Celtica*, 12/13: 349–66.

Wells, J. C. 1979. Final voicing and vowel length in Welsh. *Phonetica* 36: 344–60.

Williams, Briony 1983. An approach to the Welsh vowel system. *Bulletin of the Board of Celtic Studies* 30, 3, 4: 239–52.

6

The Cornish language

ALAN R. THOMAS

HISTORICAL AND SOCIAL PERSPECTIVE

6.0 EXTERNAL HISTORY OF THE LANGUAGE

6.0.1 Areal and demographic distribution

Tradition has it that the Cornish language died with the passing of Dolly
Pentreath, its last known native speaker, in December 1777. Though it is now
believed that Dolly was survived by a scattered handful of elderly people who
also knew the language, it is unlikely that any of them lived beyond the end of
the eighteenth century. Originally a dialect of British, Cornish began its
independent development when the Tamar became the effective boundary
between England and Cornwall in the tenth century. From then on, there was
no land contact with the dialects which ultimately developed into Welsh, nor, of
course, with Breton (itself an offshoot of the British dialect spoken in the
south-west of Britain in the sixth century). It was restricted to the area lying to
the west of the Tamar.

6.0.2 Status; institutionalisation; functional range; literacy

Three historical periods are attributed to the Cornish language: Old Cornish is
dated to the end of the twelfth century; Middle Cornish from then until the
seventeenth century; and Late Cornish for its final century or so of existence.
There are no extant literary texts in Cornish before the fifteenth century; the
division between the earlier historical periods was made on the sparse evidence
of glosses and proper names in Latin manuscripts of the time. Those texts which
do exist are mainly miracle plays, translated from English. One result of this
paucity of literary texts is that the orthography of Cornish is extremely
inconsistent, with multiple representation of almost every sound, vowel and

consonant alike; so much so, that contemporary language revivalists have – with considerable opposition – devised a new orthography as a model of pronunciation (R. Morton Nance's 'Unified Spelling'). The vowel /ə/ is variously represented as orthographic 'e', 'eu', 'u', 'uy', 'o', 'ey', so that the word with the phonological structure /mər/ 'big' appears as 'meur', 'mur', 'mer', 'meyr'; and that with the phonological structure /ləv/ 'hand' as 'leff', 'leyf', 'leuf'. There are no means of knowing whether some of the variations in spelling reflect dialectal variation. For the consonants, note that the symbol 'ʒ' is often used to represent /ð/.

In describing the phonology and morphophonology of Cornish, I will give the phonological structure which can be deduced from analysis of the written forms, with comment on its orthographic representation only where it would be excessively confusing to omit it. It goes without saying that, with no spoken record available, we can do no more than set up an abstract configuration of contrasting units, though we have for guidance Edward Lhuyd's (1707: 222–53) description of the sounds of Cornish as they were spoken in the early eighteenth century. The lack of a consistent orthography indicates that the scribes who wrote down the translated miracle plays were representing a spoken variety: all the evidence points to the absence of an indigenous literary tradition.

SYNTAX

6.2　SENTENCE STRUCTURE

The data available – being exclusively literary and almost all in verse – provides only limited information on sentence structure; the discussion takes note of major features only.

6.2.1　Simple and complex sentences

Complex sentences mainly contain adverbial subordination, as in the hypotactic example (2) in 6.2.2.

6.2.2　Parataxis and hypotaxis

Parataxis occurs as with the ellipsis of a conjunction,

(1)　　*Gans Crist　y　　tho　　cowethys. Byth nyn　　　gens y*
　　　　with　Christ PREV.PT got-he associated ever NEG (*nyn g-*) were they

> *cowethe*
> friends
> 'With Christ he had consorted. (but) they were never friends'

as do hypotactic constructions with conjunctions specified,

(2)   *Du ... dre   y skyans   bras. Pan gemert kyg a werhas*
        God ... through his knowledge great when took-he body of virgin
        'God ... through his great knowledge. When he took the body of a virgin'

6.2.3   Obligatory and optional elements of structure

Ellipsis usually involves deletion of the verbal constituent,

(3)   *Gorthyans the crist ...*
        honour   to Christ
        '(Let there be) honour to Christ ...'

and of the relative particle and the verb *bos* 'to be' in parenthetic constructions,

(4)   *... an dragon preff an pla*
        the dragon beast the plague
        '... the dragon, (which is) the beast of the plague'

Parataxis, ellipsis and parenthesis are unusually frequent, probably as poetic stylistic devices.

6.2.4   Order of elements

Word order in the simple sentence is verb + subject + object + adjunct,

(5)   *Gorthya   ihesu benitha*
        will-worship-I Jesus always
        'I will worship Jesus for all time'

where the subject is implicit in the verbal inflection. There is also an optional preverbal particle *y*, *yth* (cf. Welsh *y(r)*).

6.2.5   Affirmatives; interrogatives; negatives

The affirmative pattern is exemplified in 6.2.4. The *yes/no* interrogative is introduced by the particle *a* (with a corresponding negative form *a ny*),

(6)   *A   glewsyugh why?*
        INTER heard   you
        'Did you hear?'

though third person singular present forms of *bos* 'to be' stand alone,

(7)   *Us dour omma in oges?*
         is   water here in close
         'Is there water here close by?'

The interrogative pronominal forms are based on the particle *py* 'which', as in

(8)   *Pyw   a   whyleugh?*
         INTER.PT REL seek-you
         'Who do you seek?'

(9)   *Pyth   yw   the gallos?*
         INTER.PT is (REL form 3 sg. pres. 'to be') your power
         'What is your power?'

(10)   *Pe   feste?*
         INTER.PT were-you
         'Where were you?'

(11)   *Prag   na   ons?*
         INTER.PT NEG come-they
         'Why don't they come?'

and they have related adjectival forms, as in

(12)   *Py   dol*
         INTER.PT hole
         'What hole?'

(13)   *Py   nyl*
         INTER.PT one
         'Which one?'

(14)   *Pan   pyn*
         INTER.PT pain
         'What pain?'

Negation is achieved by placing the negative particle *ny* before the inflected verb, as in (15):

(15)   *Ny evaf*
         NEG drink-I
         'I do not drink'

There is no direct negative correlate of the fronted-subject sentence type (see 6.2.12), though there is a similar construction in which a pronominal subject is followed by the negative particle *ny* (sometimes written *na*, as in 6.2.11) and an inflected verb in agreement with the person of the subject pronoun, as in (16):

(16)   *Wy ny woðough*
         you NEG know-you
         'You do not know'

6.2.6   Active, impersonal and passive sentences

The typical active sentence is as described in 6.2.4, and impersonal constructions
follow the same word order:

(17)   *redyer   an lyver*
            may-be-read the book
            'May the book be read'

There is no formal passive form in the verb: the sense of the passive is conveyed
in an active construction, which has a form of the verb *bos* 'to be' followed by a
past-participle in a relative clause:

(18)   *The voth a   vyth   gurys*
            thy will   REL will-be done
            'Thy will (which) will be done'

6.2.7   'Being' sentences

'Being' sentences can be illustrated with a descriptive sentence (with the subject
topicalised),

(19)   *An dragon yv tebel vest*
            the dragon is evil animal
            'The dragon is an evil animal'

and with an identificatory type (again with subject topicalised):

(20)   *En gyth o   deyow   hablys*
            the day was Thursday Maundy
            'The day was Maundy Thursday'

6.2.8   Locative and possessive sentences

Location is expressed by selection of the appropriate preposition or prepositional phrase,

(21)   *Deugh geneff   ha   holyough   ve*
            come   with-me and follow-you me
            'Come with me and follow me'

Possession is expressed in a construction composed of a particle (affirmative,
negative or relative) + the appropriate infixed pronoun + third singular form of
bos 'to be':

(22)   *Ny'm   bes whane*
            NEG-me is   lust
            'I do not have lust'

6.2.9   Aspectually marked sentences

Progressive aspect is expressed in a periphrastic construction which has a form of *bos* 'to be' followed by the progressive particle *ow* and a verb–noun,

(23)   *Yma ow   kelwel ely*
         he-is PROG.PT call   Elias
         'He is calling Elias'

The perfective selects the perfective particle *re* before the verb:

(24)   *An hoyl y   lyw   re   gollas*
         the sun its colour PERF.PT lost
         'The sun has lost its colour'

6.2.10   Types of complementation

The surviving evidence, being almost exclusively religious poetry, is not productive of evidence on such topics as indirect speech, reports, requests and commands.

6.2.11   Modal sentences

There is evidence that the verb *galle* 'be able', at least, had developed as a modal auxiliary:

(25)   *Neb   na ylly gull   peghes*
         this-one NEG could commit sin
         'This one could not commit sin'

6.2.12   Types of topicalisation

Topicalisation appears to be a frequent stylistically determined feature, which can involve any major constituent of the sentence. It involves fronting of any constituent, as of the subject,

(26)   *An dragon yv tebel vest*
         the dragon is evil animal
         'The dragon is an evil animal'

of an adverb

(27)   *In hanou crist a   vercy. Me ath   worhemyn dragon ...*
         in name Christ and mercy. I REL-you order   dragon
         'In the name of Christ and mercy, I order you, dragon ...'

of an oblique object,

(28)   *Dotho oll ython   sensys*
        to-him all we-are bound
        'To him are we all bound'

or of the verb, in which case the uninflected lexical verb is followed by an inflected form of the auxiliary verb *gruthyl* 'do' in a relative clause:

(29)   *Redya a   wre*
        read   REL was-doing-he
        'He was reading'

STRUCTURE OF THE PHRASE

6.3   STRUCTURE OF THE NOMINAL PHRASE

6.3.1   Order of elements

The adjective, a nominal possessor and the demonstrative adjectives *ma* 'this', *na* 'that' regularly follow the head noun, while the article, numerals and ordinals and some adverbial modifiers precede it:

(30)   *cusyl   da*
        advice good
        'good advice'

(31)   *gras   ihesu*
        grace Jesus
        'the grace of Jesus'

(32)   *an busme*
        the world-this
        'this world'

(33)   *try   person*
        three person
        'three persons'

(34)   *ol an   tekter*
        all the beauty
        'all the beauty'

The demonstrative adjectives form a discontinuous morph *an ... ma/na* with the definite article.

6.3.2 Embedding

Relative clauses are introduced by the particles *a* (positive) or *na* (negative) immediately after the antecedent nominal (though with variations, for instance when the relative particle is governed by a preposition):

(35)   *drys ol an bestes a   gertho*
         over all the beasts REL walk
         'over all the beasts which walk'

(36)   *an ioy na   thyfyk nefre*
         the joy NEG.REL ends   never
         'the joy which never ends'

6.3.3

The 'passive' construction utilises a relative construction, too (see section 6.2.6).

6.3.4 Systems of the nominal phrase

These systems resemble those found in the other Brittonic languages.

6.3.5 Definiteness and indefiniteness

Cornish has a definite article *an*, and an indefinite article *un* 'one', both of which precede the noun: *an bys* 'the world', *un den* 'a man'.

6.3.6 Deixis

Deixis can be illustrated from the postnominal demonstrative adjectives *me*/*ma* 'these', *ne*/*na* 'those' (see 6.3.1).

(37)   *an bysme*
         the world-this
         'this world'

(38)   *an rena*
         the ones-those
         'those ones'

6.3.7 Selection

Not relevant.

6.3.8   Reflexives

There are two types, the reflexive prefix *ym-/em-* before a verb, and the
pronominal *honan* 'self' following a possessive pronoun. Both occur in (39):

(39)   emlathe   y honan
          REFLEX-kill his self
          'kill himself'

6.3.9   Reference

Pronominal back-reference is common,

(40)   ... a   ihesu del ve helheys ...
          about Jesus how he was-pursued
          '... about Jesus, how he was pursued ...'

forward reference is infrequent, but see the use of *kynsol* 'first' in (41):

(41)   Kynsol ... lues den dreys   in forth da
          first ...   many man was-brought in path good
          'first ... many a man was brought to a good path'

6.3.10   Enumeration

The numerals follow the British pattern, running in series from 'one' to 'ten',
with gender contrasts in some cases, as in:

> 1: *un*; 3: *try*, *teyr* (masc., fem.); after 10 *dek*, a new series starts,
> predicated on 10, as in
> 11: *unnek*, lit. 'one-ten': 15: *pymthek*, lit. 'five-ten'

After 'twenty' *ugens*, a further series begins, predicated on 'twenty' and
preceded by the preposition *war* 'on', incorporating the previous 'eleven' to
'nineteen' series, as in 30: *dekwarnugens* lit. 'ten on twenty'; 31: *unnekwarnu-
gens* lit. 'one-ten on twenty'. This is repeated for each further unit of twenty up
to 199, after which units of 'hundred' *cans* take over, incorporating the previous
series from 1 to 99. After 1,000 *myl*, the basic unit is *myl*, incorporating the
previous 100 and 1–99 series.

There are instances of ordinals from 'first' to 'tenth' which were formed by
suffixation of -(*v*)*es* to the numeral (but note *kynso* 'first', cf. Welsh *cyntaf*), for
example *degves* 'tenth'.

6.3.11   Possession

This is marked by the appropriate possessive adjective before the noun, *the vrodes* 'your brother'. See also 6.2.8, 6.3.1.

6.3.12   Partitives

Instances of the partitive are not common, but an example is (42):

(42)   *nep   peyth a oel a vercy*
         some thing of oil of mercy
         'some amount of oil of mercy'

6.3.13   Adjectivals

Adjectivals include the possessive adjectives (section 6.3.11) and demonstrative adjectives (section 6.3.6).

6.3.14   Agreement

Agreement within the nominal phrase centres on the gender of the noun: in some cases, nominals have gender-differentiated forms, *tryhans* 'three hundred' (masc.), *tergweth* 'three times' (fem.).

6.3.15   Pronominal phrases

Evidence for this section is minimal.

6.3.16   Nominalisations

Evidence for this section is minimal.

6.4   STRUCTURE OF VERBAL PHRASE

Verb phrases may have an infixed pronoun object:

(43)   *thom   kemeres*
         to-me take
         'to take me'
(44)   *Nyth   nahaff*
         NEG-you I-will-deny
         'I will not deny you'

The inflected verb can be replaced by a periphrastic construction which has an inflected form of the auxiliary verb *gruthyl* 'do' followed by an uninflected lexical verb:

(45)   *Omma ny   wreugh why tryge*
         here   NEG will-do you live
         'Here you will not live'

(See also 6.2.3, 6.2.4, 6.2.6, 6.2.7, 6.2.9, 6.2.11.)

6.5   STRUCTURE OF THE PREPOSITIONAL PHRASE

The prepositional phrase is very much like that of Welsh, and so is omitted from this brief description (but see 6.2.8, 6.3.10).

MORPHOLOGY

6.6   NOUNS

6.6.1   Structure: stems and endings

Nouns can be formed from stems of various word classes and nominal suffixes,

(46)   *segh* (adj.) 'dry' > *seghes* 'thirst'

and incorporate borrowings from the English suffixal system:

(47)   *marwen* + *-ans* (< Eng. *-ance*) > *mernans* 'death'

6.6.2   Inherent classes

Inherent classes are not different from those of Welsh, nor are animate/inanimate contrasts etc.

6.6.3   Gender

Nouns may be either masculine or feminine, requiring agreement of the numeral where appropriate (see 6.3.10); and soft mutation of the initial consonant of a singular feminine noun after either article, and of an adjective following a singular feminine noun.

6.6.4   Number

Nouns may be singular or plural, the plural being formed by suffixation or by loss of a suffix (original singulatives):

(48)   *corf* 'body', *corfow* 'bodies'

(49)   *guelen* 'rod', *guel* 'rods'

by vocalic alternation:

(50)   *margh* 'stallion', *mergh* 'stallions'

or by a combination of both processes:

(51)   *gurek* 'wife', *gurageth* 'wives'

6.6.5   Case

Not relevant.

6.6.6   Declensional classes

Not relevant.

6.6.7   Pronouns

In addition to the independent pronoun (see 6.6.8), there are substantive (as object of verb) and auxiliary pronouns (forming a discontinuous morpheme with the possessive adjective, the subject of an inflected verb or the object of a preposition), all similar in form to the independent one. The dependent pronouns are the prefixed possessive adjective (*ow* 'my') and the infixed possessive adjective, or objective pronoun following a verb (*-m* 'my') (see 6.4).

6.6.8   Person

There is a three-person contrast in singular and plural, with a gender contrast at third person singular, as in the independent pronoun:

	Singular	Plural
1	*my*	*ny*
2	*ty*	*why*
3	MASC *ef*	*y*
	FEM *hy*	

6.6.9   Other pronominals

These are much as in Welsh, and include such forms as *honan* 'sclf', *aral* 'other one', *pup* 'everyone', *suel* 'one', *nep* 'the one'.

6.7   VERBS

6.7.1   Structure: stems and endings

The verb–noun is typically composed of a stem and a suffix, most frequently *-e* or *-y*,

(52)   *care* 'love' < *car* + *-e*
(53)   *lesky* 'burn' < *lesk* + *-y*

Verbal forms are inflected for the person contrasts noted in 6.6.8.

6.7.2   Verb classes

These appear to be similar to those of Welsh.

6.7.3   Verb systems

These appear to be similar to those of Welsh.

6.7.4   Tense; aspect; mood

The inflected lexical verb has three contrasts of mood – indicative, subjunctive and imperative – an impersonal form for each tense and a past participle. Though each tense contrasts three persons in both singular and plural, the paradigm is illustrated with the third singular only in each case, for the verb *care* 'love':

Indicative:	present *car*, impersonal *keryr*
	imperfect *care*, impersonal *kerys*
	past *caras* impersonal *caras*
	pluperfect *carse*, impersonal ?
Subjunctive:	present *caro*, impersonal *carer*
	imperfect *care*, impersonal ?
Imperative:	*cares*, impersonal ?
Past participle:	*kerys*

For aspect, see 6.2.9.

6.7.5   Personal/impersonal: see 6.7.4

Active/passive: see 6.2.6.

6.7.6   Concord

There is strict concord with a pronominal subject,

(54)   *a   wylys vy*
          REL saw-I I
          'which I saw'

but otherwise the third singular verb form is the normal selection.

6.8   ADJECTIVES

6.8.1   Structure: stems and endings

When an adjectival form functions as a nominal, it can be pluralised with the suffix *-yon*:

(55)   *claf* 'sick one', *clevyon* 'sick ones'

6.8.2   Comparison

Comparative and superlative degrees are formed by addition of the suffixes *-a* and *-e* respectively to the base form:

(56)   *bras* 'big', *brassa, brasse*

The equative is expressed analytically, with the particles *mar* or *maga* 'as' before the adjective:

(57)   *mar hyr forth*
          such long way
          'such a long way'

(58)   *maga fuer drok*
          such great evil
          'such great evil'

6.8.3   Adjectival classes

Not relevant.

6.8.4   Adverbs

In addition to one-word adverbs like *leman* 'now', *avoyd* 'away', there is an analytic pattern in which an adjective is preceded by the predicative particle *in* (cf. Welsh *yn*), *in yagh* 'healthily'.

6.8.5   Adverb classes

No evidence.

6.9   COMPOUND WORDS

The evidence is too sparse to be useful.

6.9.1   Derivational word classes

See 6.6.1, 6.7.1.

6.10   PREPOSITIONS WITH PRONOMINALS

See 6.5.

SOUND SYSTEM

6.11   CONSONANT SYSTEM

6.11.1   Single consonants, clusters and consonant length

Most single consonants occur freely at word-initial, medial and at word-end positions. They can be exemplified thus:

Plosives:

(59)	/pen/ (*pen* 'head')	/bara/ (*bara* 'bread')
	/apert/ (*apert* 'obvious')	/neb/ (*neb* 'the one')
	/ketel/ (*kettel* 'as')	/tas/ (*tas* 'father')
	/ketep/ (*ketep* 'every')	/dov/ (*dof* 'tame')
	/karadou/ (*caradow* 'loved')	/golou/ (*golow* 'light')
	/agan/ (*agan* 'our')	/kig/ (*kyg* 'meat')

Fricatives:

(60)   /fals/ (*fals* 'false')   /ləv/ (*leuf* 'loved')
        /vil/ (*vyl* 'vile')   /avel/ (*avel* 'like')
        /arluð/ (*arluth* 'lord')   /ðe/ (*the* 'to')
        /beð/ (*beth* 'grave')
        /temtaʃon/ (*temptasyon* 'temptation')

Nasals and /r/, /l/:

(61)   /mam/ (*mam* 'mother')
        /neb (*neb* 'the one')   /anel/ (*anel* 'breath')
        /aŋou/ (*ancou* 'death')   /rag/ (*rag* 'for')

A few consonants have restricted distributions: /h/ occurs only word-initially:
/haval/ (*haual* 'like'); /x/, which is considered to be only lightly frictionalised,
occurs only medially and at word-end:

(62)   /axos/ (*ahos* 'cause')
        /brex/ (*bregh* 'arm')

The affricates are rare, occurring mainly at word-initial:

(63)   /tʃif/ (*chyf* 'chief')
        /dʒaul/ (*iaul* 'devil')

   Clusters of two consonants are very common. Initially, they are typically
composed of a plosive or fricative followed by /l/, /r/ or /n/, as in (64):

(64)   /blamjux/ (*blamyough* 'blame' (imp.))
        /bras/ (*bras* 'big')
        /knes/ (*cnes* 'flesh')
        /θron/ (*thron* 'throne')
        /dre/ (*dre* 'through')
        /klos/ (*clos* 'praise')
        /kresi/ (*kresy* 'believe')

or of /s/ followed by a plosive, as in (65):

(65)   /skians/ (*skyans* 'wisdom')
        /speris/ (*speris* 'spirit')

In final position, clusters of two consonants are typically composed of /r/ or /l/
followed by a plosive, fricative or a nasal, or of /s/ or /n/ followed by a plosive, as
in (66):

(66)   /kurt/ (*curte* 'court')
        /fals/ (*fals* 'false')
        /korf/ (*corf* 'body')
        /in misk/ (*yn mysk*, 'among')
        /jonk/ (*yonk* 'young')
        /kirx/ (*kyrgh* 'attack')

/worθ/ (*worth* 'by')
/best/ (*best* 'beast')
/hern/ (*hern* 'iron')
/pɪmp/ (*pymp* 'five')
/arv/ (*arv* 'tool')
/bern/ (*bern* 'worry')

Medially, any of the above two consonant cluster types can occur, as in (67):

(67)   /kortes/ (*cortes* 'courteous')
         /golxi/ (*golhy* 'wash')
         /helma/ (*helma* 'this')
         /mersi/ (*mersy* 'mercy')
         /termen/ (*termen* 'time')
         /bɪstel/ (*bystel* 'bile')
         /kefrɪs/ (*keffrys* 'also')

Additionally, there are sequences of two plosives, as in /baptist/ (*baptist* 'baptist'); of a nasal and a plosive, as in /gwander/ (*gwander* 'weakness'); and of /rl/, as in /arluð/ (*arluth*, 'lord').

Initial sequences of /s/ + plosive did not develop a prosthetic vowel, as happened in Welsh, so that we have Cornish /skol/ (*scole* 'school', Welsh *ysgol*).

Also, in final homorganic clusters, which had $^*lt$, $^*nt$ in British, the final /t/ developed as /s/ in Cornish, giving:

(68)   /als/ (*als* 'hill', Welsh *allt*)
         /dans/ (*dans* 'tooth', Welsh *dant*)

The same development gives Cornish final /s/ (phonetically [z]) as compared with Welsh final /d/ in words like /bos/ (*bos* 'to be', Welsh *bod*), /tas/ (*tays* 'father', Welsh *tad*). Final /-nt/ clusters in English loans retained their final plosive, however, as in /tormont/ (*tormont* 'torture').

Clusters of three consonants are rare, consisting of /s/ + plosive + /r/ or /l/ initially, as in (69):

(69)   /stretʃa/ (*streccha* 'delay')
         /skriva/ (*scryve* 'writing')

and of the same or similar types medially:

(70)   /meistri/ (*meystry* 'authority')
         /kentrou/ (*kentrow* 'nails')
         /loskvan/ (*loscvan* 'a burning')

There is no direct evidence on the length of consonants, and certainly none to suggest that it was distinctive. Phonetic realism, however, would suggest that a single consonant following a short, stressed vowel would be longer than it might be in any other context. The resonants *n, l, r* are frequently doubled in the orthography, after a stressed penultimate syllable: *teller* 'place', *terry* 'break', *mynnas* 'will'. This could suggest distinctive consonant length or gemination in this position (as in Welsh at an earlier time) or simply lengthened allophones following a short stressed vowel. In support of the latter suggestion, compare the not uncommon doubling of plosives in the same position: *otta* 'behold', *dybbry* 'eat'.

6.11.2   Consonant classes

Cornish contrasts consonants at labial, alveolar and velar positions, with an extension of alveolar contrasts. All stops, and labial and alveolar fricatives except /s/, also contrast for voice. They are shown in table 6.1.

6.11.3   Range of consonant realisations

Little can be said about contextual variation. The velar fricative /x/ is believed to have been articulated with less force than its correspondent in Welsh: this may suggest that it was phonetically velar (whereas the Welsh variant is phonetically uvular).

The orthography makes no distinction between [s] and [z], which are in complementary distribution as realisations of /s/: [s] occurs initially, following a short vowel, and at word-end following a consonant, thus:

(71)   [soːn] (*son* 'noise')
          [axos] (*ahos* 'cause')
          [sans] (*sans* 'saint')

Following /n/ in medial position, intervocalically or at word-end following a long vowel, it is realised as [z], thus:

(72)   [glaːz] (*glas* 'blue')
          [pen'zans] (*Pensance*)
          [keuzel] (*keusel* 'speak')

Cornish differs from Welsh in this respect, in that the indigenous Welsh system has no voicing opposition between sibilants, even at the level of phonetics.

6.12   VOWEL SYSTEM

6.12.1   Monophthongs, diphthongs and vowel length

There is no evidence of restrictions on the distribution of the vowels, even /ə/ occurring freely in monosyllables (contrast Welsh). The vowels can be exemplified thus:

Table 6.1. *Consonant classes*

	Labial	Alveolar	Palato-alveolar	Velar	Glottal
Plosives	p	t		k	
	b	d		g	
Fricatives	f	θ s	ʃ	x	h
	v	ð (z)	–	–	–
Nasals	m	n		ŋ	
Affricates		tʃ			
		dʒ			
Lateral	l				
Trill	r				

(73)   /i/   /ði/ (*the* 'to')   /gwiskɨs/ (*gweskis* 'dressed')
          /e/   /dre/ (*dre* 'through')   /jesɨ/ (*ihesu* 'Jesu')
          /a/   /mab/ (*mab* 'son')   /skians/ (*skyans* 'wisdom')
          /o/   /bos/ (*bos* 'to be')   /kolon/ (*colon* 'heart')
          /u/   /gur/ (*gour* 'husband')   /maru/ (*marou* 'dead')
          /ɨ/   /tu/ (*tu* 'side')   /davɨð/ (*dauyth* 'Dafydd')
          /ə/   /ləf/ (*leff* 'hand')   /brəder/ (*broder* 'brother')

The vowel /ɨ/ is of considerable interest. It appears to be the typical British 'high mixed' vowel – central with lips spread (written 'y' in Welsh). British also had a central vowel with lips rounded (written 'u' in Welsh, and by now merged with that written 'y'); it may well be that this vowel was still extant in Late Cornish, since forms like *jhesu* 'Jesu' and *dev* (a spelling variant of *du* 'God') are made to rhyme with the Norman French loanword *vertu* 'virtue' which may have retained the original frontness and rounding of the final vowel. Certainly, as in Welsh, there are two distinct representations for the close central vowel region.

Rhyming evidence suggests that the vowels /e/ and /ɨ/ were in free variation, possibly on account of their phonetic similarity, (or their being dialectal variants); for instance, the word for 'faith' appears as the doublet *feth* /feð/ rhyming with *dyweth* /diɨuð/ 'end', and *fyth* /fɨð/ rhyming with *fyllyth* /filɨð/ 'fail'.

Cornish has few diphthongs, and none closing to /i/ in the indigenous system. They can be exemplified as follows, though the vagaries of the orthography, coupled with the scarcity of the evidence, make authentic identification of any but /ou/ extremely perilous in unstressed syllables. There are plentiful examples of the latter because of its frequent occurrence as a noun plural suffix:

(74)   /ei/   /meɨn/ (*meyn* 'stone')
            /oɨ/   /moɨ/ (*moy* 'more')
            /iu/   /liu/ (*lyw* 'colour')
            /ɨu/   /dɨu/ (*dyw* 'two' (fem.))
            /eu/   /eun/ (*evn* 'right')
            /ou/   /krous/ (*crous* 'cross')
                     /lavarou/ (*lauarow* 'words')
            /au/   /nau/ (*naw* 'nine')

Again, rhyming patterns suggest either free variation or dialectal variation in the phonetic realisation of the diphthongs /eu/, /iu/ and /ou/: /deu/ (*deu* 'God') rhymes with /lɨvrjou/ (*lyfryou* 'books'), while its spelling variants *due*, *du*, can both rhyme with the Norman French loan *vertu*; and *vertu*, in turn, can rhyme with *lyw* (/liu/ 'colour'). If the previous suggestion regarding the retention of rounding in the final vowel of the borrowed *vertu* is right, it seems that the combination of high or mid tongue position with rounding, whether simultaneously or in sequence, gives rise to considerable uncertainty of the precise phonetic values involved (and could be the result of dialectal variation).

It seems, too, that English loanwords filled out the gap in the indigenous system to some extent; a form like *paynys* ('pains') was clearly borrowed before the Great Vowel Shift altered the value of orthographic 'ai', 'ay' in English, so we can predict a realisation approximating /painis/; and a form like *ioy* ('joy') would have had a realisation approximating /dʒoi/.

Since it is hazardous to give precise information on vowel length, I have left it unmarked. However, what evidence there is indicates that Cornish followed the same basic indigenous pattern as Welsh: long vowels occur in stressed syllables only; those in open stressed monosyllables are invariably long, while those followed by consonant clusters or voiceless stops are invariably short; vowels before voiced stops are long, while before fricatives and resonants long and short vowels are in contrast. Vowel length is marked in the spelling only irregularly, and in one of three ways:

1   by placing a *y* after the long vowel, as in [taːz] (*tays* 'father'), [moːz] (*moys* 'go');
2   by doubling the vowel letter, as in [graːz] (*graas* 'grace'), [miːn] (*myyn* 'edge');
3   by writing an *e* in final position after a consonant, to show that the vowel preceding the consonant is long, as in [skoːl] (*scole* 'school').

This latter convention is borrowed from English, and is one of many instances of the influence of English spelling on the Cornish orthographic system. The

evidence is too scanty for us to be able to demonstrate to what extent
word-borrowing from English may have led to the length patterns of English
words penetrating and disturbing the indigenous system (though it surely must
have done, as happened in Welsh, where extensive borrowing from English has
led to the growth of length contrasts in almost all those contexts noted as being
without in the basic system).

6.12.2   Vowel classes

The vowel system is of the 3–3–1 type, contrasting as shown in the chart:

	Front	*Central*	*Back*
Close	i	ɨ	u
Mid	e		o
Open		a	

6.12.3   Range of vowel realisations

Place-name evidence and that of Cornish dialects of English suggest that the
peripheral long and short vowels differed phonetically much as they do in
Welsh, so that we can contrast them schematically thus on the open–close
parameter.

(75)   /i/   [iː] ~ [ɪ]
        /e/   [eː] ~ [ɛ]
        /o/   [oː] ~ [ɔ]
        /u/   [uː] ~ [ʊ]

It seems, too, that long /a/ may have been raised and fronted to approximate
[eː] or the diphthongised [eə], as in *glas* 'blue, green': [gleːz], [gleəz]. This
would form a striking parallel with the neighbouring Welsh dialect of Glamorgan, which has the cognates [glæːs], [glæʌs].

6.13   SYLLABLE STRUCTURE

Syllables, whether stressed or unstressed, may be open or closed, thus:

Stressed monosyllabic:
(C)V   /le/   (*le* 'place')
(C)VC(C)   /ker/   (*ker* 'dear'), /kens/   (*kens* 'before')
Stressed penultimate:
(C)V-   /ma-ga/   (*maga* 'as')
(C)VC-   /gor-fen/ (*gorfen* 'finish')

Unstressed final:
-CV   /e-ve/   (*efe* 'drink')
-CVC(C)   /go-nis/   (*gonys* 'work')
          /whar-fos/ (*wharfos* 'happen')

6.14   STRESS

Cornish, like Welsh and Breton, has primary stress regularly on the penultimate syllable of polysyllabic words, as in /'arluð/ (*arluth* 'lord'), /'maru/ (*marou* 'dead'). There is no evidence of weakening of the vowel in a final unstressed syllable – for instance, *redya* /'redja/ 'read' is made to rhyme with *da* /'da/ 'good'; so it is likely that Cornish, like Welsh, separated rhythmic stress (on the penultimate syllable) from pitch movement (which in Welsh occurs on the post-stress syllable, giving it prominence, often greater prominence than the stressed syllable has, thus inhibiting any weakening in vowel quality). No reliable evidence can be adduced on differing degrees of stress, nor on their distribution.

6.15   PITCH

Nothing can be added to the tentative suggestion made in the previous paragraph, and so no information can be offered on intonation.

MORPHOPHONOLOGY

6.16   NOUN MUTATIONS

6.16.1   Initial mutations of consonants

There are three types of initial consonant mutation: they occur in a variety of lexical and syntactic environments which will be exemplified in part (see also 6.6.3).

Soft mutation involves voicing of the voiceless plosives /p t k/ > /b d g/; frictionalisation of the voiced stops /b m/ > /v/, /d/ > /ð/; the mutation of /g/ has passed through a historical */ɣ/ to /ð/; for example, in a singular feminine noun after the definite article /an/, as in:

(76)   /an vro/ 'the area' < /bro/
             /an voran/ 'the maiden' < /moran/
             /an dus/ 'the people' < /tus/

Spirant mutation involves frictionalisation of the voiceless plosives /p t k/ >
/f θ x/; for example, in a noun after the third person singular feminine possessive
adjective as in /i θir/ 'her land' < /tir/; /i xolon/ 'her heart' < /kolon/.

Provection involves:

> 1 Devoicing of the voiced plosives /b d g/ > /p t k/; for example, in the
>   verb–noun after the aspectual particle /ou/, as in /ou peue/ 'living'
>   < /beue/; /ou tos/ 'coming' < /dos/.
> 2 A set of secondary segmental changes to segments which were
>   themselves the historical products of soft mutation: /v/ > /f/, /ð/>/t/,
>   /ø/>/h/; for example, in an adjective following the predicative
>   particle /ən/, as in /ən ta/ 'good', < /da/ *via* *ən ða/; /ən haru/
>   'rough', < /garu/ via */ən (γ)aru/

The environments for 2 overlap with those for SM only in respect of the one
exemplified; and, of course, in that environment they displace the 'regular' SM
alternations for voiced plosives /b d g/ > /v ð ∅/.

6.16.2   Non-initial mutations of consonants

The orthographic evidence is extremely intransigent but there are examples of
all mutations in non-initial position:

> Soft: /deuiθ/ (*dywyth* 'twice' < /deu/ + /guiθ/);
> Spirant: /trixans/ (*tryhans* 'three hundred' < /tri/+/kans/);
> Nasal: /pɨm woly/ (*pym woly* 'five wounds' < /pɨmp/ + /woly/);
> Provection: /hakra/ (*haccra* 'most ugly' < /hagar/ + /-ə/).

6.16.3   Consonant mutation classes

See 6.16.2.

6.16.4   Prevocalic mutations

None.

6.16.5   Vocalic mutations

None, but note the alternation /a–e/ in the forms /mab/ *map* 'son' – /mebjon/ *mebyon* 'sons', which is an example of vowel affection before the suffix-initial /j/ of the final syllable.

Lack of space prevents detailed exemplification of the operation of mutation across the word classes. See Lewis (1946) for a full account.

REFERENCES

Lewis, H. 1946. *Llawlyfr Cernyweg Canol* (new edn), Cardiff: Gwasg Prifysgol Cymru.
Lhuyd, E. 1707. *Archaeologia Britannica*, London.

FURTHER READING

Ellis, B. 1974. *The Cornish language and its literature*, London: Routledge and Kegan Paul.
Ellis, P. B. 1971. *The story of the Cornish language*, Truro: Tov Mark Press.
Evans, D. 1956. Y Gernyweg – tranc iaith. *Y Traethodydd* 24: 34–34, 84–90.
    1969. The story of Cornish. *University of Liverpool Studies* 58: 293–308.
Gregor, D. B. 1980. *Celtic: a comparative study*, Cambridge: Oleander Press.
Jackson, K. 1953. *Language and history in early Britain*, Edinburgh: Edinburgh University Press.
Jenner, H. 1873. The Cornish language. *Transactions of the Philological Society* 165–86.
    1877. The history and literature of the ancient Cornish language. *Journal of the British Archaeological Association* (June) 137–57.
    1904. *A handbook of the Cornish language*, London: David Nutt.
Lewis, H. and H. Pedersen 1961. *A concise comparative Celtic Grammar*, Göttingen: Vandenhoek and Ruprecht.
Thomas, A. R. 1984. Cornish, in P. Trudgill (ed.) *Language in the British Isles*, Cambridge: Cambridge University Press, pp. 278–288.
Thomas, C. 1973. *The importance of being Cornish*, Exeter: University of Exeter.
Wakelin, M. F. 1975. *Language and history in Cornwall*, Leicester: Leicester University Press.

For contemporary revivalist literature, see such titles as the following:

Gendall, R. 1972. *Kernewek Bew*, Truro: Cornish Language Board.
Nance, R. M. 1929. *Cornish for all* (3rd edn. 1958), St Ives: James Lanham.
Nance, R. M. and A. S. D. Smith (Caradar) 1934.

An English–Cornish Dictionary (rev. edn by Marazion Nance, 1952), St Ives: James Lanham.

Pool, P. A. S. 1965. Cornish for beginners. Manuscript.

Smith, A. S. D. (Caradar) 1931. *Lessons in spoken Cornish*, St Ives: Federation of Old Cornish Societies.

1969. *The story of the Cornish language*, Cambourne: An Lef Kerwenek.

Stephens, M. 1976. *Linguistic minorities in Western Europe*, Llandysul: Gomer Press.

7

The Breton language

ELMAR TERNES

HISTORICAL AND SOCIAL PERSPECTIVE

7.0 EXTERNAL HISTORY OF THE LANGUAGE

The Breton language is called *brezhoneg* in Breton; Brittany is *Breizh* (written also *brezoneg*, *Breiz*, see 7.1.3). Another, now obsolete, name for the language is 'Armorican'. This is derived from *Armorica* (also *Aremorica*), the Gallo-Roman name of a Gaulish province, corresponding by and large to present-day Brittany.

In the traditional classification of the Celtic languages, Breton is (together with Welsh and Cornish) a member of the Brythonic subfamily of Insular Celtic. This may be misleading in so far as Breton is spoken now exclusively on the European continent. Strictly speaking, the division of the Celtic languages into Continental Celtic and Insular Celtic is valid only up to the fifth century AD. Breton is the descendant of the language of colonists who, from the fifth to the seventh century, emigrated under the pressure of the Anglo-Saxon invasions from south and south-west Britain and settled on the Armorican peninsula, which came to be named 'Brittany' after their country of origin. A historical account of the Breton immigration is given in Loth (1883).

The subsequent evolution of Breton in relative isolation from the languages that remained in the British Isles explains its acquisition of a number of typological traits on all grammatical levels, which neatly differentiate it now from the other living languages of Insular Celtic (see Ternes 1979).

The view that Breton is the descendant of the language brought by immigrants from Britain has always been the consensus of Celtic scholars, until a different view was advanced by Falc'hun (1962, 1963, and elsewhere). According to him, Breton is fundamentally the modern descendant of Gaulish, possibly modified to a certain extent by the language of the British invaders. Falc'hun's view seems highly improbable, however, for historical as well as linguistic reasons and has not found acceptance among other Celtic scholars. For a discussion, see Jackson (1961; 1967: 29–33) and Fleuriot (1982).

The first centuries after the beginning of the invasion are characterised by a rather unstable political situation, constantly vacillating between relative political independence and submission under Franconian sovereignty. A decisive event was the victory won over the Franconians in the battle of Ballon (north-east of Redon) in 845, after which date an independent Breton kingdom was established. Breton kings exercised their rule for somewhat less than one century, until the kingdom was dissolved as a consequence of the repeated assaults of the Normans. After the victory finally won over the Normans by Alain Barbetorte at Trans (near Cancale) in 939, the Duchy of Brittany was established. It was in existence for about 600 years, but over the centuries it came under growing French influence. In 1491 the last Breton duchess, Anne de Bretagne, was forced to marry King Charles VIII of France. Brittany was definitely incorporated into France in 1532 under the rule of King François I.

The extension of the Breton language after the settlement of the British colonists and during the Middle Ages is not precisely known. An attempt at a historical reconstruction undertaken by Loth (1907) is, however, widely accepted. Relying mainly on the evidence of place names, Loth drew a line ranging from Mont-St-Michel in the north to the mouth of the river Loire (near Donges) in the south (see map 7.1, line 1). This line is supposed to represent the eastern frontier of the Breton language in the ninth century, at which time Breton is assumed to have had its greatest geographical extension. Between the tenth and the thirteenth century, a drastic retreat of Breton is supposed to have taken place, as far as line 2 on map 7.1 (equally reconstructed by Loth). Since the thirteenth century, the linguistic frontier has retreated further westward, although much less dramatically than before. Line 3 on the map represents the eastern frontier of Breton in the second half of the nineteenth century as documented for the first time by Sébillot (1886). Since that time, the frontier has shifted only slightly, as shown by Le Roux (1924–63) and the most recent investigation (Timm 1983). Thus, for the last eight centuries, Breton has retained ground remarkably well (but see 7.1.1).

When considering map 7.1, it is to be noted especially that the two largest cities of Brittany, Nantes and Rennes, are both situated to the east of the line marking the greatest extension of Breton. These two rival cities have been the political, economic and cultural centres of Brittany from the beginning to the present day, but both of them have always been entirely French-speaking. On the other hand, no such centre ever developed within the Breton-speaking part of the country. The enormous dialectal diversity of Breton (7.1.2) indicates,

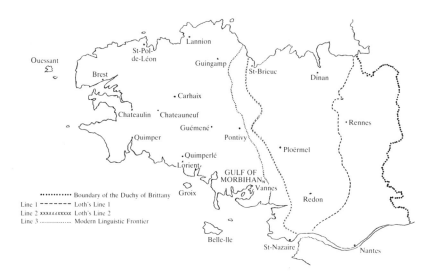

Map 7.1   The distribution of Breton (adapted from Jackson 1967:23)

among other things, that there has never been any institution or geographical centre that would have been able to exercise a standardising effect within the Breton-speaking territory as a whole. The politically and culturally leading classes of the population had gone over to French by as early as the tenth century so that, from that time down to the present day, Breton has always been the language of the 'common folk' only. In this respect, Breton occupies a rather special place among the modern Celtic languages. In Ireland, Scotland and Wales, the leading classes had retained their respective Celtic language much longer. The special case of Breton may also be seen from the fact that among the living Celtic languages, it is the only one that is practically devoid of a classical literature. It is only from the nineteenth century on that an independent Breton literature begins to emerge. Most literary productions of the earlier centuries are hardly more than calques on Latin or French models.

By the same token, Breton has the greatest number of loanwords among the modern Celtic languages. First, it shares with Welsh and Cornish a significant number of loans from Latin, taken over at the time of the Roman occupation of Britain (Haarmann 1973). From the time of the settlement in Brittany on, however, Breton underwent a different development in two respects: first, of course, it found itself under French influence, whereas all the other Celtic languages were mainly exposed to English; second, Breton at all periods of its evolution took over considerably more words from French than the other Celtic languages did from English. It is estimated that about two-fifths of the *everyday* Breton vocabulary are of French origin. The French loans are usually well assimilated and not always recognisable as such for the non-specialist. Some examples: Breton *brav* 'nice, beautiful' (French *brave* 'brave, valiant'), Breton *chom* 'to stay, to remain' (French *chômer* 'to be jobless'), Breton *kas* 'to send' (French *chasser* 'to hunt'), Breton *klemm* 'to complain' (French *clamer* 'to cry out'), Breton *paotr* 'boy' (French *poutre* 'beam' (*sic*)). Among all Celtic languages, therefore, Breton has by far the lowest percentage of native Celtic vocabulary (see Ternes 1979: 225f.).

Breton in its historical development is divided into three stages: old, middle and modern. Old Breton (from the time of the fifth–seventh–century invasion until 1100) is only imperfectly known from glosses in Latin texts and names in Latin cartularies and some other sources. There are no connected texts in Old Breton. In spite of the fragmentary preservation of this language stage, an excellent description has been provided by Fleuriot (1964a, 1964b; the latter reprinted with additions as Evans and Fleuriot 1985). Old Breton seems to have been very similar to Old Cornish and Old Welsh.

Middle Breton (1100–1659). From the beginning of this stage on, an increasing French influence manifests itself. From the point of view of language sources, Middle Breton may further be subdivided into two periods: an earlier one, extending from 1100 to 1450, for which documents, as for Old Breton, consist almost exclusively of names and glosses. The second period, from the middle of the fifteenth century on, shows the emergence of the first literary productions in Breton that have come down to us. These are mostly of religious content, such as Lives of Saints, mystery plays, Passion plays and religious edification, and are strongly marked with French influence. An important linguistic work of this period is a Breton–French–Latin vocabulary, known as the *Catholicon* of Jehan Lagadeuc, completed in 1464 and published in 1499 (re-edited by Guyonvarc'h in 1975). For a Middle Breton grammar, see Lewis and Piette (1966); for a dictionary, see Ernault (1895–6).

Modern Breton (from 1659 to the present). The year 1659 is usually regarded as the turning-point between Middle and Modern Breton, because it is the publishing date of Father Julien Maunoir's *Sacré Collège de Jésus* (Quimper, 1659), containing a Breton grammar and a French–Breton dictionary. Maunoir was the first to observe systematically the initial mutations (see 7.18.1) of Breton in writing. He also brought about a reform of Breton orthography, introducing, among other things, the famous apostrophe for the distinction of the phonemes /ʃ/ *ch* and /x/ *c'h*, both phonemes having hitherto been written indiscriminately *ch*. Modern Breton again falls into two periods, the first from 1659 to 1807, the second from 1807 to the present day. The year 1807 marks the publication of Jean-François Le Gonidec's *Grammaire celto-bretonne* (Paris, 1807). It is on this work and the same author's *Dictionnaire celto-breton ou breton–français* (Angoulême, 1821) that the contemporary standard language is based.

7.1   CONTEMPORARY POSITION

7.1.1   Areal distribution and social status

The linguistic frontier between Breton and French as described in contemporary literature can be seen from line 3 on map 7.1. It reaches from the commune Plouha (north-west of St-Brieuc) in the north to Damgan (near Muzillac, south-east of Vannes) in the south. As a rough approximation, one may keep in mind the line St-Brieuc–Vannes. The most recent investigation (Timm 1983), carried out in 1976, on the whole confirms this frontier. The most important changes of the recent past are that the peninsula Rhuys and the city of Vannes in the south as well as the small town Mûr-de-Bretagne right in the middle of the line now seem definitely to be lost for Breton.

Of the five *départements* making up the ancient Duchy of Brittany, only Finistère lies entirely within the Breton-speaking area. Côtes-du-Nord and Morbihan belong about one half each to that area, whereas Ille-et-Vilaine and Loire-Atlantique are entirely French-speaking.

The Breton-speaking part of Brittany is referred to as Basse-Bretagne (Breton *Breizh-Izel*), the French-speaking part as Haute-Bretagne (Breton *Breizh-Uhel*). The attributives *basse* 'low' and *haute* 'high' refer to the geographical position with respect to Paris: 'high' is what is nearer to Paris, 'low' is what is farther off. The French-speaking part of Brittany is also known as *le pays gallo*, the attributive *gallo* referring to anything coming from that part. Thus *une chanson gallo* is a traditional song in French, originating from the French-speaking part of Brittany.

The idea of a linguistic frontier separating a Breton-speaking and a French-speaking area is misleading to some extent. The larger and smaller towns and boroughs (French *bourgs*) have been for centuries French-speaking islands within the Breton-speaking territory. Breton is largely confined to the rural areas. In Timm's words (1983: 455): 'It is becoming more and more appropriate to think of Breton as surviving in islands strung throughout a widening sea of French speakers.' On the whole, Breton seems to be preserved better in the agricultural communities of the inner country than in the fishing communities of the coastal area.

It is difficult to give a reliable figure for the number of Breton speakers. Since the existence of minority languages in France is flatly ignored by the authorities, no official figures are to be had at all. One has to rely instead on private counts or estimates. It may be said with every due caution that the number of Breton speakers is around 600,000. This is the number of potential speakers. It is estimated that of these, only about 400,000 actually make daily use of Breton. In either case, the margin of error may be 100,000 or more. Practically all speakers of Breton are bilingual, although their French is often strongly influenced by Breton at all grammatical levels.

The difficulty of giving precise figures is aggravated by the fact that many people would be reluctant to admit that they are speakers of Breton when questioned by a person unknown to them. A group of people speaking Breton would in many cases automatically switch over to French as soon as they notice an unknown person within earshot. Local authorities such as mayors, school-masters, priests, etc., when asked whether Breton is spoken in their commune, would in many cases flatly deny this, although Breton may in fact currently be spoken and although they may even be fluent speakers themselves. On the other hand, a strong Breton accent when speaking French does not necessarily mean that the person is a speaker of Breton. He or she may very well be a monolingual French speaker. He or she may also be one of those people who have learnt neither language properly, because their Breton-speaking parents prevented them from learning Breton, but were not capable of teaching them proper French either (a phenomenon recently called semi-lingualism in sociolinguistic literature).

These and similar attitudes are a consequence of official French language policy, which has always been one of actively suppressing minority languages. Formerly as a kingdom, but even more so as a republic, France has been and continues to be a strongly centralised state. *Egalité* does not mean that all people have an equal right to speak their maternal language, but that all must speak the same language, viz. French. Thus Breton was virtually prohibited in schools until 1951. Many Breton speakers recall with bitterness the use of the so-called *symbole* (or *vache* in the school children's jargon): this was a piece of wood or the like to be hung around a child's neck. It was placed by the teacher on a pupil who had been heard speaking Breton on school premises. If this child was able to catch another one speaking Breton, he or she was, in turn, to pass the *symbole* on to the latter. Whoever had the *symbole* last at the end of the school day was a candidate for punishment. This was a fairly common practice until the early 1950s. In public places, it was not uncommon to find the authoritarian notice *Il est interdit de cracher par terre et de parler breton* ('It is forbidden to spit on the ground and to speak Breton').

By such means (and others) the Breton-speaking population acquired over the generations a deeply rooted inferiority complex. They were convinced that their language was 'good for nothing'. In fact, many people hardly ever thought of it in terms of a language. By many, even otherwise educated people, it is still regarded as a sort of unspecified ugly gibberish.

The situation began to improve slightly in the early 1950s. A milestone in the history of Breton pedagogy was the enactment of the *Loi relative à l'enseignement des langues et dialectes régionaux* ('Law concerning the teaching of regional languages and dialects') in 1951, commonly known as *Loi Deixonne* (after the name of the then minister of education of France). It allowed for the first time the teaching of Breton in schools as a facultative subject. Breton may now be taught at primary and secondary schools as well as at universities on a voluntary basis. Breton is, however, never used itself as a medium for teaching other subjects. University lectures are not, as a rule, held in Breton.

On the whole, Breton is still, as it has been for the last centuries, a language, the use of which is largely restricted to home and field. For that reason, the vocabulary of native Breton speakers is ill-suited to the requirements of modern technology and science. Breton-based neologisms have been coined in intellectual circles, but most of them are not understood by the ordinary Breton speaker.

Public opinion about Breton was hardly affected by the teaching of Breton in school. A change came about only in the wake of the so-called students' revolution in 1968 and subsequent years. From that time on, young people especially began to feel greater appreciation for regional cultures in general. As a consequence, a remarkable upsurge of national feeling manifested itself in Brittany. Extracurricular classes and summer courses in Breton started up throughout Brittany. Efforts are being made to provide very young children with an all-Breton medium of education (through a privately subsidised network). The output of literature in Breton has increased markedly over recent years. It remains to be seen, however, whether there will be a lasting effect on the maintenance of the language itself. The efforts described are largely confined to academic circles (many members of which are *néo-bretonnants*) and hardly affect the ordinary native speaker of Breton in the country.

Official institutions, government authorities, etc. do not seem to have been much affected by the revival movement. The Breton language is still not granted more than an average of half an hour of local radio per day and about half an hour of television per week. These emissions do not enjoy much dissemination, because the language variety used therein (standard Breton, based on the Léon dialect) is largely incomprehensible to many, if not most, native speakers of Breton outside Léon. There are no daily newspapers or weekly journals in Breton. On the other hand, monthly journals, mostly of a cultural nature and rather high quality, do exist, and there is indeed a very lively market in printed material of all kinds: journals, novels, short stories, verse, scientific literature, pedagogical material, translations from other languages, etc. But again, such literature does not reach the ordinary speaker of Breton in the country because most Breton speakers are completely illiterate in their first language. Literary productions are almost exclusively confined to academic circles. In Catholic church services, the role of Breton is nowadays insignificant.

Although the general atmosphere has undoubtedly improved over the last two decades, it remains true that Breton has the lowest social prestige and least official recognition among all living Celtic languages. The latest prospects are rather pessimistic as to its survival as an everyday spoken language (see Timm 1983). Although it may still be the Celtic language with the greatest number of (potential) speakers, it is unlikely to keep this place for very long. (For a general evaluation of the situation of Breton, see also Timm 1980, Fleuriot 1983, and Denez 1983.)

7.1.2   Dialect differentiation

Among the modern Celtic languages, it is Breton that has by far the greatest diversity of dialects. Many of the dialects, even within shorter distances, are not mutually comprehensible, so that in many cases speakers of Breton have to resort to French to make themselves understood to speakers of another part of the country. One reason for this remarkable dissimilarity is no doubt the complete lack of any unifying or standard-setting force or institution since the early Middle Ages (see 7.0). Geography can hardly be adduced as a determinant factor, because any part of Brittany is quite easily accessible from a geographical point of view.

In the absence of any obvious geographical boundaries, the traditional division of Breton dialects follows the frontiers of the ancient bishoprics of Brittany. Therefore the division is somewhat arbitrary from a purely linguistic point of view.

Four main dialect zones are distinguished, of which the following indications will be given below (in that order): name of the bishopric, adjective derived therefrom, place of former episcopal see, rough geographical position within the

Breton-speaking area. The respective Breton equivalent follows the French within brackets. (See map 7.2.)

1 Léon (Leon or Bro Leon), Léonais or Léonard, St-Pol-de-Léon (Kastell-Paol), north-west.
2 Tréguier or Trégor (Treger or Bro Dreger), Trégorrois, Tréguier (Landreger), north-east.
3 Cornouaille (Kernev or Bro Gernev), Cornouaillais, Quimper (Kemper), south-west and centre.
4 Pays de Vannes (Bro Wened), Vannetais, Vannes (Gwened), south-east.

Following strictly the ancient division into bishoprics, a fifth dialect is sometimes distinguished in the extreme north-east corner, known as Goélo (Goelo). It

Map 7.2   The chief dialect regions (adapted from Jackson 1967: 17)

belongs to the bishopric of St-Brieuc (Sant-Brieg), the greatest part of which lies outside the Breton-speaking area. From a purely linguistic point of view, it may be classified as a subdialect of Trégorrois.

Apart from self-explaining subdivisions such as northern, southern, central, etc. within each of the aforementioned dialect areas, a distinction is often made between an upper and a lower variety, for example Haut-Léonard–Bas-Léonard, Haut-Vannetais–Bas-Vannetais. In this case, the upper variety is always located in the eastern part, the lower variety in the western part of the respective dialect area (cf. 7.1.1).

Léonard is the most archaic dialect from a historical–comparative point of view, and therefore serves as a basis for the standard language (see 7.1.3). Dialect differences within the Léonard area are minor. Trégorrois dialects are again fairly homogeneous and are on the whole not too much divergent from Léonard. Cornouaillais, on the other hand, which occupies the largest area, represents a conglomerate of highly divergent dialects, not all of which are mutually understandable. The greatest diversity is to be found in the southern part of Cornouaille (*département Sud-Finistère*). The dialects of southern Cornouaille may at the same time be called the most progressive ones from a historical–comparative point of view. Vannetais, finally, is so divergent from all other dialects that it might be called a language of its own on purely linguistic grounds. It is at least as different from the other dialects as is Scottish Gaelic from Connacht Irish. Within the Vannetais area, dialect differences are in turn rather important. Except for the border areas, Vannetais dialects cannot be understood by speakers of any other dialect. There is, however, no sharp border line between Vannetais and the adjoining dialect areas, the transition being by degrees.

In order to accommodate the situation described, the former three dialects are often viewed as forming one bloc as opposed to Vannetais, which stands by itself. The former three are usually referred to as KLT-Breton (abbreviated from the Breton designations Kernev, Leon, Treger). If a particular feature is specifically meant to be valid for all four dialects, the abbreviation KLTGw is used (Gw for Gwened).

For the separation of KLT-Breton and Vannetais, the following two isoglosses are usually cited:

1   Segmental: Brythonic *tt* (including Latin loans in Brythonic) has given [s] or [z] in KLT, but [x] or [h] in Vannetais, all of them having developed via [θ] or [ð] in Old Breton (and preserved as such in Modern Welsh). Example: Brythonic **cattos* 'cat', KLT /kaːs/, Vannetais /kaːx/ (cf. Welsh *cath* /kaːθ/ 'cat').

2 Suprasegmental: word stress is on the penultimate syllable in KLT, on the ultimate in Vannetais. Example: *kalet* 'hard', KLT [ˊ-], Vannetais [-ˊ].

For more details about isoglosses, see Jackson (1967: 834ff.).

The number of extant descriptions of Breton dialects is very unsatisfactory, especially in view of the great linguistic diversity mentioned above. Moreover, time is pressing, because many local dialects are on the verge of extinction.

General works on Breton dialectology are Falc'hun (1963) and Jackson (1967). A dialect atlas, the first for any Celtic language, was published by Le Roux (1924–63); it is generally referred to as *ALBB*. A new one is under way, but it seems to progress only very slowly (see Le Dû 1972).

The following is a list of descriptions of specific Breton dialects, arranged according to dialect areas:

1 Léon: Sommerfelt 1920, new edn 1978 (Haut-Léonard); Falc'hun 1951 (Bas-Léonard); see also Ternes 1982.

2 Tréguier: Jackson 1960/1, 1972 (north-eastern Trégorrois).

3 Cornouaille: Humphreys 1972, 1985 (north-eastern Cornouaillais); Timm 1984 (central Cornouaillais). Regrettably, there is no description of a southern Cornouaillais dialect.

4 Vannetais: Hammer 1969 (southern Haut-Vannetais); Ternes 1970 (southern Bas-Vannetais); McKenna 1976–81 (northern Bas-Vannetais), reprinted without changes under a misleading title as McKenna 1988 (see Ternes 1991).

7.1.3   Standard language and orthography

Breton has two standard languages, based on the Léon dialect and on Haut-Vannetais, respectively. The former is of much greater importance than the latter and is often taken to be representative of the Breton language as a whole. In the remainder of this chapter, we shall refer to the former simply as standard Breton, to the latter as standard Vannetais.

It is certainly a remarkable fact that a small country like Brittany, the language of which is menaced by one of the world's greatest languages (i.e. French), should indulge in two standard languages. It has been a constant concern of people interested in the preservation and promotion of Breton to overcome this situation. The main reason for the existence of two standard languages is, of course, the great dialectal diversity of Breton.

The choice of the dialects to serve as the basis of the two standard languages (Léonard and Haut-Vannetais) has been highly unfortunate from the point of view of language planning. There are no other dialects within the whole Breton-speaking area that are more divergent from one another than precisely these two. Either of them is representative of a rather small area only and each is quite eccentric with respect to the other Breton dialects. Therefore the majority of native Breton speakers experience difficulty in understanding either of them.

Standard Breton is based on the works of Le Gonidec (born 1775, died 1838) (see 7.0). He chose the Léon dialect because of its archaic nature. Vannetais had been used as a literary language in its own right since the seventeenth century. Its use was rather fluctuating, until a standard was finally worked out by the collaborative works of Guillevic and Le Goff (1902, 1904).

A rather special feature of Breton is its multiple orthographies: there are used at present no fewer than four orthographical systems for standard Breton, and two for standard Vannetais.

The spelling used by Le Gonidec in his works was strictly based on the Léon dialect. Therefore, a group of Breton scholars known as *l'entente des écrivains bretons* brought out a new orthography in 1907. The persons most intimately associated with this project were Emile Ernault and François Vallée. The new orthography was designed specifically to accommodate better the Trégorrois and Cornouaillais dialects, without, however, departing too much from Le Gonidec's system. The Vannetais dialect was deliberately left out because it was thought to be too divergent. The new orthography is known as *orthographe KLT*. It is still used by some people hoping to avoid the political implications connected with the use of the next two orthographies (e.g. Trépos no date), but it is considered somewhat outdated at the present time.

In order to remedy the infelicitous situation of leaving the Vannetais dialect outside the standard language, a new orthography was created by an assembly of Breton writers (among them Roparz Hemon) in 1941. Among other changes, some devices were incorporated to accommodate certain aberrant Vannetais forms. The most conspicuous of these is the famous (to others: notorious) *zh* (also *sh*). These letter combinations were introduced for what hitherto had been written *z* (or *s*) in words showing the regular sound correspondence described in 7.1.2: KLT [s] or [z] vs Vannetais [x] or [h]. Thus the word 'Brittany' is [breis] *Breiz* in KLT, but [breix] *Breih* in Vannetais. By now spelling it *Breizh*, it was thought that the KLT speaker would select *z* and ignore *h* when reading, whereas the Vannetais speaker was supposed to select *h* and ignore *z*. Of course, this is hardly more than a rather transparent juggler's trick. This orthography was called *orthographe unifiée* ('unified orthography') by its authors, because it was supposed to unify KLT with Vannetais. It is also simply known as *orthographe zh* or – by using a French–Breton hybrid – as *zedachek* (*-ek* is a productive Breton suffix for forming adjectives; see (230)). The problem with this orthography is that it cannot be excluded that the idea of a 'unified' orthography was suggested, or at least approved of, by the German occupational forces at the time of its formation (1941). Therefore, for some people, this orthography still has the drawback of smacking of collaboration. At the present time, it is preferred by Breton nationalists.

After the Second World War, another orthography was designed by François Falc'hun in 1955. The name given to it by its author is *orthographe universitaire*. It is also known as *falc'huneg* after the name of its author. (The *-ek* in *zedachek* and *-eg* in *falc'huneg* represent the same suffix, but reflect differences between the two orthographical systems.) Like *orthographe KLT*, it deliberately leaves Vannetais outside its range of application. This orthography is the only one officially approved by the French Ministry of Education for school and university examinations. For some people, it smacks of compromise with the French authorities. At the present time it is used especially by the more moderate Breton circles, which may be called federalists (in contradistinction to the nationalists mentioned before).

Recently, yet another orthography has been set out by Morvannou (1975). Since Bretons have become quite versatile in inventing popular names for orthographical systems, it was immediately christened *assimileg*. It seems on the whole to be nearer to *zedachek* than to *falc'huneg*. It claims to include Vannetais, but its most important characteristic seems to be the conscious effort to get away from the strongly Léon-based character of the preceding three orthographies. It suggests certain pronunciations that are neither strictly Léonard nor strictly Vannetais and therefore may accommodate better the majority of Breton speakers. It remains to be seen to what extent this orthography, or any derivative thereof, will succeed in the future.

For Vannetais, the first orthographical standard was set by the collaborative works of Guillevic and Le Goff (1902, 1904). In conjunction with Falc'hun's *orthographe universitaire* for the KLT area, a Vannetais version of this orthography was designed in 1955. Both Vannetais orthographies are in use at the present time.

For a linguistic evaluation of the orthographies described above (except the more recent *assimileg*), see Jackson (1967: 825ff.). We shall not consider the Vannetais orthographies any further. As for the four orthographies currently in use for standard Breton, it may suffice to state here that the differences are not really of a fundamental nature from a linguistic point of view. Having learnt Breton by one particular orthography, there is hardly any difficulty in understanding a text written in any of the other orthographies. All of them are about equally well adapted for writing Breton, and they all have about the same number of deficiencies.

It is therefore hard for any person not intimately familiar with the situation in Brittany to appreciate how irreconcilable the positions taken by the advocates of one or the other orthography really are. A Breton writer chooses an orthography not for linguistic reasons, but on the basis of his or her political persuasions. On the other hand, even when a person does not have the slightest political affiliation or interest, he or she cannot help immediately being 'classified' politically through the mere choice of orthography alone. Therefore, the present author finds himself in great embarrassment, for whatever choice he takes, he is likely to have at least half of the Breton literati against him. If he has taken a decision for one specific orthography (viz. *zedachek*) – rather than add to the confusion by inventing an orthographical variety of his own – it is mainly because, by sheer coincidence, he happened to become acquainted with Breton for the first time through the medium of *zedachek*. As a result, most of his personal notes and other material at his disposal are in that orthography. He emphasises that this has no political or personal implications whatsoever. Fortunately, the present author finds himself in good company with K. H. Jackson, who has pronounced himself to the same effect (1967: 832).

A detailed correspondence between the phonemes of standard Breton and the letters of the Breton alphabet has been given in Ternes (1977a). It is based on *zedachek*, but may be used for other orthographies as well. We now give a short list of the most important correspondences (irrespective of any particular orthographical system).

> *Vowels (monophthongs)*
> i = /i/, u = /y/, e = /e/, $ê$ = /ɛ:/, eu = /ø/, a = /a/, o = /o/, ou = /u/.
> Nasality is shown by putting $ñ$ after the vowel letter: $añ$ = /ã/, $oñ$ = /õ/, etc.
> Vowel quantity may be told to a large extent from the following consonant letter or combination of consonant letters. The rules are, however, very complex.
> *Diphthongs:* ei = /ei̯/, $eü$ = /ey̆/, eo = /eo̯/, ae = /ae̯/, ao = /ao̯/, aou = /ou̯/, $aoñ$ = /ãõ̯/.
> *Consonants:* p, t, k, b, d, g = /p, t, k, b, d, g/; m, n, l, r or mm, nn, ll, rr = /m, n, l, r/; f, v = /f, v/; s, z = /s, z/ (in *zedachek* also *sh, zh*);

ch = /ʃ/; *j* = /ʒ/; *c'h* = /x/; *h* = /h/; *gn* = /ɲ/; *ilh* and *lh* = /ʎ/; *y* = /j/; *w* = /w/ or /ɥ/.

The following is a selection of works on standard Breton that may be used for reference. After each title, the orthography used in it is specified.

Grammars: Hardie 1948 (KLT); Trépos no date (KLT); Hemon 1984 (*zedachek*); Kervella 1947 (*zedachek*); Gros 1966 (*falc'huneg*) *Dictionaries:* Hemon 1978 (*zedachek*); Hemon 1974 (*zedachek*); Stéphan and Sèité 1980 (*falc'huneg*); Helias 1986 (*falc'huneg*). *Text-books* (among the modern Celtic languages, Breton is certainly the one with the greatest variety and highest quality of books for teaching and learning the language): Hemon 1975a (*zedachek*); Denez 1972 (*zedachek*); Sèité and Stéphan 1957 (*falc'huneg*); Tricoire 1955, 1963 (*falc'huneg*); Morvannou 1975 (*assimileg*). An interesting doublet is provided by Sèité 1962 and 1965. They contain the same text, the first in standard Breton, the second in standard Vannetais (both in the respective version of *falc'huneg*).

The following chapters represent a description of standard Breton as defined above. This is the variety used in all grammars, dictionaries and textbooks. Recently, a tendency has arisen to loosen somewhat the rather tight link of the standard language with the Léon dialect and to make adjustments for other dialects, especially those of the centre. These tendencies have not yet been consolidated, nor have they found expression in published material of any kind (except Morvannou 1975). Therefore, they will not be taken into account in the following description, but they will have to be watched in the future.

Examples are either our own or have been adapted from the reference works cited above. The orthography used is *zedachek* throughout.

SYNTAX

7.2   SENTENCE STRUCTURE

7.2.0   Verbal particles

It is convenient to preface any discussion of sentence structure with a summary of the use of the so-called verbal particles. They are *a* (followed by lenition, 7.18.4) and *e* (followed by the mixed mutation, 7.18.4). The particle *a* is used:

1   when the subject (nominal or pronominal) precedes the verb;
2   when a direct object (including verbal noun, 7.4.1) precedes the
    verb.

The particle *e* is used when any element other than subject or direct object (e.g. adverb, prepositional phrase) precedes the verb.

These particles are mere function words, devoid of any semantic content. They have to be used in front of any inflected verbal form, except for the following cases: the verb 'to have' (7.9.4), the situational forms of 'to be' (7.2.2.1), negated forms of all verbs (7.4.2), imperative forms (7.9.3), reflexives with *en em* (7.4.3), verbal forms preceded by a pronominal object (7.4.7), after subordinating conjunctions (7.2.8.2).

7.2.1   Order of elements

Whereas Irish, Scottish Gaelic and Welsh are typical VSO languages, Breton is the only modern Celtic language with a predominant SVO order (normal order). On the other hand, Breton is particularly flexible with respect to the order of elements, such that almost any order is permitted. Changing the order of elements from the normal order usually involves emphasis on the element placed at the head of the sentence.

7.2.1.1   Nominal subject

The normal order of elements is SVO, as in (1) and (2). When the subject of the sentence is nominal, the inflected verb is always in the third person singular, independently of the grammatical number of the subject:

(1)   SG: *ar paotr a   zigor an nor*
         the boy VPT opens the door
         'The boy opens the door'

(2)   PL: *ar baotred a   zigor an nor*
         the boys VPT opens the door
         'The boys open the door'

Every other order of elements involves emphasis on the element placed at the head of the sentence. For emphasis on the nominal subject itself, see 7.2.7 (topicalisation).

There are two ways of moving the verb to the head of the sentence, giving a VSO order. The first construction requires the use of a special set of forms of the verb *bezañ* 'to be' (known as situational forms, 7.2.2.1), followed by the present participle of the main verb (7.9.2):

(3)   *emañ ar paotr o tigeriñ an nor*
                is-SIT the boy   opening the door
                'The boy is opening the door'

The second possibility involves use of the 'auxiliary construction' (7.4.1):

(4)   *digeriñ a   ra   ar paotr an nor*
                open VPT does the boy   the door
                'The boy opens the door'

Besides imperatives, the situational forms of 'to be' are the only *inflected* verbal forms in standard Breton that may be placed at the head of the sentence.

It may be questioned whether the auxiliary construction in (4) is really an instance of VSO order. Whereas on the *sentence* level, it seems indeed to represent VSO, the auxiliary construction itself represents OV order on the *phrase* level (7.4.1). The verbal noun functions as direct object of the auxiliary *ober* 'to do', only the latter being inflected for tense and person. Sentence (5) may be translated literally 'he/she does opening', that is 'he/she opens':

(5)   *digeriñ a   ra*
                open VPT does

Placing the object at the head of the sentence gives OSV order:

(6)   *an nor a   zigor ar paotr*
                the door VPT opens the boy
                'The boy opens *the door*'

By comparing sentences (1) and (6), it becomes apparent that both sentences have the same syntactic structure and are thus syntactically ambiguous. The decision as to which noun is subject and which object has to be taken on semantic grounds. If such a decision is impossible or doubtful, it is assumed that the sentence has the normal order SVO. Sentence (7) will be translated 'Peter looks for his brother', not *'His brother looks for Peter':

(7)   *Per   a   glask   e   vreur*
                Peter VPT looks-for his brother

Sentence (7) may be disambiguated syntactically by using an inflected form of *bezañ* 'to be', followed by the present participle (7.9.2) of the main verb:

(8)   *Per   a   zo o klask   e   vreur*
                Peter VPT is looking-for his brother

Sentence (8), which has SVO order, may unambiguously be turned into OVS by using a situational form of 'to be' (cf. (3)):

(9)   *e   vreur   emañ Per   o klask*
                his brother is-SIT Peter looking-for

7.2.1.2   Pronominal subject

For the convenience of syntactical description, we use 'pronominal subject' both for sentences with a true personal pronoun, and for sentences the subject of which is expressed through a personal suffix. These two possibilities alternate according to the order of elements within the sentence.

The normal construction requires the auxiliary verb *ober* 'to do' (7.4.1), the latter being inflected for tense, person and number:

(10)   *digeriñ a   ran an nor*
   open   VPT I-do the door
   'I open the door'

Every other construction involves emphasis on the element placed at the head of the sentence.

The personal pronoun may be placed in initial position. In this case, the verb is always in the third person singular, irrespective of person and number of the subject pronoun:

(11)   *me a   zigor an nor*
   I   VPT opens the door
   '*I* open the door'

In some dialects (e.g. in Ternes 1970:253ff., 279ff.), the stylistic value of (10) and (11) is reversed with respect to usage in the standard language.

Placing any other element at the head of the sentence requires inflection of the main verb by means of personal suffixes (e.g. *-an* for 1SG PRES, 7.9.4):

(12)   *an nor a   zigoran*
   the door VPT I-open
   'I open *the door*'

(13)   *bremañ e   tigoran an nor*
   now   VPT I-open the door
   'I open the door *now*'

The auxiliary construction in (10) may be considered syntactically an expansion of (12), with two direct objects, one (verbal noun) placed in front of the inflected verb, the other placed after it.

7.2.1.3   Imperative sentences

Imperatives sentences always have the order VO:

(14)   *digor   an nor!*
   open-SG the door
   'Open (SG) the door!'

7.2.2　'Being' sentences

'Being' sentences do not present any particular syntactical feature, except that different forms of the verb *bezañ* 'to be' are used, according to the order of elements within the sentence.

The normal order is SVP (P = predicate), any other order involving emphasis on the element placed at the head of the sentence. When the subject is a noun or a personal pronoun, the verb is always in the third person singular. When there is no nominal subject and no personal pronoun, the verb is inflected by means of personal suffixes.

(15)　　*an amzer　a　zo brav*
　　　　the weather VPT is nice

(16)　　*va breur　a　zo kelenner*
　　　　my brother VPT is teacher

(17)　　*skuizh on*
　　　　tired　I-am

(18)　　*skuizh eo*
　　　　tired　he/she-is

(19)　　*skuizh int*
　　　　tired　they-are

(20)　　*me a　　zo skuizh*
　　　　I　VPT is　tired
　　　　'*I* am tired'

(21)　　*eñ a　　zo skuizh*
　　　　he VPT is　tired
　　　　'*He* is tired'

(22)　　*i　　a　zo skuizh*
　　　　they VPT is　tired
　　　　'*They* are tired'

Usage of the verbal particles *a* and *e* is similar to that described in 7.2.0: the particle *a* is used when the subject (nominal or pronominal) precedes 'to be'; the particle *e* is used when the predicate precedes. In the third person singular present *e* + 'to be' gives the irregular form *eo*:

(23)　　*an amzer　a　zo brav*
　　　　the weather VPT is nice

(24)　　*brav eo an amzer*
　　　　nice is the weather

(25)　　*an amzer　a　oa　brav*
　　　　the weather VPT was nice

(26)   *brav e   oa   an amzer*
         nice VPT was the weather

7.2.2.1   Situational forms

The verb *bezañ* 'to be' has a special set of forms known as 'situational forms'; these have two tenses only (present and imperfect; see 7.9.3). These forms always precede the subject and usually occupy initial position within the sentence:

(27)   *emañ an tad   en   ti*
         is-SIT the father in-the house
         'The father is in the house'

(28)   *emaon   en   ti*
         I-am-SIT in-the house

(29)   *edo   o vervel*
         he/she-was-SIT dying

7.2.2.2   Equative and comparative

Equative and comparative sentences do not show any syntactic peculiarities with respect to the syntax of 'to be'.

         Equative

(30)   *eñ a   zo ken kreñv hag ur marc'h*
         he VPT is as   strong and a horse
         'He is as strong as a horse'

         Comparative

(31)   *eñ a   zo brasoc'h egedon*
         he VPT is taller   than-me

7.2.3   Negation

In principle, all sentence types described in 7.2.1 and 7.2.2 have a negative equivalent, except for the auxiliary construction with *ober* 'to do' (as in (4), (5), 10)), which cannot be negated. For negation on phrase level, see 7.4.2.

7.2.3.1   Nominal subject

Nominal subject and verb usually have agreement with respect to grammatical number. There is, however, a tendency in the spoken language to conform to usage in affirmative sentences; that is, the verb may be in the third person singular, irrespective of the number of the subject. The following are the negative equivalents of selected sentences of 7.2.1.1 ((32) vs (1), (33) vs (2), (34) vs (3)):

(32)   *ar paotr ne zigor ket an nor*
the boy   NEG opens NEG the door
'The boy does not open the door'

(33)   *ar baotred ne zigoront ket an nor*
the boys   NEG open-3PI NFG the door
'The boys do not open the door'

(34)   *N' emañ ket ar paotr o tigeriñ an nor*
NEG is-SIT NEG the boy opening the door
'The boy is not opening the door'

7.2.3.2   Pronominal subject

Negative sentences with a pronominal subject (see 7.2.1.2) always require the forms with a personal suffix described in 7.4.2. Sentence (35) is syntactically neutral. It therefore is the negative equivalent of (10), although the two sentences do not correspond with respect to the order of elements:

(35)   *ne zigoran ket an nor*
NEG I-open NEG the door
'I do not open the door'

The personal pronoun may precede for emphasis. Sentence (36) is equivalent to (11):

(36)   *me ne zigoran ket an nor*
I   NEG I-open NEG the door
'*I* do not open the door'

Negative imperative: sentence (37) is equivalent to (14):

(37)   *na zigor   ket an nor!*
NEG open-SG NEG the door
'Do not open (SG) the door!'

7.2.3.3   'Being' sentences

'Being' sentences (7.2.2) do not present any further syntactic peculiarities. In negative phrases, some verbal forms are different, however, morphologically and/or morphophonologically from the ones used in positive sentences. The following are the negative equivalents of selected sentences of 7.2.2 ((38) vs (15), (39) vs (17)):

(38)   *an amzer n' eo ket brav*
the weather NEG is NEG nice
'The weather is not nice'

(39)   *ne   don   ket   skuizh*
         NEG I-am NEG tired
         'I am not tired'

7.2.4   Interrogative sentences

In word questions, the question word usually has initial position:

(40)   *piv   a   zo aze?*
         who VPT is there

(41)   *pet   eur   eo?*
         how-many hour is
         'What's the time?'

(42)   *petra a   fell   dezhañ*
         what VPT is-necessary to-him
         'What does he want?'

For sentence questions, one has to make a distinction between the written standard and the spoken standard. In the written literary language, a question may be formed from any sentence type by placing the interrogative particle(s) *ha* or *daoust ha* in front of the affirmative sentence, without any further changes. This question type is never used in the spoken language:

(43)   *(daoust) ha chom ganeomp a   reot?*
         INTER   stay with-us VPT you-PL-will-do
         'Will you (PL) stay with us?'

In the spoken language, there is no segmental grammatical device at all for forming sentence questions. Questions are distinguished from affirmative sentences by using the (rising) interrogative intonation instead of the (falling) affirmative one (see 7.17.3). Segmentally, the sentence remains unchanged:

(44)   *chom a   reot*
         stay VPT you-PL-will-do

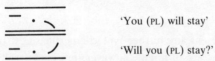

         'You (PL) will stay'

         'Will you (PL) stay?'

For answering sentence questions, *ya* 'yes' and *nann* 'no' are used. They may be used alone or, when emphasis is desired, by taking up the verb of the question in the appropriate form. In the latter case, all verbs except *bezañ* 'to be' and *kaout* 'to have' are taken up by the respective forms of *ober* 'to do'. More rarely, the verb may also be used alone. Answering sentence questions is, on the whole, rather reminiscent of usage in English.

The following are answers to the question in (44):

(45)   *Ya, (graimp)* 'Yes, (we shall do)'

(46)   *Nann, (ne raimp ket)* 'No, (we shall not do)'

7.2.5   Passive sentences

Passive sentences consist of the inflected forms of the verb *bezañ* 'to be', followed or preceded by the past participle (7.9.2) of the main verb. The agent is introduced by the preposition *gant* 'with':

(47)   *al laer a   zo bet   gwelet gant un amezeg*
          the thief VPT is been seen   with a neighbour
          'The thief has been seen by a neighbour'

(48)   *an tamm douar-se a   vo   aret   gant ar mevel*
          the piece land-that VPT will-be ploughed with the farm-hand
          'That piece of land will be ploughed by the farm-hand'

One syntactic variant of (47) is:

(49)   *gwelet eo bet   al laer gant un amezeg*
          seen   is been the thief with a   neighbour

For passive sentences without grammatical subject, see (53).

7.2.6   Impersonal sentences

7.2.6.1   The verbal forms with special impersonal suffixes (7.9.4) do not differ in syntax from verb forms with personal suffixes:

(50)   *an eil   pred a   anver   merenn*
          the second meal VPT one-calls lunch
          'The second meal is called lunch' (lit. 'One calls the second meal lunch')

(51)   *evañ a   reer   gwin da verenn*
          drink VPT one-does wine to lunch
          'One drinks wine with lunch'

(52)   *ne glever   mui   traoù evel-se*
          NEG one-hears any-more things like-that
          'One does not hear things like that any more'

7.2.6.2   Passive sentences (7.2.5) without grammatical subject:

(53)   *dornet   e vo   warc'hoaz*
          threshed VPT will-be tomorrow
          'They(IMPERS) will thresh tomorrow'

7.2.6.3   Some verbs, usually denoting features of weather and nature, are used in the third person singular only:

(54)   *skornañ a   ra*
         freeze VPT does
         'It is freezing'

(55)   *bremaik ec'h avelo*
         soon   VPT will-wind
         'There will be wind soon'

In sentences (54) and (55), as in most sentences of this type, the third person singular verb form is unspecified with respect to gender. When gender does surface, it is usually feminine:

(56)   *glav a   zo ganti*
         rain VPT is with-her
         'It looks like rain'

It is not quite clear why it is feminine. One explanation could be (perhaps too simplistic) that it refers to the noun *amzer* 'weather', which is feminine.

7.2.6.4   Another group of verbs, usually denoting subjective feelings and emotions, is used in the third person singular only. The logical subject may be expressed by means of an inflected preposition:

(57)   *ne   vern   ket*
         NEG matters NEG
         'It does not matter'

(58)   *fellout a   rae dezhi dimeziñ*
         want   VPT did to-her marry
         'She wanted to get married'

7.2.6.5   Some verbs may be inflected for all persons, but are used impersonally in the third person singular (as in 7.2.6.4) in certain fixed expressions. The logical subject may again be expressed by an inflected preposition:

(59)   *mar plij   deoc'h*
         if   likes to-you-PL
         'If you (PL) like (i.e. please)'

7.2.7   Types of topicalisation

In the absence of any phonetic means, be it through stress, pitch or length, for obtaining logical emphasis in Breton, the only way of calling attention to a particular element of the sentence is through syntactic processes (see Mangold 1975: 66f.).

7.2.7.1   The most common type of topicalisation is changing word order, especially moving the element to be emphasised into initial position of the sentence. All diversions from what is called 'normal order' in 7.2.1 imply emphasis on the initial element; see especially sentences (6), (9), (11), (12) and (13).

7.2.7.2   Stronger emphasis than through mere change of word order is obtained by the process called clefting in recent syntactic terminology. It consists in placing the element to be emphasised at the beginning of the sentence, placing the appropriate form of the verb *bezañ* 'to be' after it and making the rest of the sentence a subordinate (e.g. relative) clause. This construction corresponds to *c'est . . . que* in French, or *it is . . . who* (etc.) in English:

(60)   *ar person eo a   zeuas*
         the parson is VPT came
         'It is the parson who came'

(61)   *d' an eur-se   eo e   teu   ar gazetenn*
         to the hour-that is VPT comes the newspaper
         'It is at that hour that the newspaper comes'

The phrase preceding *eo* in sentences (60) and (61) is the predicate of the main clause. The subject is included in *eo* '(it) is'. The phrase following the verbal particle is the subordinate clause (7.2.8.2).

7.2.7.3   The sentence as a whole may be emphasised by placing *bezañ* 'to be' (often abbreviated to *bez'*) in front of it:

(62)   *bez' e   oa kalz a dud   war ar pont*
         be VPT was much of people on the bridge
         'There were many people on the bridge'

7.2.7.4   A special syntactic feature of Breton are the so-called 'sentences with double subject'. A noun phrase is placed in initial position for emphasis and functions as subject of the following verb. A second noun phrase, which may be considered a second subject, in turn follows that verb. The initial noun phrase is referred to again by a pronominal reference in the second part of the sentence. The sentence as a whole has the form: $S_1 + V + (PRO_1 + S_2)$.

(63)   *Per   a   zo klañv e   vab*
         Peter VPT is ill   his son
         'Peter's son is ill'

(64)   *ar c'hraou a   zo aet   e   doenn gant an avel*
      the stable VPT is gone his roof   with the wind
      'The stable has been unroofed by the wind'

(65)   *an tad   a   oa   mall warnañ*
      the father VPT was haste on-him
      'The father was in a hurry'

(66)   *Per   a   zo debret e   verenn gantañ*
      Peter VPT is eaten his lunch with-him (cf. 7.2.5)
      'Peter has eaten his lunch' or 'Lunch has been eaten by Peter'

7.2.8   Complex sentences: parataxis and hypotaxis

7.2.8.1   Two main clauses may be juxtaposed by means of a co-ordinating conjunction, among the most common of which are *ha* 'and', *pe* 'or', *na* 'nor', *rak* 'for, because', *met* 'but':

(67)   *Per   a   ouie neuiñ, met e   c'hoar ne   ouie ket*
      Peter VPT knew swim   but his sister NEG knew NEG
      'Peter was able to swim, but his sister was not'

When two verbs are linked by *ha* 'and', the second may remain uninflected (i.e. a verbal noun):

(68)   *Per   a   savas ha   mont d' ar prenestr*
      Peter VPT rose   and go   to the window
      'Peter rose and went to the window'

7.2.8.2   Breton has comparatively few simple subordinating conjunctions. Among the most common are *pa* 'when', *mar* 'if' and *ma* (*m'* before certain vowel-initial forms) 'that, if':

(69)   *pa   vez   leun o   c'hof,   ez eont   da gousket*
      when is-HAB full   their stomach VPT they-go to   sleep(V)
      'When their stomach is full, they go to sleep'

(70)   *mar bez   glep an douar, me a   hado   an had*
      if   is-HAB wet the earth   I   VPT will-sow the seed
      'If the earth is wet, I shall sow the seed'

(71)   *ken fall eo kouezet, m'   en deus torret   e   c'har*
      so   bad is fallen   that he has   broken his leg
      'He has fallen so badly that he has broken his leg'

(72)   *ma vijen   bet yac'h, em bije   gallet   mont ivez*
      if   I-should-be been healthy I   should-have been-able go   also
      'If I had been in good health, I should have been able to go too'

Ma (as in (71), (72)) is the most common subordinating conjunction and has a wide range of application. It therefore may express other shades of meaning as well, for example:

(73)   *ne   gare ket an noter, laeret ma oa bet   gantañ bloaz a-raok*
             NEG liked NEG the lawyer stolen that was been with-him year before
             'He/she did not like the lawyer, *because* he/she had been cheated by him the year before'

7.2.8.3   Complex subordinating conjunctions are formed by adding *ma* 'that' to various prepositions, prepositional phrases or other parts of speech: *a-raok ma* 'before' (74), *daoust ma* 'although', *dre ma* 'because' (lit. 'through that'), *e-giz ma* 'in the manner (that)' (75), *e-pad ma* 'while' (lit. 'during that'), *goude ma* 'after', *hep ma* 'without', *lec'h ma* 'where' (lit. 'place that'):

(74)   *pell e   ranko   gortoz, a-raok ma lavaro ya an tad*
             far VPT must-FUT wait   before that will-say yes the father
             'He/she will have to wait a long time, before the father will say yes'

(75)   *gra   e-giz   ma kari!*
             do-SG in-manner that you-SG-will-like
             'Do as you (SG) please!'

7.2.8.4   It is a typical feature of idiomatic Breton to avoid subordination to the advantage of various co-ordinating constructions. Two phrases may be co-ordinated without using any kind of conjunction, and the syntactical context decides which of the two phrases is to be considered logically as the main clause and which as the subordinate one. One such type, the so-called 'relative clause', will be described in 7.3.2. Examples of other types follow (in every case, verbal particles have to be used as appropriate, see 7.2.0):

(76)   *gouzout a   rit   mat e   talv   va frad   muioc'h eget-se*
             know   VPT you-PL-do good VPT is-worth my meadow more   than-that
             'You (PL) know well *that* my meadow is worth more than that'

(77)   *soñj   am-eus edo   c'hoaz en he gwele*
             thought I-have was-SIT still in her bed
             'I remember *that* she was still in bed'

The order of the second phrase in (76) may be reversed:

(78)   *gouzout a rit mat va frad   a   dalv   muioc'h eget-se*
                                   my meadow VPT is-worth more   than-that

Prepositional phrases followed by a verbal noun (see 7.5.3):

(79)   *a-raok mont en e wele, e lakaas   al levr dindan e blueg*
             before go   in his bed   VPT put-PAST the book under his pillow
             '*Before* going to bed, he put the book under his pillow'

(80)   *deuit   tostoc'h eta,   evit din   ho   klevout gwelloc'h*
         come-PL closer   REINF.ADV for to-me your-PL hear   better
         'Do come (PL) closer *so that* I may hear you (PL) better'

(81)   *evit dezhañ bezañ bouzar, klevout a   ra   pa   gar*
         for to-him be   deaf   hear   VPT does when likes
         '*Although* he is deaf, he hears when he wants to'

The so-called 'absolute clause' does not contain a verb at all. It is usually introduced by *ha* 'and':

(82)   *Yann a   oa   o klask   e   varc'h, hag eñ warnañ*
         John VPT was looking-for his horse   and he on-him
         'John was looking for his horse *while* he was on it'

(83)   *ne   yae   ket ar skeul, hag hi   hir   koulskoude, betek   an doenn*
         NEG went NEG the ladder and she long nevertheless as-far-as the roof
         'The ladder, *although* it was long, did not reach the roof'

(84)   *e   c'hoar a   oa   dimezet, ha   bugale   dezhi*
         his sister VPT was married and children to-her
         'His sister was married and she had children'

Participial phrases (7.9.2) are also often introduced by *ha* 'and':

(85)   *ha   Mikael o vezañ deuet,   a   welas anezhañ astennet war e   wele*
         and Michael being   come-PPART VPT saw   of-him   stretched on his bed
         '*When* Michael had come, he saw him stretched out on his bed'

(86)   *hejet   e   oant   un tammig, hag ar vag o vont er-maez eus   ar*
         shaken VPT they-were a   little   and the boat going   out   from the
         porzh
         port
         'They were shaken somewhat, *while* the boat was leaving the port'

7.2.9   Other sentential features

Under this heading will be treated some sentence types without a finite verb.

7.2.9.1   The so-called 'narrative construction' contains a verbal noun (7.9.2) instead of a finite verb, and is often introduced by *ha* 'and' (cf. sentences (82)–(86)). It gives a particularly vivid expression to the event related.

(87)   *hag eñ mont ha   distagañ ur flac'had   gant egile*
         and he go   and knock-off a full-of-palm with the-other
         'And he went and gave the other one a slap in the face'

7.2.9.2   The invariable *setu*, placed in initial position, introduces a noun phrase. It may be compared to French *voici, voilà. Setu* does not imply any indication of tense, person or (unlike French *voici, voilà*) distance:

(88)   *setu   ti   va zad*
           'voilà' house my father
           'This is my father's house'

(89)   *setu   hi*
           'voilà' she
           'There she is'

7.2.9.3   Petrified verb fragments of heterogeneous type, among others the invariable *arabat* 'it is forbidden, don't do', and *eme* 'says, said, quoth':

(90)   *arabat   mont pelloc'h!*
           it-is-forbidden go   further
           'It is forbidden to go beyond this point'

(91)   *arabat   koll anezho en   hent!*
           it-is-forbidden lose of-them in-the way
           'Don't lose them on the way!'

Eme usually follows direct speech. It has no indication of tense. For pronominal use it is inflected like simple prepositions (7.10):

(92)   *pelec'h emañ va lunedoù, eme   ar   vamm*
           where is-SIT my glasses   quoth the mother
           'Where are my glasses, said (says) the mother'

(93)   *Pelec'h emañ va lunedoù, emezi*
           'Where are my glasses, she said (says)'

STRUCTURE OF THE PHRASE

7.3   THE NOMINAL PHRASE

7.3.1   Order of elements

The modifiers *preceding* the head noun include articles, numerals, possessives and a very limited number of adjectives; the modifiers *following* the head noun include adjectives, attributive nouns, demonstratives and relative clauses. The elements that precede may be regarded as finite sets, whereas the elements that follow (except for demonstratives) are syntactically productive, in the sense that they allow for near-infinite variation within each set. In addition, among the elements that precede, articles and possessives may be interpreted as prefixes (a view advocated by Oftedal 1972, and exemplified by Ternes 1970). Therefore, the more substantial modifiers are those following the noun.

The main elements of the nominal phrase appear in the following order:

$$\left\{ \begin{matrix} \text{ART} \\ \text{POSS} \end{matrix} \right\} + \text{NUM} + \text{NOUN} + \text{ADJ} + \text{DEM}$$

(94) | | |
|---|---|
| *ti* | 'house' |
| *an ti* | 'the house' |
| *an ti bras* | 'the big house' |
| *an ti-se* | 'that house' |
| *an ti bras-se* | 'that big house' |
| *daou di* | 'two houses' |
| *an daou di* | 'the two houses' |
| *an daou di bras-se* | 'those two big houses' |
| *hon ti* | 'our house' |
| *hon daou di bras* | 'our two big houses' |

For the special character of the 'genitive construction', see 7.3.8.

7.3.2   Embedding: phrasal and clausal modifiers

Breton does not have a relative pronoun proper, although relative clauses are commonly referred to in Breton grammars. The following sequence may be said to include a relative clause:

(95)   an den a   welan
         the man VPT I-see
         (a) 'the man whom I see'

The verbal particle (7.2.0) is not a relative pronoun; its grammatical function is to indicate that there is *some sort* of syntactic connection between (in this case) noun and verb. Sequence (95) is in fact ambiguous and may also be translated by (b) 'I see the man' (cf. sentence (12)).

The syntactic context, supported in the spoken language by the intonation contour (final or non-final), disambiguates the two possible meanings. If the sequence is considered an independent syntactical unit, one will have to translate as in (b). If, on the other hand, there is another finite verb to follow within what is considered the same sentence, the first verb will have to be interpreted as part of an imbedded 'relative clause':

(96)   an den a   welan a   zo kozh
         the man VPT I-see VPT is old
         'The man whom I see is old'

A similar ambiguity as in (95) arises when subject and verb agree for person:

(97)   an den a   wel
         the man VPT sees

(a) 'the man who sees (...)'
(b) 'The man sees'

The nominal head may be taken up by some indicator following the verb and referring back to the head by some kind of grammatical agreement. The indicator may be an inflected pronominal preposition (7.10) as in (98), or a possessive (7.3.6) as in (99):

(98)   *an den a   gomzan anezhañ*
         the man VPT I-speak of-him
         'the man I am speaking about'

(99)   *an den a   varvas e   vuoc'h*
         the man VPT died   his cow
         'the man whose cow died'

In these sentences, a similar syntactic ambiguity arises. Example (98) may also be translated by 'I am speaking of the man', (99) by 'The man's cow died'. Compare 'sentences with double subject', 7.2.7.4.

Instead of by the verbal particle, a relative with pronominal reference (as in (98), (99)) may also be introduced by the subordinating conjunction *ma* 'that' (7.2.8.2). In this case, the sequence is unambiguously relative:

(100)   *ar puñs ma tennomp dour dioutañ*
         the well that we-draw water from-him
         'the well from which we draw water'

The nominal head may also be followed by a phrasal modifier that does not contain a verb:

(101)   *ur stêr bras he genou*
         a river big her mouth
         'a river with a wide mouth'

7.3.3   Definiteness and indefiniteness

Breton has a definite and an indefinite article. It is thus the only living Celtic language with an indefinite article (see Ternes 1979). Both articles precede the noun (7.3.1). They are invariable with respect to gender and number. The alternants depend on the initial phoneme of the following word.

Definite article: *al, an, ar*
Indefinite article: *ul, un, ur*

The *l*-forms are used before /l/, the *n*-forms before /t, d, n, h/ or vowel, the *r*-forms in all other cases:

(102)   *al loar*   'the moon'   *ar pri*   'the mud'
         an tad   'the father' *ur vro*   'a country'

un den	'a man'	*ar brioù*	'the countries'
an holen	'the salt'	*ar c'hambroù*	'the rooms'
an aodoù	'the coasts'	*ur yar*	'a hen'

In phrases with indefinite article, phrase accent falls on the indefinite article, when the noun is monosyllabic (see 7.3.5):

(103)   *ar vro*   (-́-)   'the country'   *ar gwele*   (-́-)   'the bed'
          ur vro   (-́-)   'a country'   *ur gwele*   (-́-)   'a bed'

For loss of the definite article in the 'genitive construction', see 7.3.8.

7.3.4   Demonstratives

Standard Breton distinguishes three degrees of distance: 'here (immediately at hand)', 'there (far)', 'over there (remote or out of sight)'. With a nominal head, the phrase is built up as follows (see 7.3.1): DEF ART + NOUN (+ ADJ) + DEM.

(104)   *an den-mañ* 'this man'   *an den fall-se* 'that bad man'
          an den-se 'that man'   *an ti-se*   'that house'
          an den-hont 'that man over there' *an tiez-se*   'those houses'

Demonstratives in attributive use (as in (104)) do not change with respect to gender and number. They do, however, in independent use, as in (105):

(105)   'near'   'far'   'remote'

		'near'	'far'	'remote'	
SG	MASC	*hemañ*	*hennezh*	*henhont*	'this one' etc
	FEM	*houmañ*	*hounnezh*	*hounhont*	
PL		*ar re-mañ*	*ar re-se*	*ar re-hont*	'these' etc.

The plural forms in (105) involve the dummy word *re* (plural of *hini*; see 7.3.6–7), which constructs like any noun. The demonstrative therefore takes the attributive form as in (104).

7.3.5   Enumeration

The numeral *unan* 'one' (7.8.1) does not occur in phrases with a nominal head. The indefinite article (7.3.3) is used instead. From 'two' on, there are two alternative constructions, (106) and (109), of which the former is much more common:

(106)   NUM + NOUN (SG)

daou baotr	'two boys'
div verc'h	'two girls'
dek ti	'ten houses'
triwec'h miz	'eighteen months'
kant vloaz	'100 years'

With the compound numerals involving *warn-* or *ha* (7.8.1), the noun is placed immediately after the digits:

(107)   *daou zen warn-ugent* 'twenty-two men'
          div verc'h ha tregont 'thirty-two girls'

When the noun is monosyllabic, phrase accent is on the last syllable of the numeral (see 7.3.3, indefinite article):

(108)   *dek ti* (-́-)   'ten houses'
          triwec'h miz (-́-́-)   'eighteen months'
          but: *dek aval* (-́-́-)   'ten apples'

(109)   NUM + *a* + NOUN (PL)
          dek a diez 'ten houses'

A is a preposition meaning 'of'.

7.3.6   Possession

The following set of forms is used in the formula POSS-+ NOUN. The initial mutation of the following noun (7.18.4) is noted in parentheses:

(110)   SG   1   *va* (spirant mutation)
               2   *da* (lenition)
               3 MASC   *e* (lenition)
                 FEM   *he* (spirant mutation), *hec'h* before vowel
          PL   1   *hol, hon, hor* ($k \rightarrow c'h$)
               2   *ho* (provection), *hoc'h* before vowel
               3   *o* (spirant mutation)

First person plural *hol* is used before initial /l/, *hon* before initial /t, d, n, h/ and vowel, *hor* in all other cases. This distribution is the same as for definite and indefinite article (7.3.3).

The possessives refer to the possessor. They are invariable with respect to the possessed object.

(111)   *ti* 'house'   *bugale* 'children'

SG	*va zi*	'my house'	*va bugale*	'my children'
	da di	'your (SG) house'	*da vugale*	'your (SG) children'
	e di	'his house'	*e vugale*	'his children'
	he zi	'her house'	*he bugale*	'her children'
PL	*hon ti*	'our house'	*hor bugale*	'our children'
	ho ti	'your (PL) house'	*ho pugale*	'your (PL) children'
	o zi	'their house'	*o bugale*	'their children'

hec'h anv 'her name', *hoc'h anv* 'your (PL) name'.

Special forms are used in combination with certain prepositions, for example:

(112)   *da'm zi* 'to my house'   *em zi* 'in my house'
          da'z ti 'to your (SG) house'   *ez ti* 'in your (SG) house'

For emphasis on the possessor, the above construction is followed either by the respective personal pronoun (7.6.8.1), or by the preposition *da* 'to' inflected respectively (7.10), or by both:

(113)   *va zi-me* or *va zi din* or *va zi din-me* '*my* house'
          da di-te   *da di dit*   *da di dit-te* '*your* (SG) house'
          etc.

When no specific noun is referred to, the dummy words *hini* (SG) and *re* (PL) are used (see 7.3.7):

(114)   One possessed object   More possessed objects
          va hini 'mine'   *va re* 'mine'
          da hini 'yours (SG)'   *da re* 'yours (SG)'
          etc.   etc.

7.3.7   Adjectivals

The attributive adjective as a rule follows the noun:

(115)   *un ti bihan*   'a little house'
          dour fresk   'fresh water'

A few adjectives generally precede the noun, for example *gwall* 'bad':

(116)   *gwall amzer*   'bad weather'

Some adjectives may follow or precede the noun, usually with a different shade of meaning:

(117)   *un ti kozh*   'an old house'
          ur c'hozh ti   'a miserable house'

Some adjectives generally follow the noun, but precede it in certain fixed expressions:

(118)   *ul linenn verr*   'a short line'
          e berr gomzoù   'briefly' (lit. 'in short words')

(119)   *un den fall*   'a bad man'
          fall wad   'bad mood' (lit. 'bad blood')

When no specific noun is referred to, the dummy words *hini* (SG) and *re* (PL) are used as heads (see 7.3.6):

(120)   *an hini kozh*   'the old one (MASC)'
          an hini gozh   'the old one (FEM)'
          ar re gozh   'the old ones (MASC and/or FEM)'

7.3.8 Genitive construction

Although the term 'genitive construction' is not entirely satisfactory, it will be used here in accordance with Jones and Thomas (1977: 192ff.). It has the following structure: NOUN₁ + ART + NOUN₂. NOUN₁ may be labelled *possessum*, NOUN₂ indicates the *possessor* (again after Jones and Thomas 1977):

(121)   *dor an ti*
            door the house
            'the door of the house'

NOUN₂ is attributive to NOUN₁. NOUN₂ may also have the indefinite article or any other modifier, or be a name:

(122)   *dor un ti*
            door a   house
            'the door of a house'

(123)   *dor e di*
            door his house
            'the door of his house'

(124)   *ti   Mikael*
            house Michael
            'Michael's house'

NOUN₁ never has an article itself, although it is underlyingly definite. As a consequence, it is not possible to translate a phrase like '*a* door of the (his) house' into Breton by using the 'genitive construction'.

NOUN₂ in the formula above may in turn be expanded by another attributive noun. In this case, it behaves like NOUN₁; that is, it loses the article:

(125)   *alc'houez dor an ti*
            key   door the house
            'the key of the door of the house'

7.3.9 Agreement

Agreement in nominal phrases is to be found mainly in two constructions: (a) adjectives mutate after feminine nouns (example (126) – 7.18.6); (b) the numerals 2, 3, 4 (and compounds of these like 22, 23, 24, etc.) have masculine and feminine forms which agree with the gender of the following noun (example (127) – see 7.8.1).

(126)(a)   *tad   -kozh* (MASC)
              father old
              'grandfather'

406   *Elmar Ternes*

(b)   *mamm -gozh* (FEM)
        mother old
        'grandmother'

(127)   *daou di* (MASC) 'two houses'
        div daol (FEM) 'two tables'

7.3.10   Adjectival phrases

Adjectives are modified by a following adverb (128) or by another adjective (129). The modifying element is not marked morphologically:

(128)   *mat tre*
        good very
        'very good'

(129)   *klañv fall*
        ill   bad
        'seriously ill'

7.4   THE VERBAL PHRASE

7.4.1   Auxiliary construction

The most important auxiliary verb in Breton is *ober* 'to do, to make' (inflected irregularly). The 'auxiliary construction' has the following form: VN + *a* + *ober*. The verbal noun (7.9.2) is followed by the verbal particle *a* (7.2.0). The auxiliary *ober* is inflected for tense and person. For syntactical use of this construction, see 7.2.1.1–2.

(130)   *karout a ran*
        love VPT I-do
        'I love'

(131)   Full present paradigm:

SG	1	*karout a ran*	'I love'
	2	*karout a rez*	'you (SG) love'
	3	*karout a ra*	'he/she loves'
PL	1	*karout a reomp*	'we love'
	2	*karout a rit*	'you (PL) love'
	3	*karout a reont*	'they love'
IMPERS		*karout a reer*	'one loves'

(132)   IMPERF   *karout a raen*   'I loved' etc.
        FUT   *karout a rin*   'I shall love' etc.
        COND   *karout a rafen*   'I should love' etc.
        etc.

7.4.2   Negation

Negation is shown by *ne . . . ket* embracing the verb form. The verb itself consists of stem plus suffix, the latter indicating person and tense (see the paradigms in 7.9.4). For the syntax of negated verbs, see 7.2.3.

(133)   Full present paradigm:

SG	1	*ne garan ket*	'I do not love'
	2	*ne garez ket*	'you (SG) do not love'
	3	*ne gar ket*	'he/she does not love'
PL	1	*ne garomp ket*	'we do not love'
	2	*ne garit ket*	'you (PL) do not love'
	3	*ne garont ket*	'they do not love'
IMPERS		*ne garer ket*	'one does not love'

(134)

IMPERF	*ne garen ket*	'I did not love' etc.
FUT	*ne garin ket*	'I shall not love' etc.
COND	*ne garfen ket*	'I should not love' etc.
etc.		

The negative imperative uses *na . . . ket* instead of *ne . . . ket*:

(135)   2SG *na gar ket!*   'Do (SG) not love!'
           2PL *na garit ket!*   'Do (PL) not love!'

7.4.3   Reflexive and reciprocal

There is no strict distinction between reflexives and reciprocals. Both relations are usually expressed by placing the invariable *en em* before the main verb. Examples with the auxiliary construction (7.4.1):

(136)   *en em lazhañ a   ra*
           REFLEX kill   VPT does
           'He/she kills himself/herself'

(137)   *en em glevout a   reont   mat*
           RECIP hear   VPT they-do good
           'They get on well with one another'

A reciprocal relation may also be expressed by the phrase *an eil d'egile*, lit. 'the second to the other':

(138)   *skrivañ a   reont   an eil   d' egile*
           write   VPT they-do the second to the-other
           'They write to each other'

7.4.4   Compound tenses

Breton is the only living Celtic language that has compound tenses corresponding to perfect, pluperfect, secondary future, etc. of many other European
languages (see Ternes 1979: sect. 5). The compound tenses are formed with the
present, imperfect, future, etc. respectively of the (irregular) auxiliary verbs
kaout 'to have' or *bezañ* 'to be' plus past participle of the main verb. Most verbs
take 'to have'. The verbs taking 'to be' are largely the same as in French (among
them verbs of motion like *mont* 'to go', *dont* 'to come', *kouezhañ* 'to fall').
Unlike French, however, reflexive verbs with *en em* (7.4.3) take 'to have',
whereas *bezañ* 'to be' itself takes 'to be' (for a paradigm of *kaout* 'to have', see
(208)). The inflected auxiliary may precede or follow the past participle:

(139)   *me am eus debret* or *debret em eus*   'I have eaten'
           te az peus debret   *debret ez peus*   'you (SG) have eaten'
           eñ en deus debret   *debret en deus*   'he has eaten'
           hi he deus debret   *debret he deus*   'she has eaten'
           etc.

(140)   *me am boa debret* or *debret em boa* 'I had eaten'
           etc.

(141)   *me a zo deuet* or *deuet on*   'I have come'
           te a zo deuet   *deuet out* 'you (SG) have come'
           eñ a zo deuet⎫   'he has come'⎫
                          ⎬ *deuet eo*   ⎬ 'he/she has come'
           hi a zo deuet⎭   'she has come'⎭
           etc.

(142)   *me a zo bet* or *bet on* 'I have been'
           etc.

(143)   *en em   gollet o deus   er   c'hoad*
           REFLEX lost   they-have in-the wood
           'They have lost their way in the wood'

7.4.5   Progressive form

A verb phrase not unlike the English progressive form in *-ing* is formed by
means of the *o*-participle (present participle, 7.9.2), accompanied by the
inflected forms of *bezañ* 'to be':

(144)   *emaint   o c'hoari kartoù*
           they-are-SIT playing cards
           'They are playing cards'

(145)   *edo   o vervel*
           was-SIT dying
           'He/she was dying'

7.4.6   Passive

The passive phrase is formed by means of the inflected forms of *bezañ* 'to be', preceded or followed by the past participle of the main verb, cf. 7.2.5:

(146)   *al levr-mañ a vo lennet er skol*
      the book-DEM VPT will-be read-PPART in-the school
      'This book will be read in school'

7.4.7   Pronominal object

The expression of direct pronominal objects in verb phrases is practically identical with the expression of possession for nouns (7.3.6). In other words, the verb form, to which the pronominal object refers, in fact acts as a noun, to which the respective possessive is prefixed:

(147)   *va gwelet o deus*
      my seen   they-have
      'They have seen me'

The full set of pronominal objects is identical with the possessives in 7.3.6 (including the special forms *'m*, *'z* in (112)):

(148)   SG   1   *va, 'm* (spirant mutation)
            2   *da, 'z* (lenition after *da*, provection after *'z*)
           3MASC–3PL (as in 7.36)

First and second persons singular *va* and *da* are used before verbal nouns, past participles and imperatives (except after the prepositions *da* and the negative *ne*), whereas *'m* and *'z* are used before all other verbal forms and always after the preposition *da* 'to, for' (giving *da'm*, *da'z*) and the negative *ne* (giving *ne'm*, *ne'z*).

(149)   SG   1   *va gwelet en deus*   'he has seen me'
            2   *da welet en deus*   'he has seen you (SG)'
            3   MASC   *e welet en deus*   'he has seen him'
                  FEM   *he gwelet en deus*   'he has seen her'
           PL   1   *hor gwelet en deus*   'he has seen us'
            2   *ho kwelet en deus*   'he has seen you (PL)'
            3   *o gwelet en deus*   'he has seen them'

(150)   SG   1   *ne'm c'harez ket*   'you (SG) don't love me'
            2   *ne'z karan ket*   'I don't love you (SG)'
            3   MASC   *n'e garan ket*   'I don't love him'
                  FEM   *n'he c'haran ket*   'I don't love her'
           PL   1   *n'hor c'harez ket*   'you (SG) don't love us'
            2   *n'ho karan ket*   'I don't love you (PL)'
            3   *n'o c'haran ket*   'I don't love them'

(151)   *deuit   da 'm gwelout!*
come (PL) to my see
'Come (PL) to see me!'

In the spoken language, an alternative construction is given preference to the one described above. It uses the inflected forms of the preposition *a* 'of' (7.10) instead of the possessives. The prepositional forms are placed after the verb:

(152)   (cf. (150) 3SG FEM)

ne   garan ket anezhi
NEG I-love NEG of-her
'I don't love her'

(153)   (cf. (151))

deuit   da welout ac'hanon!
come-PL to see   of-me
'Come (PL) to see me!'

7.5   THE PREPOSITIONAL PHRASE

7.5.1   Prepositions with noun phrases

A distinction has to be made between simple and compound prepositions. For simple prepositions see 7.10. Compound prepositions usually consist of a simple preposition and a nominal head following it. In many cases, the latter can be identified with an existing noun, as in:

(154)   *e-lec'h* 'instead of'   *lec'h* 'place'
e-giz 'like'   *giz* 'manner'

In other cases, however, the nominal head does not occur outside the compound preposition, as in:

(155)   *a-dreñv* 'behind' (*treñv*)

Some compound prepositions have the structure PREP$_1$ + NOUN + PREP$_2$, for example:

(156)   *en-dro da* 'around'   *tro* 'round' (NOUN)
a-dal da 'in front of'   *tal* 'forehead, front'

In noun phrases, the preposition precedes all other noun modifiers. Examples:

(157)   Simple prepositions:

war an daol 'on the table'
dindan an daol 'under the table'
gant e vamm 'with his mother'
etre c'hwi ha me 'between you (PL) and me'
goude koan 'after supper'

(158)   Compound prepositions:

> *e-giz ur bugel* 'like a child'
> *a-dreñv an ti* 'behind the house'
> *en-dro d'e di* 'around his house'

Some simple prepositions have special forms in combination with the definite article and some possessives, for example:

(159)   *en ti* 'in the house' (but: *en un ti* 'in a house')
          em zi 'in my house'

7.5.2   Prepositions with pronominals

For simple prepositions, see 7.10. With compound prepositions of the structure PREP + NOUN, the nominal head is preceded by the respective possessive (7.3.6):

(160)   *e-kichen* 'beside'

SG	1		*em c'hichen*	'beside me'
	2		*ez kichen*	'beside you (SG)'
	3	MASC	*en e gichen*	'beside him'
		FEM	*en he c'hichen*	'beside her'
PL	1		*en hor c'hichen*	'beside us'
	2		*en ho kichen*	'beside you (PL)'
	3		*en o c'hichen*	'beside them'

In compound prepositions of the structure PREP$_1$ + NOUN + PREP$_2$, PREP$_2$ behaves like a simple preposition and is inflected accordingly (7.10):

(161)   *en-dro da* 'around'

SG	1		*en-dro din*	'around me'
	2		*en-dro dit*	'around you (SG)'
	3	MASC	*en-dro dezhañ*	'around him'
		FEM	*en-dro dezhi*	'around her'
PL	1		*en-dro dimp*	'around us'
	2		*en-dro deoc'h*	'around you (PL)'
	3		*en-dro dezho*	'around them'

7.5.3   Prepositions with verb phrases

Prepositions combine with verbal nouns (7.9.2) which may in turn be expanded syntactically (by objects, adverbs, prepositional phrases, etc.). For syntactical use of this construction, see sentences (79)–(81).

(162)   *hep   kouezhañ en   dour*
          without fall   into-the water
          'without falling into the water'

(163)   *e-lec'h   chom   aze*
          instead-of remain there
          'instead of remaining there'

The verb phrase may contain a logical subject, introduced by the preposition *da* 'to'. Compare sentences (80) and (81).

(164)   *evit d' e dad   sevel un ti   nevez*
          for to his father build a   house new
          'although his father is (was) building a new house'

(165)   *hep   gouzout d' e   c'hoar*
          without know   to his sister
          'without his sister knowing (it)'

7.5.4   Spatial system of prepositions

Breton does not normally make a distinction between position and movement:

(166)   *en ti* 'in the house' or 'into the house'
          war an daol 'on the table' or 'onto the table'

The most important peculiarity in the use of spatial prepositions concerns the concept 'from'. It does not simply show a starting point in place, but implies a description of the position of the object *before* it is taken 'from' something. Hence, 'from' corresponds to a number of different prepositions in Breton:

(167)   *war an daol* 'on the table'
          diwar an daol 'from the table' (lit. 'from-on')

A picture is hung 'against' the wall, and taken 'from against' it:

(168)   *ouzh ar voger* 'on the wall' (lit. 'against')
          diouzh ar voger 'from the wall' (lit. 'from-against')

An object is taken 'from with' a person:

(169)   *ganin* 'with me'
          diganin 'from me' (lit. 'from-with')

(170)   *ne   zebr ket a voued diganin*
          NEG eats NEG of food   from-with-me
          'He/she does not accept food from me'

MORPHOLOGY

7.6   NOUNS

7.6.1   Structure: stems and endings

The minimal independent unit in noun morphology is the simple stem, for example *mor* 'sea'. In addition there are derived stems (7.11.2), for example *moraer* 'sailor', and compound stems (7.11.1), for example *morvran* 'cormorant'.

Noun stems may be inflected by suffixation, prefixation, internal inflection (umlaut; see 7.19) or suppletion (7.19). By far the most common process of these is suffixation.

7.6.2   Inherent classes: mass/count/collective/singulative

Nouns in Breton fall into two main classes: (1) singular stems (7.6.5.1), from which the plural is formed through a morphological process, for example *sac'h* 'bag' (SG) – *seier* (PL); (2) collective stems (7.6.5.2), from which the singular is formed through a morphological process, usually suffixation. Singulars derived from collective stems are referred to as singulatives, in order to distinguish them from singular stems. Semantically, collectives denominate small animals, plants, parts of plants or other objects usually occurring in great masses, for example *gwenan* 'bees (COLL)' – *gwenanenn* 'bee (SGT)', *stered* 'stars (COLL)' – *steredenn* 'star (SGT)'.

A specific subclass of singular-stem nouns are parts of the body and pieces of clothing that occur in pairs. These nouns form an obligatory dual (7.6.5.3), whereas all other nouns have no dual, for example *skoaz* 'shoulder (SG)' – *divskoaz* '(two) shoulders (DU)'.

7.6.3   Animate/inanimate etc.

The distinction animate/inanimate finds a marginal expression in plural formation: some plural suffixes are used predominantly, but not exclusively, for animate beings, especially *-ed*, *-ien*, *-on*, *-i*, *-iz*.

The distinction human/non-human (in combination with gender and number) has a bearing on the morphophonological behaviour (initial mutations) of nouns: masculine plural nouns designating human beings take lenition after the

definite article, whereas all other plural nouns take a reduced form of spirant
mutation in that position (see 7.18.5).

7.6.4   Gender

Breton has two genders: every noun is either masculine or feminine. Grammatical gender usually coincides with natural sex, for example:

(171)   Masculine   Feminine
             paotr 'boy'   *plac'h* 'girl'
             tarv 'bull'   *buoc'h* 'cow'

The numerals 2, 3 and 4 (and combinations thereof) have distinct forms for
masculine and feminine, which combine obligatorily with the respective nouns,
for example:

(172)   *tamm* (MASC) 'piece'   *daou damm* 'two pieces'
             bag (FEM)   'boat'   *div vag*   'two boats'

The noun *tra* 'thing' cannot be attributed unequivocally to one or the other
gender. On the one hand, it combines with the masculine forms of the numerals
2, 3, 4, whereas, on the other hand, it behaves like a feminine with respect to
initial mutations: it takes lenition after the article, and itself lenites a following
attributive adjective:

(173)   *daou dra* 'two things'
             un + tra + mat → un dra vat 'a good thing'

7.6.5   Number

The Breton noun distinguishes three numbers: singular, plural and dual. A
detailed description of the highly complex relations of number categories is
given in Trépos (1957).

7.6.5.1   Singular stems
From the singular stem, the plural is usually formed by adding a plural suffix,
with or without concomitant umlaut and/or various other modifications of the
stem. Sometimes the plural is formed by umlaut alone or, in some cases, by
suppletion.

There is a large number of plural suffixes. The most commonly occurring are
-où, -ioù and *-ed*. Others are *-i, -ier, -ien, -iz, -on, -en, -ez, -eier*, etc. There are
no morphological rules for predicting the plural suffix. Examples:

(174)   Various suffixes with or without stem modifications:

Singular		Plural
aval	'apple'	*avaloù*
taol	'table'	*taolioù*
labous	'bird'	*laboused*
bran	'raven'	*brini*
yalc'h	'purse'	*yilc'hier*
kloc'h	'bell'	*kleier* (suffix *-ier*)
mab	'son'	*mibien*
Breizhad	'Breton (inhabitant of Brittany)'	*Breizhiz*
gad	'hare'	*gedon*
lamm	'leap, bound'	*lemmen*
ti	'house'	*tiez*

(175)   Umlaut alone:

Singular		Plural
dant	'tooth'	*dent*
maen	'stone'	*mein*
dañvad	'sheep'	*deñved*

(176)   Suppletion:

	Singular	Plural
	ejen 'ox'	*oc'hen*
(cf. 304))	*ki* 'dog'	*chas*

(177)   Unclassifiable:

	Singular	Plural
	breur 'brother'	*breudeur*
	bugel 'child'	*bugale*

Some nouns may form two plurals, one usually in *-où* or *-ioù*, the second usually in *-eier*. The first is semantically neutral, whereas the plural in *-eier* emphasises diversity:

(178)   SG *park* 'field'   PL₁ *parkoù*   PL₂ *parkeier*

Some nouns may add a second plural suffix to a plural form. The double plurals usually have a specialised meaning:

(179)

Singular	Plural₁	Plural₂
bugel 'child'	*bugale* 'children'	*bugaleoù* 'groups of children'
merc'h 'daughter'	*merc'hed*	*merc'hedoù*

Diminutives add the plural suffix twice, after the stem and after the diminutive suffix:

(180)

Singular	Plural
bag 'boat'	*bagoù*
bagig 'little boat'	*bagoùigoù*

7.6.5.2   Collective stems

Collectives behave grammatically as plurals. From the collective stem, the singulative is formed by adding the suffix *-enn*, sometimes with concomitant modification of the stem. All singulatives are feminine.

(181)

Collective		Singulative	
merien	'ants'	*merienenn*	'ant'
gwez	'trees'	*gwezenn*	'tree'
mouar	'blackberries'	*mouarenn*	'blackberry'
blev	'hair (COLL)'	*blevenn*	'hair (SG)'

In many cases, collectives and the singulatives derived from them express semantic relations that have to be paraphrased in other languages:

(182)

Collective		Singulative	
geot	'grass'	*geotenn*	'blade of grass'
raden	'bracken'	*radenenn*	'plant of bracken'
kouevr	'copper'	*kouevrenn*	'piece of copper'
gwer	'glass (material)'	*gwerenn*	'(1) drinking-glass, (2) window-pane'

A special case is *moc'h* 'pigs' which is usually included among the collective stems. Its singulative is *pemoc'h* 'pig'.

7.6.5.3   Dual

The dual can be formed only from nouns that designate parts of the body or pieces of clothing that occur in pairs. It is normally formed by prefixing *daou-* to masculine nouns, *div-* or *di-* to feminine nouns. All three prefixes lenite the stem. Some nouns have additional modifications of the stem.

(183)

Singular			Dual
lagad	(MASC)	'eye'	*daoulagad*
dorn	(MASC)	'hand'	*daouarn*
glin	(MASC)	'knee'	*daoulin*
skouarn	(FEM)	'ear'	*divskouarn*
gar	(FEM)	'leg'	*divhar*
bronn	(FEM)	'female breast'	*divronn*

Although the dual is a relatively recent development in Breton and its formation is still transparent etymologically (i.e. it involves the numeral 'two'), there can be no doubt that it now represents an independent number category. The use of the dual is obligatory in appropriate contexts. It does not involve any emphasis on the number 'two', for example:

(184)   *gwalc'hiñ a   ran   va daouarn*
          wash   VPT I-do my two-hands
          'I am washing my hands'

If emphasis on the number 'two' is desired, the numeral 'two' is added to the dual:

(185)   *va daou daoulin* 'my two knees'

For other ways of formation and for examples of the complexity of the system, see Ternes (1970: 191f., 200f., 206–10).

7.6.5.4   Complexity of number system

This number categories of Breton (singular, plural, dual, collective, singulative) form a highly complex system, which allows very subtle shades of meaning. All categories are inter-related in a complicated way.

An example: the singular stem *pesk* 'fish' forms the plural by adding the plural suffix *-ed*. The plural form thus obtained at the same time functions as a collective stem from which a singulative is derived by adding the suffix *-enn*. From the singulative, a new plural is formed by adding the plural suffix *-où*:

(186)   SG   *pesk* 'fish (SG)'
          PL/COLL   *pesked* 'fish (PL)'
          SGT   *peskedenn* 'single fish (out of a mass)'
          PL   *peskedennoù* 'single fishes'

From the dual forms, a plural is derived. It is used when speaking of the respective organs or pieces of clothing of several people:

(187)   SG *lagad* 'eye'
          DU *daoulagad* '(two) eyes'
          PL *daoulagadoù* 'pairs of eyes'

For further details, see Trépos (1957).

7.6.6   Case

Breton has no case distinctions.

7.6.7   Declensional classes

Since there are no case distinctions in Breton, declensional classes in the traditional sense do not exist. The most convenient way of classifying Breton nouns morphologically is according to plural formation.

7.6.8   Pronouns

7.6.8.1   Person

The following set of personal pronouns occurs only under syntactically stressed conditions, comparable to French *moi*, *toi*, *eux*, etc.

(188)

		Singular	Plural
1		*me*	*ni*
2		*te*	*c'hwi*
3	MASC	*eñ*	*i* or *int*
	FEM	*hi*	

Examples:

(189)   *Setu hi.* 'There she is' (cf. (89)).

(190)   *Piv en deus graet an dra-se?. Me.*
          'Who has done that? Me.'

See also sentence (11).

For the use of pronominals as direct object in verbal phrases, see 7.4.7; for indirect objects, see 7.10.

Demonstratives
Since the majority of demonstrative forms involve nominal phrases, all demonstratives are treated in the chapter on phrase structure (7.3.4).

Interrogatives
Some of the most common interrogatives are: *piv* 'who?', *pet* 'how many?'. Most other interrogatives are compounds with *pe* 'what? which?'. All of the following are stressed on the syllable immediately following *pe-*: *petra* 'what?', *pehini* 'which (SG)?', *pere* 'which (PL)?', *pelec'h* 'where?', *penaos* 'how?', *pegoulz* 'when?', *pegeit* 'how long?', *perak* 'why?', *peseurt* 'what kind of?'

7.6.8.2   Other pronominals: 'one', 'thing', etc.
The impersonal pronoun 'one' may be translated by *an den*, lit. 'the man', or by one of the plural personal pronouns (7.6.8.1) *ni* 'we', *c'hwi* 'you', *i* (*int*) 'they'. A more idiomatic way of translating the impersonal 'one' is by using the impersonal forms of the verb (7.9.4; cf. sentences (50)–(52)).

'Nothing' is translated by *netra*, in negative sentences *tra*, lit. 'thing'; *nikun* or *den ebet* 'nobody', in negative sentences *den*, lit. 'man'.

7.7 ADJECTIVES

7.7.1 Structure: stems and endings

The minimal independent unit in adjective morphology is the simple stem, for example *nevez* 'new'. Derived stems are formed by adding a prefix to a simple stem (adjectival, nominal or verbal), for example *dis-* (privative prefix) + *heñvel* 'similar' → *disheñvel* 'different'; *di-* (privative prefix) + *skiant* 'knowledge, sense' → *diskiant* 'senseless, foolish'. Compound stems are rare: *nevez* 'new' + *ganet* 'born' → *nevez c'hanet* 'newly born'.

The only inflectional category for adjectives (apart from initial mutations, 7.18.6) is comparison.

7.7.2 Comparison

The main morphological process in adjective comparison is suffixation. There are three degrees of comparison: positive (stem), comparative (suffix *-oc'h*) and superlative (suffix *-añ*). The comparative and superlative suffixes cause the morphophonological stem alternations described in 7.18.2.

(191)	Positive	Comparative	Superlative
	brav 'nice, pretty'	*bravoc'h*	*bravañ*
	kriz 'cruel, rude'	*krisoc'h*	*krisañ*
	gleb 'wet'	*glepoc'h*	*glepañ*

Suppletive stems:

(192)	Positive	Comparative	Superlative
	mat 'good'	*gwelloc'h*	*gwellañ*
	fall 'bad'	*gwashoc'h*	*gwashañ*
	kalz 'much'	*mui, muioc'h*	*muiañ*

7.7.3 Adjectival classes

There is no need for setting up adjectival classes in morphology.

7.7.4 Adverbs

Adverbs do not form a separate morphological class in Breton. They do not differ morphologically from adjectives (see also (129)):

(193)	*un den mat*	'a good man'
	labourat a ra mat	'he/she works well'

7.8   NUMERALS

The Breton numerals combine elements of the decimal system with the vigesimal system. There is one instance of the duodecimal system: *triwec'h* '18 (=3×6)'.

7.8.1   Cardinal numbers

The numbers 2–4 and combinations thereof (22–24 etc.) distinguish a masculine and a feminine form and agree accordingly with the gender of the accompanying noun (see 7.6.4). The numbers 11–19 are combinations with *dek* 'ten' (except 18). For 21–29, *warn* (an alternant of the preposition *war* 'on') is used as the linking element, whereas the tens from 30 on use *ha* 'and'. The numeral 50 means literally 'half-hundred'.

(194)

1 *unan*	11 *unnek*	21 *unan warn-ugent*	
2 *daou* (MASC)	12 *daouzek*	22 *daou (div) warn-ugent*	
div (FEM)	13 *trizek*	23 *tri (teir) warn-ugent*	
3 *tri* (MASC)	14 *pevarzek*	30 *tregont*	
teir (FEM)	15 *pemzek*	31 *unan ha tregont*	
4 *pevar* (MASC)	16 *c'hwezek*	32 *daou (div) ha tregont*	
peder (FEM)	17 *seitek*	40 *daou-ugent*	
5 *pemp*	18 *triwec'h*	41 *unan ha daou-ugent*	
6 *c'hwec'h*	19 *naontek*	50 *hanter-kant*	
7 *seizh*	20 *ugent*	51 *unan ha hanter-kant*	
8 *eizh*		60 *tri-ugent*	
9 *nav*		61 *unan ha tri-ugent*	
10 *dek*		70 *dek ha tri-ugent*	
		71 *unnek ha tri-ugent*	
		80 *pevar-ugent*	
		81 *unan ha pevar-ugent*	
200 *daou c'hant*		90 *dek ha pevar-ugent*	
300 *tri c'hant*		91 *unnek ha pevar-ugent*	
400 *pevar c'hant*		100 *kant*	
500 *pemp kant*			
1,000 *mil*			

For the tens within the hundreds, a change has taken place over the last two or three generations. New forms are modelled on the French pattern:

(195)

	Old	New
110	*dek ha kant*	*kant dek*
120	*c'hwec'h-ugent*	*kant ugent*
130	*dek ha c'hwec'h-ugent*	*kant tregont*

140 *seizh-ugent*   *kant daou-ugent*
160 *eizh-ugent* etc.   *kant tri-ugent etc.*

For the use of numerals in nominal phrases, see 7.3.5.

7.8.2   Ordinal numbers

Ordinal numbers are formed from the cardinals by adding the suffix *-vet* (with the allomorph *-et* in some cases), but 'first' to 'fourth' have irregular forms. The ordinal numbers are usually preceded by the definite article (7.3.3), for example *ar c'hentañ* 'the first', *an eil* 'the second', *ar pempet* 'the fifth'.

(196)					
	1st	*kentañ*		11th	*unnekvet*
	2nd	*eil*		20th	*ugentvet*
	3rd	*trede*		30th	*tregontvet*
	4th	*pevare*		40th	*daou-ugentvet*
	5th	*pempet*		50th	*hanter-kantvet*
	6th	*c'hwec'hvet*		60th	*tri-ugentvet*
	7th	*seizhvet*		70th	*dekvet ha tri-ugent*
	8th	*eizhvet*		80th	*pevar-ugentvet*
	9th	*navet*		90th	*dekvet ha pevar-ugent*
	10th	*dekvet*		100th	*kantvet*

7.9   VERBS

7.9.1   Structure: stems and endings

The minimal unit in verb morphology is the simple stem, for example *gwalc'h-* 'to wash', *stag-* 'to attach, to join'. Derived stems are usually obtained through the addition of prefixes, for example the privative prefix *di-*: *distag-* 'to detach, to unbind'. Certain forms, often termed verbal particles in traditional grammars, are best interpreted as derivative prefixes, for example the reflexive *en em*: *en em walc'h-* 'to wash oneself' (see 7.4.3).

Verbal stems are usually inflected by suffixation, sometimes accompanied by umlaut. A few verbs have suppletive stems (7.19). In finite forms, the normal order of elements is stem – tense marker – person marker.

7.9.2   Verb systems: finite/non-finite; dependent/independent

The finite verb forms are treated in 7.9.3–4. The non-finite verb forms are verbal noun, past (passive) participle and present (active) participle. In conformity with usage in Celtic studies, we prefer the term 'verbal noun' to 'infinitive' because of the marked nominal properties of that form.

The verbal noun is usually formed from the stem by adding a suffix (with or without concomitant umlaut), including a zero suffix. A few verbs have suppletive stems.

There is a very high number of verbal-noun suffixes. By far the most common is *-añ*. Others are zero, *-iñ, -at, -al, -out, -a, -et, -el, -ek, -ezh, -er, -en, -n* etc. There are no morphological rules for predicting the verbal-noun suffix. Examples:

(197)	Stem	Verbal noun	
	mal-	*malañ*	'to grind'
	klemm-	*klemm*	'to complain'
	sko-	*skeiñ*	'to strike, to beat'
	gwri-	*gwriat*	'to sew'
	nij-	*nijal*	'to fly'
	kav-	*kavout*	'to find'
	pesket-	*pesketa*	'to fish' (7.18.2.)
	kousk-	*kousket*	'to sleep'
	marv-	*mervel*	'to die'
	red-	*redek*	'to run'
	laer-	*laerezh*	'to steal, to rob'
	embreg-	*embreger*	'to undertake, to handle'
	doug-	*dougen*	'to carry'
	ere-	*eren*	'to bind, to fetter'

With dissimilation (and umlaut):

(198)	Stem	Verbal noun	
	galv-	*gervel*	'to call'

Suppletion and other irregularities:

(199)	Stem	Verbal noun	
	Ø (zero)	*mont*	'to go'
	gr-	*ober*	'to do, to make'
	deu-	*dont*	'to come'

The past participle is formed from the stem by adding the suffix *-et* (selected examples from (197)):

(200)	*malet*	'ground'	*kousket*	'slept'
	klemmet	'complained'	*redet*	'run'
	skoet	'struck'	*ereet*	'bound'

The present participle is formed by particles preceding the verbal noun. In orthography, these 'particles' represent separate words. In a structural description, however, they are best analysed as prefixes. Unlike the past participle, the present participle may not be used as an attributive in a nominal phrase (see 7.4.5).

There are two particles (or prefixes) for forming the present participle: *o* (followed by mixed mutation) and *en ur* (followed by lenition); see 7.18.7.

(201)	*debriñ* 'to eat'	*o tebriñ, en ur zebriñ* 'eating'
	kerzhout 'to walk'	*o kerzhout, en ur gerzhout* 'walking'

The distinction between dependent and independent conjugation, in the sense of Old Irish and historical Celtic grammar, has not survived in Modern Breton. But other systems of syntactically conditioned conjugations have emerged instead and are of central importance in Breton syntax (see 7.2.1, 7.2.3).

7.9.3   Tense, aspect, mood

Modern Breton has six tenses: present, future, preterite, imperfect, conditional, imperative. The characteristic tense markers are as follows:

Present: zero
Future: *-o*
Preterite: *-j*
Imperfect: *-e*
Conditional: *-fe, -je* (i.e. *-f, -j* plus imperfect)
Imperative: zero

The difference between preterite and imperfect, both being past tenses, is an aspectual one: the preterite is used for a momentary action in the past, the imperfect for a habitual action or one of long duration in the past. The difference is comparable to the one between *passé simple* and *imparfait* in French. In Modern Breton, use of the preterite is restricted to the literary language. In the everyday spoken language it is usually replaced by the perfect (7.4.4). This is again in conformity with tendencies in modern spoken French.

The two conditionals are sometimes referred to as present conditional (*-fe*) and past conditional (*-je*), although this distinction is not observed any more. Both conditionals are used indiscriminately in the present-day language.

The verb *bezañ* 'to be' has, in addition to the six tenses enumerated above, two aspectual sets with two tenses each: habitual (present and imperfect) and situational (present and imperfect, see 7.2.2.1). They have the complete set of seven persons for each tense.

(202)	Habitual	Situational
	bezan 'I am usually'	*emaon* 'I am located'
	bezen 'I used to be'	*edon* 'I was located'

The verb *kaout* 'to have', which historically derives from *bezañ* 'to be', has the corresponding habitual tenses (present and imperfect), but not the situational ones:

(203)   *me am bez* 'I have usually'
          me am beze 'I used to have'

The generally accepted view is that there are no mood distinctions in Modern Breton. The future in Modern Breton, however, derives historically from the present subjunctive and may still be interpreted as such in Old Breton. This is reflected in some syntactic usages of the future in the modern language:

(204)   *fellout a   ra   din   ma teuio*
          want   VPT does to-me that will-come
          'I should like him/her to come' (lit. 'that he/she may come')

(205)   *ra vezo   ar peoc'h ganeoc'h!*
          PT will-be the peace with-you (PL)
          'May peace be with you (PL)' (cf. (295))

7.9.4   Personal/impersonal; active/passive

The Breton verb has the usual six persons (first, second and third singular and plural) plus a seventh person which is best termed *impersonal*, for example *karer* 'one loves'. The imperative has five persons (second and third singular; first, second and third plural), two of which (third singular and plural) are used very rarely.

The suffixes commonly associated with the respective persons are:

(206) | Singular | Plural | Impersonal |
          |----------|--------|------------|
          | 1 *-n* | *-mp* | *-r, -d* |
          | 2 *-z, -s* | *-t, -c'h* | |
          | 3 zero | *-nt* | |

The distinction between *-z* and *-s* in the second person singular is an artificial orthographic device to avoid homography of second person singular present and imperfect.

There are no simple finite passive forms in Breton. The use of 'passive' for the impersonal is not to be recommended. Passive forms do exist, however, on phrase level (7.4.6).

(207)   Paradigm of the regular verb

          (Example: ST *kar-* 'to love', VN *karout*)

	Present	Future	Preterite	Imperfect	Conditional I	Conditional II	Imperative
SG 1	karan	karin	karis	karen	karfen	karjen	
2	karez	kari	karjout	kares	karfes	karjes	kar
3	kar	karo	karas	kare	karfe	karje	karet

PL	1	karomp	karimp	karjomp	karemp	karfemp	karjemp	karomp
	2	karit	karot	karjoc'h	karec'h	karfec'h	karjec'h	karit
	3	karont	karint	karjont	karent	karfent	karjent	karent
IMPERS		karer	karor	karjod	kared	karfed	karjed	

The most important irregular verbs are *bezañ* 'to be', *ober* 'to do, to make', *mont* 'to go', *gouzout* 'to know'.

A very special case is the verb *kaout* (or *endevout*) 'to have'. Breton is the only modern Celtic language which possesses a verb with the meaning 'to have'. In the other Celtic languages, possession is expressed by prepositional phrases of the type 'there is . . . at me'. The existence of a specific verb 'to have' is one of the Continental (as opposed to Insular) typological features of Breton (see Ternes 1979).

The inflected forms of the verb *kaout* 'to have' consist of the element *eus* (one of the numerous suppletive stems of *bezañ* 'to be'), which expresses tense, and a preceding element which expresses person. The latter is very similar in form to the possessives in noun phrases (7.3.6). A form like *am eus* 'I have' may be translated literally by 'my being'. Morphologically speaking, therefore, the Breton verb 'to have' has nominal rather than verbal inflection, although syntactically it behaves in most respects like other verbs. The verb 'to have' has no impersonal forms:

(208)

			Present	Future	Imperfect	Preterite
SG	1		am eus	am bo	am boa	am boe etc.
	2		az peus	az po	az poa	
	3	MASC	en deus	en devo	en doa	Conditional I
		FEM	he deus	he devo	he doa	am befe etc.
PL	1		hon eus	hor bo	hor boa	
	2		ho peus	ho po	ho poa	Conditional II
	3		o deus	o devo	o doa	am bije etc.

7.10   PRONOMINAL PREPOSITIONS

Simple prepositions (See 7.5.1) like *a* 'of', *da* 'to', *evit* 'for', *war* 'on', *gant* 'with', *hep* 'without', *ouzh* 'against' and others are inflected for person, number and gender (third person singular only). There are two principal sets of suffixes:

(209)

		Singular		Plural	
	1	-on	-in	-omp	-imp, -eomp
	2	-out	-it	-oc'h	-oc'h, -eoc'h
	3	MASC	-añ		-o
		FEM	-i		

The stem used for inflection differs in most cases from the form of the preposition used before a noun in nominal phrases (7.5.1), for example *dirak* 'in front of' (*dirak an ti* 'in front of the house') is inflected on the stem *diraz-*. With respect to stem alternations and the set of suffixes used, inflected prepositions fall into eight paradigms, of which four characteristic examples are given below: (210) has no stem alternations; (211) has non-initial mutation (7.18.2); (212) has morphophonological stress shift (7.16.1); and (213) has irregular stems.

		(210) *dre* 'through'	(211) *evel* 'like'	(212) *ouzh* 'against'	(213) *a* 'of'
SG 1		*drezon*	*eveldon*	*ouzhin* (-´)	*ac'hanon*
2		*drezout*	*eveldout*	*ouzhit* (-´)	*ac'hanout*
3	MASC	*drezañ*	*eveltañ*	*outañ* (´-)	*anezhañ*
	FEM	*drezi*	*evelti*	*outi* (´-)	*anezhi*
PL 1		*drezomp*	*eveldomp*	*ouzhimp* (-´)	*ac'hanomp*
2		*drezoc'h*	*eveldoc'h*	*ouzhoc'h* (-´)	*ac'hanoc'h*
3		*drezo*	*evelto*	*outo* (´-)	*anezho*

7.11   WORD FORMATION

7.11.1   Compound words

Compounding is a common process of word formation for nouns. It is rare for adjectives and the other major word classes (but see 7.5.2).

Compound nouns: When the first element is attributive to the second, the latter always undergoes lenition (214). When the second element is attributive to the first, the second element is lenited after a feminine singular noun: lenition in (216 SG), no lenition in (215) and (216 PL).

(214)   *mor* 'sea' + *kazh* 'cat' → *morgazh* 'cuttle fish'
          penn 'head' + *kêr* 'city' → *penngêr* 'capital'

(215)   *penn* (MASC) 'head' + *glaou* 'coal' → *pennglaou* 'titmouse'
          droug (MASC) 'pain' + *mor* 'sea' → *droug-mor* 'seasickness'

(216)   *askell* (FEM) 'wing' + *kroc'henn* 'skin' → *askell-groc'henn* 'bat' (PL *eskell-kroc'henn*)

In some cases, the two elements of the compound are felt to form a particularly close unit, so that sandhi (7.15), against the rule, is shown in orthography:

(217)   *kreiz* 'middle' + *deiz* 'day' → *kreisteiz* 'noon'

Compound adjectives:

(218)   *noazh* 'naked' + *troad* 'foot' → *noazhtroad* 'barefoot'

7.11.2   Derivational word classes

Derivation by means of prefixes and suffixes is a very common process for all major word classes. Some of the most common derivational affixes are exemplified below:

Prefixes:

(219)   *di-* or *dis-* (privative):
    kargañ 'to load, to fill'   *digargañ* 'to unload, to empty'
    plegañ 'to fold'   *displegañ* 'to unfold'
    kempenn 'orderly'   *digempenn* 'disorderly'

(220)   *peur-* (perfective):
    debriñ 'to eat' – *peurzebriñ* 'to eat up'

(221)   *ken-* or *kem-* 'co-':
    breur 'brother'   *kenvreur* 'fellow, confrère'
    pred 'time, moment'   *kempred* 'contemporary (ADJ)'

Suffixes:

(222)   *-er* (agent nouns):
    milin 'mill' – *miliner* 'miller'

(223)   *-ez* (feminine), also following *-er*:
    ki 'dog'   *kiez* 'bitch'
    labour 'work'   *labourer* 'worker'   *labourerez* 'female worker'

(224)   *-ad* (inhabitant), PL *-iz* (174):
    Breizh 'Brittany' – *Breizhad* 'Breton (inhabitant of Brittany)', PL *Breizhiz*

(225)   *-ad* (content):
    dorn 'hand' – *dornad* 'handful'

(226)   *-vezh* (duration):
    mintin 'morning' – *mintinvezh* 'duration of morning'

(227)   *-ig* (diminutive for nouns), *-ik* (for adjectives):
    levr 'book'   *levrig* 'booklet'
    berr 'short'   *berrik* 'rather short'

The difference between *-ig* and *-ik* is an artificial orthographical device to differentiate nouns from adjectives. It has no foundation whatsoever in the structure of the language.

(228)   *-ezh*, *-ded*, *-der*, etc. (forming abstract nouns from adjectives):
    pinvidik 'rich'   *pinvidigezh* 'richness'
    uhel 'high'   *uhelded, uhelder* 'height'

(229)   *-adur* (result of an action):
          leskiñ (ST *losk-*) 'to burn' – *loskadur* 'burn (wound produced by burning)'

(230)   *-ek, -us* (forming adjectives from nouns):
          barv 'beard'   *barvek* 'bearded'
          mergl 'rust'   *merglus* 'rusty'

SOUND SYSTEM

7.12   CONSONANT SYSTEM

7.12.1   Single consonants

The standard Breton consonant system comprises twenty segmental units: /p, t, k, b, d, g, m, n, ɲ, l, ʎ, r, f, s, ʃ, x, h, v, z, ʒ/. For semi-vowels, see 7.13.4.

/p/:	bilabial, voiceless, aspirated stop
/t/:	apico-dental, voiceless, aspirated stop
/k/:	dorso-velar, voiceless, aspirated stop
/b/:	bilabial, voiced stop
/d/:	apico-dental, voiced stop
/g/:	dorso-velar, voiced stop
/m/:	bilabial nasal
/n/:	apico-dental nasal
/ɲ/:	predorso-palatal nasal
/l/:	apico-dental lateral
/ʎ/:	predorso-palatal lateral
/r/:	for the majority of speakers a postdorso-uvular vibrant [ʀ] or corresponding voiced fricative [ʁ], for some speakers of the older generation an apico-dental vibrant [r]
/f/:	labio-dental, voiceless fricative
/s/:	lamino-dental, voiceless fricative (sibilant)
/ʃ/:	lamino-palatoalveolar, voiceless fricative (shibilant)
/x/:	dorso-velar, voiceless fricative
/h/:	glottal, voiceless fricative
/v/:	labio-dental, voiced fricative
/z/:	lamino-dental, voiced fricative (sibilant)
/ʒ/:	lamino-palatoalveolar, voiced fricative (shibilant)

The spoken dialects of Léon have an additional phoneme /f̬/, which is not recognised by all grammarians as a phoneme of the standard language. /f̬/ is a

labio-dental, voiced, fortis fricative, as opposed to /f/, which is voiceless and
fortis, and to /v/, which is voiced and lenis (this is a re-interpretation of the
description in Ternes (1977a: 185); see also Falc'hun (1951: 33)).

7.12.2   Consonant clusters (without semi-vowels)

7.12.2.1   Initial consonant clusters
Two consonants: /pl, pr, tl, tr, kl, kr, bl, br, dl, dr, gl, gr, fl, fr, sp, st, sk/. A few
other two-consonant clusters may occur marginally. The following clusters do
not normally occur in base forms, but do appear in initial position as a result of
initial mutation (7.18.1): /xl, xr, zl, zr, vl, vr/.

Three consonants: /spl, spr, stl, str, skl, skr/.

7.12.2.2   Final consonant clusters
Two consonants: /pl, pr, tr, kl, kr, fr, mp, nt, nk, lp, lt, lk, lm, lf, ls, lx, rp, rt, rk,
rm, rn, rl, rf, rs, rʃ, rx, st, sk/. A few other two-consonant clusters may occur
marginally. There is a tendency to reduce clusters of which the second member
is /l/ or /r/ to a single consonant by dropping /l/ or /r/.

Three consonants: All final three-consonant clusters have /l/ or /r/ as their third
member: /rkl, str, skl/, and possibly a few others. All of them are of limited
occurrence. There is in addition a tendency to reduce them to two-consonant
clusters by dropping /l/ or /r/.

7.12.2.3   Medial consonant clusters
The number of medial consonant clusters is rather high. Therefore the following
lists may not claim exhaustiveness. It is also difficult to distinguish in every case
between assimilated and non-assimilated loans from French.

The following clusters occur within base forms. Clusters resulting from
morphological processes – that is, clusters immediately preceded or followed by
a morpheme boundary, as well as clusters containing a morpheme boundary –
are not included. Inclusion of these clusters would further increase the number
of items in the following lists.

Two consonants: /pl, pr, tr, kl, kr, bl, br, dr, gr, mp, mz, nt, nk, nd, lp, lt, lk, ld,
lg, lf, ls, lʃ, lx, lv, rp, rt, rk, rb, rd, rg, rm, rn, rl, rf, rs, rʃ, rx, rv, rz, rʒ, fr, fl, sp,
st, sk, sf, xl, vr/.

Three consonants: /spl, skl, spr, str, ltr, mpl, mpr, mbr/.

7.12.3   Consonant length

This is not phonemically distinctive (but see 7.12.5 and 7.13.1).

7.12.4   Consonant classes

The consonant classes emerge from the arrangement of table 7.1, which disregards phonemically redundant features. For speakers using a dental [r], the vibrant /r/ has to be assigned to the dental column.

7.12.5   Range of consonant realisations

The phonetic realisation of the standard Breton consonant phonemes corresponds to the respective values of the IPA symbols used above, except for the following cases:

> Voiceless stops are aspirated (medium degree of aspiration): /p, t, k/ = [pʻ, tʻ, kʻ].
> /n/ has the allophone [ŋ] before /k, g/.
> Uvular /r/ is ideally a uvular vibrant [ʀ], but is often realised as a postdorso-uvular voiced fricative [ʁ]. Especially in the latter case, this may lead to reduction of the consonant clusters /rx/ and /xr/ to a single consonant /x/: for example, *marc'h* 'horse' /marx/ → /max/. This reduction does not occur with speakers using dental [r].
> /r, l/ have devoiced allophones [ʀ̥] or [r̥], [l̥] in final position after voiceless consonants, that is in final clusters such as /pr, tr, fr, kl, str, skl/ etc.: for example, *istr* 'oysters' /iːstr/ [iːstʀ̥] (see 7.12.2.2 for possible reduction of these clusters).
> /n, l, r/ are slightly lengthened in intervocalic position after short stressed vowel, [nˑ, lˑ, ʀˑ]: for example, *tennañ* 'to pull' ['tɛnˑɑ̃].

7.13   VOWEL SYSTEM

7.13.1   Monophthongs, diphthongs and vowel length

For the system of monophthongs, one has to distinguish between Haut-Léon (eastern part of the Léon area) and Bas-Léon (western part). Both varieties are equally acceptable as standard pronunciations, although the former corresponds more closely to orthography. The difference is to be found in the number of long-vowel phonemes.

Table 7.1. *Consonant phonemes*

	Labial	Dental	Palatal	Velar	Glottal
Voiceless stops	p	t		k	
Voiced stops	b	d		g	
Nasals	m	n	ɲ		
Laterals		l	ʎ		
Vibrant				r	
Voiceless fricatives	f	s	ʃ	x	h
Voiced fricatives	v	z	ʒ		

Short-vowel phonemes are identical for both varieties: /i, e, a, y, ø, u, o/.

/i/:	front, close, unrounded vowel
/e/:	front, mid, unrounded vowel
/a/:	central, open, unrounded vowel
/y/:	front, close, rounded vowel
/ø/:	front, mid, rounded vowel
/u/:	back, close, rounded vowel
/o/:	back, mid, rounded vowel

The long vowels for Haut-Léon are: /iː, eː, aː, yː, øː, uː, oː/. There is in addition a marginal phoneme /ɛː/, which is of limited occurrence. The long vowels for Bas-Léon are: /iː, eː, ɛː, aː, yː, øː, œː, uː, oː, ɔː/.

/eː/:	front, half-close, unrounded vowel
/ɛː/:	front, half-open, unrounded vowel
/øː/:	front, half-close, rounded vowel
/œː/:	front, half-open, rounded vowel
/oː/:	back, half-close, rounded vowel
/ɔː/:	back, half-open, rounded vowel

Long vowels occur only in stressed syllables.

Nasalisation is phonemically distinctive for all vowel qualities. Quantity of nasalised vowels is predictable except for the open vowel. Thus, the full set of nasalised vowel phonemes is /ĩ, ẽ, ã, ãː, ỹ, ø̃, ũ, õ/.

Vowel quantity is normally regarded as being phonemically distinctive. Its functional load, however, is rather low. In fact, vowel quantity is distinctive only before /n, l, r/. A minimal pair is *dall* /dal/ 'blind' vs *dal* /daːl/ 'take!'. In all other instances, vowel quantity is predictable from the following consonant or consonant cluster, although the rules are rather complex (see Ternes 1977a: 186f., 189–91).

On the other hand, it was stated in 7.12.5 that precisely /n, l, r/ have lengthened allophones in intervocalic position after short stressed vowel. Therefore it would, theoretically, be possible to attribute the distinction of vowel quantity to consonant length. Such a solution would further reduce the functional load of vowel quantity, while it would, on the other hand, introduce a phonemic quantity distinction for consonants. The problem as a whole is not unlike the one found in Swedish and Norwegian, where it is difficult to decide whether the distinction [VC:] vs [V:C] is attributable to vowel or to consonant length.

There are several reasons that seem to speak in favour of distinctive *vowel* quantity in standard Breton: (1) the very complexity of the rules that would predict vowel quantity; (2) the phonemic diasystem of Breton dialects – there are Breton dialects where functional load of vowel quantity is higher than in Léon, and which have no lengthened consonantal allophones; (3) the typology of Celtic languages – if one adopted the alternative solution, Breton would be the only one among the modern Celtic languages without distinctive vowel quantity. This, however, seems too radical a decision. It remains a fact, however, that vowel quantity has a rather weak phonemic status in Modern Breton, probably the weakest among the modern Celtic languages.

Standard Breton has eight diphthongs (seven oral, one nasal): /ei̯, ey̆, eǫ, iṷ, oṷ, ae̞, aǫ, ãõ̯/. There is no quantity distinction for diphthongs.

7.13.2   Vowel classes

The standard Breton vowel phonemes represent a triangular system with three classes (front unrounded, front rounded, back rounded) and three or four degrees of opening. Short vowels have unequivocally three degrees of opening. Long vowels have three degrees of opening in Haut-Léon (with, in addition, a marginal phoneme /ɛ:/), and four degrees of opening in Bas-Léon.

Length is distinctive, although its functional load is low. Nasalisation is distinctive for all vowel qualities. There is only one pair of nasalised vowel phonemes differentiated by quantity, and there is only one pair of diphthongs differentiated by nasalisation.

Vowel classes may be shown graphically by the following diagrams:

Short vowels: i y   u   *Nasalised vowels:* ĩ ỹ   ũ
                    e ø o   ẽ ø̃ õ
                       a   ã(:)

Long vowels: (Haut-Léon) i: y: u:⟩
               e: ø: o: ⟩ + marginal ɛ:
                 a: ⟩

Long vowels: (Bas-Léon) i: y: u:
              e: ø: o:
               ɛ: œ: ɔ:
                  a:

Diphthongs:

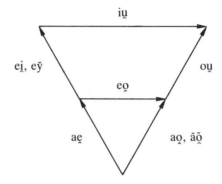

7.13.3   Range of vowel realisations

The phonetic realisation of the close vowels /i, y, u/, long and short, oral and nasalised, is close to the cardinal values [i, y, u].

The open vowel /a/, both long and short, is intermediate between front [a] and back [ɑ]. The nasalised counterpart /ã/, both long and short, has a marked back quality: [ɑ̃, ɑ̃:]

Long /e:, ø:, o:/ and /ɛ:, œ:, ɔ:/ are close to the respective cardinal values [e:, ø:, o:, ɛ:, œ:, ɔ:].

Short stressed /e, ø, o/ have the half-open quality of cardinal [ɛ, œ, ɔ]. In unstressed syllables, the precise quality of short /e, ø, o/ varies between half-close [e, ø, o] and half-open [ɛ, œ, ɔ] or any intermediate stage between the two according to a complex set of rules, the decisive factors of which are syllable structure (rather more open vowel quality in closed syllables, rather more closed in open syllables) and the quality of vowels in neighbouring syllables, especially stressed ones, of the same word. One may even speak, on the phonetic level, of a slight tendency towards vowel harmony with respect to degree of opening, for example:

(231)   logodenn /logo:den/ [lo'go:den] 'mouse'
          vs logota /logota/ [lɔ'gɔta] 'to catch mice'

The degree of opening of the stressed vowel /o:/ [o:] vs. /o/ [ɔ] in each word determines in turn the quality of the preceding unstressed /o/.

Oral vowels are often slightly nasalised when adjacent to nasal consonants. This non-distinctive nasalisation is clearly weaker than phonemically distinctive nasalisation.

Nasalised /ẽ, ø̃/ are half-open [ɛ̃, œ̃], whereas nasalised /õ/ is half-close [õ].

The precise phonetic values of the diphthongs are: /ei̯, ey̆/ = [ɛi̯, ɛy̆]; /eo̯/ = [ɛõ̯]; /ou̯/ = [ɔu̯]; /iu̯/ = [iu̯]; /ae̯, ao̯/ = [ae̯, ao̯]; /ãõ/ = [ãõ].

In unstressed syllables, all vowels are short. A phonemically long vowel is shortened when it loses stress as a result of morphological processes or sentence stress. In stressed syllables, length is phonemic for all oral vowels and for /ã/. For the remaining nasalised vowels, quantity in stressed syllables depends on the following consonant or consonant cluster (for details, see Ternes 1977a: 187–91).

7.13.4   Semi-vowels

Standard Breton has three semi-vowels: /j, ɥ, w/.

/j/:   predorso-palatal voiced approximant or fricative
/ɥ/:   front-rounded voiced approximant, corresponding phone-
       tically to non-syllabic [y̆].
/w/:   back-rounded voiced approximant, corresponding phone-
       tically to non-syllabic [u̯].

7.14   SYLLABLE STRUCTURE

Each syllable has an obligatory vocalic nucleus (short vowel, long vowel or diphthong), with or without a preceding and/or following consonant or consonant cluster. Consonant clusters consist maximally of three consonants (see, however, 7.12.2.2 for the tendency of reducing final three-consonant clusters to two-consonant clusters). This gives the following permitted syllable canons:

V	*i* /i:/	'they, them'
CV	*du* /dy:/	'black'
CCV	*fri* /fri:/	'nose'
CCCV	*stlaoñ* /stlãõ̯/	'a kind of small fish (COLL)'
VC	*eur* /ø:r/	'hour'
CVC	*koll* /kol/	'to lose'
CCVC	*brud* /bry:t/	'noise, rumour'

CCCVC	*strizh* /striːs/ 'narrow'
VCC	*erc'h* /erx/ 'snow'
CVCC	*falc'h* /falx/ 'scythe'
CCVCC	*skorn* /skorn/ 'ice'
CCCVCC	*sklent* /sklent/ 'slate'
VCCC	*istr* /iːstr/ 'oysters'
CVCCC	*riskl* /riːskl/ 'danger'
CCVCCC	*flastr* /flaːstr/ 'act of smashing'
CCCVCCC	(no example recorded)

In polysyllabic words, the vocalic nuclei may be in hiatus or separated by one to three consonants:

Hiatus	*buhez* /byːes/ 'life'
-C-	*botez* /botes/ 'shoe'
-CC-	*goustad* /gustat/ 'slowly'
-CCC-	*poultrenn* /pultren/ 'dust'.

7.14.1   Phonotactics

Restrictions for the distribution of phonemes in *isolated* words include the following:

> In word-final position, the opposition between voiced and voiceless consonants is neutralised in favour of the voiceless counterparts, for example /t/–/d/ → /t/#, /s/–/z/ → /s/# etc.

> Short vowels do not occur in stressed word-final position, cf. *du* /dyː/ 'black'.

> Short vowels do not occur in stressed syllable before hiatus, cf. *buhez* /byːes/ 'life'.

7.15   SANDHI

Further restrictions obtain in connected phrases and sentences. They may be subsumed unter the term sandhi rules. Sandhi plays an important part in standard Breton as in fact in all Breton dialects. It does so to such an extent that the understanding of a spoken utterance would be severely impaired without a notion of the respective rules. They are partly due to the fact that Breton has no phonetic indication of word boundary. Sandhi rules are extremely complex, and only very rough indications may be given here (for detailed treatment of sandhi in a specific Breton dialect, see Ternes (1970: 68–110)).

A word-final voiceless consonant followed by a word-initial vowel becomes voiced (irrespective of its morphophonological value), for example:

(232)   /-t/ + /V-/ → /-dV-/
          /-s/ + /V-/ → /-zV-/

A word-final voiceless consonant followed by a word-initial nasal or liquid becomes voiced, for example:

(233)   /-k/ + /m-/ → /-gm-/

Two adjacent stops or fricatives, one word-final, the other word-initial, both become voiceless, for example:

(234)   /-z/ + /t-/ ⎫
          /-s/ + /d-/ ⎬ → /-st-/
          /-z/ + /d-/ ⎭

Two identical consonants, occurring before and after word boundary, are reduced to one consonant, for example:

(235)   /-n/ + /n-/ → /-n-/

Under the conditions of the preceding rule, stops and fricatives always become voiceless, for example:

(236)   /-s/ + /s-/ ⎫
          /-z/ + /s-/ ⎬
          /-s/ + /z-/ ⎬ → /-s-/
          /-z/ + /z-/ ⎭

Word-initial /h-/ disappears after any word-final consonant, the latter becoming voiceless, if it is a stop or a fricative, for example:

(237)   /-z/ + /h-/ → /-s-/

There are subconditions to each of the principal rules above. In addition, many more changes occur, such as reduction of consonant clusters, complete loss of consonant clusters, alteration of vowel quality and/or quantity, etc. which cannot be described here in detail.

7.16   STRESS

7.16.1   Stressed/unstressed syllables

Word stress normally falls on the penultimate syllable. In this case, it is not marked in our phonemic transcription. There is a limited number of words (about fifty) with stress on the ultimate syllable. A full list of these is given in

Hemon (1984: sect. 273). For these words, stress is marked in our phonemic transcription. Words stressed on the ultimate syllable include base forms such as *itron* /itróːn/ 'lady', *fallakr* /faláːkr/ 'bad, malicious' and inflected forms such as *ouzhin* /uzíːn/ 'against me' (see (212) for shift of stress within the same paradigm).

It may be stated in conclusion that stress is marginally distinctive in standard Breton, although there are no minimal pairs for words differentiated by stress only. It is worth noting, however, that ultimate stress in Breton, albeit marginal, is considerably more important than in Welsh.

7.16.2   Distribution of stress (sentence stress)

In connected phrases and sentences, when uttered at normal conversational speed, individual word stresses are usually given up in favour of a group stress. Several words are strung together to form one stress group. The most prominent word within that stress group receives regular word stress, whereas the other words within the same group are either unstressed or may have secondary stress.

7.17   PITCH

7.17.1   Syllable pitch

Syllable pitch occurs as a concomitant of stress: stressed syllables are pronounced on a higher pitch than unstressed ones.

7.17.2   Word tone

There is no distinctive word tone in Breton.

7.17.3   Intonation (utterance pitch contour)

7.17.3.1   Rising–falling intonation

In the first part of the sentence, intonation rises gradually until it reaches its peak on the stressed syllable of the word which has greatest grammatical or lexical prominence in the sentence. From that syllable on, intonation falls gradually. The stressed syllable of the last stressed word in the sentence has a low-falling contour. All unstressed syllables after that contour are on a low pitch. If there is only one stressed word in the sentence, or if the last stressed

word of the sentence is the one with greatest prominence, the falling contour of
its stressed syllable is high-falling, that is, the starting point of the fall is at the
same time the intonation peak of the sentence.

This intonation is used for normal declarative sentences, for questions with a
question word and for non-emphatic imperatives:

(238)   *E-kreiz ar vourc'h e save an iliz.*
           'In the middle of the village rose the church'

Two stress groups, prominence on *vourc'h* 'village', second stress on *iliz* 'church':

(239)

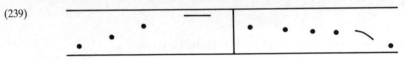

One stress group, prominence on *iliz* 'church':

(240)

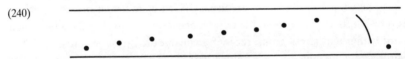

Two stress groups, prominence on *pelec'h* 'where', second stress on *nor* 'door':

(241)   *Pelec'h emañ alc'houez an nor?*
           'Where is the key of the door?'

(242)

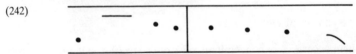

One stress group, prominence on *digorit* 'open! (PL)', secondary stress on *nor*
'door':

(243)   *Digorit an nor!*
           'Open (PL) the door!'

(244)

7.17.3.2   Rising intonation

The last stressed syllable of the sentence has a rising pitch from low to rather
high. Following unstressed syllables are slightly lower than the end of that rising
contour. Preceding unstressed syllables are on a low pitch. If any of the
preceding words is stressed, it has a medium-high pitch.

This intonation is used for sentence questions. It is the only way of forming
sentence questions in the spoken language (see 7.2.4).

One stress group, prominence on *veajiñ* 'to go on a trip':

(245)   *Mont a reot da veajiñ?*
        'Are you (PL) going on a trip?'

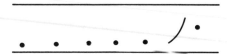

One stress group, prominence on *evel* 'like', secondary stress on *blijont* 'they please':

(247)   *Ne blijont ket dit evel-se?*
        'Don't you (SG) like them like that?' (i.e. fish cooked that way)

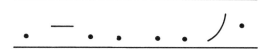

One stress group, prominence on *klañv* 'ill', secondary stress on *oc'h* 'you (PL) are':

(249)   *Klañv oc'h?*
        'Are you (PL) ill?'

7.17.3.3   Non-terminal intonation

Non-terminal intonation is similar to rising intonation. The main difference is that the rising contour of the last stressed syllable does not rise as high as for sentence questions.

(251)   *D'an deiz merket eta, an tad, ar vamm hag ar vugale a oa savet abred.*
        'On the appointed day therefore, the father, the mother, and the children had got up early.'

This sentence consists of three consecutive phrases with non-terminal intonation, followed by a declarative clause:

(252)

440   *Elmar Ternes*

MORPHOPHONOLOGY

7.18   MUTATIONS

7.18.1   Initial mutations

By initial mutations, we understand the replacement of stem-initial consonant phonemes by other consonant phonemes under specific morphological or syntactical conditions, for example:

(253)   *penn* 'head' – *va fenn* 'my head'

Initial mutations are the most common type of mutations. For details, see 7.18.4–7.

7.18.2   Non-initial mutations

By non-initial mutations, we understand the replacement of stem-final consonant phonemes by other consonant phonemes before specific suffixes, for example:

(254)   (a) *logod*   'mice'
           (b) *logodenn* 'mouse'
           (c) *logota*   'to catch mice'

Stem (a) ends morphophonologically in /d/, as can be seen from an ordinary suffixed form like (b). The suffixed form (c), however, shows stem-final replacement of /d/ by /t/.

Alternations of this type are not always referred to as 'mutations' in Celtic grammars, the term 'mutation' in a narrower sense being restricted to stem-initial alternations as defined in 7.18.4.

Non-initial mutations involve replacement of a stem-final morphophonologically voiced stop or fricative by its voiceless counterpart, for example /d/ → /t/, /z/ → /s/. These alternations occur, when one of the following suffixes is added to the stem:

(Note: The morphophonological processes involved here are more adequately reflected in *orthographe universitaire* than in *orthographe unifiée* (see 7.1.3). This is probably the weakest point of the latter orthography. We have made an effort to find examples that are written adequately. Where this was not possible, indication will be given.)

1 *-oc'h* (comparative suffix), *-añ* (superlative suffix); see 7.7.2.

(255)   *kozh* 'old'
          kozhañ 'to grow old'
          koshoc'h 'older'
          koshañ 'oldest'

2 *-añ* (3sg masc), *-i* (3sg fem), *-o* (3pl) in one paradigm of inflected prepositions; see 7.10 (211)

(256)   *evit* 'for' *evidon* 'for me'
                      evitañ 'for him'
                      eviti 'for her'
                      evito 'for them'

(Note: *evit* should in fact be written *evid*, as it is indeed in *orthographe universitaire*.)

3 *-a* (suffix deriving verbs from nouns, the latter usually plural or collective, giving the meaning 'to catch or to hunt (animals)', 'to gather or to collect (plants)'). For an example see (254).

4 *-aat* (suffix deriving verbs from adjectives, rarely from nouns)

(257)   *kozh* 'old'
          kozhañ 'to grow old'
          koshaat 'to grow old'

5 *-ad* (suffix designating measures)

(258)   *troad* 'foot (part of body)'
          troadad 'footache'
          troatad 'foot (measure)'

7.18.3   Prevocalic mutations

By prevocalic mutations, we understand the insertion of a consonant in front of a stem-initial vowel. The inserted consonant in standard Breton is usually /x/ or /z/.

Historically, this phenomenon is a direct corollary of initial mutations (7.18.1): in many cases, a specific mutation class (7.18.4) applies under the same conditions as the insertion of a specific prevocalic consonant in stem-initial position. Example: *he* poss 3sg fem (7.3.6) is followed by spirant mutation, when the stem is consonant-initial, and inserts /x/, when the latter is vowel-initial:

(259)   *ti* 'house'   *he zi*   'her house'
          anv 'name'   *hec'h anv* 'her name'

For an elaboration on the historical and structural connections between initial mutations and prevocalic mutations, see Ternes (1977b: 47–9).

Breton orthography is somewhat inconsistent in treating prevocalic mutations. The inserted consonants are sometimes added to the preceding word (as in *hec'h anv* 'her name'), sometimes written separately (as in *pa'z on* 'when I am'). However, they have to be interpreted invariantly as initials of the *following* word, for example *hec'h anv* /e xā:no/ 'her name'. This is also what the term prevocalic suggests. See Ternes 1977b (this is a re-interpretation of Ternes 1970: 177). In Irish and Scottish Gaelic orthography, the inserted consonants are indeed shown in most cases to belong to the following word.

/x/ is inserted after:

1 *he* POSS 3SG FEM, *ho* POSS 2PL (7.3.6 and 7.4.7):

(260)   *hec'h anv*   'her name'   *hoc'h anv*   'your (PL) name'
          hec'h anaout 'to know her'   *hoc'h anaout* 'to know you (PL)'

2 *o* (verbal particle forming present participle, see (201)):

(261)   *evañ* 'to drink' – *oc'h evañ* 'drinking'

/z/ is inserted after:

1 *e* (verbal particle, 7.2.0):

(262)   *neuze ez eas   kuit*
          then VPT went away
          'Then he/she went away'

2 *pa* conjunction 'when', *ma* conjunction 'if' (see 7.2.8.2), when used before inflected forms of *bezañ* 'to be' and *mont* 'to go':

(263)   *pa'z on* 'when I am'
          ma'z an 'if I go'

7.18.4   Mutation classes

This is a description of mutations in the narrower sense, that is, initial mutations (7.18.1). Standard Breton has five basic initial mutation classes. For the convenience of reference, they will be referred to here by their traditional denominations. It should be noted, however, that these denominations reflect historical sound changes and are therefore somewhat misleading from a descriptive point of view.

The mutation classes will be represented in the following way: stem-initial consonant phonemes in their base form appear in the upper vertical line. In the lower vertical line, underneath each consonant, appear the consonants resulting from application of the respective mutation. In order to avoid misunderstandings to which authors less familiar with the Celtic languages occasionally succumb, it is emphasised here that all of the consonants involved in initial mutations are *phonemes* in the respective language, none of them is allophonic.

The following lists are in orthography. Where this is ambiguous, phonemic indications will be added.

(264)   Lenition:

p	t	k	b	d	g	gw	m
b	d	g	v	z	c'h	w	v

Orthographic *c'h* resulting from *g* in lenition and mixed mutation (see (267)) is phonemically /h/. In all other cases, *c'h* is /x/.

(265)   Spirant mutation:

p	t	k
f	z	c'h

Orthographic *c'h* from *k* in spirant mutation is /x/.

(266)   Provection:

b	d	g
p	t	k

Mixed mutation (in this class, most consonants behave as under leniting conditions (see (264)), one consonant behaves as in provection (see (266)):

(267)

b	d	g	gw	m
v	t	c'h	w	v

As in lenition, *c'h* represents /h/ in mixed mutation.

Nasal mutation (this is of limited occurrence in Breton and affects only one consonant):

(268)

d
n

In many cases, the whole range of consonant changes of a specific mutation class applies. In other cases, only a reduced set of changes occurs. Therefore, each of the mutation classes (264)–(267) has one or more smaller subclasses that apply in specific cases. Examples:

> After definite and indefinite article, feminine singular nouns undergo lenition. This applies to the whole set of leniting consonants (264) except *d*. The subclass of lenition in this particular instance therefore is:

(269)

p	t	k	b	g	gw	m
b	d	g	v	c'h	w	v

> After *hor* POSS 1PL, spirant mutation (265) is limited to one consonant only:

(270)   k
         —
         c'h

These subclasses are so complex that it is not possible to take care of all cases in the following sections (7.18.5–7).

7.18.5   Noun mutations

The following remarks apply equally to sections 7.18.6–7. The conditions under which initial mutations occur are very complex, so that only some of the most important rules can be given here. There are considerably more conditioning factors than those enumerated below. On the other hand, each rule may have specific limitations or exceptions. The subdivision into noun, adjective and verb mutations is in some cases somewhat arbitrary, because the conditions may overlap, and because there is not always a clear distinction between those three word classes in Breton (when we use them, as we do here for convenience, in their traditional sense).

7.18.5.1   Lenition

Feminine nouns in the singular are lenited after definite and indefinite articles (except nouns with initial *d*):

(271)   *taol*   (FEM) 'table'   *an daol* 'the table'
         gavr   (FEM) 'goat'   *ur c'havr* 'a goat'
         mamm (FEM) 'mother'   *ar vamm* 'the mother'

Masculine nouns in the plural designating human beings are lenited after the definite article (except nouns with initial *d*):

(272)   *paotred* 'boys'   *ar baotred* 'the boys'
         breudeur 'brothers   *ar vreudeur* 'the brothers'

Nouns are mutated after any preceding attributive element, whether adjective or noun:

(273)   *izel* 'low' + *mor* 'sea' → *izel vor* 'low tide'
         mor 'sea' + *bleiz* 'wolf' → *morvleiz* 'shark'
         krenn 'middle' + *brezhoneg* 'Breton' → *krenn vrezhoneg* 'middle Breton'
         an (DEF ART) + *holl* 'all' + *tud* 'people' → *an holl dud* 'all people'

A number of prepositions make the following noun (or any other nominalised part of speech, such as verbal nouns) undergo lenition, for example *a* 'of', *da* 'to', *dindan* 'under', *dre* 'through', *war* 'on':

(274)   *kalon* 'heart' – *a galon* 'of heart', i.e. 'courageous' (as in *un den a galon* 'a courageous man')

troad 'foot' – *war droad* 'on foot'

goulenn 'to ask' (VN) – *da c'houlenn* as in: *n'ouzon ket piv da c'houlenn* 'I don't know whom to ask'

Nouns are lenited after the possessives *da* 2SG and *e* 3SG MASC:

(275)   *ti* 'house'   *da di* 'your (SG) house'
                          e di 'his house'

The same applies when the possessives are used as pronominal objects in verbal phrases (7.4.7); see example (149).

Nouns are lenited after the numerals *daou* (MASC), *div* (FEM) 'two':

(276)   *marc'h* (MASC) 'horse'   *daou varc'h* 'two horses'
               merc'h (FEM) 'girl'   *div verc'h* 'two girls'

The same applies for the dual prefixes *daou-* (MASC), *div-/di-* (FEM) (7.6.5.3).

The noun *bloaz* 'year' lenites after any numeral except after 1, 3, 4, 5 and 9. It is also lenited after *pet?* 'how many?':

(277)   *bloaz* 'year'   *dek vloaz* 'ten years'
                           tregont vloaz 'thirty years'
                           pet vloaz? 'how many years?'

Nouns are lenited after the privative prefix *di-*:

(278)   *bleuñv* (NOUN) 'blossoms' – *divleuñv* (ADJ) 'without blossoms'

7.18.5.2   Spirant mutation

Nouns undergo spirant mutation after the possessives *va* 1SG, *he* 3SG FEM, and *o* 3PL:

(279)   *ti* 'house'   *va zi* 'my house'
                        he zi 'her house'
                        o zi 'their house'

After the possessive *hor* 1PL, only *k* mutates:

(280)   *kambr* 'room' – *hor c'hambr* 'our room'

The same mutations apply when *va, he, o* and *hor* are used as pronominal objects in verbal phrases (7.4.7), see examples (149, 150).

Nouns undergo spirant mutation after the numerals *tri* (MASC), *teir* (FEM) 'three', *pevar* (MASC), *peder* (FEM) 'four', and *nav* 'nine':

(281)   *penn* (MASC) 'head'   *tri fenn* 'three heads'
                                 pevar fenn 'four heads'
                                 nav fenn 'nine heads'
             kador (FEM) 'chair'   *teir c'hador* 'three chairs'
                                 peder c'hador 'four chairs'
                                 nav c'hador 'nine chairs'

After the definite and the indefinite article, only *k* mutates with the following nouns: masculine singular nouns, all plural nouns (except masculine nouns designating human beings; see (272)):

(282)   *kastell* (MASC) 'castle'   *ur c'hastell* 'a castle'
          kambr 'room'   *ar c'hambroù* 'the rooms'

7.18.5.3   Provection

Nouns undergo provection after the possessive *ho* 2PL:

(283)   *bro* 'country' – *ho pro* 'your (PL) country'

The same mutation applies when *ho* is used as a pronominal object in verbal phrases (7.4.7); see example (149).

7.18.5.4   Nasal mutation

After the definite article, the singular of *dor* 'door' undergoes nasal mutation. This is the only occurrence of nasal mutation in standard Breton:

(284)   *dor* 'door'   *an nor* 'the door'
                          an dorioù 'the doors'

7.18.6   Adjective mutation

The only mutation that adjectives may undergo is lenition. Adjectives are lenited after feminine singular nouns, and after masculine plural nouns when designating human beings (see (272)):

(285)   *stal* (FEM) 'shop' + *bihan* 'small' → *stal vihan* 'small shop'
          breudeur 'brothers' + *mat* 'good' → *breudeur vat* 'good brothers'

Nouns immediately following another noun in attributive function behave like adjectives and lenite under the same conditions:

(286)   *loa* (FEM) 'spoon' + *koad* 'wood' → *loa goad* 'wooden spoon'

Adjectives lenite after *re* 'too':

(287)   *tomm* 'hot' – *re domm* 'too hot'

Adjectives lenite after the dummy words *hini* (FEM SG) and *re* (PL):

(288)   *kozh* 'old'   *an hini kozh* 'the old one (MASC)'
                          an hini gozh 'the old one (FEM)'
                          re gozh 'old ones (MASC and/or FEM)'

Adjectives are lenited after the privative prefix *di-* and the perfective prefix *peur-*:

(289)   *kempenn* 'orderly'   *digempenn* 'disorderly'
          dalc'hus 'persistent'   *peurzalc'hus* 'enduring up to the end'

7.18.7   Verb mutations

Personal pronouns in verbal phrases (7.4.7) are identical with possessives and therefore have been treated under noun mutations (7.18.5). This means that 'verbal' forms such as may be preceded by pronominals, are in fact nominalised forms. The distinction between noun and verb inflection is conveniently maintained for the description of Breton. It remains a fact, nevertheless, that noun inflection and a large part of what is traditionally regarded as verb inflection have many structural parallels in Breton.

7.18.7.1   Lenition
Verbs are lenited in the following contexts: after the verbal particle *a* (7.2.0):

(290)   *kerzh-* 'to walk'   *me a gerzh* 'I walk'
         gwel- 'to see'   *me a wel* 'I see'
         an den a welan 'the man whom I see'

after the negative particles *ne* and *na* (7.4.2):

(291)   *kouskan* 'I sleep'   *ne gouskan ket* 'I do not sleep'
         komzit! 'speak (PL)!'   *na gomzit ket!* 'do not speak (PL)!'
         klev- 'to hear'   *un den na glev ket* 'a man who does not hear'

after reflexive *en em* (7.4.3):

(292)   *gwalc'hiñ* 'to wash' – *en em walc'hiñ* 'to wash oneself'

after *en ur*, forming present participle (see (201)):

(293)   *dont* 'to come' – *en ur zont* 'coming'

after the conjunction *pa* 'when':

(294)   *kouezh-* 'to fall' – *pa gouezh glav* 'when rain falls'

after *ra*, forming wishes (sometimes called 'subjunctive particle'):

(295)   *bevo* 'he/she will live' – *ra vevo!* 'may he/she live!'

after the privative prefix *di-* and the perfective prefix *peur-:*

(296)   *gwiskañ* 'to dress'   *diwiskañ* 'to undress'
         moulañ 'to print'   *peurvoulañ* 'to finish printing'

7.18.7.2   Mixed mutation
Mixed mutation occurs only with verbs. Verbs undergo mixed mutation in the following contexts: after the verbal particle *e* (7.2.0):

(297)   *debr-* 'to eat'   *bremañ e tebrez* 'now you (SG) eat'
         gwel 'to see'   *bremañ e welez* 'now you (SG) see'

after *o*, forming present participle (see (201)):

(298)   *dont* 'to come'   *o tont* 'coming'
         gortoz 'to wait'   *o c'hortoz* 'waiting'

after the conjunction *ma* 'that' and its compounds such as *a-raok ma* 'before',
evit ma 'in order to':

(299)   *marv-* 'to die' – *a-raok ma varvas* 'before he/she died'
          dastum- 'to collect, to pick up' –
          Kemer a ra ur baner evit ma tastumo an avaloù.
          'He/she takes a basket in order to pick up the apples'

7.19   OTHER MORPHOPHONOLOGICAL ALTERNATIONS

A common morphophonological process in Breton is umlaut, in noun as well as
in verb inflection:

(300)   Singular   Plural
          gavr 'goat'   *givri*
          forc'h 'fork (garden tool)'   *ferc'hier*

Plural may be marked by umlaut alone:

(301)   Singular   Plural
          dant   'tooth'   *dent*
          askorn 'bone'   *eskern*

Umlaut in verb inflection is most common with the verbal noun. In the following
examples, the non-umlauted form is exemplified by the past participle (suffix
-et, see (200)):

(302)   Verbal noun   Past participle
          genel 'to give birth'   *ganet* 'born'
          terriñ 'to break'   *torret* 'broken'

Some verbs which take the verbal-noun suffix *-el*, have an alternation of *l/r* as
the result of a dissimilatory process. Since the suffix *-el* is often accompanied by
umlaut, *l/r* alternation and umlaut usually occur together:

(303)   Verbal noun   Past participle
          derc'hel 'to hold'   *dalc'het* 'held'
          gervel 'to call'   *galvet* 'called'

Suppletion is quite common in Breton morphology. It occurs in noun,
adjective and verb inflection. Nouns:

(304)   Singular   Plural
          den   'man'   *tud*
          buoc'h 'cow'   *saout*
          ejen   'ox'   *oc'hen*
          ki   'dog'   *chas*
          marc'h 'horse'   *kezeg*

The adjectives *mat* 'good', *fall* 'bad', and *kalz* 'much' have suppletive stems in
comparison (see 7.7.2).

The following verbs use suppletive stems in conjugation: *bezañ* 'to be', *kaout* 'to have', *mont* 'to go', *dont* 'to come', *ober* 'to do, to make'.

As stated in 7.14.1, the phonemic opposition between voiced and voiceless consonants is neutralised in word-final position in favour of the voiceless counterpart (a phenomenon existing also in German and known as *Auslaut-verhärtung*). As a consequence, there is an alternation of voiced and voiceless consonants in morphological paradigms. Breton orthography is usually morpho-phonological in this respect and shows the form to be used before a vowel-initial suffix (except for certain inconsistencies in *orthographe unifiée* – see the notes in 7.18.2):

(305) *fals* /fals/ 'false'   *falser* /falser/ 'falsifier'
       falz /fals/ 'sickle'   *falzer* /falzer/ 'one who handles the sickle'

Most sandhi rules in 7.15 apply also at the morphological level. Most of the resulting alternations are not shown in orthography. The following example illustrates the rule according to which two consecutive stops and/or fricatives, whether voiced or voiceless, both become voiceless (with concomitant reduction of long vowel), cf. (234):

(306) *skriv-* /skriːv-/'to write' + *-je* /-ʒe/ (conditional suffix) → *skrivje* /skrifʃe/ 'would write'

Quantity of stressed vowels is predictable in many cases from the following consonant or consonant cluster (7.13.1). These rules are very complex, however, and depend, among other things, on the number of syllables of the word (monosyllabic or polysyllabic). When a syllabic suffix is added to a monosyllabic stem, vowel quantity changes under certain conditions as a consequence of the change in number of syllables (first example, no change; second and third examples, change) (for details, see Ternes 1977a: 189–91):

(307) *ruz* /ryːs/ 'red'   DIM *ruzik* /ryːzik/ 'reddish'
       dous /duːs/ 'mild'   DIM *dousik* /dusik/ 'rather mild'
       SG *tach* /taːʃ/ 'nail' PL *tachoù* /taʃu/

Since word stress usually falls on the penultimate syllable (7.16.1), stress moves when a syllabic suffix is added to a polysyllabic stem. Since long vowels are shortened when losing stress, and short vowels may become long when receiving stress, stress movement often entails changes in vowel quantity:

(308) SG *bagad* /baːgat/ (-́-) 'herd, flock'
       PL *bagadoù* /bagaːdu/ (-́-́-)

Another consequence of this stress movement is that the stressed close vowels /iː, yː, uː/ before hiatus result in the respective semi-vowels /j, ɥ, w/ when losing stress. Under the same conditions, /oː/ also becomes /w/:

450   *Elmar Ternes*

(309)   *uhel* /yːel/ 'high'   *uhelder* /ɥelder/ 'height'
          SG *loa* /loːa/ 'spoon'   PL *loaioù* /lwaju/

A shift of stress between penultimate and ultimate syllable occurs in one
paradigm of pronominal prepositions (212).

REFERENCES

Denez, Per 1972. *Brezhoneg buan hag aes: le breton vite et facilement*, Paris: Omnivox
    (Engl. edn 1977, Cork: Cork University Press).
    1983. The present state of the Celtic languages: Breton. In G. Mac Eoin (ed.)
    Proceedings of the Sixth International Congress of Celtic Studies, Dublin: Dublin
    Institute for Advanced Studies, pp. 73–81.
Ernault, Emile 1895–6. *Glossaire moyen-breton*, 2 vols., 2nd edn, Paris: Bouillon; repr.
    1976, Geneva: Slatkine.
Evans, Claude and Léon Fleuriot 1985. *A dictionary of Old Breton. Dictionnaire du vieux
    breton. Historical and comparative*, 2 vols., Toronto: Prepcorp.
Falc'hun, François 1951. *Le Système consonantique du breton, avec une étude comparative
    de phonétique expérimentale*. Rennes: Plihon.
    1962. Le Breton, forme moderne du gaulois. *Annales de Bretagne* 69: 413–28.
    1963. *Histoire de la langue bretonne d'après la géographie linguistique*, 2 vols., 2nd edn,
    Paris: Presses Universitaires de France.
Fleuriot, Léon 1964a. *Le Vieux Breton: éléments d'une grammaire*, Paris: Klincksieck.
    1964b. *Dictionnaire des gloses en vieux-breton*, Paris: Klincksieck.
    1982. *Les Origines de la Bretagne*, Paris: Payot.
    1983. Les réformes du breton. In I. Fodor and C. Hagège (eds.) *Language reform – La
    Réforme des langues – Sprachreform*, vol. II, Hamburg: Buske, pp. 27–47
Gros, Jules 1966. *Le Trésor du breton parlé: éléments de stylistique trégorroise*, Part I: *Le
    Langage figuré*, Brest: Emgleo Breiz.
Guillevic, A. and P. Le Goff 1902. *Grammaire bretonne du dialecte de Vannes*, Vannes:
    Lafolye.
    1904. *Vocabulaire breton–français du dialecte de Vannes*, Vannes: Lafolye.
Guyonvarc'h, Christian-J. (ed.) 1975. *Le Catholicon de Jehan Lagadeuc* (Celticum 22),
    Rennes: Ogam – Tradition Celtique.
Haarmann, Harald 1973. *Der lateinische Lehnwortschatz im Bretonischen*, Hamburg:
    Buske.
Hammer, Françoise 1969. Der bretonische Dialekt von Plouharnel. Dissertation, Kiel
    University.
Hardie, D. W. F. 1948. *A handbook of modern Breton (Armorican)*, Cardiff: University
    of Wales Press.
Helias, Per Jakez (dir.) 1986. *Dictionnaire breton. Breton–français/français–breton*, Paris:
    Garnier.
Hemon, Roparz 1974. *Dictionnaire français–breton*, 2nd edn, Brest: Al Liamm.
    1975a. *Cours élémentaire de breton*, 8th edn, Brest: Al Liamm.
    1975b. *A historical morphology and syntax of Breton*, Dublin: Dublin Institute for
    Advanced Studies.

1978. *Nouveau dictionnaire breton–français*, 6th edn, Brest: Al Liamm.

1984. *Grammaire bretonne*, 9th edn, Brest: Al Liamm.

Humphreys, Humphrey Lloyd 1972. Les sonantes fortes dans le parler haut-cornouaillais de Bothoa (Saint-Nicolas-du-Pélem, Côtes-du-Nord). *Etudes Celtiques* 13: 259–74.

1985. Phonologie, morphologie et lexique du parler breton de Bothoa en Saint-Nicolas-du-Pélem (Côtes-du-Nord). Thèse d'Etat, Brest.

Jackson, Kenneth H. 1960/1. The phonology of the Breton dialect of Plougrescant. *Etudes Celtiques* 9: 327–404.

1961. Linguistic geography and the history of the Breton language. *Zeitschrift für celtische Philologie* 28: 272–93.

1967. *A historical phonology of Breton*, Dublin: Dublin Institute for Advanced Studies.

1972. The regular and irregular verbs at Plougrescant. In H. Pilch and J. Thurow (eds.) *Indo-Celtica: Gedächtnisschrift für Alf Sommerfelt*, Munich: Hueber, pp. 73–88.

Jones, Morris and Alan R. Thomas 1977. *The Welsh language: studies in its syntax and semantics*, Cardiff: University of Wales Press.

Kervella, F. 1947. *Yezhadur bras ar brezhoneg*, La Baule: Skridoù Breizh; repr. 1976, Brest: Al Liamm.

Le Dû, Jean 1972. Le Nouvel Atlas Linguistique de Basse-Bretagne. *Etudes Celtiques* 13: 332–45.

Le Roux, Pierre 1924–63. *Atlas linguistique de la Basse-Bretagne*, Paris: Droz, and Rennes: Plihon.

Lewis, Henry and J. R. F. Piette 1966. *Llawlyfr Llydaweg Canol*, 3rd edn, Cardiff: Gwasg Prifysgol Cymru; German translation by Wolfgang Meid 1990. *Handbuch des Mittelbretonischen*, Innsbruck: Innsbrucker Beiträge zur Sprachwissenschaft.

Loth, Joseph 1883. *L'Emigration bretonne en Armorique du Ve au VIIe siècle de notre ère*, Rennes: Baraise.

1907. Les Langues romane et bretonne en Armorique. *Revue Celtique* 28: 374–403.

McKenna, Malachy 1976–81. The Breton of Guémené-sur-Scorff (bas-vannetais). *Zeitschrift für celtische Philologie* 35: 1–101, 36: 199–247, 37: 249–77, 38: 29–112.

1988. *A handbook of modern spoken Breton*, Tübingen: Niemeyer.

Mangold, Max 1975. *Phonetic emphasis: a study in language universals* (Forum Phoneticum 10), Hamburg: Buske.

Morvannou, Fanch 1975. *Le Breton sans peine*. Chennevières sur Marne: Assimil.

Oftedal, Magne 1972. Modern Celtic languages. In Th. A. Sebeok (ed.) *Current trends in linguistics*, vol. 9: *Linguistics in Western Europe*, The Hague and Paris: Mouton, pp. 1202–31.

Sébillot, Paul 1886. La langue bretonne: limites et statistiques. *Revue d'Ethnographie* 15: 1–29.

Sèité, V. 1962. *Le Breton par l'image*, 2nd edn, Brest: Emgleo Breiz.

1965. *Le Breton par l'image: manuel pour le vannetais, méthode V. Sèité adaptée*, Brest: Emgleo Breiz.

Sèité, V and L. Stéphan 1957. *Deskom Brezoneg: méthode de Breton*, Brest: Emgles Breiz.

Sommerfelt, Alf 1920. *Le Breton parlé à Saint-Pol-de-Léon*. Rennes: Imprimeries Réunies (outer cover: 1921, Paris: Champion). New edn. by F. Falc'hun and M. Oftedal 1978. Oslo, Bergen, Tromsø: Universitetsforlaget.

Stéphan, Laurent and Visant Sèité 1980. *Lexique breton–français et français–breton*, 20th edn, Brest: Emgleo-Breiz.

Ternes, Elmar 1970. *Grammaire structurale du breton de l'Ile de Groix*. Heidelberg: Carl Winter Universitätsverlag.

1977a. Propositions pour un système de prononciation standard du breton. *Zeitschrift für celtische Philologie* 36: 180–98.

1977b. Konsonantische Anlautveränderungen in den keltischen und romanischen Sprachen. *Romanistisches Jahrbuch* 28: 19–53.

1979. Die Sonderstellung des Bretonischen innerhalb der keltischen Sprachen: eine typologische Untersuchung. *Zeitschrift für celtische Philologie* 37: 214–28.

1982. Review of Sommerfelt 1920, new edn, 1978. *Zeitschrift für celtische Philologie* 39: 328–32.

1991. Review of McKenna 1988. *Zeitschrift für celtische Philologie* 44: 348–51.

Timm, Lenora A. 1980. Bilingualism, diglossia and language shift in Brittany. *International Journal of the Sociology of Language* 25: 29–41.

1983. The shifting linguistic frontier in Brittany. In F. B. Agard, G. Kelley, A. Makkai and V. Becker Makkai (eds.) *Essays in Honor of Charles F. Hockett*, Leiden: Brill, pp. 443–57.

Timm, Lenora A. 1984. The segmental phonology of Carhaisien Breton. *Zeitschrift für celtische Philologie* 40: 118–92.

Trépos, Pierre 1957. *Le Pluriel breton*, Brest: Emgleo Breiz.

no date (1968). *Grammaire bretonne*, Rennes: Simon; repr. 1980, Rennes: Ouest-France.

Tricoire, J. 1955. *Komzom, lennom ha skrivom brezoneg: parlons, lisons et écrivons le breton*, Part I, Rennes: Imprimeries Réunies.

1963. *Komzom, lennom ha skrivom brezoneg: parlons, lisons et écrivons le breton*, Part II, Brest: Emgleo Breiz.

FURTHER READING

Fleuriot, Léon and Sylvie Fleuriot 1976. Studies of Celtic languages in France. *Word* 28: 12–36.

Gourvil, Francis 1966. *Langue et littérature bretonnes* (Que sais-je? 527) 4th edn, Paris: Presses Universitaires de France.

Haarmann, Harald 1972. Die Sprachen Frankreichs. Soziologische und politische Aspekte ihrer Entwicklung. In H. Haarmann and M. Studemund (eds.) *Festschrift Wilhelm Giese*, Hamburg: Buske, pp. 295–340.

Hemon, Roparz 1947. *La Langue bretonne et ses combats*, La Baule: Editions de Bretagne.

Kremnitz, Georg 1977. *Die ethnischen Minderheiten Frankreichs*, 2nd edn, Tübingen: Gunter Narr.

Marcellesi, Jean-Baptiste (ed.) 1975. *L'Enseignement des 'langues régionales'* (Langue Française 25) Paris: Larousse.

Stephens, Meic 1976. *Linguistic minorities in Western Europe*, Llandysul: Gomer Press.

Ternes, Elmar 1975. Linguistische Feldforschung in der Bretagne und im schottischen Hochland. *Zeitschrift für celtische Philologie* 34: 194–222.

Index